Saddam Hussein

Saddam Hussein

A Political Biography

Efraim Karsh
and Inari Rautsi

THE FREE PRESS
A Division of Macmillan, Inc.
NEW YORK
Maxwell Macmillan Canada
TORONTO
Maxwell Macmillan International
NEW YORK   OXFORD   SINGAPORE   SYDNEY

The Free Press
A Division of Macmillan, Inc.
866 Third Avenue, New York, N.Y. 10022

Maxwell Macmillan Canada, Inc.
1200 Eglinton Avenue East
Suite 200
Don Mills, Ontario M3C 3N1

Macmillan, Inc. is part of the Maxwell Communication
Group of Companies.

Printed in the United States of America

printing number
2 3 4 5 6 7 8 9 10

Library of Congress Cataloging-in-Publication Data

Karsh, Efraim.
    Saddam Hussein : a politicial biography / Efraim Karsh and Inari
Rautsi.
        p. cm.
    ISBN 0–02-917063-X
    1. Hussein, Saddam   2. Iraq—Politics and government.
3. President—Iraq—Biography.   I. Rautsi, Inari.   II. Title.
DS79.66.H87K37   1991
956.704'3'092—dc20
    [B]   91-10867
                                                                     CIP

Contents

Introduction: The Man and His World

"Why did we take our action against Kuwait?" Saddam Hussein leaned forward in his chair, an intense look fixed on his British interviewer. His lips twisted in barely perceptible irritation at this seemingly rhetorical question, but the tenor of his voice remained calm. He was addressing a Western audience and was determined to drive his message home to them in the clearest and least provocative manner. "We took our action because the ruling family in Kuwait is good at blackmail, exploitation, and destruction of their opponents. They had perpetuated a grave U.S. conspiracy against us . . . stabbing Iraq in the back with a poisoned dagger."[1]

A Kuwaiti conspiracy against Iraq? How conceivably could the tiny oil principality, whose entire population roughly matched Iraq's one-million-strong army, conspire against the foremost Arab power in the Middle East? Had Kuwait ever harbored aggressive designs against Iraq, or was it rather Baghdad which had challenged the legitimacy of its smaller neighbor from the latter's first day of independent existence?

To world public opinion, Saddam's explanation seemed a flimsy excuse for an unprovoked act of aggression by a regional giant against a hapless neighbor. In the eyes of the U.S. President, George Bush, the Iraqis were "international outlaws and renegades," and their leader, a modern Hitler. Even the Soviets, Iraq's traditional allies, made no efforts to disguise their contempt for

1

Saddam's tactics of trying to blame the victim of aggression for its own misfortune: "Like a thief in a market he yells: Thief! Thief! This is his way of diverting public attention from his deeds. Well, we are not surprised that the Iraqi ruler is so well versed in the laws of the underworld: what he took was not items in a bazaar, but an entire country. And now he wants to make himself out as a victim of aggression."[2]

And yet, however absurd it might seem to outsiders, for Saddam Hussein the Kuwaiti "conspiracy" was a very real threat. His distorted interpretation of the origins of the crisis illustrates the driving force of the Iraqi leader: an overriding insecurity arising from a strikingly cynical worldview. The bleak vision of humanity memorably described 300 years ago by the political philosopher, Thomas Hobbes, best describes Saddam Hussein's outlook on life. He perceives the world as a violent, hostile environment in which the will to self-preservation rules. In such a setting, as Hobbes says, the war of "all against all," is constant and man is condemned to a life that is "solitary, poor, nasty, brutish, and short."[3]

In the permanently beleaguered mind of Saddam Hussein, politics is a ceaseless struggle for survival. The ultimate goal of staying alive, and in power, justifies all means. Plots lurk around every corner. Nobody is trustworthy. Everybody is an actual or potential enemy. One must remain constantly on the alert, making others cower so that they do not attack, always ready to kill before being killed. "I know that there are scores of people plotting to kill me," Saddam told a personal guest of his shortly after assuming the presidency in the summer of 1979, "and this is not difficult to understand. After all, did we not seize power by plotting against our predecessors?" "However," he added, "I am far cleverer than they are. I know they are conspiring to kill me long before they actually start planning to do it. This enables me to get them before they have the faintest chance of striking at me."[4]

This stark worldview can be explained in part by Saddam's troubled childhood, which seldom afforded him the trusting bonds of close, family relationships, but taught him instead the cruel law of the survival of the fittest, a law he was to cherish throughout his entire political career. But to no less an extent his outlook is the product of the ruthless political system in which he has operated over the past three decades, and in which naked force has constituted the sole agent of political change.

This ruthlessness has not so much to do with personal whims as with the nature of the Iraqi state. For Iraq is a land of rival ambitions and contradictions. It is a country with a glorious imperial past, stretching back thousands of years, and far-reaching dreams for the future, and yet, geopolitically handicapped: virtually landlocked and surrounded by six neighbors, with at least two—Turkey and Iran—larger than Iraq and irredentist. It is a country that aspires to champion the cause of Arab nationalism while at the same time being, in the words of its first modern ruler, King Faisal I, no more than "unimaginable masses of human beings, devoid of any patriotic idea, imbued with religious traditions and absurdities . . . and prone to anarchy."[5] It is a land torn by ethnic and religious divisions, a land where the main non-Arab community, the Kurds, has been constantly suppressed, and where the majority of the population, the Shi'ites, have been ruled since the inception of the Iraqi state as an underprivileged class by a minority group, the Sunnis, less than one-third their size.

This wide gap between dreams of grandeur and the grim realities of weakness has generated a political legacy of frustration and insecurity. Confronted with a roiling domestic cauldron, as well as formidable external challenges, the ruling oligarchy in Iraq has been condemned to a constant rearguard action for political legitimacy and personal survival. The outcome has been the all-too-familiar politics of violence as exemplified in the summer of 1933 in the tragedy of the tiny Assyrian community in northern Iraq. The atrocities committed by the Iraqi army against some 3,000 people, as a response to their demand for ethnic as well as religious recognition, was lauded by the masses as an act of national heroism. Celebrations were held throughout the country, and in the northern city of Mosul "triumphant arches were set up, decorated with melons stained with blood and with daggers stuck into them [to represent heads of slain Assyrians]."[6]

When in July 1958 the Hashemite dynasty, which had ruled Iraq since its inception in 1921, was overthrown by a military coup headed by General Abd al-Karim Qassem, the mutilated body of the Iraqi regent, Abd al-Ilah, was dragged by a raging mob through the streets of Baghdad before being hung at the gate of the Ministry of Defense. A similar treatment was given to the body of Nuri Sa'id, the Prime Minister and "strong man" of the *ancien régime*, after it had been disinterred by the mobs.[7] When dissenting officers in Mosul tried, but failed, to unseat Qassem in March

1959, he subjected the city to one of the bloodiest retributions in Iraq's modern history. Four years later, Qassem's bullet-ridden corpse was screened on Iraqi television to the entire nation.

Qassem's successor, the Ba'th, Saddam's own party, was no kinder in its treatment of political opponents. When it was overthrown in November 1963, after merely nine months at the helm, "all sorts of loathsome instruments of torture" were found in the cellars of *Qasr al-Nihayyah*—the Palace of the End—a royal palace turned detention and interrogation center by the Ba'th, including "electric wires with pincers, pointed iron stakes on which prisoners were made to sit, and a machine which still bore traces of chopped-off fingers. Small heaps of bloodied clothing were scattered about, and there were pools [of blood] on the floor and stains over the wall."[8]

This was the political scene into which Hussein entered in 1957, at the age of 20. He did not set the rules of the game in this cruel system, although he has undoubtedly been its most savage and able player, bringing its brutal methods to awesome perfection. His natural instincts for political survival have proved impeccable. Taking Stalin as a model, he made his way to the premier position by purging actual and potential rivals for the leadership, and forging *ad hoc* alliances only to break them at the most suitable moment, betraying friends and foes alike. Once in the Presidential Palace in July 1979, he launched the bloodiest purge yet, executing hundreds of Party officials and military officers, some of whom were close friends and associates. Nothing short of absolute power and unconditional subservience would allay his fundamental insecurity. The outcome of this systemic bloodletting has been the transformation of Iraq from an autocracy, ruled by successive short-lived military regimes, into a totalitarian state, with its tentacles permeating every aspect of society, and with the omnipotent presence of the supreme leader towering over the nation.

Tragically for the Middle East, the consequences of Hussein's paranoic worldview have not been confined to Iraq. Foreign adventures have often appealed to the anxious leader, either as a means of deflecting external threats, or of boosting his domestic position by gaining regional prestige and riches at the expense of "enemy" states. Within just over a decade of his seizure of power, he had invaded two neighboring states, triggering ferocious conflicts in the war-ridden Middle East, and adding hundreds of thousands of deaths to his discredit.

The story of Saddam Hussein's political career and the means he has employed in his relentless quest for survival is a late twentieth-century tale that reveals much about the post–World War II era. By understanding Saddam's political rationale, we will not only understand more about the Middle East today, but also about a generation of leaders conditioned by the forces of nationalism and development that swept their lands and shaped their outlook.

To get beyond the popular caricature of "the butcher of Baghdad," a label which tends to demonize rather than explain the ruthless ways of Saddam Hussein, it is necessary to examine the mind of the man, his thinking and motives. Contrary to the appearance of megalomania and unpredictability, Iraq's leader has followed a consistent pattern of behavior in his ascent from obscure rural origins to a notorious role on the world stage. By closely examining the events of his life, it is possible to reveal the essential character of the man who held the world hostage and to explain his seemingly irrational determination to maintain his power no matter what the cost.

1

The Making of a Ba'thist

In 1394, as the Tartar hordes of Timurlane swept over Mesopotamia, they took the trouble of stopping at a small provincial town on the Tigris river, some hundred miles north of Baghdad, where they erected a pyramid with the skulls of their victims.[1] The name of the town was Tikrit, and its choice as the site for demonstrating Timurlane's ferocity was not accidental. A small garrison protected by a formidable fortress, Tikrit had been a center of defiance to external invaders, leading the eighteenth-century English historian, Edward Gibbon, to define it as an "impregnable fortress of independent Arabs."[2] This was the place where Saladin, the legendary Muslim military commander who defeated the Crusaders in the renowned battle of Hittin and liberated Jerusalem from Christian rule, had been born in 1138. Exactly 800 years later, it was to become the birthplace of a modern Iraqi ruler, aspiring to don the mantle of his great predecessor: Saddam Hussein.

Saddam would always hold his birthplace in great affection and pride. The few men he would choose to trust and be his chieftains would, by and large, come from Tikrit and share his strong attachment for the home of their formative years.

Yet, despite his fond thoughts of Tikrit, Saddam's was a poverty-ridden and troubled childhood. According to official sources, he was born on April 28, 1937. His place of birth was a mud house belonging to his maternal uncle, Khairallah Talfah.[3]

His father, a poor landless peasant by the name of Hussein al-Majid, died before Saddam was born and his mother, Sabha, who could not support the orphan, left him to be raised by Khairallah's family. The child's name, Saddam, meaning, "one who confronts," turned out to be strangely prophetic.

At the time of Saddam's birth, Iraq was a precarious constitutional monarchy, ruled by a non-Iraqi dynasty—the Hashemite family—originating from the Hijaz (part of today's Saudi Arabia). Established in the wake of the First World War by European great powers on the ruins of the Ottoman Empire, which had controlled the Middle East for nearly four centuries, Iraq was administered by Great Britain under a mandate from the League of Nations until 1932, when it joined the international organization as an independent state. The "founding father" of the Iraqi state, King Faisal I, who by virtue of his personality and astute leadership had managed to keep the various centrifugal forces in the country under control, died in 1933, and was succeeded by his only son, Ghazi. Faisal's premature death and Ghazi's inexperience (he was 21 years old upon ascending the throne) and weak personality ushered in a period of acute political instability. During a seven-year period between gaining independence and the outbreak of the Second World War in 1939, Iraq was governed by no fewer than 12 cabinets. In 1936 the country experienced its first military *coup d'état;* by 1941, six further coups had already taken place.[4]

The Iraq of Saddam's early years was marked by profound political instability, compounded by the gathering storm in Europe and the eventual outbreak of a general war. Resenting the continuation of British presence and influence in Iraq—despite its formal independence the country remained tied to Britain by a bilateral treaty signed in 1930, which gave the latter preferential political status and two military bases on Iraqi territory[5]—the militant Iraqi nationalists looked forward to the triumph of Nazi Germany and its allies. A Nazi victory, they believed, would dislodge Britain from the Middle East and render Iraq, and the other Arab lands of the Middle East, truly independent. As the Germans went from strength to strength, anti-British sentiments soared and Baghdad became one of the main regional centers for pro-Axis activities. A showdown between the nationalists, who enjoyed widespread support within the army, and the British seemed only a matter of time.

In April 1941 London approached Baghdad with a request to allow the landing and transfer of British troops through Iraqi

territory in accordance with the 1930 Treaty. Iraq's pro-Nazi
Prime Minister, Rashid Ali al-Kailani, who had come to power
earlier that month through a military coup, viewed the request as
a de facto occupation of Iraq. Yet, mindful that the real agenda
behind the British demand was his own overthrow, he took care to
profess his readiness to abide by the bilateral treaty. The British,
nevertheless, did not take any chances, and in late April began
landing their troops in southern Iraq. At this point Rashid Ali
ordered his army to move on the British air base at Habbaniya,
near Baghdad, and appealed for German support. In the ensuing
hostilities the Iraqi army was decisively beaten by a British
expeditionary force, and Rashid Ali and some of his supporters
fled the country. The authority of the monarchy was restored by
British bayonets. Many participants in the uprising were jailed
and some of them executed by the old-new government.

These events had a profound effect on Saddam's life. His
uncle and foster father Khairallah, an army officer and ardent
Arab nationalist, participated in the ill-fated uprising and was
subsequently dismissed from the military and jailed for five years.
The young boy was thus forced to move to the small village of
al-Shawish, near Tikrit, to live with his mother who had meanwhile remarried. Her new husband was Hasan Ibrahim, a brother
of Saddam's late father. In the following years he was to ask his
mother time and again where his uncle was, only to be given the
routine answer: "Uncle Khairallah is in jail." In Saddam 's own
account, his empathy with Khairallah had a crucial impact on the
development of his nationalist sentiments in that it fueled a
deep-seated hatred of the monarchy and the foreign power
behind it, a feeling which he was to harbor for years to come.[6] As
he would write later: "Our children should be taught to beware of
everything foreign and not to disclose any state or party secrets to
foreigners . . . for foreigners are eyes for their countries, and
some of them are counterrevolutionary instruments [in the hands
of imperialism]."[7]

The move from Tikrit to al-Shawish was quite traumatic for
Saddam. To be sure, there was nothing remarkable about the
Tikrit into which he was born. Since its destruction at the hands of
Timurlane's hordes, the town had fallen into decay. Nineteenth-
century foreign travelers passing through it in the course of their
journeys found a desolated place, remarkable only for the remains
of a ruined castle on the high cliff that overlooked the town.[8] The
town's residents, Sunni Arabs notable for their garrulousness,

earned their modest living by manufacturing *kalaks*, round rafts made of inflated animal skin.[9] Yet, in comparison with al-Shawish, Tikrit was a bustling center. Like most Iraqi rural settlements at the time, life in Saddam's small village was filled with hardships. Not only did it lack paved roads, electricity, or running water, but the appalling health and sanitary conditions made physical survival a demanding task. According to Iraqi official statistics, infant mortality in the three major cities (Baghdad, Basra and Mosul) in 1937, the year Saddam was born, amounted to 228 per 1,000 births, and the rate was admittedly much higher in rural areas.[10] This meant that one of every two or three babies in an Iraqi village was condemned to death before reaching one year of age, mainly from infirmity and malnutrition. The survival of the fittest was, literally, a reality for Saddam from the first moment of his life.

Those who were lucky enough to survive their early childhood, were to suffer throughout their lives from nutritional deficiencies and to be afflicted by numerous epidemic diseases such as malaria, *bejel* (a non-venereal form of syphilis), hookworm, tuberculosis, and trachoma.[11] This difficult existence was further compounded by the miserable poverty which permeated every household in the village. In Saddam's own recollection, "life was difficult everywhere in Iraq. Very few people wore shoes. And in many cases they only wore them on special occasions. Some peasants would not put their shoes on until they had reached their destination, so they would look smart."[12]

This was the environment into which the young Saddam was introduced upon moving to the village. Unlike Khairallah, who as a military officer enjoyed a relatively high social status, the Ibrahims were considered "local brigands." Saddam was thus condemned to a lonely existence. He had no friends among the village boys, who often mocked him for being fatherless, and he used to carry an iron bar to protect himself against attacks.[13] According to exiled Iraqi sources, Saddam often amused himself by putting such a bar on the fire and after heating it red, stabbing a passing animal in the stomach, splitting it in half. The living creature closest to his heart, as Saddam would later reveal, was his horse. Even at that early stage, he recognized the grim "reality" that "a relationship between man and animal can at times be more affectionate, intimate, and unselfish than relations between two human beings." So profound was Saddam's affection for his horse that, according to him, upon learning about the death of the beloved creature, he experienced paralysis of his hand for over a week.[14]

To make things worse, nobody in the family showed great interest in Saddam, who had to look after himself from his first days in the village.[15] His stepfather, "Hasan the liar" as he was known locally, was a brutish man who used to amuse himself by humiliating Saddam. His common punishment was to beat the youth with an asphalt-covered stick, forcing him to dance around to dodge the blows. He prevented Saddam from acquiring education, sending him instead to steal for him; the young boy was even reported to have spent some time in a juvenile detention center.[16] Saddam learnt from firsthand experience, at a very early age the cruel law of *homo homini lupus* (man is a wolf to man). Its corollaries of suspicion and distrust of one's closest associates, a need for total self-reliance, and for intimidating others so as never to be seen as prey were to guide his thoughts and acts from that time forward.

Had Saddam spent his entire youth at his mother's secluded village, he would most probably have become an undistinguished Iraqi peasant. However, to his great excitement, in 1947, shortly after his uncle's release from prison, he left his mother and stepfather and returned to Khairallah's home in Tikrit where he began attending school. Studies were quite burdensome for the young boy, who at the age of ten did not know how to spell his name. He would rather amuse his classmates with practical jokes, such as embracing his old Koran teacher in a deceptively friendly hug and then inserting a snake beneath his robe.[17] Yet, Khairallah's constant encouragement and guiding hand kept Saddam going through these difficult years. Another source of support was provided by Khairallah's son, Adnan, three years Saddam's junior and his best friend, who would later become Minister of Defense. In the fall of 1955, having graduated from primary school, Hussein followed his uncle to Baghdad where he enrolled at the Karkh high school. He was then 18 years old.[18]

Those were days of national fervor and the cafés of Baghdad were alive with intrigue and conspiracies. In 1955 Iraq joined Britain, Turkey, Iran and Pakistan in forming a regional defense organization, known as the Baghdad Pact. In taking this step, the Iraqi Prime Minister, Nuri Sa'id, was motivated by wider objectives than the containment of the "Soviet threat" which, ostensibly, constituted the raison d'être for the new security system. Faced by mounting public pressure for a unilateral abrogation of the 1930 Treaty with Britain, but reluctant to jeopardize Iraq's relations with its main international ally, Sa'id sought a magic formula that would allow him to have his cake and eat it too: to project himself as a staunch nationalist who freed his country from foreign influence, while keeping British support for Iraq intact. The Baghdad Pact, he reasoned, could offer such a solution by creating a multilateral framework that would put Anglo-Iraqi relations on a new footing, amenable to both Britain and Iraq. Besides, if joined by other Arab states, such as Jordan and Syria, the Baghdad Pact could give Iraq a springboard for outshining Egypt, its traditional rival for leadership of the Arab World. Since the ancient struggle for regional hegemony between Mesopotamia and Egypt, the relationship between Iraq and Egypt had been a competitive one.

These expectations turned sour. By the time the pact was established, it was already evident to Sa'id that he had lost the battle over the minds and souls of the Arab masses to the young and dynamic Egyptian President, Gamal Abd al-Nasser. In September 1955 Nasser dealt a blow to the West by concluding a large-scale arms deal with the Soviet Union (known as the "Czech deal" since Prague was the official signatory to the agreement), which gave Moscow a doorway to the Middle East, hitherto an almost exclusive Western "preserve." (It was the Western great powers that had defeated the Ottoman Empire in the First World War and carved up the Middle East between them in a series of League of Nations mandates in accordance with the Sykes-Picot Agreement of 1916.) Ten months later Nasser publicly snubbed Great Britain by nationalizing the Suez Canal. The British response was not slow in coming: in October Egypt was attacked by an Anglo-French-Israeli war coalition. Even though the Egyptian army was defeated by the Israelis and suffered significant losses at the hands of the British and the French, and although it was the United States (and to a lesser extent, the Soviet Union) that saved the day for Nasser by forcing the invading forces to relinquish their gains, in Arab eyes Nasser was the hero of the Suez Crisis; the person who had taken on "world imperialism" single-handedly and managed to emerge victorious.

While Nasser was steadily establishing himself as the standard-bearer of the anti-imperialist struggle and the embodiment of Arab nationalism, the Iraqi leadership was increasingly viewed as a "lackey of Western imperialism," a reactionary regime out of

step with the historic march of Arab destiny. Hence, not only did
Iraq fail to attract other Arab partners to the Baghdad Pact,
finding itself in glaring regional isolation, but the formation of the
pact met with considerable domestic disapproval. The left-wing
factions resented Iraq's involvement in what they viewed as direct
aggression against the USSR. The nationalists, for their part,
considered the pact a submission to Western imperialism and a
betrayal of the cause of pan-Arabism.[19]

Public dissatisfaction in Iraq reached its peak in the fall of 1956
when widespread riots engulfed Baghdad in reaction to the regime's passivity during the Suez Crisis. One of the many people
who roamed the streets during those heated days was Saddam, who
felt in his element in this turbulent environment. The political
milieu was not daunting to him; indeed he was well suited to it. His
uncle's example had inspired him to political activism and his lack
of close, emotional ties in his early childhood had taught him to
scheme and manipulate to survive. Finding anti-government activity far more gratifying than studies, he plunged wholeheartedly
into the seething streets of the capital. In early 1957, at the age of
20, he joined the Ba'th Party.

The Ba'th Party, meaning the party of the Resurrection, or
Renaissance, was established in Damascus in the early 1940s by
two Syrian schoolteachers, Michel Aflaq, a Greek Orthodox
Christian, and Salah al-Din al-Bitar, a Sunni Muslim. A radical,
secular, modernizing party, its ideology is a patchy mixture of
pan-Arabism and socialism, which can be reduced to three
organizing principles: unity, liberation, and socialism. This "holy
trinity," as the Ba'thists tend to call it, constitutes a unified
metaphysical whole. None can be fully achieved without the
attainment of the other two; all are means to promote the ultimate
goal of the spiritual rebirth of the Arab nation.

This rebirth, according to Ba'thi doctrine, should be a profound and revolutionary process, extending far beyond such
practical considerations as international boundaries, to encompass
the "liberation" of the individual from former tribal, religious, or
regional loyalties. Yet, high ideals apart, from its early days of
activity the Party's agenda has been essentially predicated on one
issue: elimination of the "traces of colonialism" in the Middle East
and unification of the Arab nation. Since, in Ba'thi thinking, the
great powers carved up the Middle East in the early twentieth
century in such a fashion as to satisfy their particular interests and

keep the Arab nation divided and weak, this wrong has to be rectified. The colonial powers must be pushed out of the region, and the artificial boundaries left behind should be abolished to accommodate the advent of a unified Arab state. Israel, which in Ba'thi thinking was a colonialist creation designed to fragment the Arab nation, had to be eliminated altogether.

This pan-Arab agenda has been illustrated not only by the main Ba'thi motto—"One Arab Nation with an Eternal Mission"—but also by its organizational infrastructure. The Party's supreme decision-making body, the National Command, is international in composition, comprising representatives from branches in the various Arab countries. These local branches are called Regional Commands, implying that all Arab states are merely parts of the wider Arab nation.[20]

Ba'thi ideas began infiltrating Iraq in the late forties through Iraqi students studying in Syria and Lebanon, and Syrian students in Iraq. In 1952 the Iraqi branch of the Ba'th received official recognition from the Party's National Command, and Fuad Rikabi, a Shi'ite engineer from the southern Iraqi town of Nasiriya, was appointed Secretary of the Regional Command in Iraq. Yet, whereas the Syrian Ba'th developed into a significant political force during the late 1940s and early 1950s, the Iraqi branch remained an ephemeral organization, numbering fewer than 300 members in 1955. This was partly due to the lack of intellectual interest in the complex Ba'thi ideology. Although Baghdad had once been a major center of learning and the arts in the more distant past, particularly under the Abbasid Caliph Harun al-Rashid (786–809), 400 years as one of the more desolate corners of the Ottoman Empire had left a deep intellectual void.

An even more important reason for the failure of the Ba'th to make deep inroads into Iraqi society was the tough competition it faced from other political parties and groups. The socialist message of the Ba'th did not stand much chance against that of the communists who, at the time, were a significant movement on the Iraqi political map.[21] On the nationalist front the Ba'thi position was even more precarious. A fragmented society, beset by unbridgeable ethnic and religious divisions, Iraq hardly represented a model nation. And yet from its early days of statehood, modern Iraq has vigorously and persistently championed Arab nationalism. At the highest level of abstraction this aspiration can be viewed as a continuation of the historical struggle between Mesopotamia and Egypt for regional mastery of

the ancient world. At a more proximate level, however, it reflects
the inextricable mixture of great personal ambition and perennial
vulnerability characterizing twentieth-century Iraqi politics. On
the one hand, the mantle of the pan-Arab cause offered the
regime a potent instrument to assert its leadership role in the
region. On the other, it provided the political elite with a unifying
concept that might transform the "unimaginable masses of human
beings, devoid of any patriotic idea" into a cohesive social and
political entity. If all Iraqis are Arabs, and all Arab states are
merely regions of the wider Arab nation, what difference does it
make if the ruling few are Sunni or Shi'ite?

Hence, not only did the regime propagate its own ambitious
nationalist schemes (such as Premier Nuri Sa'id's plan in the
1940s for the unification of the Fertile Crescent under Iraqi
leadership), but the Ba'th had to outbid several nationalist groups
which predated it and offered a much more straightforward
program. These ranged from the right-wing militant *Istiqlal*
(Independence) Party, to the centrist *Ahrar* (Liberal) Party, to the
leftist *Sha'b* (People's) Party. Each offered its own unique concoc-
tion of nationalism and social reforms. Each was more established
in the Iraqi political system than the Ba'thi newcomer.[22]

Precisely what drove Hussein to join the Ba'th Party at such a
low ebb in its development is difficult to say. In later years he was
to argue that the Party's commitment to the idea of Arab
nationalism was particularly appealing to him. Yet such inclinations could have been readily satisfied within the other, more
prominent, nationalistic parties. It is true that Ba'thi radicalism
provided an outlet for the unbounded energies and discontent-
ments of the young Tikriti, but so could have the rest of the
radical factions that abounded at the time in Iraq. The main
reason for Hussein's preference for the Ba'th over the seemingly
more promising alternatives seems therefore to be less romantic
and more prosaic, less related to his ideological predilections than
to his relations with his uncle and foster father, Khairallah Talfah.

Khairallah probably had the most influence on molding
Saddam's character. It was he who played the role of father to the
boy and was his object of male identification. As both model and
mentor, he nurtured the nationalistic sentiments of the young
Saddam. He introduced Saddam to people who were to play a key
role in his rise to power, including the future President, Ahmad
Hasan al-Bakr, Khairallah's cousin and close friend throughout
the 1940s and 1950s.[23] Following in his uncle's footsteps, Hussein

applied to the prestigious Baghdad Military Academy, but failed
the entrance examinations. His unfulfilled desire to don an
officer's uniform was to haunt Saddam Hussein for nearly two
decades until in 1976, while number two in the Iraqi leadership,
the man who had never served in the Iraqi military had the rank
of General conferred upon him by his then superior, President
Bakr.

In Hussein's eyes, Khairallah, who became headmaster of a
local school following his expulsion from the army, was an
intellectual "who understood the value of going to school."[24]
What kind of values the uncle managed to instill in his nephew is
not entirely clear. To judge by Khairallah's public and political
behavior in future years, however, it would seem that his home
provided a useful workshop in which Saddam took his first lessons
in manipulation and intrigue, vital tools for survival in the devious
corridors of the Iraqi political system.

After his nephew began rising in power, Khairallah became
the Mayor of Baghdad, a position he exploited to the full in order
to accumulate fabulous wealth. A greedy and exploitative person,
his corruption reached such preposterous proportions that Saddam was eventually forced to remove him from office: shortly
before the occupation of Kuwait in the summer of 1990, seventeen
companies run by Khairallah were closed and their executives
arrested.[25] A chilling insight into Khairallah's outlook was afforded in 1981 when Saddam, already President of Iraq, arranged
to have his uncle's philosophical thoughts published by the state
press. In a slim treatise entitled *Three Whom God Should Not Have
Created: Persians, Jews, and Flies,* Khairallah defined Persians as
"animals God created in the shape of humans." Jews, in his view,
were "a mixture of the dirt and leftovers of diverse people," while
flies, the least appalling of the three, were trifling creatures
"whom we do not understand God's purpose in creating."[26] To
judge from Saddam's diatribes against Israel and Iran throughout
his career, Khairallah's ideas about Persians and Jews had fallen
on fertile soil.

That Saddam Hussein was a man of action rather than of letters,
an operator rather than an intellectual, was evident from his
earliest days of political activity. A low-ranking new member of
the Ba'th, Saddam's initial assignment was to incite his high-
schoolmates into anti-government activities. This he did with
great enthusiasm, rallying the students (as well as some local

thugs) into an organized gang that struck fear into the hearts of many inhabitants of his Baghdad suburb of Karkh by beating political opponents and innocent passers-by. In late 1958, at the age of 21, Saddam was implicated in the murder of a government official in his hometown of Tikrit and thrown into jail.[27] He was released six months later, apparently due to insufficient evidence against him. However, shortly after this initial notoriety, he was given, together with several other young and relatively obscure Ba'thists, his most important party assignment until then: participation in an attempt on the life of Iraq's ruler, General Abd al-Karim Qassem.

Relations between the Ba'th and Qassem, who headed a group of "Free Officers" in overthrowing the Hashemite monarchy in a bloody coup on July 14, 1958, were initially warm. The Ba'thists wholeheartedly embraced the coup. They did not hesitate to participate in Qassem's cabinet and to capitalize on the nationalist fervor which swept the country in order to expand their narrow popular base and to consolidate their organization. Yet relations quickly soured as the two parties found themselves hopelessly polarized over the key political issue facing Iraq at the time: whether or not to join the Syro-Egyptian union called the United Arab Republic (UAR), established in February 1958. This was a political union of Egypt and Syria, with Nasser as its President and Cairo as its capital. Yemen joined in 1958 to form a federation called the United Arab States. The union was, however, short-lived, for Syria withdrew in 1961, soon followed by Yemen.

While the Iraqi Ba'thists, like their Syrian counterparts, pressed for a speedy merger with Egypt, which they viewed as a major stride toward the ultimate unification of the "Arab nation," Qassem was vehemently opposed to such a move. His position was essentially pragmatic. He would not transform Iraq into yet another part of an Egyptian-dominated wider state, thereby subordinating himself to Nasser, whom he disliked and feared. He also anticipated that such a union would strengthen the position of his second in command, Colonel Abd al-Salam Aref, who had his eyes set on the country's leadership. These fears were fully justified. In a meeting with Nasser in Damascus a week after the July 1958 coup, Aref had promised Nasser that Iraq would soon join the UAR and that Qassem would be removed from his post. Word of this conversation soon reached Qassem.[28]

Anxious to shore up his position against what he perceived as an imminent threat to his leadership, Qassem swiftly took on the "unionists." Aref and Rashid Ali al-Kailani, the veteran Arab nationalist and former Prime Minister, were put on trial and sentenced to death (their sentences were later commuted to life imprisonment). Simultaneously, as a result of its support for the union, the Ba'th Party rapidly lost its newly acquired influence in military and political institutions, with many Party members being thrown into the overcrowded prisons. In his struggle against the "unionists," Qassem chose to rely on the communists, whose influence consequently grew. In a desperate bid to stem this mounting tide of communist influence, in March 1959 non-Ba'thist Arab nationalist officers staged an abortive uprising in the northern city of Mosul. Qassem's retribution was prompt and ominous. One of the bloodiest episodes in Iraq's modern political history ensued. The communist militias were given a free hand in Mosul to take revenge. Rapes, murders, lootings, summary trials and executions in front of cheering mobs followed. Hundreds lost their lives, most of them Arab nationalists.

The horrors of the Mosul massacre forced the Ba'th underground. They were now convinced that Iraq's salvation lay with the killing of Qassem. Despite the growing deterioration in Qassem's relations with the communists, following yet another massacre carried out in Kirkuk, this conclusion remained unchanged. Hence, in the early evening hours of October 7, 1959, a group of young Ba'th activists, including Saddam, ambushed Qassem's car on his way home from his office and shot him at close range.[29] Wounded, but narrowly escaping death, the shaken dictator ordered a nationwide clampdown on the Ba'th Party from his hospital bed. Although the ensuing purge severely disrupted the Party's organization and curbed its activities, the defiant stand of many Ba'thists in the public trials which were held put them in the national spotlight and exposed the still-small party to widespread recognition and respect.

The abortive attempt on Qassem's life became a major landmark in the evolution of the Iraqi Ba'th, as well as in the life of Saddam Hussein. Suddenly he emerged from complete obscurity to become one of the country's most wanted men. A fanciful story came to embellish his role in the assassination attempt. Saddam, the young idealist waits pistol in hand for the hated dictator, ready to martyr himself for a national cause. Wounded in the act, the revolutionary on the run is denied proper medical aid. Unflinchingly, he uses a knife to extract the bullet from his flesh and gallops through the desert on his horse, resourcefully escap-

ing numerous military patrols in hot pursuit. The determined
fugitive warrior swims to freedom in the icy water of the Tigris
river, knife between tightly clenched teeth.[30] The assassination
attempt and Saddam's escape would become an essential component of the Iraqi President's legend, glorified in numerous
publications, television programs and even a movie. The story
contains all the essentials of the making of a national hero:
patriotism, courage, manliness, iron discipline.

The truth about Saddam's role in the assassination attempt is
less glamorous. His original task was secondary: to provide
covering fire for his partners as they were shooting Qassem.
However, according to his semi-official biography, "when he
found himself face to face with the dictator, he was unable to
restrain himself. He forgot all his instructions and immediately
opened fire."[31] While this sympathetic account seeks to glorify
Saddam's behavior by underlining his initiative and eagerness to
rid the country of a detested dictator, it nevertheless implies that
he risked the entire operation, if not failed it altogether, through
his premature action. By ignoring the original plan and acting
independently, he confused his partners and enabled Qassem's
bodyguards to recover from their initial shock and to respond
more effectively. In the ensuing confusion one member of the "hit
squad" was killed by friendly fire, and Saddam himself was
injured by one of his comrades. Whatever the actual outcome of
Saddam's impetuous behavior, this episode constitutes one of the
few documented accounts of Saddam losing his nerve when faced
with grave danger. His public exposure and later glorification of
the incident notwithstanding, the young Saddam must have been
disconcerted by his contribution to the failure of the Ba'th's most
important political mission until then. Nor was the need to flee his
home country for an unknown period of time a welcome development for the young man, who had never before been
outside Iraq, and had cherished no such plans for the immediate
future. Apart from marking an important milestone in his political career, the abortive attempt had a sobering impact on
Saddam, teaching him the merits of self-control, patience and
caution.

In any event, Saddam managed to cross the border to Syria
where he was very warmly received by the Ba'th leadership, then
part of the joint leadership of the United Arab Republic. Michel
Aflaq, a founding father of the Party and its chief ideologue,
reportedly took a personal interest in the young political exile and

promoted him to the highest rank of Party membership, full member.[32] Even though Aflaq later recollected having met Saddam only after 1963,[33] there is little doubt that they quickly established a close rapport, and their friendship proved highly rewarding for Saddam Hussein. In 1964, largely due to Aflaq's efforts on his behalf, he was elected to the Iraqi Party's highest decision-making body, the Regional Command. Later on, Hussein would use the elderly spiritual figure to strengthen his own ideological credentials and legitimize his regime. Like the Soviet dictator, Joseph Stalin, who used Lenin's name as a source of legitimacy for his personal rule, so Saddam "had a living Lenin who could be wheeled out on suitable occasions to ratify his decisions and above all his status as guardian of party orthodoxy against successive groups."[34] Even Aflaq's death in 1989 was used to promote Saddam's political purposes. The Iraqi leader spread the word among his subjects that he personally paid to build a tomb for the founding father of the Ba'th Party.[35]

In February 1960, after a pleasant stay of three months in Damascus, Saddam left for Cairo, still the undisputed center of pan-Arabism, since the United Arab Republic was still in existence; indeed it was to be sustained until September 1961 when Damascus unilaterally seceded from the merger. The Egyptian capital abounded with political activists and exiles of all sorts, and Saddam quickly integrated into this vibrant community. Together with his close friend Abd al-Karim al-Shaykhli, who had also participated in the abortive attempt on Qassem's life, he joined the local Egyptian branch of the Ba'th Party. Within a short while Saddam became a member of its Regional Command. Yet, his foremost preoccupation in the Egyptian capital had less to do with revolutionary activity than with the advancement of his formal education. In 1961, at the age of 24, he finally graduated from high school in Cairo, and a year later he enrolled for law studies at the University of Cairo.

Contrary to what might be expected, Saddam's brief spell of academic learning did little to cultivate his radicalism or political awareness. Unlike the West, where universities were seething centers of intellectual activity, university life in Egypt in the early 1960s was intellectually dull. While professing a radical, indeed revolutionary ideology, the Egyptian authorities ruthlessly suppressed any manifestation of independent thinking on the campuses, imposing a "stifling uniformity" on teachers and students alike. Lecturers as well as students were often imprisoned for their opinions and forced to avoid taking provocative political stands. Demonstrations by students were forbidden except on rare occasions. Academic standards were exceptionally low, particularly in the liberal arts which offered a rather undemanding route to a degree. Students were often admitted on the basis of meager grades, were required to memorize rather than interpret material, and could obtain a degree after committing perhaps a dozen books to memory.[36]

Saddam, nevertheless, would never complete his law degree. Nine years after abandoning his studies in Egypt, having enrolled in law studies at the University of Baghdad, he appeared at the university with a pistol in his belt and accompanied by four bodyguards to receive his certificate. Four years later, in 1976, he would arrange to have an M.A. in Law awarded him by the university.[37]

During his stay in Egypt Saddam decided to marry his cousin, Sajidah Talfah. The two had known each other from their early childhood. They had been brought up together at Khairallah's home like brother and sister and, according to Saddam, when they were still children Sajidah had been betrothed to him by his grandfather. Following the traditional custom Saddam wrote his stepfather, Hasan Ibrahim, requesting him to approach Khairallah on his behalf and ask for his daughter's hand. Ibrahim did exactly that and Khairallah gave his consent to the couple's marriage. They were engaged while Saddam was still in Cairo and got married shortly after his return to Iraq in early 1963. A year later their first son, Udai, was born.[38] Their wedding picture shows a happy, good-looking couple. Saddam had not yet grown his famous mustache. His expression is soft, the look in his eyes tender and reconciled, nothing resembling the all-too-familiar tough, bullish expression he would assume from the mid-1970s onwards.

Before returning to Baghdad, however, Saddam had to endure three unpleasant years in Egypt. Even though the Iraqi Ba'th was indispensable to Nasser in his protracted confrontation with Qassem, his clashes with the Syrian Ba'th Party in the Egyptian-Syrian union leading to the withdrawal of Syria from the union in 1961, made him wary of anything that smacked of Ba'thism. This presidential state of mind had direct implications on Saddam Hussein's daily life. The maintenance allowance he received from the Egyptian government as a member of the Iraqi

Ba'th in exile was often delayed and at times suspended. Not only was he kept under surveillance and subjected to occasional harassment by the security services, but once he was even thrown into jail for a short while. Accounts of the reasons for his detention differ. According to Shi'ite opposition sources, Hussein was arrested on suspicion of murdering another Iraqi political exile. An alternative explanation linked Saddam's detention to the authorities' disaffection with his political activities (he was even reported to have paid occasional visits to the American Embassy in Cairo).[39] In either case, there was no basis for a legal prosecution and before long Hussein found himself a free man again.

If there was one ray of light in Saddam's Cairo period, it was the opportunity he had to observe President Nasser in action. According to Saddam's own account, he was then an admirer of the Egyptian President who "expressed the opinion of the whole Arab nation before the world," and was keen on adopting his political tactics.[40] Nasser's skillful dismantling of political pluralism in the UAR and its replacement by a single-party system (the so-called National Union) probably influenced Saddam's view on the nature of Iraq's future regime. Nor did Nasser's attempt to confer a semblance of democracy on his formation of a National Assembly escape Saddam's eye: in 1980 he would resort to a similar tactic by re-establishing Iraq's parliament after more than two decades of inactivity. Saddam also took account of the currents of pragmatism underlying Nasser's impassioned rhetoric. When Abd al-Karim Qassem challenged Kuwait's independence in 1961, the Egyptian President collaborated, albeit indirectly, with "imperialist" Great Britain in shielding the conservative Gulf monarchy from "revolutionary" Iraq: Qassem was his sworn enemy, and to allow him any gain that could boost his position was inconceivable.[41]

These important observations notwithstanding, Saddam was no "blind follower of Nasser," as the acrimonious exchanges between the two after the Ba'thi takeover in 1968 would reveal. He was correct in judging that the fundamental difference in their personalities would make any indiscriminate imitation look ridiculous. An introvert and restrained person, Saddam lacked Nasser's charismatic appeal. Unlike the Egyptian President who was often carried away by his own rhetoric and used it to inflame his listeners with fiery speeches, Saddam addressed his audience like a radio announcer, enumerating his points quietly, almost impersonally. His flat tone of voice and somewhat inhibited manner of speaking made him appear detached from his own rhetoric, and often turned the most ardent language into a boring monologue. Because of these differences Saddam knew that the substance could be borrowed from Nasser, but the appearance would have to be molded along the lines of his own personality. If he were to be a prominent Arab leader, he would do it his way.

The Egyptian period in Hussein's life ended in February 1963 when the Ba'th Party in Iraq, together with sympathetic military officers, managed to overwhelm Qassem and to seize power. Like the ascendancy of the deposed regime, five years earlier, the Ba'thi takeover was excessively bloody. Qassem and some of his close associates were immediately executed and his supporters, the communists in particular, combatted the army and the Ba'thi militia, the National Guard, in the streets of Baghdad for several days. By the time they had laid down their weapons, between 1,500 and 5,000 people had perished.[42] This, however, did not end the bloodshed. Having established themselves in power, the Ba'thists turned to settle scores with political opponents. Thousands of leftists and communists were arrested and tortured. Hundreds were executed.

Saddam, nevertheless, had nothing to do with these events. Upon arriving in Baghdad he found himself very much an outsider. At the time of his escape from Iraq he had been too junior in the Party to build up a power base, and his three years in Egypt had kept him isolated from its development. Hussein's major credential, participating in the attempt on Qassem's life, failed now to buy him a ticket to the Party's inner circle. The frustrated young man had, therefore, to linger on the fringes of the newly installed Ba'thi administration and to content himself with the minor position of a member of the Party's central bureau for peasants. Without delay, he began building up his position within the Party by joining the faction co-headed by his fellow Tikriti and blood relative Brigadier Ahmad Hasan al-Bakr, who now served as Prime Minister of Iraq, and Colonel Salih Mahdi Ammash, the Defense Minister.

Hardly had the Ba'th gained power when it was torn by a bitter ideological struggle between two main rival camps. The first, a leftist and militant group headed by the Party's Secretary-General, Ali Salih al-Sa'di, preached a fundamental, rapid transformation of the Iraqi socio-political system to a socialist state. It was opposed by a dovish, right-wing faction that advocated a more gradual evolution to socialism and supported collaboration with non-Ba'thist military officers. Among its members was the-then Commander of the Air Force, General Hardan al-Tikriti. Bakr's faction struck a middle course between these two extremes with a certain bias toward the right-wing camp. This centrist faction lacked the ideological commitment and political zeal of the other two camps. It did not share their willingness to commit political suicide for a theoretical position. Practical and pragmatic to the core, Bakr and his associates worked assiduously to reconcile the rival wings. They knew that the Party's only hope lay in its unity. Either it stuck together or it would hang together.

They were fighting a hopeless rearguard action. Not heeding words of moderation, the extremist factions continued their relentless infighting. In a special session of the Party's Regional Command on November 11, 1963, the leftist group was expelled from the Party. Secretary-General Sa'di and four of his closest aides were arrested during the session, driven to the airport and flown to exile in Spain. This coup sparked off a wave of violence in Baghdad, bringing the capital to the verge of civil war. The National Guard, Sa'di's political instrument, raged in the streets, killing and looting. In a desperate attempt to mediate a compromise solution, a high-ranking Syrian delegation headed by Michel Aflaq rushed to Iraq, only to realize that reconciliation was no longer feasible and that the only way out of the crisis was to purge the Party of the two extremist camps. Within a day, the visiting members of the National Command expelled the right-wing group from the Regional Command, and its leaders found themselves on a plane to Beirut.[43]

By way of filling the ensuing power vacuum in the Iraqi leadership, the National Command in Damascus stepped on the scene and assumed responsibility over the Iraqi branch. This proved a fatal mistake. With the Iraqi Ba'th leadership effectively removed and the National Command's interference in Iraqi politics viewed by the public as a blatant violation of their country's sovereignty, the Party's national standing plummeted to its lowest point. This in turn enabled President Abd al-Salam Aref, who had been installed in his position by the Ba'th as a titular figure, to move against his previous benefactors. In November 1963, after nine turbulent months at the helm, the Ba'th found itself outside the corridors of power.

Their ouster was a traumatic event in Ba'thist history. The

general feeling was one of a great loss, of a missed historic
opportunity. A soul-searching process began amid an acrimonious
exchange of accusations and a strenuous jockeying for positions.
Yet, just as the general good does not necessarily benefit every
single individual, so a collective adversity does not bode ill for all.
For Saddam Hussein, the Party's setback was a blessing in
disguise, a major turning point in his career which would transform him within a few years into one of the most powerful figures
in the Party.

As a junior member in the centrist faction of the ruling Ba'thi
administration, Hussein's chances for rapid promotion had been
virtually nil, given the prior balance of forces within the Party.
Once the Ba'th had been thrown into disarray, however, new
promising avenues were opened to the young and ambitious
Tikriti. By the mid-1960s Bakr's camp had developed into the
dominant power within the Ba'th. Bakr himself was elected in
1964 as a member of the National Command and a year later he
became Secretary-General of the Iraqi Regional Command. And,
in his train, Saddam followed. He quickly gained Bakr's trust,
becoming his close confidant and, ultimately, his right-hand man.

The reward for his fidelity followed soon after. In February
1964 the Seventh Congress of the National Command sought to
invigorate the debilitated Iraqi branch by establishing a provisional Regional Command that excluded those involved in the
Party's fall from power. Due to Michel Aflaq's efforts, and Bakr's
support, Hussein was appointed Secretary of the new organ.
When the permanent Regional Command was re-established later
that year, the two introduced their young protégé into this
institution as well.

From his first moments in the Party's supreme decision-making
body, Hussein was adamant on assuming responsibility for security affairs. If there was one single lesson he drew from his
experience, it was that in the violent Iraqi political world there was
no substitute for physical force; that physical force was indispensable both for coming to power and staying there, as well as for
subordinating any and all political factions to one's will. It was
armed force which had enabled Qassem to overthrow the monarchy in 1958 and which then accounted for his own destruction
five years later. And it was lack of control over the state's
legitimate organs of violence which had prevented the Ba'th from
effectively resisting the military takeover by Aref. Hence, if the

Ba'th were to return to power, it would have to be achieved through military means.

Faithful to this reasoning, Hussein, who in 1964 was put in charge of the Party's military organization, quickly moved to plot a *coup d'état* against President Aref. Before long two alternative courses of action had been devised, both scheduled for execution by mid-September 1964 at the latest. According to first plan, a group of armed Ba'thists headed by Hussein was to infiltrate the Presidential Palace during a cabinet meeting and to eliminate the entire Iraqi leadership. The second course of action envisaged the downing of Aref's plane on his way to Cairo to attend an Arab summit meeting. Both these violent plans proved stillborn. The hopes of infiltrating the palace were dashed when an officer of the Republican Guard, who was to lead the conspirators to their destination, was unexpectedly removed from his post. To make matters worse for the Ba'th, the plan to shoot down the presidential plane was betrayed by one of the pilots, who turned out to be working for the secret services. Aref responded to this revelation by clamping down on the Party and its leadership.[44]

As one of the few senior Party members outside prison during Aref's purge of the Party, Hussein faced an agonizing decision: either to try to escape to Syria and continue the struggle from there, or to stay in Baghdad and run the likely risk of being caught and arrested. Choosing the second alternative, he defied the National Command in Damascus which instructed him to leave for the Syrian capital. The reasons for this decision are not difficult to gauge. Fleeing Iraq at the time when most of the Ba'th leaders, including Bakr, were rotting in jail was likely to be interpreted as an act of cowardice which could tarnish Hussein's prospects within the Party. Masterminding the Ba'thi campaign against the regime, on the other hand, contained the seeds of future glory and involved far smaller risks than those he had already run during the attempt on Qassem's life a few years earlier. No death penalty awaited Hussein this time. The gravest punishment he faced was to join his colleagues behind bars which could only "martyr" him on "the altar of the revolution."

Given this balance of risks and opportunities, Hussein's decision to remain in Baghdad seemed reasonable. Like the numerous risky decisions he was to take in subsequent years, this move was anything but impetuous; rather it was made after a careful consideration of the costs and benefits involved. As in many of Hussein's future actions, the calculated risk paid off, though not without paying a certain price: in mid-October 1964 Hussein's hideout was surrounded by security forces, and, after an exchange of fire, he ran out of ammunition and was forced to give himself up.

Hussein's account of his two years in Aref's prison is conspicuously reminiscent of the prison term served by another young revolutionary whom the Iraqi leader has unabashedly admitted admiring: Joseph Stalin. He "imposed upon himself a rigid discipline, rose early, worked hard, read much, and was one of the chief debaters in the prison commune."[45] This routine enabled Hussein to sharpen his skills and assert his leadership over fellow political prisoners. More importantly, he managed to maintain close contacts with Bakr, who had already been released, by transmitting and receiving messages hidden under the robe of his baby son, Udai, who was brought by Sajidah on her weekly visits to the prison. Hussein had already established himself as Bakr's closest aide, the "fixer" who would handle all bureaucratic and organizational problems, the single-minded strategist whose determination to reinstate the Ba'th in power would not be sidetracked by ideological or moral niceties. The extent of Bakr's confidence in his younger associate was best illustrated when he later appointed Hussein Deputy Secretary-General of the Iraqi Regional Command.

Like many other stories relating to his underground days, Saddam's road to freedom from behind bars was to become part of the Saddam legend. According to the escape plan which was devised by Saddam, together with two other Ba'thist friends, Abd al-Karim al-Shaykhli and Hasan al-Amiri, the three were to persuade the guards accompanying them to court to stop at a certain Baghdadi restaurant for lunch. Two of them were then to go to the washroom, which opened directly to the street, and to get away by a special car that would be waiting for them. The third was to engage the guards and try to persuade them to desert. The scheme was executed as planned. Amiri remained behind while Saddam and Shaykhli left the room, rushed into a car which was waiting outside with the doors open, and were driven away by Sa'dun Shakir, Saddam's cousin and an active Ba'thist.[46]

The first major challenge facing Hussein after his escape revolved around relations with the sister party in Syria. On February 23, 1966, a military coup had brought the radical, Marxist faction of the Ba'th to power in Damascus. Aflaq, al-Bitar and the other members of the Old Guard were arrested, and the

National Command, the Party's supreme decision-making organ, was temporarily dissolved. This development was viewed by Hussein and his close associates with grave concern. The radicalization of the Syrian regime and its aspirations to re-establish the National Command under Damascus's wings threatened to turn the Iraqi Ba'th into a mere extension of the Syrian will. The fact that the Syrian leadership consisted of military officers set an example which Hussein would later seek to avoid. Though keenly aware of the need to collaborate with the military in overthrowing Aref, Hussein had no intention of sharing political power with them. He had already learned that a powerful and independent military always posed a threat to civilian government. Above all, the ascendancy of the Marxist faction in Syria rekindled fears of a possible resurgence of the leftist faction of the Iraqi Ba'th, subdued but not completely eradicated since 1963.

Unwilling to accept Damascus's authority, Hussein initiated an Extraordinary Regional Congress to determine the Iraqi Ba'th's response to the Syrian challenge. The conference which was convened in September 1966 became a watershed in Ba'thi history. Although it would not be until February 1968 that the Iraqi Ba'th formed its own pan-Arab National Command, the Extraordinary Congress which met in 1966 cemented the ideological and organizational schism between the branches of the Ba'th Party in Iraq and Syria. A unified Ba'th with Regional Commands in the respective countries ceased to exist. It was replaced by two separate parties, one in Damascus and the other in Baghdad, both claiming to be the lawful successor of the original Party; and both with a pan-Arab National Command comprising representatives from other regions. It is from this time that the bitter inter-Arab rivalry between Syria and Iraq, which was to characterize many periods of Saddam's career, began.

Having played the key role in precipitating the breach with Damascus, Hussein concentrated on reconstructing the Party's organization in Iraq, but not before purging the remaining leftists in the ranks of the Ba'th. He completed the formation of the Party's security apparatus (which he personally headed),[47] laid the foundations for a new party militia, and expanded the Party's network of branches throughout Iraq. Above all, together with Ahmad Hasan al-Bakr and a narrow circle of associates, he began to calculatingly weave a tangled web which was to close on President Aref a couple of years later.

The Ba'thist conspiracy was largely facilitated by a rather lenient attitude on the part of the Iraqi authorities toward the Party's activities. In April 1966 the Iraqi President, Abd al-Salam Aref died in a helicopter crash and his brother, Abd al-Rahman Aref, assumed the Presidency. A weak and colorless character, the new president found it increasingly difficult to reconcile the rival factions within the military, and virtually impossible to balance the various political forces in the country. Treading cautiously on the uncertain paths of the Iraqi political system, Aref sought to improve his position by using the carrot rather than the stick. Repression of Ba'thist activities eased significantly, and on several occasions the President even sounded out the Party's readiness to collaborate with the regime. This, in turn, enabled the Ba'th to consolidate its power base and to wait patiently for the right moment for a renewed bid for power.

Such conditions appeared to have developed following the humiliating Arab defeat in the Six Day War of 1967. In a brilliant *blitzkrieg,* within six days Israel managed to defeat the armies of Egypt, Syria, Jordan, and an Iraqi expeditionary force, and to occupy the Sinai Peninsula, the Golan Heights, and the West Bank, including East Jerusalem with its holy sites. Coming in the wake of a month of escalating tensions and high Arab nationalist rhetoric, in which President Nasser succeeded in orchestrating an all-Arab coalition against Israel, the extent of the Israeli victory stunned the Arabs. Nasser's personal prestige suffered a decisive blow. So did the idea of Arab nationalism. Pan-Arabism had liberated the various Arab states from colonial domination, but it succeeded neither in advancing the unification of the Arab nation, nor in uprooting the perceived major threat to this nation—Israel. If the Arab states could be so easily defeated by the "Zionist entity," as Israel was called by the Arab states, how could they aspire to achieve the ultimate goal of unity? Even Nasser seemed disillusioned with the cause he had so vigorously championed throughout his career. "You issue statements but we have to fight," he told a gathering of the heads of Arab states in Cairo. "If you want to liberate, then get in line in front of us."[48]

As huge crowds of Iraqis took to the streets to demonstrate their anger and frustration over the defeat, the Ba'th quickly capitalized on the country's minimal participation in the war in order to delegitimize the regime. During the last months of 1967 and the early months of 1968, it conducted a series of strikes and demonstrations which denounced the regime's corruption and ineptitude and called for its replacement. The Party's public activities reached their peak in April 1968 when 13 retired officers, five of whom were Ba'thists, submitted a memorandum to Aref demanding the removal of the Prime Minister, Tahir Yahya, the establishment of a legislative assembly and the formation of a new government.

These demonstrations notwithstanding, the Ba'thists were fully aware of their inability to bring down the Aref regime on their own. In a political system that thrived on physical force, they simply lacked the necessary means to overwhelm their opponents. Hence, in early 1968 the Party began sounding out the readiness of the armed forces to participate in a coup attempt. Before long they established contact with the "Arab Revolutionary Movement," a group of young officers formed in 1966 to protect President Aref but who had become increasingly unhappy with his leadership.[49] The foremost targets of the Ba'thi persuasion campaign were four senior officers who constituted the pillars of the Aref regime: Colonel Abd al-Razzaq Nayif, Head of Military Intelligence; Colonel Ibrahim Abd al-Rahman Da'ud, Commander of the Republican Guard (the President's praetorian guard); Colonel Sa'dun Ghaydan, Commander of the Republican Guard's armored brigade; and Colonel Hammad Shihab, Commander of the Baghdad Garrison.

Fortunately for the Ba'thists, these officers, each of whom could easily have foiled an attempted coup against the regime, were open to negotiations. Ghaydan and Shihab were sympathetic to the Ba'thi cause in the first place, and in Shihab's case this positive attitude was reinforced by blood relations: he was a Tikriti and a cousin of Bakr. Nayif and Da'ud, for their part, were motivated by the all-too-familiar combination of impulses dominating Iraqi politics: greed and fear. On the one hand, they considered themselves the natural successors to Aref and viewed the Ba'th as a junior partner that could be easily tamed. On the other hand, they had been alienated from Aref for quite some time and had good reasons to anticipate their own impending purge. Besides, they lacked the organizational infrastructure and ideological appeal which the Ba'th could possibly offer. The reward they demanded, though, was exorbitant: the Premiership for Nayif and the Ministry of Defense for Da'ud.[50]

The price of the two officers' participation confronted the Ba'th at an emergency meeting of its Regional Command, convened at Bakr's home on the evening of July 16, 1968. While the

Ba'thists viewed this last-moment decision as an unscrupulous attempt to blackmail them into further concessions, Nayif and Da'ud needed to move abruptly: a few hours earlier they had been summoned to President Aref and asked whether there was truth in the rumors about an impending coup. The two denied any such rumors and tearfully kissed Aref's hands, assuring him of their unswerving loyalty. He believed them, but they feared that their conspiracy would soon be uncovered and decided to throw in their lot with the Ba'th.[51]

However irritated with the extortionist demands and however wary of the two, the Ba'thists saw no other choice but to comply. A negative response was bound to antagonize Nayif and Da'ud and would have required a dramatic revision of the coup plan, if not its indefinite postponement. This possibility was eminently clear to Saddam who distinguished himself as one of the foremost proponents of a tactical alliance with the officers. "I am aware that the two officers have been imposed on us and that they want to stab the Party in the back in the service of some interest or other," he told his comrades, "but we have no choice now. We should collaborate with them but see that they are liquidated immediately during, or after the revolution. And I volunteer to carry out this task."[52]

Saddam's speech offers a vivid illustration of the ruthless pragmatism that was to become his main hallmark, and was to bring him within a decade to the Presidential Palace. The end justified all means. Collaboration with the most despised partners was perfectly legitimate if it served the ultimate goal of political survival. Nor was there anything morally wrong in forming an alliance with the foreknowledge that it would be dissolved at the first opportune moment. Since all political opponents were virtually "spies and agents," they should be given their own medicine. As Saddam himself put it during the discussion: "It is a legitimate and a moral necessity that the Party should not be betrayed a second time [the first being the fall from power in 1963], and that it should be protected from harm."[53]

Emboldened by Saddam's emotional plea, the Party decided to accept the officers' demands and to proceed with its *putsch*. A few hours later a new era in Iraq's modern history was to dawn.

2

Second among Equals

It was not yet morning when President Abd al-Rahman Aref was awakened by the telephone beside his bed. At the other end of the line was the veteran Ba'thist officer, General Hardan al-Tikriti. "I am empowered to inform you that you are no longer President," Tikriti said dryly, "the Ba'th has taken control of the country. If you surrender peacefully, I can guarantee that your safety will be ensured." The President, still hoping that it was only a nightmare, made desperate, last-minute phone calls to Da'ud and Ghaydan, only to be told that the army had turned against him. Deeply shaken, Aref proceeded to the entrance hall of the palace where Tikriti was already waiting for him, and gave himself up. A few hours later he was in a plane on his way to London. Shortly afterwards the Iraqi people learned that the Ba'th "had taken over power and ended the corrupt and weak regime, represented by the clique of the ignorant, the illiterate, the profit-seekers, thieves, spies, and Zionists."[1]

Thus started the "July Revolution," the fourth change of regime in Iraq since the overthrow of the monarchy exactly a decade earlier. In contrast to the harsh overtones of its 1963 predecessor it was conspicuously bloodless. As Aref had been betrayed by the guardians of his regime—Da'ud, Nayif, Ghaydan, and Shihab—there was virtually no fighting and the only shots were those fired later in the day to celebrate victory. Nothing in

31

the air indicated the dark cloud of repression that was to settle over Iraq before too long.

Saddam's whereabouts on this momentous day in Ba'thi history are not entirely clear. According to the official account he was in the first tank to storm the Presidential Palace, but there is no evidence to substantiate the claim which seems more of a retrospective attempt to embellish Saddam's "revolutionary" credentials. The July 1968 takeover was yet another military *coup d'état* rather than a popular uprising, and was carried out essentially by the military officers within the Party such as Bakr, Hardan al-Tikriti, and Ammash. The coup was not even a purely Ba'thist enterprise, since it owed its success largely to Da'ud and Nayif, who had been harnessed to the venture shortly before the zero hour.

Due to their less critical roles, the civilian members of the Party, Saddam Hussein included, were forced to bide their time during the coup in nervous anticipation of news. This was a particularly unwelcome situation for Saddam who, as Deputy Secretary-General of the Ba'th, had no choice but to watch potential contenders for leadership, such as his fellow Tikriti, Hardan, outshine him. His only consolation might have been that in the event of the coup's failure, he would be better poised for a future leadership role since his military colleagues would be killed, arrested, or discredited for their failure. Yet, the coup succeeded and though Saddam had not played a highly visible role at the initial transfer of power to the Party, he soon occupied a central place in its hierarchy.[2]

Fortunately for Saddam, his organizational and operational skills proved indispensable for the Party's survivability. From the moment Aref was driven from the Presidential Palace to his comfortable exile, a fierce jockeying for power within the new leadership ensued. From its inception, the coalition between the Ba'th and the Nayif-Da'ud faction was an unholy alliance aimed at destroying a joint enemy rather than building a common future. Neither camp trusted the other; both were bent on ridding themselves of an unwanted partner at the first available opportunity. Nayif and Da'ud regarded the Ba'th as a free rider on the revolution that had been made possible only by their participation. The Ba'thists, for their part, felt victimized. They had been blackmailed into the coalition and had paid an exorbitant price to buy the acquiescence of the two officers who could easily have jeopardized their bid for power. Now that they shared leadership with the Nayif-Da'ud faction, the Ba'thists felt that unless they moved immediately against their unwanted partners, they would find themselves yet again outside the corridors of power.

This task, however, was easier said than done. The Party's power base within the military, the key for any political change, was extremely precarious. Although Hardan al-Tikriti was appointed Chief of Staff and once again Commander of the Air Force, he had been outside the military for quite some time and was consequently less intimate with the officer corps than his superior, Minister of Defense Da'ud. Nor did the Ba'th enjoy unequivocal superiority in the state institutions. Even though Bakr, Saddam's relative and protector, succeeded Aref as the Iraqi President, the Premiership, and the Ministries of Defense and Foreign Affairs fell to the Nayif-Da'ud faction. The Revolutionary Command Council (RCC), the foremost decision-making body in Iraq which was set up immediately after the takeover, consisted of seven officers: three Ba'thists (Bakr, Ammash, and Hardan al-Tikriti), Nayif, Da'ud, and two neutrals (Shihab and Ghaydan) who leaned toward the Ba'th but whose loyalty was by no means a foregone conclusion. The 26-member cabinet, headed by Nayif, was similarly divided, with the Ba'th and the Nayif-Da'ud faction each having eight supporters.

If the removal of Nayif and Da'ud was to be achieved without a military *putsch* or a political coup within the state's ruling bodies, it had to be accomplished through a sophisticated conspiracy. And it was here that Saddam proved his creative imagination and operational skills, playing a pivotal role both in plotting and in delivering the *coup de grace* to the rival faction. On July 29, 1968, Da'ud was lured out of the country, ostensibly for an inspection tour of the Iraqi forces stationed in Jordan. Totally unaware of the real motive behind the mission, Da'ud gave full control of the army in his absence to the Chief of Staff, Hardan al-Tikriti. The next day, Nayif was invited for lunch with President Bakr at the Presidential Palace. As the unsuspecting Premier was preparing to leave the Palace, Saddam dashed in accompanied by four officers. What happened next was related by his semi-official biographers:

> Hussein drew his revolver and ordered Nayif to raise his hands. When Nayif saw the revolver pointed at him he put his hands over his eyes and said: "I have four children." Saddam was adamant. "Do not be afraid," he said, "nothing will happen to your children

if you behave sensibly. Abd al-Razzaq, you know you forced your
way into the revolution and that you are a stumbling block in the
way of the Party. We have paid for this revolution with our blood,
and now it has come out. The decision of the Party is that you
should be put out of the way. You should leave Iraq immediately."

Matters did not end here. Once Nayif had accepted, Saddam
Hussein ordered a plane prepared to convey him from the Rashid
Military Camp to Morocco. Saddam Hussein ordered Nayif to act
naturally, to salute the guards when they saluted him, and to walk
normally to the official car awaiting him. He warned Nayif that his
gun was in his jacket, and that if he saw the slightest sign that Nayif
was about to disobey his orders, he would end his life then and
there. He asked some of his comrades to remain at the Palace to
protect President Ahmad Hasan Bakr. Saddam sat next to Nayif all
the way to the Rashid Military Camp. The plane was waiting. After
it took off, Hussein felt tears come to his eyes.[3]

The sincerity of Saddam's alleged tearfulness is certainly dubious.
Nayif was made ambassador to Morocco, but in fact he was exiled
for fear he would mount a countercoup to oust the Ba'thists. His
life was to end a decade later in London, where he was gunned
down at his doorstep in July 1978, after at least one previous
abortive attempt on his life. Even in exile he was considered too
dangerous by Saddam, who suspected him of continuing to
conspire against the regime. Da'ud was instructed to remain in
Jordan as head of the military mission there. In 1970 he was
retired from his post, and was never allowed to return to Iraq.

By July 30 the Ba'th had carried out its second successful coup
within two weeks, this time gaining exclusive control over the
country. As Nayif headed toward Morocco, his followers were
being stripped of their state positions. Bakr consolidated his
powers by assuming two new posts in addition to the Presidency
and Chairmanship of the RCC which he had held since July 18:
he was made Prime Minister and Commander-in-Chief of the
armed forces. Hardan al-Tikriti became Minister of Defense
while Abd al-Karim al-Shaykhli was appointed Minister for Foreign Affairs. Ammash retained his post as Minister of the Interior.[4] The most significant nomination, though, was the promotion
of Saddam Hussein to the second most important position in the
ruling hierarchy: Deputy Chairmanship of the RCC.

Bakr's choice of Hussein as his right hand was hardly surprising. Hussein had been his deputy at the Party's Regional Command since 1966. Both were relatives and fellow Tikritis and both

had known each other well for a long time. Bakr had closely followed Hussein's personal development from a young boy at Khairallah Talfah's home to an efficient *apparatchik* at the party's supreme organs. This formed the core of Saddam's reliability in Bakr's eyes. But no less important for the President was the complete lack of any military education in Saddam's personal background.

To Saddam, his failure to enter the Military Academy had been a personal disgrace, a humiliating reminder of his inadequacy vis-à-vis his uniformed colleagues and relatives, and an exclusion from one of the country's most powerful channels of social mobility. Ironically, however, it was exactly this exclusion that appealed so much to President Bakr. Until 1966 the Ba'th had been headed by a civilian Secretary-General, but chronic disunity within the Party had led to the ascendancy of the military faction.[5] As long as the Party was in opposition, the primacy of the military faction was indispensable since the army was the only institution which could help the Party regain power. Having achieved the country's top position, Bakr no longer needed a strong military faction. On the contrary, ambitious independent officers around him posed a permanent threat to his position, and in light of past experience Bakr knew all too well that it was a potentially fatal threat indeed. In these circumstances, an able and ruthless, yet loyal operator like Saddam Hussein, who was equally determined to break the military's hold on Iraqi politics, seemed the ideal number two man.

At the age of 31 Saddam Hussein could view his political career with a sense of achievement. Within less than a decade the tall, slim, yet powerfully built young man had developed from an obscure Party member into the second most influential person in Iraq. Though he had not played a significant role in the actual execution of the coup which brought the Ba'th to power in 1968, he was largely responsible for the "second revolution" which enabled the Party "to rule rather than merely reign."[6] Given his intimacy with Bakr and his dynamic character, Saddam wielded far greater power than an ordinary number two man, particularly since his prominent position was reinforced by control over the Party's security apparatus, which he created.

Despite his youthfulness, Hussein adjusted ably and quickly. He was realistic enough to know that holding on to his position, let alone moving forward to the Presidential Palace, would be a precarious and tortuous process. Yet he also was confident that he possessed the necessary qualities for this hazardous journey: great caution, endless patience, intense calculation, and utter ruthlessness. A vivid illustration of Saddam's caution was afforded by the ostensibly inexplicable fact that his position as Deputy Chairman of the RCC was not made public until November 1969, more than a year after he was actually appointed. Saddam would later explain this decision on grounds of pure altruism. In his own account, he initially surprised Bakr by refusing to assume any executive duties. Since he believed that the Ba'th's fall from power in 1963 had resulted from unbridled personal ambitions, he thought it would be better if, after the "1968 Revolution," he quit his senior position in order to demonstrate humility and Party discipline. The reason why he eventually decided to acquiesce to Bakr's plea and to remain at the steering wheel was his realization that the Party's future would be jeopardized by his retirement from power: even as early as the summer of 1968 he had uncovered plots against Bakr and was aware of Hardan's ambition to subvert the President's position.[7]

Who would not declare in public the substitution of the national interest for personal ambition? But even if humility is not one of his most visible virtues, Saddam's explanation clearly reflects his extreme caution, stemming from distrust of his environment and constant anticipation of plots. Experts on Iraqi politics tend to attribute Hussein's apparent modesty and shortsightedness—by avoiding public exposure he ran the risk of sliding into relative obscurity—to his fear that the success of the Ba'thi revolution was by no means a foregone conclusion. By remaining behind the scenes, they have argued, Saddam could presumably hope to insure himself against the dire consequences of the Party's possible fall from power.[8]

The fear was there, it is true, but it was not a fear of a mass uprising. Iraq's historical experience revealed that, given the country's social and religious fragmentation, changes of regime were not executed by popular uprisings but, rather, by military coups. Keeping Saddam's official status from public knowledge could hardly guarantee his chances for survival, since his actual position was fully known inside the Party and the military. Everybody who counted knew that Bakr and Hussein were a duo. If the former were to be overthrown by a *putsch* of sorts, the latter was bound to go down with him.

The projection of humility on Saddam's part, therefore, was

targeted at the Party's political and military leadership, not at the public. He knew all too well that, however prominent, the Deputy Chairmanship did not enable him to impose his will over the coalition of the Ba'thist officers facing him: Hardan, Ammash, Ghaydan and Shihab. It is true that this coalition was beset by mutual jealousies and enmities. It is also true that not all of the four were hostile toward Saddam. Shihab, for example, had a close friendship with his fellow Tikriti, and it was Saddam who had even convinced him, in a prolonged conversation, to join the Ba'thi bid for power in July 1968.[9] Yet by virtue of their stature, Saddam viewed Hardan and Ammash as potent rivals who would have to be removed from the scene sooner or later. Since his position was weaker than theirs, initially, he avoided a direct confrontation, preferring instead to lure the officers into a false sense of complacency by donning the mantle of modesty. A humble Saddam with no personal ambitions for national leadership would appear harmless to the officers who, in turn, would leave him alone to conspire against them. But before he would feel secure enough to turn against his comrades, Saddam was faced with the more urgent task of ensuring the Party's hold on the newly regained reins of power.

The Ba'thi takeover was no popular revolution. The Party did not rise to power on a wave of public demand. In fact, the national attitude toward the "July Revolution" ranged from deep anxiety to apathetic indifference. The ruthless Ba'thi experience of 1963 was still very much alive in the collective mind and was remembered with awesome fear and quiet, deep-seated resentment. The July 1968 Revolution had occurred so swiftly that it hardly touched the daily life of ordinary Iraqis.[10] During the decade preceding the "revolution," they had grown accustomed to military officers succeeding one another at the Presidential Palace, without any alteration or alleviation of the hardships of daily life. Not surprisingly, the Ba'thi coup was initially perceived as one of the endless succession of others like it. The Ba'th leadership was largely anonymous to the Iraqi people; while some officers were known on a local basis, Bakr was the only figure of national standing. Grassroots support for the party was meager. According to Ba'thi estimates, in 1968 the Party numbered approximately 5,000 full members, and even this modest figure seems lavish. The Ba'th's actual strength at the time was apparently no more than half of its own estimates.[11] The social foundation of the

Party was glaringly slim. While Shi'ites account for some 60 percent of the Iraqi population and Sunnis for nearly 20 percent, by the late 1960s the Ba'th had become a virtual Sunni party. The historical legacy of the Sunni Ottoman Empire, social fragmentation, and geographical constraints kept the Shi'ite community internally divided, and prevented it from becoming an effective political force. Although a few Shi'ites managed to reach high-ranking positions (such as Sa'dun Hammadi who in 1969 became Minister of Oil and Natural Resources), there were no Shi'ites in the party's top echelon which was dominated by the so-called "Sunni triangle," Iraq's main Sunni concentration, lying between Baghdad in the south, Mosul in the north, and Rutba in the east, near the Jordanian and Syrian border. The hard core of leadership was even narrower and was predicated, by and large, on army officers from Tikrit, Saddam's home region. The rise of the Tikritis to political prominence, which played a crucial role in Saddam's personal career, can be traced to the impoverishment of the town in the early twentieth century, which drove many of its inhabitants to move to Baghdad and other major cities in search of a living. Many of the emigres found their way into the cost-free Royal Military Academy, embarking consequently on a military career.

The person who opened the doors of the Academy to the steady flow of young Tikritis was one of the more influential Arab nationalists in Iraq in the 1920s—Mawlud Muklis. Born of a Tikriti father, he participated in the "Arab revolt" against the Turks during World War I, becoming a close confidant of King Faisal I and Vice President of the Senate under the monarchy. Until his death in the 1950s, he used his power and influence to place young Tikritis in the army and the police, as well as in governmental posts. This practice was repeated later by Muklis's protégés who placed kinsmen and town members in military and political posts, a common practice in Middle Eastern societies where one's first loyalty is to immediate clan and place of origin.[12]

Given their narrow base, the Ba'th had never had any intention of establishing a liberal democracy in Iraq. In one of Saddam's public statements at the time, he straightforwardly spelled out his authoritarian vision of Iraq's political system: "The ideal revolutionary command should effectively direct all planning and implementation. It must not allow the growth of any other rival center of power. There must be one command pooling

and directing the subsequent governmental departments, including the armed forces."[13]

Given the Ba'th's narrow popular base, the subordination of
the nation to its will and the legitimization of its rule required
heavy reliance on coercion. The masses had to be "re-educated"
and incorporated into the Party's organizational machinery. Rivals
had to be eliminated and a deep sense of fear and respect had to
be struck into people's hearts. These tasks fitted Saddam's abilities
perfectly. They gave him an ideal opportunity to outbid the
military officers in the service of the Party and, in turn, to boost
his own standing and that of his security apparatus.

The fall of 1968 witnessed the launching of a wave of
ferocious purges which was to be sustained for nearly a year. The
operation began by removing all non-Ba'thists from the various
state institutions, proceeded to repress organized political opposition and individual political dissidents, brutally suppressing
several alleged "plots," and—at long last—hit at the military
faction within the Party. Saddam's declared goals were to purify
the government and the society from plotters and conspirators.
The undeclared objective, however, was to extend his control
throughout the Party and state machinery, and to demonstrate
beyond any doubt that his and Bakr's Ba'th Party was there to
stay.

These purges were not only planned and executed by Saddam
in his capacity as the head of the security services, but there is
some evidence that he took close interest in their practical
implementation. A Shi'ite dissident who survived the torture
chambers of *Qasr al-Nihayyah* gave a hair-raising description of
how Saddam personally killed another Shi'ite detainee by the
name of Dukhail: "He came into the room, picked up Dukhail
and dropped him into a bath of acid. And then he watched while
the body dissolved."[14] Although this episode, like numerous
Shi'ite stories seeking to blacken Saddam's image, can be neither
confirmed nor denied, the Deputy Chairman's personal involvement in the persecution of political opponents is also illustrated by
the account of a Jewish survivor of the notorious palace, who was
much luckier than his Shi'ite counterpart. Na'im Tawina, now a
65-year-old Israeli, was a member of the Iraqi Jewish community
when he was jailed in the early 1970s as "a Zionist spy." One day,
as he was about to be tortured, Saddam suddenly entered the
room. He cast a quick glance at Tawina and addressed the

investigator. "Do not touch this man," he said, "he is a good man. I know him. Let him go." The startled Tawina was released from jail and sent away. Shortly afterwards he fled the country and emigrated to Israel. For years he wondered what drove the "strong man in Baghdad," whom he had not personally known, to show such close interest in his fate. It was only much later, when he saw a picture of the young Saddam, that the pieces of the jigsaw puzzle were put together. He recollected that Saddam had been the slim youth at the Baghdadi street corner from whom he used to buy his cigarettes on his way to work, and whom he had often tipped handsomely. Saddam apparently remembered his anonymous benefactor and rewarded him in the most significant manner possible.[15]

This story sheds a somewhat brighter light on the commonplace image of Saddam as a bloodthirsty ogre. It shows that notwithstanding his ruthlessness, indeed brutality, he is not immune to a feeling of gratitude, even if the person involved is a "Zionist spy." It also indicates that, however arbitrary Saddam's blood trail may seem to external observers, it has its own rationale. Saddam does not engage in purges for their own sake. He does so because he is convinced that they are vital for his survival, and that if he does not strike at his opponents, real or imaginary, they will get him first. The underlying impulse for his purges is insecurity, the fear that his ambitions will be thwarted. Every purge, every execution, has its purpose. This means that nobody, not even the closest associates, can feel completely secure. Yet, it also implies that those whose persecution does not serve a direct or indirect purpose for Saddam may be spared.

With government offices swiftly cleansed of unwanted non-Ba'thists following the initial turmoil of July, the Party moved to tighten its grip on the military. In December 1968, Faisal al-Ansari was retired from his position as Chief of Staff to which he had been appointed after the "second revolution." Shortly afterwards he was arrested and sentenced to 12 years' imprisonment on a charge of conspiracy. He was replaced by Hammad Shihab, the most sympathetic person toward Saddam within the military faction. Officers of questionable loyalty to the Party were replaced by Ba'thists or their sympathizers, including several division commanders. Many of them were arrested and tortured. By the end of 1970, an elaborate system of political commissars belonging to Saddam's security apparatus had been deployed throughout the military, effectively bypassing the formal chain of command and tightly controlled by Saddam Hussein.[16]

In September 1968 Saddam resorted for the first time to a technique which he was to bring to awesome perfection during the following two decades: the exposure of fabricated "plots," and the detention and execution of their perpetrators. The uncovered "plot" was allegedly planned by a Masonic group in the southern town of Basra, and the "conspirators" were reportedly caught red-handed in a church.[17]

The copyright for the "plot technique" was not Saddam's: in the two years following the attempt on Qassem's life in October 1959, the Iraqi dictator boasted he had uncovered 27 plots against him.[18] Even though this figure is obviously inflated, Qassem did actually face several coup attempts. For Saddam, conversely, plots were from the outset an excellent tool for eliminating actual and potential opposition, sending pointed signals to external enemies (such as Syria and Iran) and terrorizing the population into total subservience. Among the numerous "plots" which were "uncovered" during the 1970s and 1980s, only one can be verified without equivocation—that of Saddam's henchman and Head of Security Services, Nadhim Kazzar, in 1973. The rest may well have simply been used as a means to bolster Saddam's position and ward off criticism of his stringent security measures.

Three months after the "exposure" of the September 1968 "plot," a special "Revolutionary Court" was set up to try "spies, agents, and enemies of the people." Consisting of three military officers with no legal training, the court was a mockery of the legal process, even by Iraqi standards. The common accusations brought before the court were "conspiracy to overthrow the government" and "espionage on behalf of the United States, Israel, or Iran." Selected trials were televised and the Iraqi people could watch and hear contrived confessions by prominent ex-officials and politicians. On one such occasion the former Minister of the Interior, Rashid Muslih, who had left the Ba'th and joined Aref in 1963, confessed to having spied for the CIA, and was executed. Abd al-Rahman al-Bazzaz, an ex-Premier, and Abd al-Aziz al-Uqayli, a former Minister of Defense, who were put on trial with Muslih in the summer of 1969 but did not confess, were given lengthy periods of imprisonment.[19]

Not everyone was "lucky enough" to "benefit" from this "revolutionary justice." In November 1968 Nasser al-Hani, Foreign Minister in the July coalition cabinet and a former member of the Nayif-Da'ud faction, was kidnapped by a group of Ba'thists in the middle of the night. A few days later his body was found riddled with bullets, lying in a ditch.[20] According to the official explanation, he was murdered by criminals. A similar explanation was to be given four months later, following the murder of Colonel Abd al-Karim Mustafa Nasrat, a former minister and a sympathizer of the Syrian Ba'th. This time the security services went out of their way to cover up their act, by producing a public "confession" from a petty criminal who admitted having stabbed Nasrat to death at his home in the course of a robbery.[21] A year later the first Secretary-General of the Iraqi Ba'th, Fuad al-Rikabi, who a decade earlier had deserted the Party, was also stabbed to death. In 1969 he was sentenced to one-and-a-half years' imprisonment. A few days before he was due to be released, "the authorities brought in a hooligan armed with a knife. Rikabi was stabbed in the chest and then dragged on foot to the hospital. They left him unattended until he died."[22]

One of the jewels in the crown of the "new justice" was the trial, in January 1969, of an "Israeli ring of spies." The spies were accused of passing intelligence information to Israel, planning and carrying out sabotage in Iraq, and transferring large sums of money from Israel, via Iran, to the Jewish community in Iraq, who then passed the money to the Kurdish rebels. Fourteen people, nine of whom were Jews, including the leader of the Jewish community in Iraq, were found guilty of espionage charges and publicly hanged. Their bodies were left in the public square "as a warning to others." In a macabre spectacle, some half a million men, women and children danced past the scaffolds and throughout Baghdad chanting "death to Israel," "death to all traitors."[23]

The Jewish community in Iraq, one of the oldest of the Jewish diaspora, dates back to the sixth century B.C. when the triumphant Babylonian King, Nebuchadnezzar, brought the "children of Israel" to Mesopotamia, having occupied Jerusalem and destroyed the Temple there. An established and prosperous community, it suffered periodic persecutions whenever Arab nationalist sentiments rode high. Following Rashid Ali's defeat in 1941, for example, ecstatic Arab mobs attacked the Jewish community in Baghdad, killing hundreds of people and looting and damaging much property. After the establishment of the State of Israel in 1948, the 100,000-strong community was reduced to approximately one-tenth its size, as most of its members emigrated to the

newly established Jewish state. Those who stayed behind became
social outcasts, having to bear the burden of Arab frustration and
hostility toward Israel. By the Ba'th's return to power in 1968, the
number of Iraqi Jews had fallen to a mere 2,500.[24]

For Bakr and Saddam the Jews were an extremely useful scapegoat that enabled them to prove their commitment to the pan-Arab
cause, and thus to legitimize their regime in the eyes of their
followers, without actually having to confront Israel. When in
December 1968 Israeli aircraft bombed the Iraqi forces deployed
in Jordan as part of the Arab "eastern front" against Israel, killing
16 and wounding twice as many, President Bakr incited a hysterical
crowd gathered in the Square of Liberation against Israel and the
Jews. Promising "to strike with a fist of steel at those exploiters and
fifth columnists," Bakr paused occasionally to ask his audience for
their wish. "Death to the spies" came the thunderous reply.[25] This
wish was fulfilled in the form of the ghastly hangings of January
1969, to the indignation of the outside world. International protest
that the killings were motivated by ethnic and religious discrimination was laconically rebuked by the response that all convicted
Muslims, Jews and Christians were executed alike.

Indeed, as would be exemplified two decades later with the
execution of an Iranian-born British journalist, Farzad Bazoft, on
espionage charges, Saddam's witch-hunt for "spies" and "plotters"
seemed to thrive on Western remonstrations. Appeals for leniency
from world dignitaries, such as the United Nations Secretary-
General, only drove Hussein to prosecute the execution spree
with greater vigor: in February 1969 seven more people were
executed, to be followed two months later by another fourteen. As
in January, the masses were urged to come and watch the
hangings, and the grisly scenes which took place in central
Baghdad were deftly described by a British journalist:

> For eight hours on the day of the hangings the police virtually
> handed over central Baghdad to the youths. Directed by Ba'th
> Party Commissars they erected the gibbets in flower beds, patrol-
> ling the approach roads, controlled the tens of thousands of
> watchers, and chanted for more executions. Each of the three
> soldiers among the executed had a bandage on an ankle or wrist;
> the joints were so clearly misshapen that they had clearly been
> broken.[26]

Most of the executions in February and March, however, were
carried out in the southern city of Basra (a predominantly Shi'ite

community near the Iranian border) with the clear aim of sending
a direct warning both to the Shi'ite community and to the Iranian
Shah who, at the time, was increasing his pressure on the Ba'th
regime in an attempt to assert Iran's hegemony in the Gulf.
Purges had become not only a means to suppress domestic
opposition but also an expedient foreign policy tool.[27] Indeed, on
January 21, 1970, the Iraqi security services announced that they
had uncovered an anti-government conspiracy supported by
"Iran, the CIA, and the Zionists."[28] The alleged plot involved
several dozen military personnel, and was reportedly led by two
retired senior officers: Abd al-Ghani al-Rawi, a protégé of the
Aref brothers, and Colonel Salih Mahdi al-Samarra'i, a former
military attaché at the Iraqi Embassy in Beirut under the monarchy. According to the official account, the plotters formed "hit
squads" that were supposed to kill Party and governmental
officials. The zero hour was set for 10:00 P.M. on January 20, but
most of the plotters had been arrested beforehand. The hard core
of the plot, some 50 armed men headed by al-Samarra'i, managed
to set out for the Presidential Palace. Once they reached their
destination, the gates were thrown open, and after entering
without resistance, the group was led into a large hall. As they
weighed their options, the door was thrown open and Saddam
entered the hall, accompanied by several officers. The plotters
surrendered peacefully, after recognizing that they had been
lured into a trap.[29]

On the same day that Baghdad declared the crushing of the
plot, a special court, presided over by Captain Taha Yasin
al-Jazrawi (Ramadan), a member of the RCC and a close associate
of Saddam, and including Saddam's henchman, Nadhim Kazzar,
was set up to try the plotters. Thirty-seven officers were sentenced
to death for attempting to overthrow the government, and were
executed with the weapons they had allegedly received from the
Iranian security services. Fifteen others were imprisoned. A death
sentence was also passed on the exiled Prime Minister, Nayif, who
was alleged to have engineered the coup attempt on behalf of
"foreign elements." The Iraqi government ordered the Iranian
Ambassador to leave Baghdad within 24 hours. The Iranian
consulates in Baghdad, Karbala and Basra were closed and
several Iranians residing in the country were hastily deported.[30]

Although the harshness of the Iraqi response lends some
credence to the belief that a pro-Iranian coup did actually take
place, the confused atmosphere in Baghdad where everyone was

a potential, if not an actual spy makes confirmation of the real
extent of Iranian involvement virtually impossible. At the time,
the alleged chief conspirators, Nayif and al-Rawi, were not even in
Iraq. What is clear, though, is that from Saddam's point of view
the incident sent a resounding signal to the Iranian Shah that the
Ba'th would not be intimidated by his growing regional power. It
was also a bright feather in Saddam's cap. The implication of
members of the armed forces in the "coup" damaged the military
faction within the leadership and enabled the vigilant Deputy
Chairman to make the point that it was he and his formidable
security services, rather than the military, which provided for the
Party's security.

This was no hollow claim. By that time, the long arms of the
security apparatus had already reached the average Iraqi. Streets
were patrolled by the Ba'thist militia. Surprise raids on private
homes in the middle of the night drove home the message that
nobody was beyond its control.[31] As a British journalist put it,
Iraq was being transformed into "a place where men vanished,
and their friends were too frightened to inquire what had
happened to them; people arrested on trivial charges 'committed
suicide' in prison; former officials were mysteriously assassinated;
politicians disappeared."[32]

The security services under Saddam also carried on the
struggle against the communists, the Ba'th's erstwhile enemies. It
is often the case that ideological proximity generates the worst of
rivals. Competition for the souls and minds of the same constit-
uency through similar recipes for salvation is bound to sharpen
differences and create harsh chords, as each Party seeks to prove
why its slightly different means is superior to its adversary's. In
the case of the Ba'th and the Iraqi Communist Party (ICP), the
two standard-bearers of "socialism," the debate had been not only
acrimonious but exceedingly bloody. In the late 1950s, being the
main foundation of the Qassem regime, the communists carried
out widespread atrocities against the "Arab nationalists," including the tiny party of the Ba'th. Several years later, during the first
Ba'thi regime, Bakr had had hundreds of leftists executed and
thousands arrested.

Saddam, however, had always viewed relations with the communists in purely practical terms. He had never been overly
concerned about the ideological challenge of this doctrine. As far
as he was concerned, communism was a foreign ideology which
did not suit the national, spiritual and economic needs of the

Arabs: "Traditionally Marxism attracts the oppressed. This, how-ever, is not the case in the Arab nation. . . . The socialist programs in Arab history did not always come from the poor, but from men who had known no oppression and became the leaders of the poor. The Arab nation has never been as class-conscious as other nations."[33] What troubled him deeply, though, was the popular base of this movement and its effective organizational infrastruc-ture, particularly in such sensitive segments of Iraqi society as the disadvantaged Kurds and Shi'ites.

Faithful to his habit of adopting the indirect approach when-ever faced with staunch opposition, Hussein suggested that Bakr try to gain the goodwill and collaboration of the communists, in order to give the Ba'th a much-needed respite to secure itself in power. At the beginning of August 1968, the communists were invited to join the government. A month later, within the frame-work of a general pardon, many communist prisoners were released from jail while communist exiles were allowed to return to Iraq. The communist response, however, was disappointing. While praising the Ba'thi regime's zealous anti-Zionist and anti-imperialist stance, the ICP criticized its "suppression of the working class" and refused to join the government as long as the Ba'th did not liberalize Iraq's political life: allow the formation of a multi-party system, establish a democratic coalition government and offer true autonomy for the Kurds. The Ba'thi evasive readiness to accede to these demands at a later date was declined by the ICP.

Even though Bakr and Saddam had no intention of giving the communists any real share in power, and their offer of some ministries to the ICP was designed merely to better contain the communist challenge, the duo was profoundly irritated by the communist response. They interpreted the contradictory signals coming from the ICP as an indication that it was not really interested in collaboration but rather sought to oust the Ba'thi regime. The outcome of this assessment was horrifying. Before long Saddam's security services embarked with their customary ferocity on yet another extensive purge: hundreds of communists were arrested, tortured and executed in mysterious circumstances.

This time, however, Saddam found a rival who measured up to his size. The communists would not be a lamb led to the slaughter. Attacks on their ranks were met with harsh retaliation and the more militant elements of the ICP formed small armed detachments to overthrow the Ba'thi regime. These raided and looted official Ba'th quarters. They even fired on Saddam's house. The Deputy Chairman met iron with iron: on March 23, 1970, a prominent communist leader, Muhammad Ahmad al-Khadri, was found dead in a Baghdad street, heralding a fresh wave of arrests, tortures and executions of communists which continued throughout the year and expanded well beyond Baghdad. While Saddam beat the communists with the Party's big stick, Bakr was offering them a carrot: he allowed the publication of a communist periodical and in December 1969 even admitted a communist, Aziz Sharif, to his cabinet as Minister of Justice.[34]

In the fall of 1969 Bakr and Saddam felt confident enough to make their first move against the military faction. The Party's hold on the reins of power seemed secure. The purges were still under way but the unmistaken message that the Ba'th "had come to stay" had been effectively driven home in the minds of both political opponents and the public at large. The moment seemed ripe for the consolidation of the duo's position within the Party's decision-making bodies. On November 16, 1969, the *Iraqi News Agency* declared that all Regional Command members and all the Iraqi members of the Party's National Command had joined the Revolutionary Command Council. Since eight of the nine newcomers to the RCC were civilians, the balance of power within the country's foremost institution was decisively tilted in favor of the Bakr-Hussein axis. It was at this point that Saddam's position as Deputy Chairman of the RCC was officially announced, thus reflecting his growing power and confidence within the Party.

To be sure, this development was more beneficial for Bakr than for Saddam. To the President it signified a net gain, an unequivocal improvement in his position vis-à-vis the military faction. Saddam, though, had to pay a certain price for his drive forward: acquiescence in the entry of some opponents into the RCC. Yet just as one of Hussein's models, Joseph Stalin, used his lesser rivals to destroy his archenemies, and then turned against them, so Saddam knew that there was no escape from striking a tactical alliance with his opponents. The time of reckoning would have to be postponed until the military faction had been overwhelmed.

The two key figures in the military faction were Hardan al-Tikriti and Salih Mahdi Ammash, both of whom had a distinguished Party record and many constituents both inside the Party and the military. Hardan had served as Commander of the Iraqi Air Force during the Ba'th's brief reign in 1963, becoming Chief of Staff, Minister of Defense and Deputy Premier following the Party's return to power in 1968. An arrogant, ruthless person, whose huge physique was matched only by his unbounded ambition, he was detested and feared by Saddam who knew that their common Tikriti origins would not guarantee his safety should Hardan become too powerful. Ammash, for his part, though less ruthless than Hardan, was equally ambitious and was feared by Saddam as one of the most long-standing members of the Party. Having joined the Ba'th in the early 1950s, he drew closer to Bakr and together they headed the centrist faction of the Ba'th. Following the "July 1968 Revolutions," Ammash assumed the influential positions of Minister of the Interior and Deputy Premier together with Hardan, alongside his membership of the Party's Regional and National Commands, as well as the RCC.

Since a direct assault on these two formidable foes seemed suicidal, Saddam resorted to his favorite strategy of divide and rule. First, he took great pains to discredit the two in Bakr's eyes by spreading the word that they, Hardan in particular, had set their sights on the Presidency. Once Bakr's trust in his colleagues had been shaken, he backed his Deputy's efforts to pit Hardan and Ammash against one another in an attempt to neutralize them. The next stage in Saddam's and Bakr's strategy was to drive a wedge between Hardan and Ammash and the other two prominent members of the military faction, Shihab and Ghaydan. This task proved relatively easy as the latter were promised their counterparts' posts. The scene was thus set for the decisive move.

In November 1969, Hardan and Ammash lost substantial ground with the abolition of the Deputy Premiership. This meant that neither of them could chair cabinet meetings in Bakr's absence (in 1969 the Premiership was merged with the Presidency). Six months later, on April 3, 1970, the two were made Vice Presidents, but it soon became apparent that it was a hollow promotion since they were relieved of their key ministerial positions. Shihab replaced Hardan as Minister of Defense while Ghaydan took over the Ministry of the Interior from Ammash.

Once the two had lost their power base, their fate was sealed. It was only a matter of time before the final blow would come. In October 1970 Hardan was stripped of all his posts, allegedly for failing to adhere to the Ba'thi commitment to the Arab cause. He was accused of not helping to rescue the Palestinians who were slaughtered in large numbers by the Jordanians in the bloody events of September 1970 (the "Black September"). He was also criticized in harsh terms for his temporary "defection" from the Ba'th in 1963. These accusations were in truth baseless. Having already lost his job as Minister of Defense in April 1970, Hardan was in no position to dictate Iraq's military reaction to the events of "Black September." If somebody had to pay a price for the Iraqi inaction it was Shihab and his Chief of Staff, Abd al-Jabbar Shanshal, or, above all, the Commander-in-Chief of the armed forces, President Bakr himself. Moreover, Hardan was not the only one to oppose an Iraqi intervention in the Jordanian civil war; most of the Iraqi leadership—Saddam in particular—were equally opposed to such a move. Nor was Hardan the only person to "collaborate" with Aref after the Ba'thi fall from power in 1963. Bakr himself had done the same until he became disillusioned with Aref and decided to seek his overthrow.[35]

In any event, Hardan heard the bitter news in Madrid, where he had been sent at the head of an Iraqi mission. He did not suspect this move as Saddam had taken great care to deceive him into complacency. He personally came to the airport to bid Hardan farewell, affectionately kissing his rival on both cheeks to demonstrate that he harbored no hostility toward him. This, in fact, was the kiss of death. Surprised and furious at the unexpected development, Hardan disobeyed a government order to assume a new appointment as the Ambassador to Morocco and returned to Iraq to plead his case. Upon arriving in Baghdad, however, he was immediately put on board a special plane and flown to an undistinguished exile in Algeria. A few months later he moved to Kuwait where he was assassinated in March 1971 by the Iraqi security services.[36]

Ammash did not have to wait too long for his turn. Increasingly isolated and subjected to a constant smear campaign by Saddam and his supporters, in September 1971 he lost his Party and government positions and was sent as an ambassador to the USSR. His fate, though, was less violent than Hardan's. Since he no longer posed any political threat, in the mid-1970s, after a string of ambassadorial duties, he was allowed to return to Iraq, where he reportedly died in complete obscurity.

As several senior officers followed Hardan and Ammash in withdrawing from power, Saddam could proudly declare that "with our party methods, there is no chance for anyone who disagrees with us to jump on a couple of tanks and overthrow the government."[37] He was undoubtedly right. The power of the military faction had been broken beyond repair. The political loyalty of the new military leadership was unquestioned. The officer corps, under constant surveillance by the security services, was steadily purged and filled with Bakr's and Saddam's loyalists. The young Deputy Chairman was now free to devote his full energies to the next stage in his consolidation of power. Before long he was immersed in a systematic purge of actual and potential competitors within the "civilian" faction of the Party.

The purge of the "civilian" camp, to be sure, did not start overnight. Already during his sustained campaign against Hardan and Ammash, Saddam was ridding himself of those members of the Party whose support was not required for the titanic struggle against the military faction, but who could endanger his position in the future. The first victim on Saddam's list was the Minister of Culture and Information, Abdallah Sallum al-Samarra'i. A Ba'thist since the late 1950s and a member of the RCC, he was removed from all his duties in March 1970 and made the Iraqi Ambassador to India.[38] Another member of the RCC, Shafiq al-Kamali, was dislodged from this prestigious body during the same month. They were followed by Salah Umar Ali, a fellow Tikriti and a relative of Bakr, who lost both his seat in the RCC and his ministerial post in the summer of 1970, after a hostile encounter with Hussein.

It was only after the neutralization of the military faction, however, that Saddam dared to move against more prominent members of the civilian leadership. On September 28, 1971, the same day that Ammash was removed from his post, the Iraqi Foreign Minister since July 1968, Abd al-Karim al-Shaykhli, was relieved from all his duties. Like the rest of the demoted leaders, he was sent abroad as Ambassador to the United Nations, where he no longer posed any conceivable threat to Saddam.

One of the leading figures of the young generation of the Ba'th, Shaykhli had become a member of the Regional Command as early as the mid-1960s, and joined the RCC in November 1969. What was particularly striking about this case was his close relationship with Saddam. While the two diverged on certain policy issues—Shaykhli, for example, advocated a rapprochement with the twin Ba'th regime in Damascus while Saddam was vehemently opposed to such a move—they had a long record of

intimate friendship and fruitful collaboration. Both took part in
the abortive attempt on Qassem's life and spent several years
together as political exiles in Egypt; both were political prisoners
during the Aref regime, escaped from prison at the same time,
and worked closely together, after the setback of 1963, to pave the
way for the Party's return to power.

On one occasion in 1964, Shaykhli even saved Saddam from
arrest, if not from certain death. This incident took place when
the two were sitting together at Shaykhli's apartment, reconsid-
ering their strategy. "It was just one o'clock in the morning.
Saddam rose from his seat and was about to leave. 'Where are you
going?' 'To sleep in the hideout where the arms are hidden.' 'The
police patrols are very active these days,' said Abd al-Karim, 'you
had better spend the rest of the night here.' That very night the
arms cache was raided. Saddam had been saved by pure
chance."[39] It was no mere chance. It was due to Shaykhli's advice.

Al-Shaykhli's purge provided the first glaring proof that even
Saddam's closest associates were not immune to the cruelest of
retributions, should he perceive them as a potential threat to his
position. Personal feelings apart, Shaykhli, by virtue of his organizational abilities and popularity inside the Party, was a potential
contender for the national leadership and had to be removed
from the scene: in 1980, several months after Saddam's ascendancy to the Presidency, the retired Foreign Minister was shot
dead in Baghdad. Such treatment of close associates was repeated
on several occasions, most notably the execution in 1979 of Adnan
Hussein al-Hamdani, a member of the RCC and an intimate
friend of Saddam, and the mysterious death of Adnan Khairallah
Talfah, Saddam's cousin and Minister of Defense a decade later.

The most significant "civilian" purge, from Saddam's point of
view though, was that of Abd al-Khaliq al-Samarra'i, his most
dangerous opponent after Hardan and Ammash. Samarra'i and
Saddam were born the same year, both came from poor families,
and both made their way rapidly from the lowest-ranking Party
membership to the top. Samarra'i's base of support among the
Party's rank and file was wide and solid. He enjoyed the aura of a
leading "theoretician," and, like al-Shaykhli, was a possible future
candidate for the Party's leadership.[40] Yet, one of the general
lessons of history is that the struggle between the "prophet" and
the "king," the theoretician and the *apparatchik,* is more often than
not decided in favor of the latter. Al-Samarra'i's case was no

exception: in July 1973 he was sentenced to prison and six years later, while still behind bars, he was executed for alleged participation in a new coup against the regime.

The scope of the *apparatchik*'s triumph over the theoretician was all the more impressive given the fact that Saddam operated from a (temporarily) precarious position. While the widespread purges within and outside the Party had apparently removed any conceivable contender for the leadership, in the summer of 1973 Bakr and Saddam were unexpectedly faced with the gravest challenge to their regime since the "July Revolution." What was so galling for Saddam was that the threat came from within his own creation, the security apparatus. Even worse, this threat was posed by one of his most prominent protégés, Nadhim Kazzar, Head of Security Services. Coming from a humble family in the small town of Amarah, Kazzar was one of the few Shi'ites to reach a key position in the Ba'thi administration. He joined the party in the late 1950s and made his career in the Security Services, taking an active part in the massacre of the communists during the first Ba'thi regime in 1963. A brutal operator, he soon caught Saddam's eye and was appointed to head his Security Services in 1969. Thereafter, Kazzar became Saddam's right hand, implementing his master's extensive purges with sadistic pleasure. One of his favorite methods of interrogation was to extinguish cigarettes inside his victims' eyeballs. It was exactly this carefully nurtured horrendous reputation which enabled Kazzar to build his power base within the Party.[41]

What drove Kazzar to bite the hand that had fed him so generously? Apparently the familiar combination in Iraqi politics of hatred, fear and ambition. It was common knowledge that Kazzar harbored a deep grudge against the Sunni domination of the Ba'th in general, and the privileged status of the Tikritis in particular. Surprisingly, he freely expressed his resentment and was even reported to have pledged "to wipe Tikrit off the map of Iraq."[42] Under normal circumstances such frankness would have cost Kazzar his position if not his life; but since he proved indispensable to his master's political designs, Saddam was willing to ignore his subordinate's misconduct. What he would not tolerate, though, was an excessive consolidation of Kazzar's power, particularly in light of his hatred of the Tikritis. Since Kazzar was busily building up a personal empire within the security apparatus, he reckoned that a collision with Saddam at a certain stage was inevitable. Rather than allowing his boss to choose the time and method of such a confrontation, he decided to preempt him by making the first move.[43] In this sense he was adopting Saddam's own confrontational tactics.

Kazzar's plan was to kill Bakr at Baghdad Airport as he returned from a state visit to Poland. The zero hour was set for 4:00 P.M. of June 30, 1973. To guarantee the success of his plot, Kazzar had detained Minister of Defense Shihab and Minister of the Interior Ghaydan. This way he hoped not only to neutralize the response of the military and the police but to provide himself with valuable hostages for any negotiations with the regime. Tragically for Kazzar, Bakr's plane was delayed for four hours, thereby leading the "hit squad" awaiting the President at the airport to believe that the plot had been uncovered and to disperse in panic without informing their mastermind. Meanwhile, with Shihab and Ghaydan stuffed in a cellar, Kazzar anxiously watched the television, only to see Bakr arriving safely. By now, Kazzar, too, concluded that the plot had been foiled. Taking his hostages with him, he set out to flee in the direction of Iran. In a message to Bakr he threatened to kill the hostages if he were not granted free access to Iran and offered to meet the President to discuss their differences.

Kazzar was in no position to dictate terms, and Bakr would hear nothing of negotiations. Instead, he gave strict orders to the army and the air force to capture the fugitive dead or alive before he managed to cross the Iranian border. Saddam Hussein quickly volunteered to command the seizure operation, and shortly afterwards he could proudly report the accomplishment of his task: Kazzar was intercepted by planes and helicopters and captured, but not before killing Shihab and wounding Ghaydan. The shaken Ghaydan would later reveal that he had managed to stay alive only by lying underneath Shihab's body and pretending to be dead.[44]

The regime's revenge was prompt and decisive. On July 7, a special court led by Izzat Ibrahim al-Duri, member of the RCC, convened to try Kazzar and his co-plotters. Eight security officials, including Kazzar, and 13 military officers were executed. The following day, another 36 men were put on trial, including al-Samarra'i, and of these 14 were sentenced to death.[45]

Saddam's eagerness to play the key role in seizing Kazzar is not difficult to understand. Not only did the coup attempt, which was aborted only due to superior force, expose a criminal negligence on Saddam's part, causing him and his formidable security apparatus a public embarrassment, but it was even rumored in Baghdad that he had been behind the conspiracy.[46] Hence, he had a desperate need to redeem himself in the eyes of his superior, the Party, and the public at large. He fully achieved these objectives by the lethal effectiveness with which he conducted the seizure operation. Moreover, Saddam managed to do the impossible and turn this highly embarrassing event into a springboard for ejecting his erstwhile opponent Abd al-Khaliq al-Samarra'i.

When Kazzar had offered to negotiate with Bakr before his trial, he suggested Samarra'i's house as a possible venue for a meeting. This was a gift from heaven for Saddam. It enabled him to divert attention from his own negligence to anticipate the plot by putting Samarra'i on trial for failing to pass on information about the coup to higher authorities. Notwithstanding Samarra'i's vehement denials of the allegation, he was found guilty of treason and sentenced to death. There is little doubt that Saddam would have gladly had him shot together with the conspirators, but the glaring lack of evidence against Samarra'i and the strong appeals on his behalf by Michel Aflaq forced the reluctant Deputy Chairman to agree not to execute his opponent.

Saddam could afford this concession. By the summer of 1973 his position seemed unassailable. Though facing a brief moment of great uncertainty during the "Kazzar affair," he managed to rebound in a remarkable way. His most dangerous enemies had been removed from the political scene. The military, the most influential actor in Iraqi politics in the decade preceding the July Revolution, had been brought under Party control following a thorough process of "Ba'thization." The security services had been cleansed of "unreliable elements" after the Kazzar affair. The nation was being subordinated to the Party's will through the ominous state machinery and kept away from any rebellious thoughts by the waves of purges and show trials.

All of these developments bore the hallmarks of Saddam Hussein; and all of them were particularly impressive in light of the Party's meager popular support at the time of the July Revolution and its crippling dependence on the military.

These achievements, however, would not have been feasible without the strong backing Saddam got from his superior, Ahmad Hasan al-Bakr. From the outset their partnership was no typical relationship between number one and his number two. While Bakr was far from a titular figure at the time, he rendered Saddam much greater powers and responsibilities than a leader would normally give his Deputy, especially in an autocratic and ruthless political system like Iraq's. This was partly due to Bakr's failing health (as early as in 1971 he was suddenly hospitalized for what was described by the official press as "a slight indisposition"),[47] and partly to the fact that the President was made of softer stuff than his Deputy. In public Bakr was the frontline leader while Saddam took refuge in his shadow as a humble and loyal subordinate; in actual fact, it became common knowledge that theirs was a dual leadership where decisions were taken jointly, and, more often, at Saddam's instigation.

Saddam, for his part, vehemently discounted such insinuations. "I know there are some who claim that Saddam Hussein is the number one man in Iraq," he was quoted by the Iraqi radio as saying in 1971, "but we have a President who exercises his constitutional powers. In our view he is the number one man, and, even more, we consider him the father and the leader."[48]

This demonstrated humility was not accidental. In the early 1970s Saddam's strategy for political survival was to keep the lowest possible public profile so as to gain the unquestioning confidence of his superior and lure his political opponents into complacency. While systematically purging political enemies and potential contenders for national leadership, he kept away from the limelight. His public appearances and press interviews were minimal, and it was only after the removal of Hardan and Ammash that he allowed himself to become a more public persona. Yet, it was only with the suppression of Kazzar's plot that the Iraqi people began to be exposed to the personality of the country's second most important man.

This rather exceptional symbiosis between Bakr and Saddam suited them both. Shrewdly they toiled to implant loyalty to their dual authority under the public cloak of the collective Ba'th. Their aim was to make the nation loyal to the Party, and to make the Ba'th malleable to their own designs. Both were bent on gaining absolute power; neither could achieve this goal on his own. Without the dogged determination of Hussein and his nearly paranoic wariness, it is doubtful whether Bakr would have been able so successfully to overwhelm the military faction or spread the Party's tentacles throughout the nation. Without Bakr's relentless support, Hussein's ability to purge his actual and potential rivals would have been seriously impaired. For Bakr, the operational and organizational skills of Hussein, as well as his pragmatic ruthlessness, were indispensable. To Saddam, the President complemented and legitimized his own position, since he possessed everything that Saddam still desperately lacked. As a member of the "young officers" who overthrew the monarchy in 1958, Bakr gave the Ba'th an air of respectability and legitimacy and, moreover, was publicly known as a champion of Arab nationalism. No less important, his long-standing connections within the military could be exploited by Hussein. In short, Bakr provided Hussein with the protective shield behind which he could comfortably and patiently lay the groundwork for his ultimate goal: the country's Presidency.

3

The Ruthless
Pragmatist

No single issue touches a more sensitive nerve among Arab nationalists than the question of Palestine. In their view, the establishment of the State of Israel in 1948 was a Western imperialist plot to usurp Arab lands. By implanting an artificial entity, Israel, in the midst of the Arab nation, a wedge was driven between the Arab states, and the Palestinians were prevented from exercising their right to self-determination. As Saddam saw it, Zionism is nothing but "hordes migrating from Japan, from the United States, from the Soviet Union and from everywhere else, who came and gathered in [Palestine] at the expense of the people who were expelled and were left to live in the wilderness."[1] Since the road to Arab unity runs through the "liberation of the Arab Homeland," the struggle over Palestine involves nothing less than the Arab national existence. As long as Palestine remains occupied, the Arab cause will remain imperiled.[2]

Bakr and Saddam, needing to heal the wounds of their recent purges, viewed the Palestinian problem as a trump card both in rallying the masses behind the regime and providing an outlet for popular frustration. The Iraqi state radio had lauded the public hangings of Jews in January 1969 as "a courageous first step toward the liberation of Palestine" and called upon the public to come in great numbers and "enjoy the feast."[3] Since the "liberation of Palestine" required the disappearance of the "Zionist entity," the regime unequivocally rejected United Nations Reso-

lution 242 of November 1967 which called for an Israeli withdrawal "from territories occupied in the recent conflict" in return
for a lasting peace between Israel and its Arab neighbors. Armed
struggle, not a political solution, was seen as the only way to
liberate Palestine.

The impassioned rhetoric of the Ba'th Party promoting the
Palestinian cause did not, in fact, translate into action. Faced with
the first major opportunity to extend crucial support to the
Palestinians, during their desperate struggle against King Hussein of Jordan in September 1970, Bakr and Saddam remained
glaringly aloof.

Following the Six Day War of 1967, the Palestinian guerrilla
organizations had begun using Jordanian territory as a springboard for attacks against Israel. King Hussein was deeply disturbed by this strategy as he could not adequately protect his
country against Israeli retaliation. With the rise in the power and
influence of the Palestinian organizations in Jordan over the
years, however, they had gradually established a state within a
state, gaining full control over the Palestinian refugee camps on
Jordanian soil and disregarding the Jordanian authorities altogether. This development was viewed by the King as life-
threatening to his kingdom and he was determined to check it.

The tensions between Jordan and the Palestinians were
brought to a head in September 1970 when Jordan was rocked by
a series of violent events, including an attempt on the life of the
King, the hijacking and destruction of several Western commercial aircraft, and the eruption of armed clashes between the
Jordanian army and the Palestinians. Confronted with an open
Palestinian call for his overthrow, King Hussein moved resolutely:
on September 10, he appointed a military government which
embarked on an all-out campaign against the Palestinians. By the
time fighting subsided some two weeks later, the Jordanian army
had regained full control of the country while the Palestinian
organizations had been totally shattered. At least 5,000 Palestinians had been killed and twice that number wounded. The violent
confrontation was dubbed the "Black September."

While the Jordanian army was slaughtering the Palestinians *en
masse* in the fall of 1970, an Iraqi contingent some 20,000-strong
was deployed in Jordan. Baghdad openly threatened to use them
to protect the Palestinians: "Go struggling Ba'thists to help your
valiant brother heroes who are fighting in Jordan for victory and
the liberation of Palestine . . . the National Command places all

the Party resources at the national level in a state of alertness and readiness to wage the battle side-by-side with their struggling Fedayeen comrades."[4]

Given these vociferous pledges of support, the desperate Palestinians pleaded with Iraq to make good on its promises. But not a single Iraqi soldier moved to the rescue of the Palestinians. The Iraqi forces remained in their barracks and, according to one report, even allowed Jordanian units to pass through their lines.[5]

From a purely military point of view, this inaction was fully justified. The "Saladin Force," as the Iraqi contingent in Jordan was called (after the great Muslim leader who had liberated Jerusalem from the Crusaders), was in no position to take on the larger and better equipped Jordanian army. Yet for a regime inscribing on its moral banner the championship of the Palestinian cause, it was a humiliating acknowledgment of weakness which exposed it to Palestinian criticism and Syrian ridicule. The Syrians had good reason to mock the rival Ba'thi regime for, unlike the Iraqis, they came in strength to the rescue of the Palestinians. Even though the Syrian decision to intervene was taken half-heartedly, and although their expeditionary force was decisively beaten by the Jordanians, Damascus had doubtless scored an important ideological victory in the competition with Baghdad that dated from the 1966 schism between the Ba'th parties in the two countries. Black September forced the Iraqi Ba'th to argue unconvincingly that "the revolutionary commitment to support Fedayeen action does not necessarily mean embarking on a direct military battle against the Jordanian armed forces."[6]

Ba'thist sensitivity to the Palestinian question was further underlined by the fact that the events of Black September were followed by decapitations both in Damascus and in Baghdad. In Syria, the "civilian faction" of the Ba'th, which had engineered the Jordanian intervention, reprimanded the head of the "military faction," General Hafiz Asad, who had been opposed to it, only to be overwhelmed by the latter who seized full control over the country. In Iraq, conversely, it was the military faction which was to be the main loser: utilizing the events in Jordan as a heaven-sent opportunity to strike at his main rival, Saddam made Hardan al-Tikriti the scapegoat for Iraq's disgrace. In a heated debate at the Revolutionary Command Council, in which the two reportedly drew their pistols and threatened to shoot each other, Hussein blamed the ex-Minister of Defense for failing to respond to the Palestinian plight.[7] What probably happened next at the meeting was perceptively described by a British journalist: "It must have been at that moment that a slight smile flickered over the faces of the members of the RCC present. For all of them knew that the move to keep the Iraqi forces in Jordan inactive had been a joint one, agreed to by all of them in the light of military reports that their troops could not be sustained and supported so far from their base in the face of outright Jordanian hostility."[8]

Not only had Saddam supported the collective decision not to intervene, but his opposition to such a move had been so vehement that some observers concluded that Hardan was removed because he had supported an intervention in Jordan against the view of Saddam and Bakr, and not vice versa.[9] Eleven years later, in an interview with a Kuwaiti newspaper, Saddam would implicitly admit his role in the events of September 1970, justifying his position at the time by his opposition to the use of armed force by "one Arab against another."[10] Saddam's explanation could not be more far-fetched. If anything, his behavior in 1970 had been motivated by purely pragmatic considerations, namely, reluctance to risk a military defeat, however limited, that could tarnish the Ba'th regime and, by extension, his own position.

The outbreak of the Yom Kippur War in October 1973, when Egypt and Syria launched a joint surprise attack against Israel in order to break the political stalemate in the region, gave Saddam a valuable opportunity to redeem Iraq's nationalist credentials. By that time he had already developed into the de facto "strong man" in Baghdad. His main opponents had been purged and his influence on Bakr was growing by the day. Shortly after the outbreak of hostilities he convinced the hesitant President to send an armored division to the Syrian front. This time the decision to intervene was far easier, since the attendant risks were significantly lower. Iraq was not going to fight Israel on its own but was a negligible part of a formidable Arab buildup. Even if the expeditionary force were to be beaten, this would not be viewed as a direct Iraqi defeat but rather as part of a general Arab setback. The merits of such an intervention, on the other hand, were manifold. At a relatively low cost Iraq would be able to portray itself as a selfless champion of the Palestinian cause and as the military power that saved the day for the Arabs. "In the October 1973 War Iraq was the only Arab country to fight on two fronts," Saddam boasted at a later stage. "Its Air Force bombed Israeli missile bases in the first attack on the Egyptian front, and its Army moved to the Syrian front as soon as war broke out in Syria. Iraq left its own land undefended in order to safeguard that of the Arab nation." In his opinion, it was Baghdad's heroic stand which prevented the collapse of the Syrian front: "The Iraqi Army fought with courage and honor, to the dismay of the enemy Minister of Defense, Moshe Dayan, who had, before the Iraqi army's arrival on the Golan Heights, stated that he planned to have lunch the next day in our beloved Damascus. That is how we applied the national principles of our Party."[11]

The real facts were far less heroic. Arriving at the Golan front ten days after the war began, the Iraqi division was ambushed by the Israeli forces and lost some 100 tanks within a few hours. This, to be sure, was not only due to Iraqi incompetence. Given the hostility between the rival Ba'th regimes in Damascus and Baghdad, the Syrians were not too eager to see Iraqi troops on their soil, and the reception they gave to their self-styled saviors was less than lukewarm:

> The commander of the Iraqi force, Colonel Imami, arrived in Damascus at about 1900 hours to find he was not expected and neither instructions nor information were available. He was simply told "go forward and fight," the direction of the front being vaguely pointed out to him. . . . The Iraqis had only the maps they brought with them; none were issued by the Syrians. They were given no codes, call signals, radio frequencies.[12]

Iraq's meager contribution at the operational level was matched by a complete lack of input on the politics and strategy of the war. Baghdad was given no advance notice about the impending campaign, nor any indication of the intention to cease-fire. Indeed, Saddam quickly accused his Arab partners of keeping him in the dark, saying that the Iraqis heard the news of the cease-fire over the radio, the same way they had learned about the outbreak of the war.[13] Within a week of the cessation of hostilities, the Iraqi expeditionary force had been withdrawn from Syria amidst vociferous Iraqi accusations that Damascus's agreement for a cease-fire on the basis of Security Council Resolutions 338 and 339 compromised "the rights of the Arab nation in its usurped land."[14]

Saddam's public explanation did not reveal the real agenda behind the withdrawal of the expeditionary force. By the time of the cease-fire, Israel had recovered its initial territorial losses and, moreover, had managed to capture additional Syrian territory, thus putting Damascus within the range of its artillery fire. The Syrian army was in a state of total exhaustion, and it was evident to Saddam that Damascus was in no condition to continue the war. The Iraqi contingent in Syria was equally incapable of resisting the Israeli pressure, given its high level of casualties. On the other hand, debilitated as it was, this force was required back in Iraq to bolster the regime's ability to confront other more direct threats: sustained Iranian pressure arising from the Shah's regional ambition and an imminent ethnic conflagration in the northern part of the country, Kurdistan. By sending Iraqi troops to Syria, Saddam had been less interested in helping the Ba'th regime in Damascus, a bitter rival since 1966, than in boosting Baghdad's standing in the Arab World: Iraq's military contribution was too limited and too late to have any impact on the course of the war beyond a symbolic gesture of solidarity. Having proved Iraq's pan-Arab credentials through a token participation in the war, Saddam seized the first available opportunity to recall the troops to Iraq, while simultaneously rebuking Damascus for its alleged defeatism. As in the case of Iraq's inaction during the Black September, Saddam's commitment to the wider Arab cause went only as far as it did not clash with Ba'thi, hence his own, interests. Political survival, not the lofty ideal of Arab unity, was the true guide to his behavior.

Baghdad's fiery Palestinian rhetoric did little to promote the desired goal of Arab unity. Quite the contrary, Iraq's virulent attacks were not solely directed against Israel but also against Arab regimes, which were accused of betraying the Palestinian cause and therefore deserving to be overthrown. The Ba'th soon found itself on a collision course with most of the Arab World. The harshest confrontation was with Syria, where the Ba'th regime sought to discredit its counterpart and each of the twin parties sought to present itself as the bastion of Arab nationalism. Relations with Egypt did not fare much better. At the turn of the decade the two countries were immersed in a bitter controversy regarding which of them really carried the Arab banner in the liberation of Palestine. Saddam ridiculed Nasser's credentials and questioned his right to remain in power following his humiliating defeat in the Six Day War of 1967. He also blamed Egypt for paving the way for the tragic events of Black September by supporting the U.S. peace initiative at the time (the so-called Rogers Plan to exchange Israeli territory for peace).[15] The Egyptian President responded in kind, accusing the Iraqi Ba'th of evading its pan-Arab responsibilities during the crisis.

Iraq was equally isolated in the Persian Gulf area, where the conservative monarchies abhorred the harsh rhetoric coming from Baghdad. What frightened them was not merely Iraq's subversive activities, such as support for the Marxist regime in South Yemen or the radical Popular Front for the Liberation of the Occupied Arabian Gulf, which challenged the legitimacy of the conservative Gulf monarchies, but also the Ba'th Party's outspoken pretension to become the "protector" of Arab interests in the Gulf: "The responsibility of the Party and Revolution for the Arabian Gulf arises from their Pan-Arab principles and aims. Furthermore, Iraq, as the most important and advanced Arab country in the area, and the one with the largest potential, must bear the heaviest burdens in protecting it against dangers and encroachment."[16]

For the Gulf states the best proof that Iraq was a power to be feared rather than befriended, was afforded by the sustained Iraqi pressure on its tiny neighbor to the south—Kuwait. Until the turn of the twentieth century Kuwait had been officially part of the Ottoman Empire. Since the eighteenth century, however, the Empire's rule over the principality had been nominal. The al-Sabah family, descendants of the Bedouin Utub clan, had settled around the Gulf's finest natural harbor, and in 1756 they established an autonomous sheikdom in Kuwait. It was a patriarchal desert society where authority was based on traditional tribal rule without elaborate administrative hierarchy.

Toward the end of the nineteenth century, Kuwait and Britain discovered each other due to common interests: Kuwait feared the reassertion of Constantinople's authority while Britain resented Germany's growing ambitions in the Gulf. On January 23, 1899, the two parties signed a bilateral agreement which gave Britain responsibility for Kuwait's defense and foreign affairs.[17] When news of the agreement reached Constantinople, the Sultan hurried to declare Kuwait a district of the *velayet* (province) of Basra and nominated the sheikh of Kuwait as *qaimaqam* (district officer), implying that Kuwait was subordinate to the Governor of Basra. This move, however, was purely symbolic and in October 1913 Britain and Kuwait renewed the 1899 agreement with its exclusivity clause to cover oil as well: Britain was the sole country to be given an oil concession, should the precious commodity be found.

Earlier that year, on July 29, 1913, Britain and the Ottoman Empire concluded a significant agreement, "The Draft Convention on the Persian Gulf Area," which restricted Ottoman sovereignty over the sheikhdom, recognized the autonomy of the sheikh of Kuwait and acknowledged Britain's status in Kuwait. According to this agreement, the territory of Kuwait proper was to be delineated by a semi-circle to indicate the area within which the tribes were to be subordinated to Kuwait, and the Ottomans were not allowed to establish garrisons or undertake any military action in the sheikhdom without London's approval or to exercise administrative measures independently of the sheikh of Kuwait. The agreement also stipulated the inclusion of the Warba and Bubiyan islands, strategically located at the northern tip of the Gulf, within Kuwait's boundaries. However, as a result of the outbreak of the First World War the agreement was not ratified.[18]

The collapse of the Ottoman Empire in the wake of the First World War created a pressing need for delineating the borders of the new entities established on the ruins of the regional empire. This problem was especially acute in the Arabian peninsula not only due to the lack of a historical legacy of precise permanent territorial boundaries, but also because there were no outstanding topographical landmarks or clear-cut ethnic divisions. At an international conference in the early 1920s, the boundaries of Kuwait were established, both on its northern side with Iraq and in the south with Saudi Arabia. Since some differences remained unresolved, the so-called Kuwait Neutral Zone was created, where both Kuwait and Saudi Arabia were to share jurisdiction and oil resources, should these be discovered.[19]

On June 19, 1961, Kuwait was proclaimed an independent state, and a month later was admitted to the Arab League. Britain guaranteed the newly established state military support if the latter so requested. That same year the monarchy elected a Constituent Assembly, which adopted a constitution for the independent state in November 1962.

Kuwait's anxiety to promptly assert its newly gained independence was not motivated by domestic considerations alone, but rather by the desire to affirm its determination to cling to its independence. A tiny state in possession of mammoth wealth, with a large natural harbor and some 120 miles of Gulf coastline, Kuwait was painfully aware that it would be a greatly coveted

prize for greedy neighbors. This fear was not difficult to understand. Although immediately after Iraq's independence in 1932
Premier Nuri Sa'id recognized the boundaries set in the 1913
treaty, Baghdad never shied away from either pressuring Kuwait
to lease it the islands of Warba and Bubiyan, which could improve
its narrow access to the Persian Gulf, and which, according to its
claim, belonged to Iraq, or from trying to subvert the al-Sabah
regime. Moreover, in the late 1930s King Ghazi began openly
demanding the incorporation of the whole of Kuwait into Iraq.

The same demand was reiterated, with greater vehemence, by
Abd al-Karim Qassem. In the same month that Kuwait gained
independence in 1961, Qassem claimed that the sheikhdom had
always been part of the *velayet* of Basra and therefore belonged to
Iraq. He went so far as to allude to the possibility of using armed
force in redressing this "historical wrong," backing his threat by
the deployment of troops along the joint border. Alarmed by the
brazen demand, the Kuwaitis quickly approached Britain with a
request for military support. On July 1, 1961, British troops
landed in the tiny principality while British naval units were
patrolling the Gulf. Arab support was coming too, though more
slowly: in September, after prolonged and arduous negotiations,
the Arab League acquiesced to a Kuwaiti request and sent a
multinational force comprising Saudi, Egyptian, Jordanian and
Sudanese troops. Iraq's cooperation with the Arab League soured.
In December Baghdad announced that it would "reconsider"
diplomatic relations with any state recognizing Kuwait. Thus, as
Kuwait was recognized by a growing number of states, a procession of Iraqi ambassadors throughout the world was making their
way home.

In 1961, following the breakup of the United Arab Republic,
Egyptian and Syrian forces, now separate countries again, were
withdrawn from Kuwait. The rest of the Arab contingent remained until February 1963, when Qassem was overthrown by
the first Ba'thi coup. By then, it had become clear that the
aggressive policy toward Kuwait had brought Iraq nothing but
growing isolation in the Arab World. Hence, without much delay
the Ba'th regime changed tack, and in October 1963 recognized
Kuwait's independence. This concession was, reportedly, made in
return for a substantial Kuwaiti financial contribution to Iraq.

The second Ba'thi regime was much less kind to the Kuwaitis
than its predecessor. In 1969 Baghdad requested that Kuwait
allow Iraqi forces to take up positions on the Kuwaiti side of the

common border in order to protect the Iraqi coastline against an
impending Iranian attack. Despite the evasive Kuwaiti response,
the Iraqis deployed troops in a narrow strip along the border.[20]
Having presented the Kuwaitis with a *fait accompli,* an Iraqi
delegation arrived in Kuwait to gain the government's formal
approval. Although this permission was not granted, the Iraqi
forces, which were augmented in the spring of 1973 by additional
troops, remained on Kuwaiti territory for nearly a decade against
Kuwait's wishes, allegedly to fend off an Iranian threat. Whenever
the Kuwaitis requested the withdrawal of these forces, Iraq,
pretending innocence, would decline the demand on grounds
that the troops could not be pulled out as long as the permanent
border had not been delineated. When Kuwait sought to reach an
agreement on the final status of the border, the Iraqis made it
plain that they would recognize the "de-facto borders only if the
islands of Warba and Bubiyan be either included within Iraq or
leased to it."[21]

In building up the Iraqi pressure campaign on Kuwait, Saddam
was undoubtedly driven by the traditional Iraqi motives toward
this country, such as nationalistic aspirations and yearning for the
fabulous wealth and geo-strategic advantages it offered. At the
same time, his actions were underpinned by a deep sense of
anxiety dictated by the growing Iranian threat.

While there has never been much love lost between Iraq and
Iran—the hostility between the two countries may be traced back
to the "age-old struggle between Persians and Arabs for domination of the Gulf and the rich Tigris and Euphrates Valley to its
north"[22]—until the late 1960s bilateral relations were conspicuously correct. Both countries were saddled with domestic and
external problems and they lacked the willingness and stamina to
engage in mutual hostilities. Consequently, the periods of convergence and cooperation between twentieth-century Iran and Iraq
exceeded by far those of hostilities and antagonism. During the
late 1920s and early 1930s, Iraq and Iran collaborated in quelling
ethnic insurgencies such as those of the Kurdish minority in both
countries. In 1937 they resolved their dispute over the strategic
Shatt al-Arab waterway separating Iraq from Iran at the head of
the Gulf and the same year established a regional security defense
pact ("the Saadabad Pact"), together with Turkey and Afghanistan. In 1955 the two, together with Britain, Turkey and Pakistan,
established the Western-orchestrated Baghdad Pact for regional

defense, and, with the exception of *ad hoc* brief crises, maintained working relations well into the late 1960s.

This peaceful coexistence came to an abrupt end by the close of the 1960s. Because of a series of events—the announcement in 1968 of Britain's intention to withdraw from its military bases east of Suez, the diminution of a direct Soviet threat following the significant improvement in Iranian-Soviet relations beginning in the early 1960s and rising oil revenues—the Iranian Shah, Muhammad Reza Pahlavi, embarked on an ambitious drive aimed at asserting Iran's position as the leading power in the Gulf. To justify this policy, the Shah argued that the responsibility for maintaining Gulf security lay solely with the local states and that no external powers were to be allowed to interfere in the affairs of the region. As the largest and most powerful Gulf country, he believed Iran had a moral, historical and geo-political obligation to ensure stability in this region not only for regional benefits but also for the good of the world.[23]

The Shah's perception of Iran as the "guardian of the Gulf," a regular theme in his pronouncements in the 1970s, manifested itself in an impressive buildup of Iran's military capabilities that turned it into the most powerful country in the Persian Gulf. This new prowess was demonstrated by a series of Iranian actions intended to signal—both to the Gulf countries and the great powers—exactly who had the final say in the region. These included, inter alia, the occupation on November 30, 1971, of the strategically located islands of Abu Musa and the Greater and Lesser Tunbs, near the Strait of Hormuz, which were at the time under the sovereignty of the emirates of Sharja and Ras al-Khayma, respectively. Also included was the Iranian military intervention in Oman from 1972 to 1976 at the request of Sultan Qaboos to suppress the radical Dhofari rebels then operating along Oman's border with Marxist South Yemen (and supported by the latter).

To the newly installed Ba'th regime in Iraq, the Iranian ambitions were an awkward development that jeopardized its own ability to hold onto power. Nobody recognized this fact better than Hussein, the main architect and executor of the Party's struggle for political survival. He knew that the Ba'th was bound to be the foremost victim of the Iranian drive for regional hegemony, for the simple reason that no matter how weak Iraq was in relation to its larger neighbor, it constituted the only potential obstacle on Iran's road to military supremacy; the other

Arab Gulf states were simply too weak to be viewed by the Shah as a hindrance to his hegemonic aspirations.

Saddam was not mistaken. On April 19, 1969, Iran unilaterally abrogated its 1937 Treaty with Iraq on the navigation rules in the Shatt al-Arab, that waterway which runs from the confluence of the Tigris and Euphrates rivers to the Persian Gulf, and for decades the object of disputes between Iran and Iraq. According to this agreement, the frontier between the two countries had been fixed at the low-water mark on the eastern side of the river. This had given Iraq control of the entire waterway, except the area near the Iranian towns of Abadan and Khorramshahr where the frontier had been designated at the *thalweg* (the median, deep-water line). Another advantage accruing to Iraq by the treaty had been the stipulation that ships sailing the Shatt were to have Iraqi pilots and fly the Iraqi flag, except in the area where the frontier was fixed at the *thalweg*.[24]

Now that Iran no longer considered itself bound in any way by the old treaty, it refused to pay tolls to Iraq and to comply with the requirement that all vessels using the Shatt fly the Iraqi flag. In response, Iraq declared that Iran's unilateral abrogation of the 1937 Treaty was a blatant violation of international law. Emphasizing that the entire Shatt al-Arab was an integral part of Iraq, and the country's only access to the Gulf, Baghdad threatened to prevent Iranian vessels from using the waterway unless they abided by the flagging regulations. In complete disregard of the warning, on April 24, 1969, an Iranian merchant ship escorted by the Iranian navy, with cover provided by fighters, passed through the disputed waters of the Shatt to Iranian ports and paid no toll to Iraq as required by the 1937 Treaty. Iraq did not stop the Iranian ship, but before long the two countries were deploying military forces along the Shatt.

Saddam was deeply disturbed by the Iranian move. "In the last quarter of the twentieth century no one is allowed to abrogate international treaties," he said, ironically undermining his own later arguments to justify the Iraqi invasion of Kuwait. "The argument that this treaty was concluded under imperialist domination and must therefore be unilaterally abrogated is not valid. The Second World War imposed conditions which might somehow be unjust to this or that party, but they have become a political reality. Changing these conditions might lead mankind to a Third World War."[25] The intensity of Saddam's anxiety was also illustrated by the expulsion of some 10,000 "Iranians" from Iraq, as well as by the revival of Iraq's ancient claim to the Iranian region of Khuzistan (Arabistan in the Arab jargon) and the formation of the Popular Front for the Liberation of Arabistan. This region consisted of a mixed Arab-Persian population; the Arabs in Khuzistan had received independence from the Persian Shah in 1857, but were re-incorporated into Persia in the early twentieth century. Nevertheless, irredentist Arab feelings remained widespread, at times incited by pan-Arab leaders such as Nasser and the Syrian Ba'th Party. As Saddam began to use this card in his dealings with Iran, bilateral relations soon plunged to their lowest ebb.[26]

However important, the question of the Shatt al-Arab was not the most distressing aspect of Tehran's imperial ambitions for Iraq. Had the Shah confined himself to this issue, the Ba'th might have grudgingly endured. Yet, to Saddam's exasperation Iran did not restrain its activities to the Shatt issue but, rather, found a new-old channel to destabilize Iraq: the Kurdish problem.

By virtue of history and geography, the Kurdish question has been one of the thorniest problems of twentieth-century Iraq. A distinct ethnic group of Indo-European origins and of Muslim, mainly Sunni faith, the Kurdish community comprises about 20 percent of Iraq's population, and resides in the northern part of the country. In the wake of the First World War, as the great powers re-carved the Middle East following the collapse of the Ottoman Empire, the Kurds were promised autonomy by the Treaty of Sèvres (1920), with an option for complete independence, only to realize three years later that they had been cheated out of this pledge: the Treaty of Lausanne between Turkey and the victorious allies bore no specific reference to the Kurds, promising only tolerance for the minorities.

Since then the Kurds have been one of the largest aggrieved national minorities in the Middle East, the intractability of their situation stemming from their dispersion in four Middle Eastern countries—Iraq, Iran, Turkey, and Syria (there is also a small Kurdish minority in the Soviet Union)—each having a vested interest in suppressing the Kurds' national aspirations. The Kurdish predicament has been further aggravated by the fragmentation of the community along linguistic, clan and tribal lines, which has impaired the crystallization of a collective Kurdish identity and has facilitated their suppression by the respective governments.[27]

In the Iraqi case, Kurdish separatism has been particularly disconcerting for the central government. It threatens Iraq's fragile sectarian edifice, thereby raising the fearful specter of the possible disintegration of the entire state into three entities: Kurdish, Shi'ite and Sunni. This, in turn, might have rendered Iraq a non-viable whole, given the fact that approximately two-thirds of the country's oil production and oil reserves come from a predominantly Kurdish area, and Kurdistan's fertile lands make it Iraq's main granary.

Because of these weighty considerations the central government in Baghdad had always been adamant on keeping Kurdistan an integral part of Iraq. The Kurds, for their part, sheltered by the rugged mountainous terrain which made military operations in the area extremely difficult, embarked on a sustained struggle against the regime, which has continued with varied intensity to date. They asked for a proportional representation in Iraq's official institutions, including the cabinet, the parliament and the army, and demanded a proportional share in the country's economic resources. These demands were to no avail, as was their claim for autonomy in Kurdistan.

When the first Ba'thi regime was established in February 1963, the Kurds quickly presented it with a far-reaching plan for an autonomous region in Kurdistan. The plan was dismissed out of hand, and in the summer of 1963 the Ba'th launched a ferocious military campaign in Kurdistan. This proved a serious mistake. War operations dragged on inconclusively for several months, driving yet another nail into the coffin of the first, short-lived Ba'thi regime. Fighting in Kurdistan continued throughout the 1960s, and by the time of the Ba'th's return to power in 1968, Kurdistan appeared to be heading toward a civil war. In the fall of 1968, and again in the following spring, guerrilla fighters attacked oil installations in Kirkuk, causing severe economic damage and sending a painful reminder to the central government about the stakes involved.[28] The regime responded to the mounting rebellion by rushing most of the Iraqi army (four out of six divisions) to northern Iraq. Fierce fighting ensued in which the military did not shy away from indiscriminate attacks against helpless civilians. One of the better-known atrocities took place in the Kurdish village of Dakan in August 1969 and was painstakingly recorded by the *Kurdish Affairs Bulletin*:

The children and the women of the village escaped to one of the caves in the vicinity, for fear of artillery shelling and bombing by aircraft.

After burning the village, the officers and mercenaries assembled near the entry of the cave. They collected wood, and after sprinkling the wood with petrol, they set fire to it. The cries of the children and the women began rising to God. They were shooting at the entry of the cave so that no one could escape, and so were burnt, 67 children and women in the cave.[29]

The events in Kurdistan were viewed by Saddam with grave concern. He was mindful of the destabilizing impact of the Kurdish problem on the previous Ba'thi regime and feared that an overriding preoccupation with it yet again would threaten the Ba'th's rule and, more importantly, undermine his position within the Party. He knew that suppression of an all-out Kurdish rebellion would require a sustained military effort, particularly in light of the massive Iranian support likely to be given to the Kurdish rebels. It was clear that the economic costs of such a civil war would be exorbitant, especially if the Kurds were to handicap Iraq's oil industry, a mission that was not beyond their capabilities, as the attacks on the Kirkuk oil fields had illustrated. He was fully aware that Iraq's immersion in Kurdistan would play into Iran's hands and would enable it to impose its will on Iraq on a variety of issues, most notably the navigation rules in the Shatt al-Arab, Iraq's sole access to the Gulf.

Saddam's dilemma was even more complicated, since the specter of a decisive military victory over the Kurdish rebels was not a heart-warming scenario for him. He was not in charge of the war operations and was consequently unlikely to harvest the spoils of victory. Rather, the fruits of success would likely accrue to the military leadership in general, and his archenemy, Minister of Defense Hardan al-Tikriti, in particular, who, indeed, pressed for a military solution to the Kurdish problem. In fact, a military stalemate in Kurdistan was more in Saddam's political interest since it carried the potential for discrediting Hardan. Yet, since such a development would have entailed grave consequences for the survival of the entire Ba'th regime, its disadvantages overshadowed by far the potential personal gains.

The only way for Saddam to square the circle was to seek a peaceful resolution to the Kurdish problem, a mission which he pursued with his typical determined doggedness. His initial inclination was to try to drive a wedge into the Kurdish camp by

opening talks with the intellectual and "modern" faction of the
Kurdish national movement, headed by Jalal Talabani and Ibrahim Ahmad. This policy backfired. Not only was the Talabani-
Ahmad faction too small and too powerless to deliver any political
solution, but the mainstream camp of the Kurdish resistance, led
by Mullah Mustafa al-Barzani, which resented its exclusion from
the political process, escalated its struggle against the regime.
Realizing that there was no viable settlement of the Kurdish
problem without Barzani, in the autumn of 1969 Hussein entered
into secret negotiations with the Kurdish leader. During the
following months he was to toil wearilessly to reach an agreement,
going so far as to travel to the north for a personal meeting with
Barzani. On March 11, his efforts culminated in a 15-point
agreement which contained far-reaching concessions to the
Kurds, most importantly, the first Iraqi recognition of the Kurds
as a distinct national entity and their consequent right to autonomy. Other concessions included a recognition of cultural, linguistic and administrative rights, the appointment of a Kurd as
Vice President of Iraq and the enhancement of Kurdish representation within the state's ruling institutions.[30]

It is true that the March Manifesto, as the agreement was
called, involved several important gains for the central government, such as Barzani's undertaking to cut off relations with Iran
and to integrate his guerrilla force (the *Peshmerga*) into the Iraqi
army. Yet even these gains could hardly disguise the fact that the
Manifesto, with its substantial concessions to the Kurds, was the
product of great anxiety on Hussein's part. He desperately
needed a period of stability on the domestic front in order to free
his energies to deflect the mounting Iranian pressure and to shore
up his position vis-à-vis the military faction. No wonder, therefore,
that Saddam went out of his way to present the agreement as an
extraordinary achievement. A three-day "peace holiday" was
announced, and the Iraqis heard their Deputy RCC Chairman
lauding the Manifesto as "equal in every way to that of the July 17
Revolution."[31]

This careful cultivation of national euphoria was intended to
preempt criticism by his opponents within the Party who, Saddam
knew, were bound to attack the agreement as a "sellout" to the
Kurds. Barzani's long-standing relationship with Israel was defi-
nitely not a factor that could reinforce Hussein's position as the
self-styled champion of the Palestinians, indeed the pan-Arab
cause, either within the Party or the public at large. Saddam's

outspoken enthusiasm was also related to his desire to lull his co-signatories into complacency. Having concluded the Manifesto at a moment of Ba'thi vulnerability, he had no intention of abiding by it when circumstances changed. Yet, since he required Kurdish quiescence as long as he was consolidating his political power, Hussein, once again a pragmatic opportunist, observed the agreement in part while undermining its basic understandings. Thus, the March agreement was followed by a series of token gestures to the Kurds. A general amnesty was declared and the government promised to subsidize Barzani's party, the Kurdish Democratic Party (KDP). Five of Barzani's followers were admitted into the cabinet while government support for the intellectual Talabani faction was by and large withheld. However, on the most important issue, the implementation of autonomy, Saddam was not only evasive but, indeed, obstructionist.

According to the Manifesto a census was to be held in Kurdistan to delineate the exact areas where Kurds constituted the majority, so as to determine the scope of the proposed autonomy. The idea was that mixed areas in which no ethnic group formed a clear majority were to be kept out of the Kurdish autonomous rule. The issue of delimitation was particularly critical with regard to the Kirkuk province where Iraq's main oil fields lay. Barzani, who wanted Kirkuk to be the capital of the Kurdish autonomous region, laid claim to the province on the basis of its having a Kurdish majority. The central government, which did not consider for a moment allowing the country's economic heart to be under Kurdish control, countered this request by arguing that the Kurds constituted a majority only in certain parts of Kirkuk, and therefore only those areas were to be included in the autonomous region. Carefully planned by Saddam, the March Manifesto, and the secret understandings attending it, provided for a four-year period for the *complete* application of the treaty, which gave him ample time to rearrange the demographic balance in Kurdistan. In September 1971, some 40,000 Shi'ite Kurds were expelled to Iran on the grounds that they were not really Iraqis, and in 1972 alone tens of thousands of Kurds of Iranian origin were forced out of Iraq to make room for the growing numbers of Iraqi Arabs arriving in the area. Saddam's justification for disinheriting the Kurds was quite simple. "There is nothing wrong for members of the larger national group [i.e., Arabs] to move to live on the land of the smaller national group [i.e., Kurds] which enjoys autonomous rule," he said. "Any opposition to such a development is nothing but pure separatism."[32]

Barzani got increasingly disillusioned with Saddam's devious tactics. He demanded that the main bulk of the Iraqi army be withdrawn from Kurdistan in accordance with the agreement, but Saddam refused on the grounds that the treaty had to be implemented over a four-year period. Barzani chose a close associate of his, Muhammed Habib Karim, Secretary-General of the KDP, as the Kurdish candidate for the position of Vice President, but Baghdad would not accept this choice because of Karim's "Persian background." Barzani also accused Saddam of dragging his feet on the census and of "Arabizing" Kurdistan.[33] Furthermore, in December 1970 Barzani's son, Idris, narrowly escaped an attempt on his life, and a year later, on September 29, 1971, the Kurdish leader himself survived a similar experience. The trail led to the doorstep of Nadhim Kazzar, the then still-obedient henchman of Saddam.

The attempt on Barzani's life took place in the course of a meeting he held at his headquarters with eight religious dignitaries, sent by Saddam to discuss the implementation of the March Manifesto. As Barzani was talking to his guests, two explosions rocked the room, killing two of the clerics. Barzani's bodyguards immediately opened fire, shooting dead five sheikhs and capturing one survivor. At his interrogation it transpired that the clerics had been innocent couriers of deadly explosives. Prior to the meeting, they had been provided with tape recorders by Kazzar, who had also asked them to record their conversation with Barzani without the latter's knowledge. When two of them operated the machines, the explosions took place.

What made this incident particularly galling for Barzani was the fact that the meeting with the clerics had been agreed upon with Saddam, when the two met a short while before the assassination attempt. Even worse, Saddam involved in the conspiracy one of Barzani's sons, Ubaidallah, who had been alienated from the Kurdish leader for quite some time. In return for Saddam's pledge that he would succeed his father, Ubaidallah was asked to convince a prominent cleric of the Barzani tribe to participate in the talks with Mullah Mustafa. The participation of the sheikh removed Barzani's suspicions and made the assassination attempt possible.[34]

While putting on a brave face in public, Barzani interpreted the attempt on his life as a de facto declaration of war by Hussein.

"Iraq is a police state run by Saddam Hussein who is a power-obsessed megalomaniac," he said. "He eliminated Hardan and Ammash; he tried to eliminate me; he will eliminate Bakr."[35] This prognosis was prophetic. With Saddam's political position far stronger after the removal of his political rivals, and with the situation in Kurdistan seemingly less volatile than ever, the Deputy Chairman felt less inhibited about violating the Manifesto which he had personally engineered and so highly praised two years earlier. This time, however, his confidence was premature, as Barzani was gradually driven to rekindle the flame with his old supporters, the Shah of Iran and Israel. Barzani even went beyond his traditional alliances and, despite his decades-long association with the Soviet Union, which had supported him with arms and political advice, allowed himself to be seduced into a partnership with the United States. He was immediately rewarded: in May 1972, the U.S. President, Richard Nixon, approved a CIA plan to grant Barzani some $16 million over a three-year period.

To Barzani the U.S. connection held potential gains. For one thing, he believed that the United States, in its capacity as Iran's foremost ally, could provide a safety valve that the Shah would not be able to remove at will. For another thing, he wanted to insure himself against the possible adverse consequences which, he feared, were bound to ensue from the perceptible warming of Iraqi-Soviet relations. Barzani's first assumption was to be proven wrong with catastrophic consequences for the Kurdish national struggle. The United States did not move a finger to prevent the Shah from betraying the Kurds when, after the 1975 Algiers Agreement, the Iranian leader felt sufficiently placated by Baghdad to withdraw his support from the Kurds. Barzani's fear of the dire implications of an Iraqi-Soviet honeymoon, though, turned out to be fully vindicated. Again, to the detriment of Kurdish national aspirations.

By spring 1972 Saddam had come to the conclusion that the Ba'th's multitudinous problems could be solved with one stroke: alignment with the "non-imperialist" superpower, the Soviet Union. There was little ideology in this decision. Despite the secular socialism advocated by the Ba'th, Saddam had never been a serious student of Marxism-Leninism, and his perception of the Soviet Union had always been purely instrumental. For him, Moscow offered the possibility of resolving several conflicts at

once. It was an important counterweight to the Iranian threat. As
a direct neighbor of Iran—the Soviet Union and Iran share a
1,000-mile-long border—Moscow had traditionally been Tehran's
prime security concern. As long as Iran feared its large neighbor
to the north, it could not threaten its smaller neighbors. It was
only when this fear significantly diminished in the early 1960s,
due to the improvement in Irano-Soviet relations, that the Shah
could confidently pursue his aggressive ambitions against Iraq.
The creation of a Soviet-Iraqi axis, Saddam reasoned, was bound
to bring the Shah back to his senses.

Apart from providing a powerful ally that could improve
Baghdad's international standing, the Soviets could also boost
Iraq's military potential through massive arms supplies. This, in
turn, would enable Iraq to enhance its deterrent posture vis-à-vis
Iran, and, no less importantly, to pursue the campaign against the
Kurds with renewed vigor. In addition, Moscow appeared to hold
the keys to some of the Ba'th's more intractable problems. Soviet
relations with the Kurds were still close, a fact which enabled
Moscow to play the role of a mediator between Barzani and
Saddam; and it had, of course, influence over the Iraqi Communist Party. Last but not least, the Soviet Union provided Saddam
with vital backing for a decisive move he was contemplating at the
time: the nationalization of Iraq's oil industry. Mindful that two
decades earlier the nationalization of oil had caused a direct
confrontation between Iran and the West that led to the collapse
of the Iranian government headed by the radical Premier Mo-
hammed Mossadegh, Saddam was reluctant to make a move
before shielding Iraq from a possible Western backlash.

All together, these considerations made a compelling case for
a major breakthrough in Iraqi-Soviet relations. Fortunately for
Saddam, a similar rationale prevailed in Moscow. The Soviet
Union's bilateral relations with Egypt were steadily declining due
to President Anwar Sadat's resentment of the USSR's attempts to
obstruct his war preparations against Israel. And, Soviet-Syrian
relations still precarious given President Asad's wariness of Moscow, a strategic alliance with one of the most important Arab
states seemed irresistible at that moment. Accordingly, following
an official visit to Moscow by Saddam Hussein in February 1972,
the Soviet Prime Minister, Alexei Kosygin, flew to Baghdad,
where on April 9 he signed a bilateral Treaty of Friendship and
Cooperation.[36]

The treaty, a standard agreement between the USSR and its

Third World allies, stipulates wide-ranging military, economic, political, scientific and technical cooperation between the two countries. It contains no Soviet guarantee to come to Iraq's aid in the case of war, nor even a commitment to enter into mutual consultations in the case of an armed attack against one of the signatories, or threat thereof. Yet it provides for regular consultations on international affairs affecting the two signatories, as well as a commitment for mutual consultations to meet military attack or threat to world peace.

This was the second treaty of its kind signed by the Soviet Union with a Middle Eastern country in the post–World War II era; the first had been concluded with Egypt in May 1971. But whereas the Egyptian treaty came at Moscow's initiative, in a desperate attempt to arrest the deterioration in bilateral relations, the Iraqi treaty was of Saddam's making and was aimed at further intensification of an already warm relationship. Indeed, shortly after the conclusion of the treaty the Iraqi communists were brought into the government, and a year later, into the National Patriotic Front, a loose alignment established by the regime in July 1973 to create a semblance of democratization in the political system. The Soviets reciprocated by pressuring Barzani not to escalate his activities against the central government. More importantly for Saddam, however, the conclusion of the treaty removed his last reservations regarding the nationalization of Iraq's oil.

Until 1972, the Iraq Petroleum Company (IPC), a consortium owned by several Western countries with some local associates, accounted for the entire oil production of Iraq and effectively controlled prices and quotas. This state of affairs had always been a painful thorn in the flesh of the nationalists who viewed it as a kind of "foreign occupation" of the Iraqi economy. Qassem had tried to redress this wrong by expropriating most of the IPC's concessions and forming the Iraq National Oil Company (INOC) to exploit the new areas. Yet, since the IPC was allowed to continue to operate its existing facilities, it was not severely affected by Qassem's move, which remained essentially of symbolic value—albeit the first real challenge to Western oil interests in Iraq.[37]

Another attempt to challenge the IPC was made in December 1967 when President Aref signed a "Letter of Intent" with the Soviet Union on the development of Iraq's oil industry.[38] Nearly two years later, in June 1969, the Ba'th capitalized on this accord to conclude several technical agreements with the Soviet Union for the development of the Rumaila oil fields in southern Iraq, expropriated by Qassem from Western oil companies some eight years earlier. Although production did not start until April 1972, these agreements implied that Iraq was, for the first time ever, on its way to building an independent infrastructure, however modest, for its oil production. Yet Saddam had no intention of waiting for the development of an indigenous oil industry alongside IPC. On June 1, having reproached the international consortium for reducing its oil production during the previous months, the Ba'th nationalized the IPC.

This was indeed a revolutionary move of national assertion and a brilliant political gambit in which Saddam justifiably took great pride. In future references to the momentous event, he would never fail to claim that the move had been his brainchild, emphasizing that he was the one who made the decision to nationalize, despite general opposition to the idea: "All the experts and advisors warned me against nationalization; not one was in favor. Yet the decision was taken. . . . Had I listened to the experts and advisors, had I listened to the Oil Minister, the decision would never have been made."[39]

While the move to nationalize was fraught with considerable risks and uncertainties, forcing the government to impose austerity measures, it is doubtful whether Saddam actually needed to swim against such a strong current as he would like his audience to believe. The dream had been there for a long time, and only the right circumstances were required. Once these had been created by the conclusion of the Friendship and Cooperation Treaty with the Soviet Union, the move seemed more than natural. Moreover, Saddam had taken great care to reduce the attendant economic risks of such a move to the barest minimum by ensuring that Moscow would, quite literally, pay for the nationalization, in the form of "a commitment of replacing the lost Western markets for Iraqi oil, at least until Iraq readjusted its relations with its previous clients,"[40] a commitment which was not fully respected later.

The nationalization affords yet another vivid illustration of Saddam's calculated risk-taking style of operation. He proved himself a cautious, yet daring decision maker who did not flinch before a challenge. Weighing his options carefully and taking the necessary precautions, he did not rush into a hasty decision. But, once he had made up his mind, he moved swiftly and resolutely toward his target. Cautious until the last minute, he disguised his real intentions in an interview with a Lebanese newspaper in early April when he cleverly evaded a direct question regarding Iraq's intention to nationalize the foreign oil companies.[41]

Apart from paving the way for the nationalization of oil, the alignment with the Soviet Union gave a significant boost to Iraq's military expansion. Spending some $1.5 billion on arms procurement during the first half of the 1970s, Iraq doubled the order of battle of its ground forces from 600 tanks and 600 armored personnel carriers (APCs) deployed in 1970 to 1,200 and 1,300, respectively, in 1975. The air force rate of growth was less impressive at around 10 percent, from 229 to 245 combat aircraft. The Iraqi navy hardly grew at all in this period.

The pattern of military expansion reflected the government's security priorities. The glaring neglect of the navy (an integral part of the army rather than an independent branch) and the consuming interest in the development of the ground forces, underlined the regime's essentially defensive posture toward the outside world, namely, the absorbing preoccupation with the Kurdish insurgency, and the need to deter Iraq's two main enemies, Iran and Syria.[42]

Indeed, in these two important respects the Soviet alliance failed to live up to Hussein's expectations. While offering its good offices to mediate between Baghdad and the Kurds and between Iraq and Iran, Moscow was unable to bring about a political solution. Alarmed by the improvement in Soviet-Iraqi relations, the United States and Iran stepped up their support for the Kurdish insurgency. This, in turn, made Barzani more defiant than ever. He dismissed Saddam's offer to join the National Patriotic Front, accused the government of consistent evasion of its commitments in the March Manifesto, and resumed the guerrilla warfare against the Iraqi forces in Kurdistan.[43] The oil nationalization was particularly galling for Barzani who viewed this move as a blatant violation of the Manifesto, aimed at disinheriting the Kurds of their right to the oil-rich area of Kirkuk. Thus, he was not deterred from hitting Hussein at his most sensitive point. "The Kurdish territory is rich in petrol," Barzani declared, "and it is our territory. It is ours, and therefore we commit no act of aggression by taking it." To rub salt in Saddam's wounds he did not fail to specify, in an interview with the *Washington Post* in the summer of 1973, what he intended to do with the Kirkuk oil fields, once they had been returned to their "lawful owners": "we are ready to do what goes with American policy in this area if America will protect us from the wolves. If support were strong enough, we could control the Kirkuk field and give it to an American company to operate."[44]

To Hussein, these statements vindicated his belief that Barzani's real aim went far beyond his demand for autonomy; that the Kurdish leader was after an independent state that would be tied to Iraq's archenemies—Iran, Israel and the United States.[45] This disturbing prospect was totally out of the question, and Hussein did not fail to declare his determination to prevent the disintegration of Iraq. "We must understand," he said, "that this country will remain as it is within its present geographic boundaries forever."[46] Nearly a decade later, a similar fear would ultimately drive Hussein, then already President, to the bold move of invading Iran. In the early 1970s, being too weak to even entertain such an idea, he resorted to a "stick and carrot" policy, combining relentless efforts to suppress the rekindled Kurdish rebellion, with expressed readiness for a political solution, directed particularly toward the Kurds' main backer, the Shah of Iran.

Amidst intensifying clashes in Kurdistan, punctured by a brief lull during the Yom Kippur War of October 1973 and by a UN-orchestrated cease-fire in the spring of 1974, the two parties put forward several compromise solutions, but to no avail. A detailed Kurdish autonomy plan, submitted in March 1973, was vehemently rejected, as was the government's scheme which was unveiled six months later.[47] Negotiations between the KDP and the government, resumed in January 1974, quickly ran into a blind alley. In March, Saddam gave an ultimatum to the Kurds to accept the government's autonomy plan as agreed in 1970, only to be rebuffed by Barzani, who demanded instead an extension of the autonomous area proposed by the regime. On March 11, 1974, exactly four years after the March Manifesto, the government's autonomy plan was unilaterally put into effect.

For the Kurds, this was proof that their worst fears had been justified. The very same day that the Autonomy Law was passed, the pro-Barzani Kurdish ministers left the cabinet, and the KDP, having outwardly rejected the new law, braced itself for a full-scale confrontation with the Ba'th regime. This erupted without much delay and, although Barzani by no means enjoyed the unconditional support of the entire Kurdish community, the region was soon in flames.

The Iraqi campaign was initially successful, but by the fall of 1974 it had already ground to a halt. Having failed to sever the Kurdish supply lines with Iran (and Syria, which also extended material support to the Kurds), the Iraqi army was confronted by Barzani's well-equipped guerrillas, armed with heavy artillery and surface-to-air missiles. The Iraqi predicament was decisively compounded when the Iranian army entered the fighting on the side of the Kurds, going as far as to deploy two regiments inside Iraq in January 1975.[48]

Saddam's confident statement a month later that "the political and military situation in the northern area has never been so good"[49] could not, therefore, have been more far-fetched. The threat posed by the Kurdish problem to the Ba'th regime was the deadliest since its rise to power in 1968. The exorbitant cost of the rebellion—over $4 billion according to some estimates—threatened to bring the country to the brink of economic disaster. The consequences for the armed forces were no less alarming. As Saddam was to admit candidly several years later, the human toll exacted by the Kurdish campaign in the year between March 1974 and March 1975 exceeded 60,000 casualties.[50] The logistical situation, in his own account, was equally desperate. The army suffered from "a great shortage of ammunition" which reached preposterous dimensions in March 1975, when "there were only three bombs left for the air force to fight the Kurds."[51] Last but not least, the war in Kurdistan threatened to alienate the regime from Iraq's largest community, the Shi'ites, who, due to their sheer size, constituted the backbone of the armed forces and consequently took the brunt of the campaign against the Kurds.[52]

With the Iraqi army on the verge of collapse and the economy severely afflicted, the Iranian Shah was virtually holding Baghdad by its throat. At will, he could dismember Iraq; at will he could topple the Ba'th regime. Fortunately for Saddam and his associates, the Shah was not after their heads in a way that his fundamentalist successors would be half a decade later. All he wanted was an unequivocal Iraqi recognition of Iran's geopolitical hegemony in the Gulf which, concretely, required a legal revision of the navigation rules in the Shatt al-Arab and some minor territorial concessions. Moreover, while using the Kurds as a pawn in imposing his will on Iraq, the Shah had no intention of allowing the Kurds to gain excessive power. Since Iran was burdened with its own Kurdish problem, an autonomous, let alone independent, Kurdistan would inevitably bode ill.

The nature of the Shah's ambitions was fully recognized by Saddam. He was far from enthusiastic about complying with them, particularly in light of the Shatt al-Arab's strategic importance for Iraq. Yet he felt that he had no choice. Should the Iraqi forces in Kurdistan collapse, he was the most likely person to have to pay the price. He could no longer hold others responsible as he had done following the events of Black September. It was common knowledge, both within the Party and among the public at large, that it was he who was in charge of the Kurdish problem. After all, had he not been the self-lauded architect of the March Manifesto of 1970?

Therefore, even by the fall of 1974 Saddam seemed anxious to reach an understanding with the Shah that would lead to the withdrawal of Iranian support from the Kurdish insurgency. Following the Arab summit in Rabat in October 1974, King Hussein of Jordan succeeded in arranging a meeting between Iranian and Iraqi representatives.[53] Thereafter, the contacts between the two parties continued intermittently until March 1975 when, during an OPEC summit in Algiers, President Boumedienne brought together the Iranian Shah and Saddam Hussein. On March 6, 1975, Hussein and the Shah concluded the Algiers Agreement which, at one stroke, terminated the armed confrontation between the two countries, settled the Shatt al-Arab dispute and paved the way for the suppression of the Kurdish rebellion.

According to the agreement, the land frontier between the two countries was to be demarcated in accordance with the 1913 Protocol of Constantinople and the verbal accord of 1914. This implied, first and foremost, the renunciation of the Iraqi claim to Khuzistan. No less important from the Iranian point of view, the agreement stipulated the delimitation of the river boundaries in the Shatt al-Arab along the old medium, deep-water line, that favored the Iranians. Hussein, for his part, was greatly relieved by the bilateral provision to re-establish security and confidence along the common borders and to undertake to exercise a strict and effective control with the aim of finally putting an end to "all infiltrations of a subversive character from either side." Finally, the two parties undertook to regard the provisions negotiated at the 1975 OPEC meeting as indivisible elements of a comprehensive settlement, so that a breach of any one would be considered a violation of the spirit of the Algiers Agreement.[54] The settlement was confirmed in Baghdad on June 13, 1975, and known

officially as the Iran-Iraq Treaty on International Borders and
Good Neighborly Relations.

There is little doubt who in the Algiers Agreement made the
most concessions. Whereas Saddam went out of his way to placate
the Shah by acknowledging Iran's sovereignty over half of the
Shatt al-Arab, the Shah made no practical concessions unless
non-interference in the domestic affairs of another sovereign
state can be considered one. In the Algiers Agreement, Hussein
"bought" the inviolability of Iraq's frontier, a fundamental and
self-evident attribute of statehood, by paying the high price of
territorial concessions. The severity of these concessions is evident
in light of the supreme importance of the Shatt, Iraq's sole access
to the Gulf, for Iraqi politico-strategic and economic needs. While
Iran has a long Gulf coastline of about 1,240 miles, Iraq is
virtually landlocked, with a Gulf coastline of only 15 miles. While
Iran had five naval bases along the Gulf coast, some of them
beyond Iraq's effective operational reach, Iraq had to rely on two
naval bases, Basra and Umm Qasr, both very vulnerable and well
within the range of Iranian artillery.

Saddam's willingness to make these weighty concessions reflected his painful realization that the effective enforcement of
Iraq's internal sovereignty in general, and his political survival in
particular, depended on the goodwill of Iraq's neighbor to the
east. It did not stem from Arab pressures to end the Iranian-Iraqi
conflict so as to free the overall resources of the Arab World for
the struggle against Israel.[55] Egypt, still Israel's main Arab foe,
was edging at the time toward a second agreement with Israel on
the disengagement of forces from the Sinai Peninsula. Syria, for
its part, not only did not push Saddam toward an accommodation
with Iran but harshly deplored him for signing the agreement
which, in its view, involved the surrender of the Arab lands of
"Arabistan" (Khuzistan).[56]

The truth is that, in concluding the Algiers Agreement,
Saddam's mind could not have been more removed from the
Palestine question and the struggle against Israel. For him, an
immediate resolution of the Kurdish problem, on his own terms,
was a matter of life and death. Had he not reached such a
solution, his entire future would have been jeopardized; had he
not bowed to the superior Iranian power, such a solution would
not have been feasible. Faced with the choice between a humiliating foreign policy concession and political demise, the way out
was self-evident. Saddam opted for the former and achieved his

objective: 48 hours after the signature of the Algiers Agreement Iran had withdrawn its support for the Kurds, and within two weeks the Kurdish rebellion had been effectively suppressed.[57]

Years later, one of Saddam's main chieftains, Taha Yasin Ramadan, would vividly describe the depth of Iraqi anxiety preceding the conclusion of the Algiers Agreement. "Our signing of the agreement," he told a London-based Arabic magazine, "came in circumstances under which we had to make calculations as to whether we would lose either Iraq or half of the Shatt al-Arab. We chose what was in the best interests of Iraq."[58]

This move was in Iraq's best interests, it is true, but what Ramadan failed to mention was that his master had been essentially responsible for confronting Iraq with such grim choices. It was the first occasion on which, due to a strategic miscalculation on his part, Saddam boxed Iraq into a corner and tied its national interest, indeed its very existence, to his political survival. Had he adhered to the spirit of the March 1970 Manifesto, which he had personally engineered, and implemented it to the letter, the Kurdish revolt might have been averted. This would have still left Saddam exposed to the hegemonic aspirations of the Iranian Shah, but his vulnerability would have been greatly reduced. As things developed, Saddam overestimated his ability to impose his own solution on the Kurds, and was consequently forced to fight simultaneously on two fronts. This proved to be beyond Iraq's power and the only escape from the dire straits into which he had maneuvered himself, and his country, was to make a humiliating concession to Iran, and to try to project this as an important achievement.

Fortunately for Hussein this strategy worked, and his road to the Algiers Agreement was to become a crucial watershed in his career. From now on there would be no doubts who "the strong man" of Baghdad was. Saddam had managed to carry his Party with him through a four-year crisis and to emerge victorious, though at the price of one of the most significant political concessions of his career. During this tortuous journey he proved to be anything but a rigid doctrinaire unwilling to bend. Overwhelmingly pragmatic, he displayed a remarkable degree of flexibility, shifting tacks and twisting ideological tenets in accordance with the pressure of events. High rhetoric apart, Saddam's activities reflected a striking single-mindedness, geared toward one paramount goal: his own political survival.

4

The Strong Man
of Baghdad

"It is certain that matters would have been accomplished faster had I become the Republic's President five years earlier," Saddam Hussein said shortly after assuming the Presidency. "This was also President Bakr's conviction. But I used to contradict him because I did not want him to leave his post as President."[1] Saddam was not ready to assume the country's top spot in 1974 although he may have thought that such a move would have promoted Iraq's national interest. In his own account, his behavior was motivated by noble ideals. "If I had not behaved in this moral way, what would I have told the people?" he pleaded emotionally. "My situation would have been exactly like any other revolutionary situation in the world or in the Arab nation, with no clear-cut moral difference. If the one who is better takes over his friend's place and seeks only the reward, then we would be exactly like so many other revolutionary movements, whereas this is far from the truth."[2] Professing respect and fidelity, Saddam remained second in command.

While there is not much in Saddam's political record to support his claim of altruism—in 1979 he eventually forced his superior into "retirement" on the alleged grounds of poor health—Hussein's account reveals that in the mid-1970s he did not yet want President Bakr out of the way. Lurking behind his seemingly deferential reticence were the practical and patient considerations of a fundamentally cautious man who would only

85

risk supplanting the President when he felt confident of success.

On the face of it, Saddam was well poised to make a bid for the Presidency in 1975. He had effectively purged all potential contenders for the leadership, tightened his grip over the military and maintained the security apparatus as his personal preserve. His imprint was on every major domestic and foreign policy decision. It was he who masterminded the nationalization of oil, and appeared to have resolved the Kurdish problem by suppressing Barzani's rebellion; it was he who had engineered the Treaty of Friendship and Cooperation with the Soviet Union and deflected Iranian pressure on the Ba'th regime, albeit at the exorbitant cost of the Algiers Agreement. Everybody knew that Saddam was the "strong man of Baghdad" and that Bakr was gradually fading into the background as nothing more than a titular figurehead. The division of labor between the two was simple and straightforward: Hussein made policies, while Bakr sanctioned them by virtue of his official position and national prestige. The voice was Bakr's—but the hands were Saddam's.

Later on, when in the Presidential Palace, Saddam would recall the nature of his relationship with Bakr during that period: "It might have seemed that, in an emergency, I conducted myself with an authority of a head of state[;] this may also have happened in private, but I never turned this 'emergency status' into one that was permanent. When the emergency was over, I became once more the Vice-President of the Revolution[ary] Command Council. . . . I would respectfully return to my place."[3]

He returned to his place, but only *pro forma*. In public Bakr was the Head of State. He was President, Chairman of the Revolutionary Command Council and of the Party's Regional Command, Prime Minister, Defense Minister, and Commander-in-Chief of the Armed Forces. In private, however, Saddam did not hesitate to indicate to his superior who "called the shots." He insisted on being called "Mr. Deputy," the only person addressed by such a title, and was most particular about observing ceremonial forms. He understood full well the importance of symbolic representations of status and their effect. "Some find it strange," he revealed in 1979, "that, when President Bakr used to telephone me and ask me to step into his office, I refused to do so until his aide-de-camp went in and announced me. I truly believe in this code of behavior and it certainly does not make me a weak character or personality; it is a source of strength."[4]

Saddam had his reasons for remaining in the shadows. To

him, Bakr was still indispensable. While the President was not
devious and powerful enough to derail Saddam from his determined thrust forward, Bakr, with his impeccable revolutionary
record, provided his Deputy with the public respectability and
prestige he himself lacked, a formidable shield behind which
Saddam could allay the fears of potential rivals and pursue his
policies with virtual impunity. Should shining successes be scored,
it was common knowledge who "the strong man of Baghdad" was.
Should something go fundamentally wrong, there would always
be a higher authority to be blamed.

Well protected by this comfortable symbiosis, Hussein could
plot and implement his long-range strategy. Predictably enough,
the first item on his agenda was the further consolidation of his
position within the Party and the armed forces. In January 1977
ten new members joined the Regional Command, bringing Saddam a comfortable majority of 14 followers out of the organ's 21
members. Seven months later all Regional Command members
joined the Revolutionary Command Council, thereby significantly
boosting Saddam's power within the country's foremost decision-
making body. In the process of these changes Saddam managed
to remove another formidable foe, Dr. Izzat Mustafa.

One of President Bakr's most entrusted confidants, Mustafa
had joined the RCC in November 1969 and had held several
cabinet appointments, the most recent being Minister of Municipal Affairs. The official pretext for his dismissal, which took place
together with that of another rival and member of the Regional
Command, Fulayyih Hasan al-Jasim, was their "failure to shoulder
the Revolutionary Command responsibilities and negligence in
performing their Party duties." The two were accused of too lax
an attitude toward participants in violent Shi'ite demonstrations
earlier that year, but this accusation was only an excuse. The
tribunal on which they had sat sentenced 8 Shi'ite *ulama* (religious
authorities) to death and 15 others to life imprisonment—hardly
a lenient verdict. Moreover, shortly after the trial the Regional
Command confirmed that the sentences reflected the Party line,
which sought to limit the death penalty to the riots' leaders only.[5]
Besides, it was common knowledge among diplomatic circles in
Baghdad that Mustafa and al-Jasim were opposed to the formation of the court in the first place, and that their appointment as
judges was a ploy by Saddam to discredit them. In doing so,
Saddam not only removed two personal opponents from the
political scene, but also deprived Bakr of two loyal supporters,

thereby further isolating the President and paving the way for his replacement.[6] Like former disgraced rivals of Saddam, Mustafa was to be assassinated some three years later. Stripping rivals of their power apparently was insufficient to stifle Saddam's anxieties. Mindful of Qassem's and Aref's leniency in leaving their opponents alone, only to be overwhelmed by them later, Saddam was determined not to repeat the mistake.

Beside ensuring his control over the state's machinery, Saddam sought to reduce his dependence on Bakr, who as a veteran senior officer and Minister of Defense, was his primary link with the armed forces. To win over the officer corps, Saddam tried to convince them that he, and not only the President, was one of them. Although he had never served in the military, in January 1976 Saddam had his superior appoint him to the rank of Lieutenant General (retroactively from July 1973), equivalent to the Chief of Staff.[7] Furthermore, to make the military more subservient to his wishes, Saddam installed relatives and members of his Tikriti clan in key military positions, most notably the promotion of his favorite cousin, Colonel Adnan Khairallah Talfah, to Minister of Defense in October 1977, a post until then held by the President. This nomination was an important milestone on Saddam's road to the Presidency. At the symbolic level, it represented the first executive function to be stripped from Bakr; the fact that Adnan was the President's son-in-law may have smoothed the President's readiness to relinquish this powerful post. More practically, Adnan's takeover from Bakr placed the armed forces under Hussein's direct control. Indeed, as early as in the summer of 1978 Adnan launched his first large "cleansing operation": dozens of officers were purged, including the Commander of the Air Force and several divisional commanders, while some 60 military personnel were executed. In July 1978 the RCC enacted a decree rendering non-Ba'thist political activity an illegal act, punishable by death, for members of the armed forces.

With his grip over the military secured, Saddam pressed forward with an ambitious program of military buildup, which he funded from Iraq's growing oil revenues. Such a move had been in the cards for quite some time to counterbalance the formidable and threatening Iranian military expansion which had been under way since 1975. Yet, as long as Saddam was not absolutely certain of the military's loyalty to him, he refrained from meeting Iraq's operational needs. It was only after Adnan's nomination that he felt confident enough to move in this direction. Consequently, between late 1977 and mid-1979 the Iraqi armed forces absorbed the most advanced Soviet weapons systems, hitherto unavailable to them, including some 450 T-72 tanks, dozens of 122 and 152 mm self-propelled guns, Tu-22 bombers, Mi-24 helicopters and Il-76 transport aircraft. The Iraqi air force underwent extensive modernization. Forty Mirage-F1 fighters were ordered from France and Iraq's anti-tank potential received significant reinforcement with the purchase of 60 Gazelle helicopters.[8]

Hussein's meticulous preparation for his decisive leap to the Presidency went far beyond the gradual subordination of the Ba'th and the military to his will. It had been evident to him, from early on, that even the least democratic form of government required substantial popular support, however loosely defined. He knew that a regime ruling at the points of bayonets was condemned to a precarious existence, and bound to come to an abrupt end. In order to ensure the absolute loyalty of the masses to unelected leaders, they had to be incorporated into a total system, which would indoctrinate them and permeate every aspect of their daily lives. On a visit to Baghdad in 1975, a British journalist was told by his government interpreter that "Saddam's half-brother and Head of Intelligence, Barzan al-Tikriti, had asked him to procure books on Nazi Germany. He believed that Saddam himself was interested in this subject, not for any reason to do with racism or anti-semitism, . . . but as an example of the successful organization of an entire society by the state for the achievement of national goals."[9]

An indispensable component of such radical reorganization was the complete subordination of the economy to the needs of the ruling elite. " 'L'Etat c'est moi' (I am the state) is almost a liberal formula by comparison with the actualities of Stalin's totalitarian regime," wrote the Soviet revolutionary, Leon Trotsky, on the man who had purged him and eventually had him murdered. "Louis XIV identified himself only with the State. The Popes of Rome identified themselves with both the State and the Church. The totalitarian state goes far beyond Caesars and Popism, for it has encompassed the entire economy of the country as well. Stalin can justly say, unlike the Sun King, 'La Société, c'est moi' (I am society)."[10]

While Stalin was one of Saddam's main political models, he did not have to go that far afield in order to appreciate the

importance of controlling the economy for one's political ends.
Such a notion is deeply embedded in Middle Eastern political
culture and not confined to Ba'thi thinking. The far-reaching
economic reforms of the nineteenth-century Egyptian ruler,
Muhammad Ali, for example, had been essentially geared to the
consolidation of his regime and the creation of an infrastructure
that would allow him to embark on external expansion. For the
founding father of modern Turkey, Mustafa Kemal (Atatürk), a
state-controlled economy was a means of Westernizing Turkish
society.[11] For Saddam Hussein, the economy was an effective
vehicle for rallying popular support behind the regime and
bolstering his own political position. For Saddam and his party,
socialism was not a coherent body of ideas, but rather a catchword
to win the support of the masses. It is not surprising that Ba'thi
writings fail to convey a clear vision of socialism, preferring
instead to divert their energies to the main tenet of Ba'thi
thinking: unity of the Arab nation. By deliberately leaving the
socialist agenda vague, the Ba'th Party could adapt its economic
policies to the needs of the moment, so as to satisfy popular
demands for economic well-being. For what could create a greater
sense of public gratitude than a decisive improvement in social
and economic conditions?

Fortunately for Saddam, his populist perception of socialism
developed against the backdrop of unprecedented economic
prosperity. The nationalization of Iraq's oil industry and the
breathtaking rise in oil revenues during the 1970s led to the
accumulation of great wealth during the Ba'th regime. In 1968
Iraq's oil revenues totaled some $476 million; by 1980 they had
reached $26 billion.[12] This, in turn, enabled Hussein to embark
on a wide-ranging program of economic development in an
attempt to transform Iraq into a socialist state according to his
own modifications of the Ba'thi agenda. Some of the new wealth
was redistributed directly, either in the form of tax cuts and wage
rises, or through subsidies on basic foodstuffs. Moreover, lands
were expropriated from the upper classes without compensation
and given to peasants, and ambitious development schemes were
launched in the critical areas of housing, health and education.[13]

Some of Saddam's social projects were decidedly progressive.
Major efforts were invested in education, including massive campaigns to eradicate illiteracy. Free education, from kindergarten to
university, was hammered down by an official law, and a special
coordinating body for the eradication of illiteracy among the adult

population was established.[14] Laws for the compulsory education of illiterate people were passed, stipulating strict punishments, including imprisonment for those who failed to attend classes. Heavy emphasis was also placed on the emancipation of women, including legislation ensuring equal pay and outlawing job discrimination on the basis of sex. The family law code, known as the Code of Personal Status, was similarly revised, rendering polygamy more difficult to practice and expanding women's freedom to choose to marry and to divorce. Women were allowed to enroll in the military and the Party's militia (the Popular Army).[15]

Nevertheless, the secularization and modernization of Iraq was by no means a painless enterprise or an unqualified success. For one thing, the implementation of Ba'thi socialism was plagued by the same chronic problems experienced in Soviet and East European socialism: inefficiency, waste, mismanagement and corruption. Consequently, the unprecedented influx of funds into the country did little to narrow the social inequities. They remained essentially unchanged since the days of the monarchy: the share of the bottom 5 percent of families in the gross national income was 0.6 percent, while the top 5 percent earned 22.9 percent. The economic disparities between rural and urban areas even widened. According to various estimates, in 1978 more than four million people still lived in mud houses, and some 250,000 in tents. The proposed land reform progressed unevenly, and agriculture, which in the past had not only been capable of feeding the Iraqi population but also of exporting its products, declined at an alarming rate to make Iraq dependent on imported foodstuffs.[16]

Rapid urbanization caused its own severe social and economic dislocations. A new underprivileged class was developing on the fringes of the cities, alienated and frustrated at its poor lot. This phenomenon was particularly disturbing in Madinat al-Thawra, a predominantly Shi'ite town outside Baghdad, which quickly exploded to reach nearly two million people, far beyond what it could and was designed to accommodate.

In an effort to deal with the inadequacies of the socialist economy, Hussein decided to encourage the evolution of a private sector in the Iraqi economy. By the mid-1970s he was offering ample incentives to entrepreneurs and giving private companies, both domestic and foreign, growing portions of the state's development programs. Such deviation from a socialist centralized economy, to be sure, was not unusual in the 1970s. A growing number of Arab regimes, without relinquishing their hold on the levers of economic power, sought to introduce a measure of liberalization into their tightly controlled economies. In a major break with his predecessor's centralist socialism, President Anwar Sadat embarked on a policy of economic openness (*infitah*), allowing the flow of domestic and foreign private capital into the Egyptian economy. Even Saddam's archrival in Damascus, President Hafiz Asad, did not pursue a dogmatic economic line, but rather tried to marry some elements of a free market economy to the state-controlled Syrian socialism. Yet, while Sadat's policy of *infitah* was largely economically motivated (due to the far less authoritarian nature of the Egyptian political system), the rationale behind Saddam's policy of measured liberalization was no less political than economic: the creation of a new social class of "national bourgeoisie" whose economic interests cut across sectarian lines, and which owed its allegiance to the person who had made its emergence possible—Saddam Hussein.[17]

Since he constantly promised the Iraqi people "not to deviate from the path of socialism either now or in the future,"[18] Saddam felt obliged to rationalize his economic innovations and pragmatism. Arab socialism, he argued, is more difficult and more complex than ordinary capitalism and communism:

> As capitalism advocates total freedom, regardless of the fact that there must be exceptions, it shows indifference to the harm that might be caused to society. As for communist thought, it says there can be no private ownership. Thus, it chooses the temporary and easy way. As for us, we have a socialist sector and a private one . . . our option is more complicated, because the easy solution is not always the correct one.[19]

And what about the socio-economic inequities inherent in the existence of a private sector? Here Hussein is similarly pointed: "Socialism does not mean the equal distribution of wealth between the deprived poor and exploiting rich; this would be too inflexible. Socialism is a means to raise and improve productivity."[20]

The emancipation of the Iraqi woman affords an equally compelling example of Saddam's rather eclectic, superficial commitment to Ba'thi secularist doctrine. Even though this issue had been one of the cornerstones of the Party's secular policy— "There can be no genuine radical change of the Arab society towards unity, liberty and socialism while women remain inferior and unequal partners," read the Political Report of the Eighth Congress of the Ba'th Party[21]—and even though some important steps were taken in this direction under Hussein, they were a far cry from the Ba'th's far-reaching goals. While loosening the grip of the patriarchal family on the Iraqi woman, "male dominance in the spirit of Islamic law held sway in those areas that most directly affected women as individuals: polygamy, divorce, and inheritance," where Ba'thist measures were "considerably less radical than the 1956 Tunisian Code, for example, or the Shah's family reforms, to say nothing of Atatürk's radical break with Islamic family law in 1926."[22]

Nor was the involvement of women in the labor force or their social mobilization anathema to traditional Islamic values. Saddam did not need to fear a backlash from Islamic fundamentalists in Iraq in response to his ostensible liberation of the Iraqi woman. Indeed, the revolutionary regime in Tehran, perhaps the embodiment of Islamic fundamentalism, used masses of veiled women "not only against the Shah, but to break up some of the early feminist demonstrations against Khomeini's edict on the veil."[23] Above all, the weakening of the patriarchal foundations of the society was less motivated by a sincere concern for the status of the Iraqi woman, than by the desire to substitute the Party, and by implication its leader, for the extended family as the main source of social loyalty. In Saddam's own words: "The unity of the family must be based on congruence with the central principles of the policies and traditions of the revolution in its construction of the new society. Whenever there is a contradiction between the unity of the family and these new principles, it must be resolved in favor of the latter."[24]

Given his expedient political perception of the emancipation of the Iraqi woman, Saddam did not hesitate to slow down this process whenever such a move suited his needs. "There is no justification," he told a Party seminar in 1976, "for putting forward hasty measures which would place a section of our people—who so far have been with us—in a hostile attitude to the Revolution."[25] More than a decade later, Saddam would take a decisive step in emptying Ba'thi ideological commitment to the emancipation of women of any real substance. Disturbed by the collapse of the communist dictatorships in Eastern Europe on the one hand, and by the spread of public discontent in Iraq following the regime's inability to improve economic conditions in the wake of the Iran-Iraq War on the other, he sought the

support of the Muslim masses by reversing a decade-long policy
and restoring awesome, indeed medieval, patriarchal control over
the Iraqi woman. On February 18, 1990, the RCC issued a special
decree which stipulated that "any Iraqi who, on grounds of
adultery, purposely kills his mother, daughter, sister, maternal or
paternal aunt, maternal or paternal niece, maternal or paternal
female cousin, shall not be prosecuted."[26]

The most vivid illustration of Hussein's readiness to subject his
vision and strategy to utilitarian considerations was, perhaps,
offered by his oil and trade policy. While the nationalization of oil,
despite its short-term economic setbacks, built up Saddam's
credentials as an ardent nationalist who freed the country's
economy from "foreign occupation," he was not deterred from
cultivating close commercial relations with exactly those "occupying forces." "The nationalized oil should not be sold to the same
parties whose share had been nationalized," he argued heatedly.[27]
Yet, as early as in June 1972 he paid an official visit to Paris, the
only Western capital he had visited until then, where he agreed to
sell France nearly a quarter of the oil produced by the Iraq
Company for Oil Operations (ICOO), the new, nationalized Iraqi
oil company. In no time, Saddam was welcoming representatives
arriving in Baghdad from Europe, Japan, India and Latin America to conclude lucrative deals.[28]
    The driving force behind Hussein's oil policy was the desire
for the maximum economic, and in consequence, political gains.
Following the Yom Kippur War of October 1973, when oil was
employed for the first time as a political weapon against the West
by dramatic oil price increases and the boycotting of certain
countries, Saddam collaborated with his fellow Arab oil producers
only to the extent that their policy served Iraq's economic needs.
He did not make any effort to prevent Iraqi oil from reaching the
boycotted countries, and refused to reduce his production quota,
and thus allow prices to go down, once the crisis had reached its
zenith and high prices had outlived their political usefulness for
the Arab cause.[29] Similarly, while Iraq's economic ties with France
were presented as a reward for the "correct" French policy during
the Six Day War of 1967 (in which Paris refrained from supplying
weapons to Israel in accordance with previously signed agreements), they actually offered Saddam urgently needed income
and prospects of access to much-desired French technology.
    This was indeed the West's main attraction for Saddam.

During the early 1970s, the Soviet Union had been Baghdad's primary trade partner both in the civilian and in the military spheres. With the accretion of oil revenues, Saddam gradually came to the conclusion that, as far as economic considerations were concerned, Moscow had outlived its usefulness for Baghdad. The Soviet Union was markedly inferior to the West in each of the economic spheres that mattered to Saddam: as a contributor to his development programs, as a purchaser of Iraqi oil, and as a provider of modern technology. Cash was to form the basis for Iraq's economic transactions, and if this meant more extensive contacts with the more affluent West at Moscow's expense, so be it. Hence, during the latter half of the 1970s the Soviets were forced to anxiously watch the evolution of intensive trade relations between Iraq and Japan, West Germany and even the United States, at the same time as Baghdad's economic transactions with the communist bloc declined to only 5 percent of its overall trade.[30]

No less worrisome from Moscow's point of view was Saddam's growing determination to diversify Iraq's sources of arms, so as to avoid a crippling dependence on the Soviet Union. "I do not care where my weapons come from," Saddam told the startled Soviet Foreign Minister, Andrei Gromyko, who protested Iraq's growing interest in Western weaponry, "what counts is that these weapons will serve my purposes."[31] And indeed, by the end of the 1970s he had established procurement ties with Italy, West Germany, Belgium, Spain, Portugal, Yugoslavia and Brazil. While the Soviet Union still remained Iraq's major arms supplier, its share in Baghdad's overall arms acquisitions dropped from over 95 percent in 1972 to around 63 percent in 1979.[32]

The main beneficiary of Saddam's "policy of diversification" was France which, from the mid-1970s, managed to develop into Iraq's second-largest arms supplier after the Soviet Union. The Iraqi-French arms relationship can be traced back to 1968, when Iraq showed interest in the purchase of Mirage-III aircraft, but nothing came of it, and no progress was made in this respect until the second half of the 1970s. In the summer of 1977 Iraq signed its first arms deal with France for the supply of Mirage-F1 fighters, to be followed a year later by further agreements on the sale of Alouette attack helicopters, Crotale-I surface-to-air missiles and electronic equipment.[33]

Until the Algiers Agreement with Iran this diversification policy had not been feasible. Diversification of weapons presents complications even for advanced, modern armies operating in peacetime conditions. It took Egypt no less than a decade to satisfactorily complete the Western re-armament of its forces. It was inconceivable for Saddam to entertain such an idea as long as the Iraqi army was bogged down in an exhausting conflict in Kurdistan. Saddam's desperate need for Soviet military support and political backing in his confrontation with the Kurds and Iran had left him no room for maneuver vis-à-vis his larger ally. Also, Saddam's political standing was not stable enough to allow him to establish close relations with the "imperialist" West. This concern led him to conduct his dealings with the West in great secrecy. In the late 1970s he forbade the state-controlled media to publish any details of Iraq's commercial deals except for the laconic announcement of the conclusion of contracts "with a foreign company."[34] Publication by Iraqi sources of their country's oil sales to the West became a capital offense, punishable by death.

Revelation of details about Iraqi oil transactions with the West was not the only "offense" punishable by death. Being a member of the Communist Party in the late 1970s was equally perilous. In early 1979, a foreign guest of Saddam Hussein learned to his horror how his host had personally purged the two communist ministers in his cabinet. According to a member of Saddam's entourage, the two were invited to the Deputy Chairman's office to discuss their possible promotion. While they were sitting unsuspectingly in Saddam's office, having their coffee, Hussein suddenly drew his pistol and shot both of them to death. Their blood spurted all over the office, to such an extent that it was necessary to replace the carpets.[35]

Unlike most stories regarding Saddam's predilection for personally executing senior dissidents, this incident can be easily refuted: the two communist ministers in the cabinet after 1974— Mukarram Talabani and Amir Abdallah—were purged but not executed.[36] The question, therefore, is why a member of Saddam's inner circle, a highly intelligent and well-educated person, would fabricate a story which could embarrass his master and might cost him a good deal? He was evidently proud of Saddam's supposed deed and eager to share with others the toughness of his leader. "The communists deserve such a punishment," he said, "for their atrocities against the Iraqi people in the late 1950s." The most plausible explanation would seem to be that the dissemination of such stories, a common practice of Saddam's coterie, has always been a useful means of magnifying their master's powerful image, so as to deter would-be plotters against him.

The incident, apocryphal as it may be, symbolized the end of an era in Hussein's relations with the ICP, and reflected his diminishing tolerance for any opposition to his growing absolutism. From Saddam's point of view, the communists had always been an irritant, a major obstacle to the transformation of Iraq into a truly one-party state. He had been willing to enter into an uneasy coexistence with them in the early 1970s only because he desperately needed a respite on the domestic front and a *rapprochement* with the Soviet Union. And, as he would reveal in March 1975 to the Algerian President, Huari Boumedienne, and to the Iranian Shah, he had turned to Moscow only because of Iraq's international isolation and the pressures applied on it by Iran.[37] Once these reasons had lost their validity, both the Soviet Union and the communists had become redundant.

The communists, for their part, apparently believed that in joining the National Patriotic Front (established in July 1973 to give a semblance of democracy to the regime) at a time when the Ba'th was becoming increasingly dependent on the Soviet Union, they stood a genuine chance of consolidating their position. And, for a short while they did appear to resume normal political activities: they were allowed greater freedom of expression and could openly strengthen their grassroots organizations. However, it did not take long for the communists to realize that they were not a party to the decision-making process and that they were being subjected to behind-the-scenes harassment by Saddam. Their disillusionment deepened following the conclusion of the Algiers Agreement. Given their traditionally strong power base in Kurdistan, the communists were appalled by the brutal Iraqi suppression of the Kurds that followed their betrayal by the Iranian Shah. Equally disturbing was the fact that, as Saddam's domestic and international problems subsided and his hold on the reins of power tightened, his persecution of the communists intensified. By the end of 1975 and over the next few years, communists were again arrested indiscriminately and persecuted. The communists responded by escalating their criticism of the Ba'th: its methods of repression, its policies on the Kurds, and its bias toward the West.[38]

This last accusation in particular touched a sensitive nerve in Saddam who was adamant about keeping his relations with the

West away from the public eye. As he edged away from Moscow, the ever-wary Deputy Chairman began to suspect an impending Soviet-orchestrated plot against him by the ICP. His fears were further fueled by a Soviet-directed coup in Afghanistan in April 1978, which brought to power a Marxist regime under the leadership of Nur Muhammad Taraqi. Against this backdrop Hussein moved promptly. Clearly implicating the Soviet Union, he accused the Iraqi Communist Party of not being based on genuinely Iraqi foundations, but rather of taking its cue from Moscow. He charged it with violating the principles of the National Patriotic Front through its vehement criticism of the Ba'th and of plotting to overthrow the regime.

The signal for the letting of communists' blood was given in May 1978 when 21 communists, who had been in prison for several years on charges of organizing communist cells within the army, were executed, despite appeals from the Soviet Union and several East European countries to pardon them.[39] The following months witnessed an extremely ferocious campaign against the ICP. Arrests, tortures and executions followed suit, driving many communist leaders out of the country, and the Communist Party underground again. By the summer of 1979 the ICP had been virtually removed as a political factor, and the National Patriotic Front had effectively ceased to exist.

The destruction of the Communist Party coincided with the sustained crushing of the remnants of Kurdish opposition. Saddam's unilateral implementation of the 1970 March Manifesto, begun in 1974, continued apace after the collapse of the Kurdish rebellion following the Algiers Agreement. Boundaries of problematic areas, such as the district of Kirkuk, were redrawn to ensure that they did not have a Kurdish majority, and Saddam acted to insure that the Kurds would not profess nationalistic determination in the future. To this end he renewed his systematic effort to reshape the demographic balance in Kurdistan by a forceful relocation of Kurds and their replacement by Arabs. In a move to be replicated a decade later, in the final stage of the Iran-Iraq War, numerous villages along the Iranian (and to a lesser extent, Turkish) frontier were razed and their population moved to various parts of the country, to make room for a "security zone" between Iraq and its neighbors. Many settlements in other parts of Kurdistan were similarly destroyed, or reoccupied by Arabs. Large numbers of Kurds were transferred to southern parts of Iraq, where they were settled in Arab villages in groups of no more than five families per village. By 1979 over 200,000 Kurds had been relocated.

Even though the military infrastructure of the Kurdish national movement had been broken beyond repair in 1975, and although its main source of military supplies had been completely cut off, the government's repressive measures did not fail to rekindle armed Kurdish resistance. Guerrilla operations were resumed in 1976, and were soon becoming an irritant for the central government. In the spring of 1978 there were several reports of large-scale military movements in northern Iraq and of clashes between the army and Kurdish guerrillas. According to some sources, more than 1,000 Iraqi troops and Kurds were killed, and nine villages burnt. The state-controlled media conspicuously denied these reports, arguing instead that "a few dozen spies and terrorists who had carried out bombings and assassinations in Suleimaniyya in April," had been executed.[40]

To Saddam's great relief, the Kurdish nationalist movement was beset by communal and tribal divisions. Also fragmenting the Kurds was the death in March 1979 of the exiled Mullah Mustafa Barzani, the embodiment of Kurdish defiance, which denied the resistance movement a unifying inspirational leader. All of this made Kurdish opposition to the regime a far cry from the armed struggle of the early 1970s. Following the 1975 catastrophe for the Kurds of the Algiers Agreement, when the Iranians withdrew their support, the Kurdish movement broke into two camps, the KDP-Provisional Leadership under Mas'ud Barzani, and the Patriotic Union of Kurdistan (PUK), led by Jalal Talabani. While both advocated armed struggle against the regime, Barzani's was a "traditional" nationalist party, while the PUK declared it was guided by Marxist-Leninist ideology. The former would later sympathize with Khomeini's Iran and be supported by it; the latter was backed by Syria.

Instead of joining forces against the central government, the two factions engaged in a futile struggle for power and influence within the Kurdish community, thereby enabling Saddam to pit one against the other. Even though the Kurds, like the communists, had never been spared the harshest blows from Saddam's stick, they were also given a taste of his carrot. In an attempt to make his repressive policy more amenable to the Kurds, Saddam accompanied it by occasional gestures, such as an increased flow of funds for economic and municipal projects, and the introduction of several Kurds into the central government and the National Patriotic Front. Much ado was made in early 1979 about the repatriation of some 30,000 families of Kurdish refugees from Iran to Iraqi villages. Each family received a color television and a cash allowance, and the authorities announced allocations of financial resources for the development of Kurdish areas. Saddam wanted everyone to know that he did not discriminate against his own ethnic minorities.

The more Saddam got immersed in Iraq's smoldering domestic problems, the less inclined he was to engage in foreign ventures. The ideological extremism of pan-Arabism in the early 1970s (as manifested in subversive activities abroad and Iraq's bold claim to be the "protector" of Arab interests in the Gulf) had, he reckoned, won Iraq no friends, leaving it isolated and exposed to external enemies. By the mid-1970s he no longer had to heed his colleagues and their agendas in any significant way; instead the Party had to fall into line with his wishes. Nor was he any longer engaged in jockeying for political power; rather, he was grooming himself patiently for the country's top spot. What he needed least of all were hazardous enterprises abroad that could rock the Iraqi boat in the wrong direction at the wrong time.

Accordingly, the conclusion of the Algiers Agreement ushered in a "new Saddam," reconciled to his immediate environment and abounding with conciliatory gestures. Gone was the fierce rhetoric on the export of the Arab revolution; in its place was the peaceful hope that the spirit of the agreement would extend to every part of the region.[41] This outspoken friendliness was accompanied by a subtle, yet visible, change in one of the main Ba'thist ideological tenets: the unity of the Arab nation. Like Joseph Stalin, who had discarded the notion of the "permanent revolution" in favor of a policy of "socialism in one country," Saddam was slowly tilting in the direction of "Ba'thism in one country." To justify his declining commitment to the notion of pan-Arabism, he argued that only upon the complete Ba'thization of Iraq would the revolution be able to spread further, under Iraq's leadership, to the rest of the Arab world. As he put it, "the glory of the Arabs stems from the glory of Iraq. Throughout history, whenever Iraq became mighty and flourished, so did the Arab nation. This is why we are striving to make Iraq mighty, formidable, able and developed, and why we shall spare nothing to improve its welfare and to brighten the glory of the Iraqis."[42]

The first beneficiaries of Saddam's change of heart were the conservative regimes of the Gulf, the primary targets of Iraqi harassment in the early 1970s. A visit to Baghdad in June 1975 by Crown Prince Fahd marked the beginning of a new era in Iraqi-Saudi relations and paved the way for a series of bilateral agreements, including an agreement on the demarcation of a neutral zone on their joint border. The following spring Saddam reciprocated Fahd's visit and traveled to Jedda, where he emphatically affirmed the need for collaboration among the Arab Gulf states. Diplomatic relations were also established with Oman, whose monarch, the Sultan Qaboos, had been on Baghdad's "subversive list" only a few years earlier. The staunch support for the radical Marxist regime in South Yemen was curtailed in 1978, as Saddam increasingly assumed the role of a mediator between it and its more moderate neighbor, the Yemen Arab Republic.

Saddam's attempts to integrate Iraq into mainstream Arab politics were also reflected in his approach to the Palestinian problem. Already at the Rabat Summit of October 1974 Iraq abandoned its relentless commitment to the "armed struggle" against Israel and accepted the "phased strategy" which envisaged the establishment of a small Palestinian state on the West Bank and the Gaza Strip as an interim stage in the "final liberation of Palestine." By supporting this policy change Saddam hoped to kill two birds with one stone: to project a moderate image of Iraq to the conservative Arab regimes, and to reduce Iraq's military commitment to the Palestinian cause. As he was to admit candidly, the liberation of Palestine through military means was not feasible before building up a "scientifically, economically, and militarily strong Iraq."[43]

Not surprisingly, this approach failed to satisfy the PLO which held a long-standing grudge against Iraq for not coming to its rescue in the Black September of 1970. Baghdad, for its part, responded by supporting the extremist factions within the Palestinian movement, such as the notorious Sabri al-Banna, better known by his *nom de guerre* Abu Nidal, who was allowed to operate from Iraq. Although Iraq sided with the PLO against the Syrian military intervention in Lebanon in 1976 (initially designed to support the Christians against the Palestinians), its policy was more motivated by the desire to undermine the Syrian position than by a feeling of empathy for the PLO's plight. Relations between Iraq and *al-Fatah*, the largest constituent group within the PLO and Arafat's own organization, reached their lowest point in early 1978. Amidst an exchange of terrorist attacks against Iraqi and Palestinian targets, *al-Fatah* closed its offices in Baghdad and withdrew its funds. The Palestinian organization distributed pamphlets depicting Saddam as a professional killer and attacked Iraq for remaining outside the "progressive" camp opposing Anwar Sadat's peace negotiations with Israel. Baghdad retorted by accusing the *al-Fatah* of "slander against the Iraqi Ba'th Party and Government."[44]

But, as is often the case, the prospect of détente between Egypt and Israel was sufficient to bring the two camps together once more. Their antagonism ended abruptly in late 1978 as Hussein, seeking to play a prominent role in the all-Arab effort to block Anwar Sadat's drive toward peace with Israel, moved swiftly toward reconciliation with Yasser Arafat. The two met in Baghdad in November 1978 and yet again in March 1979, and Baghdad curbed Abu Nidal's activities against the PLO, as well as his virulent propaganda campaign.

A particularly revealing insight into Saddam's growing moderation in the late 1970s is reflected in his relations with Egypt. Historically, the relationship between Egypt and Iraq had been one of competition rather than cooperation: from the ancient struggle for regional hegemony, via twentieth-century monarchial rivalries, to Qassem's acrimonious relations with Nasser and Saddam's exchange of diatribes with the Egyptian President in the late 1960s, when he accused Nasser of responsibility for the humiliating Arab defeat in the 1967 Six Day War. Yet, paradoxically, it was at the very moment that Egypt's commitment to the pan-Arab cause seemed weakest that Saddam chose to thaw their relations. Under President Nasser, the champion of Arab nationalism, relations had soured. As his successor Anwar Sadat distanced himself from the pro-Soviet "progressive camp" and courted the "imperialist" Americans, Saddam Hussein was fostering economic ties with Cairo. Sadat's overt interest in a *rapprochement* with Israel initially proved no hindrance to Saddam, who continued to give the Egyptian President political backing as late as his historic visit to Jerusalem in November 1977. Thus, when in September 1975 Sadat concluded an agreement with Israel on the disengagement of forces in Sinai, Hussein accused Nasser, Sadat's predecessor, of planting the seeds of the shameful agreement, and, oddly enough, argued that Damascus "used the Egyptian regime as a mine detector, letting it absorb the explosions, so that when the road is cleared, the Syrian regime can march on with few casualties."[45] Saddam's anxiety to introduce Iraq into the mainstream of Arab politics, so as to free his hand for the consolidation of his domestic political position, seemed stronger than unquestioning commitment to lofty Ba'thi ideals of pan-Arabism.

Even Sadat's Jerusalem visit did not provoke Hussein to a virulent response. While Damascus went out of its way to condemn the Egyptian "betrayal of the Arab cause," Baghdad's tone in response to Sadat's move remained relatively subdued. When in January 1978 the radical Arab states established the Front of Steadfastness and Confrontation to resist the Egyptian "capitulation," Iraq remained outside the militant grouping. Even though the Iraqis justified their non-participation on account of the Front's lenient response to Egypt, in March 1978 they did not shy away from resuming diplomatic relations with the Egyptian state.[46] As in 1975, the Iraqis did not fail to point an accusing finger in Syria's direction. In a letter to several heads of Arab states in November 1977, President Bakr blamed Syria for "shouldering a basic responsibility for the deterioration of the Arab situation, [for] after the October [1973 Yom Kippur] War it followed the same line as Sadat, though differing at times on details and methods of implementation and expression."[47]

The marked difference between the Syrian and Iraqi reactions to the Israeli-Egyptian peace process reflected their contrasting interests. For Hafiz Asad, the Sadat visit was a traumatic event. Apart from breaking the most sacred Arab political and ideological taboo, Sadat's move undermined Syria's ability to advance its national goals. It seriously upset the strategic balance between Israel and the Arabs, leaving Syria alone, "like an orphan," to face the Israeli threat. For Saddam Hussein, conversely, the visit was a blessing in disguise. He did not share the intensity of Asad's anxiety over the adverse implications of the upset for the strategic balance. Unlike Syria, Iraq does not share a border with Israel and was unlikely to face an Israeli invasion. At the same time, the disappearance of Egypt from the center of inter-Arab politics gave Saddam an ideal opportunity to achieve two inter-related goals: to thrust himself into regional prominence without any conceivable risk, and to exploit Asad's heightened threat perception, due to Egypt's "defection," in order to force this archenemy to recognize Iraq's supremacy. Saddam moved resolutely on both fronts.

Following the conclusion of the Camp David Accords between Israel and Egypt in September 1978, Saddam quickly disabused himself of his previous moderation toward Egypt, and called upon the heads of Arab states to meet in Baghdad to coordinate a collective response to the disturbing development. When it convened in Baghdad between November 2 and 5, the summit turned out to be a shining success for Saddam. While chaired by President Bakr, it was common knowledge who had pulled the strings behind the scenes. This was the first all-Arab summit to be held in Baghdad, and even though it failed to halt Anwar Sadat's determined drive toward a formal peace treaty with Israel, it allowed Hussein, for the first time in his career, to play a key role in an Arab gathering of the utmost importance. He exploited his inter-Arab exposure to the full. On March 17, 1979, following the conclusion of an Israeli-Egyptian peace treaty a few days earlier, the Foreign and Finance Ministers of the Arab League convened in Baghdad for a follow-up meeting which expelled Egypt from the all-Arab organization. Baghdad had effectively become the center of inter-Arab politics, and Saddam, a politician of regional stature and a champion of the Arab cause.

A no less significant gain accrued to Saddam as a result of Sadat's peace policy. This was the *rapprochement* with Syria in late 1978 and early 1979.

Despite the moderate thrust of Iraqi foreign policy in the late 1970s, before this *rapprochement* relations with Syria had remained as turbulent as ever. Whatever the issue at stake, it seemed, Baghdad and Damascus had been on opposing sides. When Saddam concluded the Algiers Agreement with Iran, Damascus had no qualms about accusing the "Tikriti regime" of surrendering "Arab lands." When Syrian troops entered Lebanon in June 1976 to try to put an end to the intensifying civil war there, Iraq quickly sided with Syria's opponents at the time—the Muslim-PLO coalition—and emphasized that no settlement of the Lebanese problem was possible before the elimination of the "Syrian intervention." To underline its resentment of the Syrian action in Lebanon, Iraq went so far as to deploy a significant military force along the joint border, forcing President Asad to respond in kind and bringing bilateral relations to the verge of armed confrontation. During the following years the two countries remained embroiled in their relentless hostility, exchanging diatribes on a regular basis and carrying out occasional terrorist attacks against each other.

Against this backdrop it is highly doubtful whether the two regimes would have been able to patch over their mutual disdain, had it not been for the Egyptian-Israeli peace process. The acute attack of anxiety overtaking Asad, and the window of opportunity seen by Saddam to assert Iraqi supremacy coincided to drive these two leaders, who could hardly bear each other's presence in the same room, into a strong embrace.

On October 1, 1978, in a clear attempt to appease the rival Ba'th regime in Damascus, the RCC announced Iraq's readiness "to despatch immediately effective military forces to the Syrian arena" in order to fill the void left by Egypt's "desertion" of the Arab camp, calling upon the Syrian government "to respond fully to this historic pan-Arab step."[48] Three weeks later Asad arrived in Baghdad for a summit meeting with Bakr and Saddam, the first of its kind for nearly five years, where the two parties signed on October 26 a Charter for Joint National Action, aimed at "bringing about the closest form of unity ties between Iraq and Syria." A Joint Higher Political Committee was set up to promote this goal and on November 7, Baghdad and Damascus declared that the two countries were "one state, one Party and one people" and that preparatory measures leading ultimately to complete unity between the two states would immediately be set in motion.[49] For a short while, relations perked up: mutual propaganda attacks stopped altogether, air traffic between the two countries was resumed, and some political exiles in both capitals were shown the way out of the country.

This sudden reconciliation was all the more remarkable in light of the exceptionally acrimonious legacy between the two regimes. Not only had Syrian-Iraqi relations vindicated the general geo-political rule that "vicinity, or nearness of situation, constitutes nations [sic] natural enemies,"[50] but they had been compounded by a host of additional factors such as ideological rivalry over Ba'thist doctrine, competition for regional prominence, and, above all, personal animosities. For Saddam, Asad was probably his most dangerous Arab rival. He was young, dynamic, extremely competent and harbored undisguised ambitions for championship of the Arab cause. No less importantly, he was a permanent reminder of Saddam's unfulfilled dreams. He was a military officer, something the Iraqi leader had failed to achieve and in his eyes a disgrace he felt compelled to compensate for throughout his career. Moreover, Asad had been the undisputed ruler of his country since 1970 while Saddam, though the de facto leader of Iraq, had to bide his time in patient anticipation of the ripening of conditions for his decisive leap forward. During his years in power Asad had succeeded in transforming Syria from a weak country—the object of inter-Arab competition, whose name had been synonymous with internal instability—into a regional and political power whose wishes and interests could not be ignored.

Yet the compulsory honeymoon between Syria and Iraq did not last long. The Joint Higher Political Committee did not travel far. Its first meeting, during the Baghdad Summit of November 1978, was euphoric. Its second meeting, which took place in Damascus in January 1979, was disillusioning. The third meeting in June 1979 was "the funeral party for the entire project."[51] A month later, the newly installed President, Saddam Hussein, would deal the *coup de grace* to this unlikely *rapprochement*.

While the deeply entrenched enmity between the two regimes constitutes the underlying cause for the failure of the unity scheme, several explanations have been advanced regarding the short-term motivations of the main actors. It has been suggested that the unity talks were not to Saddam's liking from the outset and that he was forced into them by President Bakr, who was more committed to the Ba'thi precept of Arab unity. It has also been argued that Saddam's resentment of the projected union stemmed from his knowledge that Bakr was to become its President and Head of the unified Ba'th Party, while Asad was to serve as his deputy, thereby leaving Saddam without any real position or power.[52] Hence, he seized the first available opportunity after Bakr's resignation to reverse an unfavorable course of events. According to Saddam's own account he was adamant on achieving the unity, but was forced to back down immediately upon assuming the Presidency, having exposed a Syrian plot to overthrow him.[53]

None of these explanations seems satisfactory. Whatever Bakr's personal inclinations, and Syrian radio hastened to report upon his resignation on July 16, 1979, that "President Bakr stressed the importance of continuing the march toward unity between fraternal Syria and Iraq," the bilateral negotiations did not collapse after Saddam's seizure of power: they had been clinically dead since the beginning of 1979. More significantly, the assumption that Saddam was forced into the negotiations is at odds with the actual relationship between him and Bakr. Saddam had been behind all of Iraq's major foreign policy decisions since the early 1970s, when his power base had been markedly weaker. He had masterminded the Soviet-Iraqi bilateral treaty and the Algiers Agreement. He had been the person who mellowed Iraqi foreign policy after 1975. Would Saddam be inclined to play second fiddle at a time when he was effectively (though not yet officially) the undisputed leader, particularly in an issue which entailed such decisive implications for his political survival? Certainly not. Indeed, not only was Hussein not dragged into the negotiations against his will, but he played the key role on the Iraqi side, and from January 1979 onward—the almost exclusive role.

Saddam's disillusionment with the unity scheme, therefore, seems to lie in his realization that Asad would never fall into the secondary niche, assigned to him by Hussein. Having recovered from his initial shock following the Camp David Accords, Asad began to question the military unity of the projected union, particularly in light of Moscow's unmistaken indications that it would not support a unified Syria as generously as an independent one. Faced with the choice between the dubious benefits of a Syro-Iraqi federation and the humiliation of being under Saddam's (de facto) rule, the Syrian President decided to drag his feet.

This behavior antagonized Saddam. For him the union was purely instrumental: a means to put Iraq in the driver's seat of the Arab World. He had never envisaged placing the unification on an equal footing. In his view, since Iraq was superior to Syria in every important respect, its predominance should be institutionalized in the federative arrangement; and since it was Syria which needed Iraq and not vice versa, it had to reward its larger sister handsomely. There was no room for sharing power with Asad. The Syrian leader had to come under Iraqi control. If he was unwilling to comply, it was better to drop the unification scheme altogether.

Saddam's dwindling interest in unification may also have been affected by the resurgence of an old-new threat at Iraq's doorstep: Iran. During 1978 the Pahlavi monarchy, which had ruled Iran since the early twentieth century, was rocked by a mounting wave of public disturbances which, by the end of the year, had turned into a popular uprising. These events could not have been more unwelcome to Saddam. It was only four years after he had managed to find, at an exorbitant cost, an acceptable *modus vivendi* with Iran. To him the Algiers Agreement had been the basis on which he had anchored his political survival. It had given him a desperately needed respite to consolidate his position and to prepare for the crucial leap forward. There was nothing that he wanted less than renewed instability on Iraq's eastern border. Now that Tehran was convulsed by domestic strife, the fearful specter of such an eventuality loomed larger than ever.

With great anxiety Saddam followed the waning fortunes of his former enemy, the Shah, ready to help him in any possible way. At the Shah's request, in October 1978 Saddam had the exiled Iranian religious leader, Ayatollah Ruhollah Khomeini, who had lived in Iraq since the early 1960s, expelled from the country. A month later Empress Farah visited Baghdad and was received by Hussein with much pomp. It was only after the Shah's position became clearly hopeless, that Baghdad distanced itself from the monarch and began courting the Iranian opposition, including Ayatollah Khomeini, who moved to Paris following his expulsion from Iraq.[54] Once the Ayatollah made his triumphant return to Iran, Saddam immediately endorsed the revolutionary regime and extended his friendship to Iran.

At this stage, however, Saddam apparently concluded that he would have to make his bid for formal Iraqi leadership sooner rather than later. Mindful of the gathering storm in the east, in revolutionary Iran, he no longer felt able to remain "Mr. Deputy." He was the "strong man of Baghdad" all right, but in order to confront the Iranian challenge he needed more than that. He needed the official seal that would enable him to unite the nation behind his leadership. Besides, in his view, President Bakr was getting increasingly out of touch with his environment and might become a serious liability in a future predicament. As one of Saddam's semi-official biographers put it:

This military man spends his spare time on things that have no bearing on affairs of state. He wakes up early in the morning and goes into his garden; he waters the plants and trims the rose bushes. When he tires, he rests awhile in the company of his grandchildren. He lives with his memories, which are for the most part tragic. His son was killed in a car accident when he was only twenty-three, at a time when Ahmad Hasan Bakr was still recovering from the shock of his wife's death. Then his son-in-law died, and Ahmad Hasan Bakr was left to care for his daughter and her children.[55]

Even though this description should by no means be taken at face value, but rather as a justification for Saddam's decision to reshuffle his superior, it reflects Saddam's mood in the winter and spring of 1979. Regardless of Bakr's political capabilities at the time, he was no longer of any use to Saddam, and had therefore to be gently, but firmly, pushed to the sidelines.

Saddam's last leap to the coveted post was made with his typical caution. From 1979 onward he hectically toured the country, visiting urban and rural population centers, military camps and Party branches, without forgetting the Shi'ite and Kurdish communities. His speeches focused on one issue: his own glorification. At the same time the mass media launched an intensive personality cult campaign. Pictures, speeches, slogans and poems hailed the "leader," as if Bakr was no longer the official leader of Iraq. When the Yugoslav President, Josip Broz Tito, visited Baghdad in February, Saddam—and not Bakr—was awarded the highest Yugoslav medal, traditionally bestowed upon the Head of State.[56]

The stage had been set. On July 16, 1979, the eve of the eleventh anniversary of the Ba'thi takeover, President Bakr appeared on television and told the entire nation of his retirement from all his public duties due to health reasons. That very same moment Saddam was sworn in as President of the Republic of Iraq.

5

President at Last

"It has never happened before, either in ancient history (including that of our nation since its dawn) or in modern times, that two leaders have been in power for eleven years within one command, without this resulting in a dangerous moral or practical imbalance in leadership, and without their relationship ending in one of them driving the other out."[1] Saddam's words in his first address to the nation as Iraq's supreme ruler, shortly after purging his former superior and taking his place, disguised the true nature of his relation to Bakr and his assumption of Iraq's highest office. In one fell swoop he had not only become President of the Republic, but now held all key posts. He was Chairman of the Revolutionary Command Council, Secretary-General of the Ba'th Party Regional Command, Prime Minister, and Commander-in-Chief of the Armed Forces. With his long-standing de facto position as "the strong man of Baghdad" and the enforcer of Iraq's internal security, Hussein had succeeded in gathering in his hands power hitherto unknown to any Iraqi ruler. He headed a country with enormous oil riches, he commanded a rapidly expanding and modernizing army, and he wielded fearsome control over his subjects. He could boast a developing Iraq where health services and education were free, and where basic foodstuffs were in good supply and low in price. And he was only 42 years old. Here was a man in his prime, full of ambitious plans and, above all, grim determination to keep his hold on the levers of power at all costs.

Saddam's rise to power was remarkable. It was characterized by tenacious perseverance, skillful manipulation and merciless elimination of rivals. He had proved that in the devious corridors

110

of the Iraqi political system nothing must be left to chance. For more than a decade he had been patiently and doggedly striving toward the country's top spot until the time was ripe to remove Bakr. He had purged actual and potential opponents. He had even structured the economy in a way that would cement his power with the support of a new, entrepreneurial middle class. Furthermore, his domestic and foreign policies had been subordinated to the promotion of his political fortunes. The long march ended with a spectacular success: on July 11, 1979, a special closed session of the Revolutionary Command Council decided to relieve President Bakr from all his duties and to transfer them to Saddam Hussein.

The changing of the guard was a surgical operation. It had been kept under the strictest secrecy to the very last moment to prevent any unexpected disruptions. The timing of the move, the anniversary of the "July Revolution," was also carefully chosen to symbolize the historic continuity of the regime. The icing on the cake was provided by Bakr himself, who agreed to collaborate with Saddam in portraying his own purge as a natural, indeed inevitable, transition of power. For years, Bakr had been the de facto captive of his young protégé, whom he had personally cultivated. Now he had to accept that the time for his departure had come. In his address to the nation, the 65-year-old former President explained his decision to resign on the grounds of poor health. "For a long time," he told his listeners, "I have been talking to my Comrades in the Command, particularly cherished Comrade Saddam Hussein, about my health, which no longer allows me to shoulder the responsibilities with which the Command has honored me. I would repeatedly ask them to relieve me of this burden, but the magnanimity of Comrade Saddam Hussein and the Comrades in the leadership prompted them to refuse to discuss this. They always expressed their readiness to lift from my shoulders some of the burdens that could be lifted. "However," he continued, his voice shaking, "my health has recently reached the stage where I could no longer assume responsibility in a manner that satisfies my conscience and is commensurate with the magnitude of the missions with which the Command has entrusted me. Therefore, I insisted that Comrade Saddam Hussein and my Comrades in the Party leadership and the Revolutionary Command Council respond to my request to be relieved of my responsibilities in the Party and the State."[2]

At this stage Bakr proceeded to laud the person who had just

purged him from power as "the man best qualified to assume the
leadership." Applauding Saddam's political credentials, the ex-
President emphatically said,

> During the bitter years of struggle prior to the revolution, Comrade
> Saddam Hussein was a brave and faithful struggler who enjoyed
> the respect and trust of the Party's strugglers. On the eve of the
> revolution, he was at the head of the brave men who stormed the
> bastions of dictatorship and reaction. During the revolution's
> march he was the brilliant leader who was able to confront all the
> difficulties and shoulder all the responsibilities.[3]

Hussein, for his part, donning the mantle of modesty and
humility especially reserved for such occasions, took great pains to
tell the nation of his initial reluctance to replace Bakr and of his
tireless efforts to prevent the ailing President from retiring. It was
only after Bakr had insisted on quitting his position that he,
Saddam, half-heartedly agreed to accept his nomination due to
"Party consensus." Praising his predecessor effusively, Hussein
described the transition of power as "unique in ancient and
modern history" due to the "natural, moral and constitutional
manner" in which it had been effected.[4] What he failed to
mention was that it was he who had orchestrated the entire
transition.

Having rendered his last valuable service to his former
protégé, Ahmad Hasan al-Bakr faded gracefully from the scene,
after 11 years in power. Three months later he was stripped of his
last duty, that of Deputy Secretary-General of the Ba'th Party
National Command, a post which was added to those already held
by Saddam. In late 1982, at one of Iraq's darkest moments during
the Iran-Iraq War and amidst rumors about Bakr's possible
restoration to power, the retired President died in complete
obscurity. This, in turn, provoked speculation regarding the real
cause for his death, but there is no evidence to tie it to Saddam.

Once at the helm, Saddam moved swiftly to assert his position.
Despite the seeming ease of Bakr's resignation, resistance to
Saddam's usurpation of the Presidency existed and had to be
eliminated. During the special meeting which decided on Bakr's
resignation, the RCC's Secretary-General, Muhie Abd al-Hussein
Mashhadi, "suddenly stood up and demanded that they vote on
the question of President Bakr's relinquishing his responsibilities

in the Party and the State to Saddam Hussein. He insisted that the decision be carried unanimously. 'It is inconceivable that you should retire,' he told Bakr. 'If you are ill why don't you take a rest?' "[5]

Such dissent was intolerable from Saddam's point of view. He was not content with the comfortable majority he had enjoyed in the state's ruling institutions. He was on his own now, without Bakr's fatherly figure to shield him whenever the need arose, and with a great deal more to lose. He was at once far more powerful than all his comrades put together, and far more vulnerable to attack from them. He was determined to shield himself at all costs. This combination of prowess and fear, which, at a later stage would drive Saddam to the extreme moves of military aggression against Iran and Kuwait, manifested itself within two weeks of his inauguration in the most brutal, far-reaching purge in his entire career.

Already on July 15, a day before Bakr's public resignation, the Iraqi people learned that Mashhadi had been relieved of his duties three days earlier.[6] The explanation for this move was given only two weeks later, when the state-controlled mass media suddenly announced the exposure of "a treacherous, low plot perpetrated by a gang disloyal to the Party and Revolution." According to the official statement, the conspiracy had been planned over a period of several years and the authorities had been aware of its existence for a long time. A foreign power was implicated, but, "in the national interest," it was decided not to "expose its identity for the time being." Like the earlier purges of the late 1960s and early 1970s, the "conspirators" were subjected to the nebulous accusation of being part of "a capitulationist design led by U.S. imperialism in the interest of Zionism and the forces of darkness."[7]

What the ordinary Iraqis learned on July 28 had been common knowledge within the Party for a few days. On July 22, Saddam convened an extraordinary conference of senior Party cadres. The gathering opened with Taha Yasin Ramadan, a longtime close associate of Saddam and Commander of the Party's militia, the Popular Army, taking the podium and announcing the exposure of "a painful and atrocious plot." Ramadan spoke in a sad and melancholy voice, trying to convey his pain at the "betrayal" of the Party by some of its most prominent and long-standing members. Astonishment in the audience reached its peak when Ramadan announced that all the plotters were present in the hall, and that they had been invited to the meeting without prior knowledge of its content. Ramadan then asked Mashhadi, who had been brought from prison, to take the platform and narrate the details of the "horrible crime."

Conspicuously reminiscent of Stalin's great purges of the 1930s, Mashhadi's fabricated confession was long and detailed. His tone of voice was subdued. His appearance was that of a broken person, reconciled to his imminent death. He told the audience that since 1975 he had been part of a Syrian plot aimed at removing Bakr and Saddam Hussein, in order to pave the way for a Syrian-Iraqi union, headed by Hafiz Asad. When the conspirators realized that Bakr was about to step down in favor of his Deputy, they decided to try to persuade the President to change his mind, knowing that Saddam's ascendancy would consolidate the Party and, in consequence, obstruct their plans. In Mashhadi's account, the plot was headed by another RCC member, Muhammad Ayesh Hamad, and President Asad had been in the picture from the outset. He met the plotters on several occasions, and was the person who decided to try to forestall the transfer of power from Bakr to Saddam.

When Ayesh's name was mentioned, Saddam, who until then had sat calmly enjoying a Havana cigar, as if the entire affair had nothing to do with him, interrupted Mashhadi. "I noticed that Muhammad Ayesh was behaving strangely during the meetings of the RCC," he said,

> he was nervous and I noticed that he was looking at me with hatred. So I summoned Tariq Aziz and told him: "Go and spend an evening with Muhammad Ayesh. I feel that there is a black spot in his heart against me, try to learn what this black spot is." Aziz came from his mission and said that Ayesh had nothing in his heart against me. So did my half-brother Barzan al-Tikriti and Izzat Ibrahim (Deputy Chairman of the RCC under Saddam), whom I had also sent to Ayesh. This was because we always watch the enemies of the revolution but not our own leadership. We did not expect them to exploit their immunity by this plotting.

As Mashhadi ended his testimony, Saddam took the podium. He told the audience how stunned he was to discover that he had been betrayed by his closest associates. "After the arrest of the criminals," he said, "I visited them in an attempt to understand the motive for their behavior. 'What political differences are there between you and me?,' I asked, 'did you lack any power or money? If you had a different opinion why did you not submit it

to the Party since you are its leaders?' They had nothing to say to
defend themselves, they just admitted their guilt." As Saddam
mentioned the name of Ghanem Abd al-Jalil Saudi, one of the
alleged plotters, he began to weep. He took a handkerchief from
his pocket to hide his tears and, having overcome his emotions, he
unfolded a piece of paper which he held in his hand and began
reading the names of the supposed traitors. He read slowly and
theatrically, pausing occasionally to light his cigar. Sixty-six people, including some of Saddam's close associates, were named and
led away from the hall, one by one. The audience erupted into
hysterical chants hailing Saddam and demanding death for "the
traitors." Saddam, anticipating the propaganda value of his
action, had the entire event filmed and distributed to the top
echelons of the Ba'th and the military, as well as to officials of
other Arab countries. He had sent an unmistakable signal to one
and all that he would brook no opposition.[8]

The hard core of the alleged plot consisted of five of the
Revolutionary Command Council's 21 members: Mashhadi, Ayesh, Adnan Hussein al-Hamdani, Muhammad Mahjub Mahdi,
and Ghanem Abd al-Jalil Saudi. All of them were also members of
the Party's Regional Command. Among the five, Mashhadi and
Ayesh stood out as the most outspoken critics of Saddam. The
fatal mistake, which eventually cost them their lives, was their
blatant opposition to Saddam's *putsch* against Bakr. Hamdani's
principal "crime," on the other hand, was apparently his being a
potential overachiever. For unlike his comrades he had never
been among Saddam's enemies. On the contrary, the two had
been close friends and collaborators on a host of issues, including,
reportedly, the development of Iraq's non-conventional arms
industry. What made this case particularly striking was that in a
cabinet reshuffle carried out by Hussein on the day of his
ascendancy, Hamdani was appointed Deputy Prime Minister and
Head of the President's Office. Why then, one may ask, did
Saddam appoint a "plotter" to a key governmental position, only
to remove him a few days later? Was it because of his ignorance of
Hamdani's "devious machinations"? Probably not, since the authorities publicly admitted that they had known about the existence of the "plot" for quite some time. Perhaps it was a shrewd
move by Saddam to conceal his designs until the transition had
been effectively completed. By promoting Hamdani, Saddam
apparently sought to project himself as the aggrieved party, so as
to remove any doubts about the authenticity of the "plot." After

all, he had done nothing wrong. Wrong had been done to him.
How could he know that "the evil clique would go so far as to sell
trust, conscience and honor to the forces of evil"?[9] This technique
of blaming his victims for their misfortune, which Saddam had
frequently used in his ascent to power, was to be employed on
numerous future occasions, most notably in the summer of 1990
when he justified his occupation of Kuwait on the grounds of a
deadly Kuwaiti conspiracy against Iraq.

On the day the "plot" was made public, a special court
comprising seven RCC members was set up, under Deputy
Premier Na'im Haddad, to try the accused. The court found 55
men guilty. Twenty-two were sentenced to death through "democratic executions," by their fellow Party members, including the
five members of the RCC. Thirty-three were given prison sentences. One person escaped, while 13 were released. Saddam
seized the opportunity to rid himself of an old enemy as well. Abd
al-Khaliq al-Samarra'i, who had spent the past six years in prison
for his alleged role in the Kazzar coup attempt, was also implicated
in the new "coup" and sentenced to death.[10] The price of dissent
in Saddam's Iraq was very high.

As in 1969, Baghdad was rife with rumor and agitation and
Saddam moved to mobilize popular sentiment on his behalf.
Hundreds of thousands marched through the streets of the
capital to demonstrate their support for the sentences. All Party
divisions and branches throughout the country were requested to
send an armed delegate to join the firing squads. Hundreds of
such delegates, headed by their President and the entire Revolutionary Command Council, took part in the "unprecedented
event in the history of the Party," the popular purge and
execution of their "traitorous" members. The state radio proudly
reported that the executions were carried out "amid cheers for
the long life of the Party and the Revolution, and the Leader,
President, Struggler, Saddam Hussein."[11] One voice remained
mute, however, that of ex-President Bakr who refrained from any
response to the execution of veteran colleagues.

Saddam, conversely, was more than articulate. In a public
speech on August 8, the day of the executions, he presented the
exposure of the "plot" as a great achievement of the "Ba'thi
Revolution." It was not merely opponents in Iraq who had been
defeated but broader external forces whose puppets they had
been. "We pity the traitors and conspirators outside Iraq," he told
a huge crowd gathered in the gardens of the Presidential Palace,

"who labored for more than five years and all they could win over
from the Iraqi people were these 55 individuals." "There are now
16 members of the RCC," he continued to chants demanding
death for the traitors, "seven of them were in the tribunal and
three in the investigatory body. This is the first time in the history
of revolutionary movements without exception, or perhaps the
first time in the history of human struggle, that over half of the
supreme leadership took part in a tribunal and investigation to
guarantee justice and voice the truth."[12]

The term "historic" was doubtless appropriate, for a new era
had dawned upon Iraq in July 1979, that of the "Leader,
President, Struggler, Saddam Hussein." Iraq had effectively
crossed the Rubicon between an "ordinary" politico-military dictatorship and a totalitarian state, whose influence extends to every
aspect of the society. The purges marked the beginning of the
"Saddamization" of the Ba'th, and in consequence, of the entire
nation. The Ba'th would no longer be the same, as it was now
reduced to an extension of Saddam's will. The purges provided
the ultimate proof of Saddam's naked manipulation of others to
achieve his ends and of his unbridled ruthlessness. Nobody was
now safe, not even his very close associates, as Hamdani's fate
indicated. As Hussein himself put it: "We are now in our Stalinist
era. We shall strike with an iron fist against the slightest deviation
or backsliding beginning with the Ba'thists themselves."[13]

At the pragmatic level, the fabricated plot enabled the new
President to achieve several simultaneous objectives. By fueling
the xenophobic sentiments of his subjects against the "evil forces
of imperialism and Zionism," he managed to rally the masses
behind his leadership. He sent a resounding warning both to
would-be "plotters" and to problematic segments within Iraqi
society, particularly the Kurds and Shi'ites, that he would not
tolerate any "treacherous acts" or any contacts with "foreign
elements." By implicating Syria in the alleged "coup," he managed
to terminate the inconclusive talks on Iraqi-Syrian unification
which had been under way for some time, thus publicly humiliating his archenemy, Hafiz Asad. The Syrian Foreign Minister,
Abd al-Khalim Khaddam, shuttled back and forth between Damascus and Baghdad bearing messages from Asad professing
Syria's innocence and emphasizing that "a plot is not in Syria's
interest." But as the London weekly, the *Observer*, put it, Hussein
had "won the round."[14]

Last but not least, he managed to inextricably implicate the

entire Ba'th Party, the RCC in particular, in his policies. He was
not the only person responsible for trying and executing the
"plotters." It was a collective act performed in front of the entire
nation. Nobody could shrug off responsibility. This responsibility
was especially visible in the case of Na'im Haddad. As a Shi'ite, his
position as head of the special court was designed to ensure that
the execution of two of the most prominent Shi'ites in the Ba'thi
administration, Mashhadi and Hamdani, at a time of mounting
Shi'ite restiveness, would not be interpreted in the context of
inter-communal strife. At the same time, Haddad's key position
on the court was certain to buy him the hostility of many in his
community, thus increasing his dependence on his master.

Even though, in his August 8 speech, Saddam vehemently
denied reports in the Western media regarding widespread
arrests in Iraq, it soon became evident that the purges extended
far beyond the 55 people Saddam had so diligently singled out,
and continued well after July. They were not only aimed at
removing immediate threats. They were intended to ensure the
Party's full submission to its new master. Accordingly, hundreds
of Party members and military officers were purged and many
were executed, including Major General Walid Mahmud Seirat,
Commander of one of Iraq's three Army Corps. In August 1979
the Assistant Secretary-General of the Ba'th National Command,
Munif al-Razzazz was arrested, and in the spring of 1980, following rumors of yet another alleged "coup," further executions
were reported. As in the case of al-Samarra'i, Saddam seized the
opportunity to settle old scores. In April 1980, Saddam's old
friend-turned-victim, Abd al-Karim al-Shaykhli, who had been
removed from his duties as long ago as 1971, was gunned down in
Baghdad. Another retired Ba'thist, Sa'd Abd al-Baqi al-Hadithi,
relieved of his membership in the RCC and the RC in 1974, was
murdered in Baghdad two months later.[15] Saddam would shore
up his Presidential power with total terror, a policy he would
pursue to the present day. No dissent was too trivial or slight in
the eyes of Saddam. All were equated with aggressive acts which
required absolute punishment and eradication. There could be
only one power in Iraq and it would be Saddam's.

The purges were accompanied by organizational changes aimed
at further tightening Saddam's grip on the reins of power. On the
day he assumed power he merged several cabinet ministries,
replaced eight Ministers, and created the post of First Deputy

Premier and five posts of Deputy Premier. The first new slot was manned by Taha Yasin Ramadan, while the rest were filled by Saddam's cousin and Minister of Defense, Adnan Khairallah Talfah, together with four close confidants: Na'im Haddad, Tariq Aziz, Sa'dun Ghaydan, and the ill-fated Adnan Hussein al-Hamdani. Another relative of Saddam, Sa'dun Shakir, was made Minister of the Interior to replace Izzat Ibrahim al-Duri, the newly appointed Deputy Chairman of the RCC. To boost the position of the pro-government elements within the Kurdish community, Saddam also appointed several Kurdish figures to senior Party roles.

Having restructured the cabinet, Saddam moved to enhance its power at the expense of the state's foremost institution—the Revolutionary Command Council. He had never had full trust in the RCC, though he knew that his way to the Presidency had to pass through the authority of this body. During the 1970s he had secured a comfortable majority in the RCC, and his first act after assuming the Presidency was to cleanse it of any conceivable sources of independent thinking. He more than achieved this objective. Apart from removing the last potential bastion of dissent, the July 1979 purges also cowed the remaining members of the RCC into unquestioning subservience. Yet even this failed to satisfy Saddam who now opted to strengthen the President's formal and operational powers and curb those of the RCC. To this end he activated the cabinet which until then had been a rather inoperative body. He began holding regular meetings to discuss state affairs, presiding over them in his capacity as Prime Minister. For Saddam, the cabinet offered a useful executive instrument that lacked any ability to strike an independent course. Another means used by Saddam to circumvent the RCC was his growing reliance on Presidential regulations, defined variously as "directives," "instructions," and "guidelines" to run the country. In March 1980, to this end he enacted the National Assembly Law which conferred wide-ranging powers on the President at the expense of the RCC.[16]

The decision to awaken the state legislature from two decades of deep sleep into which it had fallen after the overthrow of the monarchy in 1958 was apparently taken a short while after Saddam's takeover. Invoking a law passed by the RCC in 1970 for the establishment of a National Assembly,[17] in December 1979 a draft law on the assembly was circulated and finally approved in March 1980. According to the law, a 250-member assembly was to

be elected by secret ballot every four years by all Iraqi citizens over
the age of 18. To qualify as a candidate, though, one had to fulfill
a long list of requirements, which made the election of non-
Ba'thists virtually impossible. Not only did a potential candidate
have to be a 25-year-old native Iraqi of paternal Iraqi origins; not
only was he forbidden to have a foreign wife and to belong to a
family whose property or land had been expropriated under the
various state laws, but, above all, he had to be "a believer in the
principles of the July Revolution."[18] Special election committees
were formed to ensure that these qualifications would be strictly
observed. And as if to banish any thoughts of heresy on election
day, Saddam made his expectations of the Iraqi nation deadly
clear: "We must ensure that the thirteen and a half million [Iraqis]
take the same road. He who chooses the twisted path, will meet
the sword."[19]

The elections were held on June 20, 1980. Not surprisingly,
few if any chose to take "the twisted path." Seventeen so-called
independent representatives were elected to the 250-member
body. Hussein himself laconically summarized the elections as an
indication that the Iraqi people supported Ba'th candidates and
not any other political party. Among the elected were four RCC
members, and four Ministers. Na'im Haddad was made Speaker
of the Assembly.

To give widespread exposure to the first act of "democratic"
participation in Iraq in over two decades, several foreign journalists were flown to Iraq and taken to different parts of the country.
The *New York Times* provided the following glimpse into the
process:

> Here in Najaf, a city near the banks of the Euphrates holy to Shi'i
> Muslims, the Governor, Mizban Khider, greeted the visitors in an
> office equipped with 8 telephones and 6 portraits of President
> Hussein. Telling them that he expected a large turnout to give
> thanks to "the leadership of the party and the revolution," he said:
> "They will show that they like and love Saddam Hussein. Saddam
> Hussein is the hope of the Arab nation and the Arab homeland."[20]

These words of the local official captured the underlying motive
behind the re-establishment of the National Assembly. It was not
only another bureaucratic creation to improve Saddam's hold on
the levers of power and to impart a semblance of democracy on

his personal rule. It was a vehicle established within the framework of an unprecedented personality cult campaign, by which Hussein was projected as the embodiment of both the Iraqi state and the popular sovereignty. He knew all too well that fear was not enough to secure absolute power; that if he were to stay at the helm for an indefinite period of time, and he had never had any other intention, then the Iraqi people had to be made to love and adore him, to identify themselves with his person. He was to become Iraq. He was to become the Iraqi nation, the voice of the collective people.

The nurturance of Saddam's personality cult involved widespread material inducements and demonstrative shows of goodwill, aimed at portraying him as the generous benefactor of the nation. Pay increases were announced for a wide range of wage earners, with an especially substantial pay rise given to all members of the armed forces. A solemn presidential pledge was made to speed up the country's economic development projects. A general amnesty was declared, with the exception of prisoners convicted of plots against the regime, espionage, economic sabotage and drug smuggling. A direct telephone line to the Presidential Palace was established, so that citizens could supposedly call and talk to their supreme leader.

The Iraqi people were increasingly exposed to the personality of their omnipotent, omnipresent, fatherly leader, who was portrayed as strict, but righteous. His image sprang up everywhere. Numerous sites were named after him. His life story was featured in a special edition of the Baghdad newspaper *al-Jumhuriyya,* a film and an exhibition mounted in Baghdad. The Iraqis learned that Saddam was a devoted family man and a loving father to his two sons, Udai and Qusai, and three daughters, Raghd, Rina, and Hala; a father who would not shy away from sewing on his daughter's button in front of his aides and guards. They also learned that he was fond of working in his garden, fishing, or looking after the sheep, and preferred bitter black coffee to tea, since in his prison years he had been denied tea and got accustomed to drinking coffee.[21]

Many Iraqis were taken by surprise when their young and dynamic President popped in on them in factories, hospitals, mosques and farms. Saddam used these unannounced visits to make himself appear close at hand and potentially at any place at any time. Occasionally he would try to disguise his real identity by wearing a big hat or an Arabic *kefiya* (cotton headdress), so as to (ostensibly) receive candid replies from his unsuspecting audience. In a regular television program featuring such meetings, Saddam was often shown sitting at an ordinary Iraqi home, exploring his hosts' views about himself and his policies. The hosts, pretending not to recognize their President, whose picture adorned every street corner, did not spare their praise for his great achievements. Whenever Saddam felt that the subject had been exhausted, he unveiled his real identity to the staged surprise and delight of his hosts. At this moment a big and genuine smile would creep into Saddam's face. He had won the love and admiration of his subjects.

Looking at these television scenes, one cannot but recall the eighth century Abbasid Caliph, Harun al-Rashid, who used to tour Baghdad incognito in order to get first-hand impressions of the public mood in his capital. Yet, Saddam's quest for national symbols that could reinforce his personal absolutism extended far beyond the cultural flowering of the Abbasid period. Ancient Iraq, or Mesopotamia as it was called, offered everything he could possibly wish for in this respect. This was the cradle of civilization: the land where monotheism emerged, where the basic principles of mathematics and astronomy were developed and where the first legal code was laid down by Hammurabi. This was a land of great kingdoms, of conquests and grandeur. In their turn, each of the two Mesopotamian empires, Babylon and Assyria, had been the hegemonic powers in the region, bringing vast territories of today's Middle East under their control. Many of the rulers of these empires were fearless warriors and able bureaucrats, worthy of emulation and capable of stirring up nationalistic sentiments. The Assyrian King, Shalmaneser III (858–824 B.C.), for example, spent 31 of the 34 years of his reign in expansionist wars, taking his soldiers to the farthest corners of the Middle East, from the Persian Gulf in the southeast to Palestine and the Taurus mountains in the West.[22] Sargon II (722–705 B.C.), the founder of a ruling house which governed Assyria for nearly a century and brought the empire to its farthest territorial limits, spent most of his reign suppressing domestic disorders, before he was eventually killed in war. One of Sargon's predecessors, Tiglathpileser III (744–727 B.C.), developed an original method for repressing such disorders—mass deportations of rebellious populations. More than a millennium later his methods would be replicated by Saddam in his dealings with Iraq's Kurdish minority.

What made most Mesopotamian rulers particularly appealing

to Saddam was not merely their regional prominence, but their victorious campaigns in Palestine. Senacherib, Sargon's successor (704–681 B.C.), set out for an expedition in Palestine, and, though failing to occupy Jerusalem, managed to subdue several important cities in Judah and to exact a heavy levy from the Jewish king, Ezekiah. What Senacherib failed to achieve was accomplished a century later by the Babylonian king, Nebuchadnezzar: in 587 B.C., following a Jewish revolt in Palestine, he effectively put an end to the kingdom of Judah, destroying Jerusalem, including the Jewish Temple there, and deporting thousands of Jews to Babylon. This historic event was often narrated by Saddam who, on several occasions, unabashedly admitted his desire to follow in the footsteps of the great Babylonian king.

Such a desire is hardly surprising. The glorious Mesopotamian past seemed to offer an ideal route to bypass Iraq's present problems. By making all Iraqis—whether Arabs, Kurds, Sunnis, or Shi'ites—perceive themselves as heirs to the great Mesopotamian civilizations, Saddam hoped to create a unifying concept that would transcend their divisions. Once such collective identity had been established, it would be linked to the glorious past through the personality of Saddam Hussein, the natural heir to the great Mesopotamian kings.

Hence, from his early years in power Saddam embarked on a sustained attempt to create a new and specifically Iraqi identity out of the disparate elements of the country's population. Without divorcing Iraq from the Arab World, Saddam emphasized its unique Mesopotamian heritage in an attempt to create a new "Iraqi man." This policy began in a low key in the early 1970s and gained considerable momentum during the latter part of the decade. Intensive cultural campaigns were launched to underscore the uniqueness of the Iraqi people. The various Mesopotamian periods were "Arabized" and portrayed as part of the Iraqi heritage. The most conspicuous effort to revive the long-buried past was the beginning, in 1978, of a reconstruction of Babylon, including a triumphal arch and a giant ziggurat, although at half their original scale.[23]

Already in 1974 Hussein lauded the Party's success in transforming the Iraqi national identity. "The man of Iraq is now a new man," he said in an interview with Arab and foreign journalists. "It may be that not everyone in Iraq is the 'homo sapiens' of the future, but he is certainly a new man who has evolved from ancient man in every respect. This is our achieve-

ment and this is the source of our confidence that the future
belongs to us and not to any evil individual whether in Iraq or in
the Arab homeland."[24] Six years later, on the twelfth anniversary
of the "July Revolution," the direct linkage between Saddam's
personality and the Mesopotamian heritage was unequivocally
established. "Iraq was more than once the springboard for a new
civilization in the Middle East," ran an official two-page statement
by the Iraqi government published in the London *Times*,

> and the question is now pertinently asked, with a leader like this
> man, the wealth of oil resources and a forceful people like the
> Iraqis, will she repeat her former glories and the name of Saddam
> Hussein link up with that of Hammurabi, Ashurbanipal, al-Mansur
> and Harun al-Rashid? To be sure, they have not really achieved
> half of what he has already done at the helm of the Ba'th Arab
> Socialist Party, [and] he is still only 44.[25]

This pretentious statement was correct in one important
respect. Having established himself at the Presidential Palace,
Saddam ran the country through a combination of deep fear and
awesome grandeur, typical of Iraq's imperial rulers. Although his
appetite for pomp was not to assume preposterous proportions
until the last stages of the Iran-Iraq War, it was already visible in
the first days of his Presidency. In contrast with the humble image
he sought to project to his subjects, Saddam quickly got accustomed to the small privileges attending his new position. His
wardrobe expanded to no fewer than 200 expensive suits, uni-
forms and tribal costumes for every occasion. A luxurious yacht
was ordered from a Danish shipyard. One of Saddam's visitors
gave a vivid description of the President's pomp: "he was dogged
by an obsequious flunky carrying a large box. Every few minutes,
Saddam, without turning round, would reach for a giant Havana,
light up, take a few puffs, [and] stub it out, only to reach for
another."[26]

Another personal guest of Saddam at the time, a Western
surgeon flown to Baghdad to operate on him (Iraqi surgeons
were presumably reluctant to undertake this hazardous task), was
struck by the more fearful side in Saddam's personality: his
excessively suspicious mentality and the fear he evoked among his
coterie. In the long conversation between the two after the
operation, Saddam was relaxed and unassuming. He made no
effort to impress his prowess upon his guest, and for most of the

time even avoided direct eye contact with him, looking instead sideways and downwards. He paid close attention to the explanations given to him, and his manner was that of a person recognizing a higher professional authority. And yet, despite this reception the surgeon felt chilled. He did not know Saddam's political history—at the time the Iraqi President was still anonymous to many outside the Middle East—and had no preconceptions about him. However, he was disturbed by the oblique look in Saddam's eyes, and the deep tension and anxiety among those present in the room.

At a certain point during the conversation, Saddam complained of his many headaches and asked whether there was a way of reducing them. The surgeon answered that it was possible in principle, depending on the causes of the headaches. He then proceeded to ask Saddam if he were aware of any particular circumstances that might put him under stress. The expression on the face of Saddam's personal physician, who acted as a translator during the meeting, revealed that the question had better remain unasked. Sweating heavily, he translated the question to his master, waiting nervously for the answer. Saddam, nevertheless, did not show the slightest sign of irritation. "Of course I have weighty reasons for distress," he answered, embarking on a lengthy exposition of the tangled web of conspiracies surrounding him. This is doubtless a clear case of paranoia, the surgeon thought to himself.[27]

One person who could still feel safe near Saddam in the turbulent summer of 1979 was his cousin, Adnan Khairallah Talfah. When, following his takeover, Saddam sought to reinforce his hold over the military by establishing the new position of Deputy Commander-in-Chief of the Armed Forces, Adnan was appointed to the influential post, alongside his position as Minister of Defense. For himself Hussein assumed the highest military rank of a Field Marshal in late 1979. He intensified the military buildup, which had already accelerated since late 1977. Between Saddam's ascendancy and the invasion of Iran in September 1980, the Iraqi ground forces were increased by some 800 tanks, 650 armored vehicles, and approximately 100 artillery pieces, most of them self-propelled. This equipment enabled the army to increase its order of battle from 10 divisions to 12. The Iraqi air force did not grow much during the same period, apart from the addition of 40 helicopters, but modernization accelerated.[28]

The expansion of Iraq's conventional capabilities was only part of Saddam's enormous military expansion. Already in the mid-1970s Saddam had embarked on a determined covert thrust toward the acquisition of non-conventional capabilities: chemical, biological, and most importantly, nuclear weapons. These last weapons, in particular, occupied a special place in his plans. For Saddam, nuclear weapons have always meant much more than the "great equalizer," the weapons that can erode Israel's military edge. They have been a personal obsession. A symbol of Iraq's technological prowess, a prerequisite for regional hegemony, the triumphant achievement of the self-styled Nebuchadnezzar, for him they represent the ultimate guarantee of absolute security. "For the Arab nation, the need for scientific advancement is tantamount to the need to live," he said in 1975, "since it is impossible for any nation to lead a dignified existence . . . without respect for science and a defined role in its exploration and exploitation."[29] When asked by an Arab journalist what he would like to be when he grew up, Saddam's eldest son, Udai, then a 16-year-old boy, unhesitatingly answered: "a nuclear scientist."[30]

While Udai never became a nuclear scientist, his father brought Iraq to the verge of nuclear military capability.[31] The main country on which Hussein placed his hopes for nuclear capability was France. The Soviet Union, then his foremost ally, while supplying Iraq with a research reactor as early as the late 1960s, was too cautious to be relied upon in such an ambitious and hazardous enterprise.

Franco-Iraqi relations gained momentum in the fall of 1974 when the French Premier, Jacques Chirac, paid an official visit to Baghdad. Saddam reciprocated the following year by visiting Paris, only to host another French Premier, Raymond Barre, in Iraq in the summer of 1977. In 1976 Saddam purchased the Osiraq research reactor from France, which he renamed Tammuz after the month of the Ba'thi Revolution. The reactor was supposed to have the power of about 70 megawatts thermal and was scheduled to become operative at the end of 1981. According to the original agreement, France was to supply Iraq with 72 kilograms of highly enriched uranium, which could be directly used for the development of nuclear weapons. Since this deal aroused a wave of international concern, the French hurried to suggest a substitute fuel that was unusable for military purposes. Saddam was infuriated. Iraq had been promised a certain fuel, he argued, and would not settle for less. Any substitute would not allow the full range of research activities planned at Osiraq. His insistence was partly rewarded. The French would provide Iraq with the highly enriched uranium, though only about one-third of the original quantity promised.

Saddam persistently denied any intention to produce atomic weapons, arguing instead that his nuclear program was being developed for purely peaceful purposes. Ridiculing the growing number of reports on Iraq's nuclear ambitions as the product of Zionist propaganda, he argued: "These Arabs, the Zionists said, could do nothing but ride camels, cry over the ruins of their houses and sleep in tents. Two years ago, the Zionists and their supporters came up with a declaration that Iraq was about to produce the atom bomb. But how could a people who only knew how to ride camels produce an atomic bomb?"[32] Saddam's sardonic comment revealed the defensive anger and pride of a Third World nation on the brink of modern technological power.

Many in the West seriously doubted Saddam's disclaimers. Leading experts on nuclear proliferation pointed out that the Osiraq reactor was exceptionally large and capable of irradiating uranium to produce the necessary plutonium for an atomic bomb. They pointed out that Iraq had a small laboratory-scale reprocessing facility at Tuwaitha, based on three radiologically shielded cells from Italy, which enabled it to extract plutonium from irradiated uranium. Indeed, there was evidence that Iraq had received Italian equipment for the purification of uranium oxide. In 1980, when Osiraq was about to be made operational, Baghdad was hectically shopping for exceptionally large quantities of natural uranium from a string of countries, including Italy, Brazil, and Portugal. One expert put the doubts regarding Osiraq's real purpose succinctly. Such a reactor, he argued, "was designed primarily for nations engaged in the indigenous production of nuclear power reactors. Iraq has no such program; Osiraq is not an electric power generating reactor. With its large oil reserves, Iraq would have no great economic or energy incentive to establish a nuclear power generating capacity."[33] This left only military purposes for the reactor.

These doubts were obviously shared by the Israelis who were Saddam's oft-stated enemies and whose destruction he hoped for. The closer Saddam got to his coveted goal, the more prevalent mysterious accidents aimed at delaying Iraq's nuclear program became. In April 1979, the core of a nuclear research reactor and other parts of the reactor, which were about to be shipped to Iraq, were blown up in France, thereby delaying their delivery by several months. In June 1980, an Egyptian-born nuclear scientist by the name of Yahya al-Meshad, who played a key role in the Iraqi nuclear program, was murdered in a Paris hotel. Two months later, the offices of an Italian company linked to the Iraqi nuclear program were severely damaged by a bomb explosion. Although there was no evidence to implicate any party in these incidents, the common assumption was that they had been perpetrated by the Israeli security service, the Mossad.[34]

Saddam remained undeterred by these serious delaying tactics. "Whoever antagonizes us must know that the nation he is antagonizing today will be different in five years," he declared, and pressed ahead with the plan to operate the Osiraq reactor as scheduled.[35] In mid-1980 France delivered the first consignment of enriched uranium fuel. Three months later, on September 30, 1980, Iran, which had been invaded by Iraq a week earlier, launched an air raid against the Osiraq reactor. The attack failed, but on June 7, 1981, the Israeli air force bombed Osiraq, shortly before it was to become operational. The reactor was completely destroyed, though fissionable material that had been stored in a deep underground canal was not damaged.

Saddam responded angrily by pointing to Iranian-Israeli collusion. "Had you not ably and sincerely faced the challenge imposed on you by the Persian enemy," he told the Iraqi people in his annual address on the anniversary of the Ba'thi takeover, "the Zionist enemy would not have raided Iraq in June because he would have been afraid of you." "However," he promised, "we will not succumb to the Zionist aggression and will not deviate from the war we have chosen."[36] He would make good his promise during the 1980s, reconstructing his nuclear program with foreign, particularly French and to a lesser extent German, support. This process was significantly accelerated in 1988 during the Iran-Iraq War, before being decisively reversed two years later during the Gulf War, when allied aircraft reportedly knocked out Iraq's nuclear installations.

The development of the other two components of Iraq's non-conventional arms industry, chemical and to a lesser extent biological weapons, had a less troublesome existence. Since in terms of damage and destruction chemical means are a far cry from nuclear weapons, and as their development requires a significantly less advanced technology, the Iraqi chemical program did not alarm potential enemies, such as Israel and Iran, and was allowed to continue in almost complete obscurity. Iraq's project of chemical and biological armament was reportedly launched as early as 1974 when a three-man committee, headed by Saddam Hussein, was formed for this purpose. The committee, whose other members were Adnan Khairallah Talfah and Adnan Hussein al-Hamdani (who was to be executed in 1979) soon established contact with a Beirut-based consulting firm by the name of Arab Projects and Development (APD), owned by two Palestinian construction tycoons. At the firm's advice, and through its good offices, Saddam began recruiting Arab scientists and technicians from all over the world. Between 1974 and 1977 more than 4,000 research personnel had been lured to Iraq by substantial financial rewards, and assigned the task of constructing chemical and biological plants.

Since this Arab scientific effort still failed to make Iraq self-sufficient in chemical warfare, Saddam decided in the late 1970s to seek the support of foreign companies for his chemical and biological programs. Procurement teams were sent to Europe and the United States, again disguised as commercial representatives of the APD, to search for the necessary technological know-how and supplies. Before long the Iraqis established contacts with an American company which provided the blueprints for the construction of the first Iraqi chemical weapons plant. The plans were labeled as "flow charts for a pesticide plant," but "even a novice would have recognized that at least two of the chemicals it was supposed to produce, Amaton and Paratheon, could be used to make nerve gas."[37] Although the American company eventually did not receive the necessary license to export the machinery for constructing the chemical plant, Saddam had managed to obtain a key element for his project: the plans of the enterprise.

The Iraqi efforts in Europe were not much more successful. Several companies in Britain, Germany and Italy were approached with the request to assist Iraq in assembling a chemical plant, but to no avail. On at least one occasion, that of the large British chemical corporation, ICI, the Iraqi agents even aroused suspicion which, in turn, drove the company to inform the Foreign Office of the nature of the Iraqi interest. Although the British authorities failed to take any action, Hussein was deterred by the incident and decided that Iraq would assemble the plant on its own. Subsequently, Baghdad began purchasing the required components on a piecemeal basis under the guise of constructing a pesticide plant.

By his takeover in July 1979, at the cost of nearly $60 million Saddam had completed the assembly of the first chemical warfare plant near the northwestern town of Akashat. During the next decade he was to recruit to Iraq's expanding non-conventional arms industry a host of foreign companies, German in particular, which would enable Iraq to produce significant amounts of chemical weapons, including a refined form of Distilled Mustard (HD), as well as Tabun nerve agent and the more potent VX nerve agent. The biological industry, too, was to expand significantly and to produce such agents as anthrax, typhoid and cholera.[38]

The massive expansion of Iraq's military potential was accompanied by an effort to project the Iraqi President as an international statesman of the rarest stamp. The main channel for promoting this goal was Iraq's declared policy of non-alignment, which gained considerable momentum after Saddam's rise to power. In the fall of 1979 he made his presidential debut at the Sixth Non-Aligned Summit in Havana, where Iraq was chosen as the venue for the next summit, scheduled for 1982. Saddam was ecstatic. In his own eyes, he was becoming "the leading Arab figure in the non-aligned movement."[39]

In accordance with his professed policy, Hussein was eager to indicate that Baghdad was keeping its distance from Moscow. The term "strategic alliance," which Saddam had so lavishly used in the early 1970s to describe the state of Soviet-Iraqi relations, disappeared from his vocabulary; it was replaced by the far milder term of "friendly relations."[40] Yet even this reference overstated the nature of the bilateral relationship following Saddam's ascendancy. His need for Moscow had decreased significantly. From his point of view the Soviet Union had largely played its role. By providing the necessary military support and political backing it had enabled him to nationalize the oil industry and to confront both crippling domestic problems and Iranian pressures. But this was nearly a decade ago. With the Iranian threat withering away following the Algiers Agreement and the domestic situation manageable, there was little the Soviet Union could offer Saddam. Even its main means of support, military aid, was no longer exclusive, as Western countries, France in particular, were steadily contributing greater shares to Iraq's arsenal.

Hence, as the decade neared its end, Soviet-Iraqi relations were experiencing some of their most trying moments. The first major breach between the two countries took place as early as in 1975, when the Soviets resented Hussein's conclusion of the Algiers Agreement without prior consultations with them. In the coming years the Soviets would clash with Iraq over its intransigent rejection of Israel's right to exist, as well as its growing openness toward the West. In 1976 Saddam ordered that the Soviet Embassy, situated next door to the Presidential Palace, be moved to new premises. When the Soviets refused to obey, the Embassy had its water and electricity cut off. Two years later, Iraq threatened to break off diplomatic relations with Moscow if the Soviet Union continued to support the Marxist Ethiopian regime against the "fraternal" Eritrean rebels who for a long time had sought to secede from that Ethiopian state. By that time Hussein was diligently persecuting the Iraqi communists and openly attacking Moscow's "expansionist" intentions. "The Soviet Union," he said in a famous interview in the summer of 1978, "will not be satisfied until the whole world becomes Communist."[41]

The poor state of Iraqi-Soviet bilateral relations was further underscored by the Iraqi reaction to the Soviet invasion of Afghanistan in December 1979. While Moscow's other Middle Eastern ally, Syria, went out of its way to support the Soviet invasion, Iraq did not hesitate to express vociferous condemnation of the action.[42] When the Syrian President, Hafiz Asad, hosted the Soviet Foreign Minister, Andrei Gromyko, in Damascus in a public show of support for the Soviet stance, Saddam participated in an all-Islamic gathering in Islamabad, which came out with a call for the immediate and unconditional withdrawal of all Soviet troops from Afghanistan. The Soviets were to repay Saddam later that year when, following his invasion of Iran in September 1980 (yet another move taken without prior consultations with Moscow), they declared their neutrality and suspended all arms supplies to Iraq.

In his dealings with the West, Saddam chose a pragmatic path, taking care to differentiate between "friends" and "imperialists" in accordance with his changing needs. As he admitted in an interview with an Egyptian journalist in January 1977, "we deal with some people as friends by virtue of the convergence of our strategies or interests, and we deal with others as enemies or opponents on account of the divergence of our strategies or interests."[43] Accordingly, his attitude ranged from open warmth toward Paris, with whom relations were flourishing, to vehement attacks on the United States, which he often labeled as "the Arab nation's Enemy number one," to manifest coolness toward Britain.

Yet even Saddam's perception of the "Enemy number one" had nothing dogmatic about it. "The rupture in our diplomatic relations with the United States of America," he said, "is a political matter based on principle. It will continue as long as American policy persists in the same way which prompted us to sever diplomatic relations with it in the wake of the 1967 Six Day War." In the meantime, "we have no complex or feeling of sensitivity about dealing with any company in the world on a basis that preserves our sovereignty and ensures legitimate mutual bene-fits. . . . Sometimes we deal with them on strategic matters, as in the case of the socialist states. Sometimes we deal with them on the basis of temporary mutual interest, as is the case with some Western and American companies."[44]

He meant what he said. The lack of diplomatic relations proved no hindrance to the development of close trade contacts. From the mid-1970s onwards, Iraqi civilian imports from the United States increased substantially, eventually surpassing those from the Soviet Union. By the early 1980s the U.S. interest section in the Belgian Embassy in Baghdad, which included 15 U.S. diplomats, had expanded significantly. Some 200 American busi-nessmen were stationed in the Iraqi capital. In 1977, American exports to Iraq reached $211 million; two years later they had surpassed $450 million. In 1978 some 700 Iraqis studied in the United States; by 1980 this number had tripled. Thus, it did not come as a total surprise when in February 1979 Saddam implied his readiness to establish direct diplomatic relations with the United States if that was found to be in the best interest of the Arab World.[45]

Interestingly enough, Saddam's perception of Britain was more negative in certain respects than his view of the United States. For one thing, Britain's potential political and economic utility for Saddam's designs was markedly lower than that of the United States. For another thing, there was the historical experi-ence with British imperial power. Saddam was further infuriated by the British readiness to allow Iraqi political exiles, first and foremost communists, to publicly voice their grievances against his regime. Equally irksome for him was the British criticism of France's nuclear deal with Baghdad, as well as its treatment of

Iraqi diplomats involved in acts of terrorism. In July 1978, for
example, after the assassination of the exiled Iraqi Premier, Abd
al-Razzaq Nayif, in London, the British government declared 11
Iraqi officials *personae non gratae* and ordered them to leave the
country. Iraq responded in kind. In September a British national
was arrested in Baghdad for alleged economic espionage and
attempted bribery, and Iraqis were banned from traveling to the
United Kingdom. A special directive was issued instructing ministries and state organizations not to sign contracts with British
companies without special permission from the authorities. A
year later, in May 1979, a British businessman was sentenced to
life imprisonment on charges of "economic espionage."[46] This
was one of Saddam's typical tactics, to have his cake and eat it, to
extract what he needed from the West while keeping the latter at
arm's length, so as not to damage his nationalistic credentials. It
was only in July 1979 that relations began to thaw when, following
a visit of the British Foreign Secretary, Lord Carrington, to
Baghdad, Iraq lifted its trade embargo on Britain.

Saddam's flurry of international activism did not neglect the
Middle East, where he returned to his old theme of Arab
nationalism, which he had toned down since the mid-1970s. His
bid for championship of the Arab cause was made on February 8,
1980. Addressing cheering crowds celebrating the seventeenth
anniversary of the 1963 Ba'thi takeover, Hussein announced an
Eight-Point National Charter, an elaborate program to shape the
unity and policies of the Arab states in Saddam's own image. The
Charter underlined Iraq's policy of non-alignment and, playing
on a sensitive issue in the Arab collective consciousness, called for
the rejection of any foreign presence on Arab soil. Condemning
superpower presence in the area, it stressed that Arab interests
"can only be protected and promoted by Arabs and no one else."
The Charter then moved to ban, in line with the 1945 Arab
League Charter, the use of force by one Arab state against
another: "Disputes that might arise between Arab states should be
settled through peaceful means, under the principles of joint
national action and the supreme Arab interest." Significantly
enough, the ban on force was extended to nations and countries
"neighboring the Arab Homeland," with the exception of Israel
("Naturally," ran the Charter, "the Zionist entity is not included
because the Zionist entity is not considered a state, but a deformed
entity occupying Arab territory"). The Charter also confirmed

Arab commitment to international law governing territorial waters, airspace and land "by any country not in a state of war with
any Arab state." Most importantly, perhaps, it stipulated the need
for close Arab collaboration in the economic, political, and
military fields, to promote the integration of the Arab nation and
to rebuff aggression against it: "Arab states shall embark upon
collective solidarity in the event of any aggression or violation by
a foreign party against the sovereignty of any Arab state, or the
launching of an actual state of war against any Arab state."[47] This
last provision, in particular, reflected the real agenda underlying
the National Charter. Ostensibly it was a decisive bid for Arab
mastery by a confident and powerful leader. But behind this
apparent prowess lurked Saddam's great anxiety, which was
growing by the day, over Iraq's rapidly deteriorating relations
with its large neighbor to the east—Iran. The emphasis on
banning force against the Arabs' neighbors was meant to signal to
Tehran that Saddam harbored no hostile intentions against it. In
underlining Arab commitment to observe international legislation
governing territorial waters, he indicated his keen interest in
abiding by the 1975 Algiers Agreement on the navigation rules in
the Shatt al-Arab. Above all, the solidification of the Arab World
into a unified front against "any aggression or violation by a
foreign party against the sovereignty of any Arab state," was
aimed at convincing the vehemently hostile Ayatollah Khomeini
that Iraq did not stand alone. The Ayatollah despised Saddam
and his secular Ba'th regime, and hoped to export the Iranian
Revolution to Iraq's 60 percent Shi'ite population. Saddam Hussein was intent on showing that Iraq might well be "the eastern
flank of the Arab World," but the weight of the entire Arab nation
was behind it.

Hussein's eagerness to project an imposing image to Tehran
was not difficult to understand. The Iranian threat was rearing its
fanatical head again, and Hussein had been around long enough
to grasp the full consequences of this development to his political
survival. Five years earlier he had managed to buy Iran's quiescence at a heavy price. This time, however, he felt that such
concessions would not suffice to appease Iran. It was not territory
which interested the mullahs; nor even the re-assertion of Iran's
superiority over Iraq. They had raised the stakes above Saddam's
acceptable threshold: they openly demanded his head.

6

Deciding on War

On September 17, 1980, Saddam Hussein addressed his newly reinstated National Assembly. His face was tense and somber. He spoke slowly, occasionally waving his finger to stress his point. It was clear to everyone in the audience that this was no ordinary presidential speech. "The frequent and blatant Iranian violations of Iraqi sovereignty," he said, "have rendered the 1975 Algiers Agreement null and void. Both legally and politically the treaty was indivisible. Now that its spirit has been violated, Iraq sees no alternative but to restore the legal position of the Shatt al-Arab to the pre-1975 status." "This river," he continued to a barrage of applause, "must have its Iraqi-Arab identity restored as it was throughout history in name and in reality with all the disposal rights emanating from full sovereignty over the river."[1]

The implications of this speech were not long in coming: on September 22, emulating the brilliant Israeli gambit of the Six Day War in 1967, Iraqi aircraft pounded ten airfields in Iran in an attempt to destroy the Iranian air force on the ground. A day later Iraqi forces crossed the Iranian border in strength, igniting what was to develop into one of the longest, bloodiest and costliest armed conflicts in the post–World War II era, and for Iraq, the most traumatic experience in its modern history until then.

What exactly was on Saddam Hussein's mind when he took such a grave political decision will probably never be known. The most common explanation views the invasion of Iran as evidence of Hussein's aggressive personality and his unbridled regional ambitions. In this explanation his war aims ranged from the occupation of Iranian territories (the Shatt al-Arab and Khuzistan), through the desire to inflict a decisive defeat on the Iranian

135

Revolution, to the need to assert Iraq as the pre-eminent Arab and Gulf state. In this view, by defeating Iran, Saddam Hussein might well have hoped to become the most influential leader of the non-aligned movement.[2]

It is true that Saddam Hussein is an ambitious man. Merely eight months before invading Iran he had boasted that "Iraq is as great as China, as great as the Soviet Union and as great as the United States."[3] It is equally true that the Algiers Agreement, which established Iran's sovereignty over half of the Shatt al-Arab and recognized its superiority to Iraq, was anathema to him. And yet, despite the humiliation attending the conclusion of the 1975 Agreement, the outbreak of war in September 1980 could not have been more ill-timed for the young and dynamic President. Due to the world oil boom in 1979 and 1980 the Iraqi economy enjoyed unprecedented prosperity. Oil export revenues rose from $1 billion in 1972 to $21 billion in 1979 and $26 billion in 1980. During the months preceding the war, these revenues were running at an annual rate of $33 billion, enabling Saddam to carry out ambitious development programs. Numerous construction projects mushroomed throughout the country. Baghdad was grooming itself to host the summit of the non-aligned movement in 1982. Living conditions of many groups within Iraqi society were on the rise.[4] War could only risk these achievements and, in consequence, render Saddam's domestic standing more tenuous.

But even if these weighty disincentives to war had not existed, explanations that concentrate on Hussein's ambitions present only one aspect of the determination that drove him to invade Iran. The other aspect was most certainly his insecurity, a gnawing fearfulness bred by the precariousness he perceived in his own regime and by Iraq's glaring vulnerability vis-à-vis Iran. To the contemporary state of Iraq, Iran represented the major geo-political challenge. A much larger country in territory and population, with its major strategic centers located deep inside the country and with a long Gulf coastline, Iran easily towered over its smaller neighbor to the west. Recognizing Iran's fundamental superiority, Iraq had no aspirations of competing with its larger neighbor for Gulf supremacy. Instead, it directed its energies toward the Arab World (as evidenced by Saddam's Eight-Point National Charter of February 1980), a less risky and potentially more rewarding arena. In concluding the 1975 Algiers Agreement Saddam virtually acquiesced in a new regional order based on Iranian hegemony in the Gulf in order to stave off any threat to Iraq's lands and his political position. There were no indications whatsoever during the latter part of the 1970s that he was seeking to upset this peace with Iran, let alone go to war for this purpose.

Against this backdrop Hussein followed with much concern the growing revolutionary turmoil in Iran in the late 1970s, which threatened to undermine the status quo set up by the 1975 Algiers Agreement. It is true that a weakened and fragmented Iran could augur well for Iraqi security. Yet as often as not, revolutionary turbulence is channeled outside a state's boundaries to engulf its neighbors. The ability of a popular uprising to overthrow a well-entrenched dictatorship was not a heart-warming prospect for Saddam Hussein. Still, as there was nothing Iraq could do to influence the momentous events in its neighboring country, the wary Hussein decided to welcome the new revolutionary regime in Tehran. Not only did he not attempt to take advantage of the civil strife in Iran in order to revise the Algiers Agreement, but he was quick to recognize the newcomers to power in Tehran and to indicate his willingness to abide by the status quo existing between the two states: "a regime which does not support the enemy against us and does not intervene in our affairs, and whose world policy corresponds to the interests of the Iranian and Iraqi people, will certainly receive our respect and appreciation."[5] This hospitable statement was backed by an official memorandum to the Iranian Prime Minister, Mehdi Bazargan, underlining Iraq's desire to establish "the strongest fraternal relations on the basis of respect and non-interference in domestic affairs," and expressing its sympathy and support for the struggle of the Iranian people for "freedom and progress."[6]

Saddam's positive attitude toward the revolutionary regime continued well throughout spring and summer 1979. When Iran decided to pull out of the Central Treaty Organization (CENTO)—an organization for military and economic cooperation formed in 1959 by Britain, Iran, Pakistan and Turkey as a successor to the Baghdad Pact—Iraq offered its good services in case Iran should decide to join the non-aligned movement. When in June 1979 Iraqi aircraft mistakenly bombed the Iranian side of the border in the course of operations against the Kurds, Baghdad quickly filed an official apology. By that time President Bakr was referring to Iran as a brotherly nation, linked to the Arab people of Iraq by "strong ties of Islam, history and noble traditions," and praising the revolutionary regime in Tehran for pursuing a policy that underlined these "deep historical

relations."[7] In July 1979, the newly installed President Saddam
Hussein of Iraq reiterated his interest in establishing close relations with Iran "based on mutual respect and non-interference in
internal affairs." The dismissive Iranian response to his appeal
did not dissuade Saddam Hussein: as late as August 1979 he
extended an invitation to Bazargan to visit Baghdad.[8]

Tehran did not, however, reciprocate Hussein's goodwill. On
the contrary, from its early days in power the revolutionary
regime sought to overthrow the Iraqi regime. Even though Iran's
revolutionary zeal was directed against the rest of the Gulf states
as well, several fundamental factors made Iraq the primary target
for the export of Iran's Islamic Revolution. With Shi'ites account-
ing for approximately 60 percent of Iraq's total population, the
revolutionary regime in Tehran could, and certainly did, entertain hopes that this community, which had always viewed itself as
a deprived and disenfranchised group, would imitate the Iranian
example of overthrowing the Shah's Pahlavi monarchy and rise
against its own Sunni "oppressors." These expectations were
further fueled by the secular, "heretic" nature of the Ba'th, which
was adamantly opposed to the very notion of an Islamic political
order, and by the location of the holiest Shi'ite shrines—Karbala,
Najaf, Kazimain—on Iraqi territory, a combination that could
serve as a potentially powerful weapon in the hands of the Islamic
regime.

Above all, the mullahs in Tehran were confronted with the
same geo-strategic dilemma that the Shah had faced a decade
earlier: Iraq's position as the major potential obstacle to Iran's
quest for regional hegemony. Just as the Shah's road to supremacy
necessarily entailed subduing Iraq, so in the mullahs' eyes the
replacement of the status quo in the Persian Gulf by an Islamic
order had to begin with the removal of the primary hindrance to
this goal—the secular Ba'th regime and its absolute leader. In the
words of a militant member of the Iranian leadership, Hujjat
al-Islam Sadeq Khalkhali: "We have taken the path of true Islam
and our aim in defeating Saddam Hussein lies in the fact that we
consider him the main obstacle to the advance of Islam in the
region."[9]

In June 1979, the revolutionary regime began publicly urging
the Iraqi population to rise up and overthrow "the Saddamite
regime."[10] A few months later Tehran escalated its campaign by
resuming support for the Iraqi Kurds (which had been suspended
in 1975), providing aid to underground Shi'ite movements in

Iraq and initiating terrorist attacks against prominent Iraqi officials. These reached their peak on April 1, 1980, with a failed
attempt on the life of the Iraqi Deputy Premier, Tariq Aziz, while
he was making a speech at Mustansirriya University in Baghdad.
Two weeks later, the Iraqi Minister of Information and Culture,
Latif Nusseif al-Jasim, narrowly escaped a similar attempt. In
April alone, it was estimated that at least 20 Iraqi officials were
killed in bomb attacks by militant Shi'ite underground organizations.

The Iranian pressures were all the more disconcerting for Saddam since they coincided with a huge wave of Shi'ite unrest. By
the turn of the decade it had become evident that the Shi'ite
problem had succeeded the Kurdish one as Iraq's foremost
domestic predicament, posing a far deadlier challenge to Saddam's regime than its predecessor. However acute, the Kurdish
problem had never threatened the Ba'th in a way that Shi'ism
could do. Although the Kurds had always provided a channel for
foreign interference in Iraqi domestic affairs and had even raised
the specter of Iraq's disintegration and the downfall of the Ba'th
regime, they remained a non-Arab minority. Their national
aspirations had always been anathema to most Iraqis and, consequently, the masses could always be rallied behind a regime that
rejected Kurdish attempts to "rob the Arab nation of part of its
lands." The Shi'ite community, on the other hand, was an integral
part of the Arab nation, and the largest religious community in
Iraq. Its open defiance of Ba'thi legitimacy, therefore, endan-
gered the regime's survival in crucial respects. At the ideological
level, Shi'ite separation cut the ground from under the Ba'th's
feet, for how could it aspire to be the standard-bearer of pan-
Arabism if it could not preserve the unity of the Iraqi "region"? At
the practical level, unrest on the part of the overwhelming
majority of the Iraqi people could not but entail grave consequences for the stability of the regime.

The origins of Shi'ism date back to the political struggles
attending the demise of the Prophet Muhammad in June 632.
Immediately after Muhammad's death, his cousin and son-in-law,
Ali Ibn-Abi-Talib, laid claim to the succession as the Prophet's
closest relative. His will did not prevail, and Muhammad's father-
in-law and one of his old companions, Abu Bakr, succeeded him
as the first Caliph, head of the community and the state. When Ali
eventually succeeded to the Caliphate in 656, his leadership was

constantly challenged, most seriously by the Governor of Syria, Mu'awiyah Ibn-Abi-Sufiyan.

In his capacity as head of the Umayyad house, a distinguished family related to the Prophet's Hashemite clan, Mu'awiyah sought to avenge the murder of Ali's predecessor and a fellow Umayyad, the Caliph Uthman-Ibn-Affan. The feud between him and Ali evolved through various stages, some of them violent. As Ali braced himself for the decisive battle against his contender, he was murdered in January 661 in the capital city of Iraq, Kufah. Mu'awiyah seized the Caliphate and established the Umayyad ruling house, with its capital in Damascus.

Some two decades later Ali's second son, Hussein, was urged by the inhabitants of Kufah to challenge the Umayyad dynasty. Succumbing to the temptation he complied with their wish, only to realize that his Iraqi compatriots would not back his daring venture. Fleeing from the advancing Umayyad forces he reached the town of Karbala, some 60 miles south-southwest of Baghdad, where he soon found himself under siege. The commander of the Umayyad expeditionary force called upon him to surrender but Hussein, believing his inviolability as the Prophet's grandson, remained defiant. He was killed in the ensuing battle, on October 10, 680, and his head was sent to Damascus.

Hussein's death was to become a crucial watershed in the history of Shi'ism. It cemented the small group of Ali's followers, *Shiatu Ali,* the party or faction of Ali, into a significant and cohesive religious movement. Hussein's grave in Karbala was to become the most sacred site of pilgrimage for all Shi'ites, Iranians in particular. His day of martyrdom (*Ashura,* the tenth day of the Arabic month of Muharram on which he was killed), is commemorated every year in the most emotional way.[11]

Though by far the largest religious community in Iraq, the Shi'ites have not only failed to play the key role commensurate with their sheer magnitude (60 percent of the population), but have been ruled as an underprivileged class by the small Sunni minority (20 percent of the population). Thus, for example, under the monarchy Arab Sunnis held 44 percent of all governmental posts and 60 percent of the top posts, as compared with 32 and 21 percent, respectively, held by Shi'ites. In the decade following the overthrow of the monarchy the Sunnis occupied 80 percent of the top spots, while Shi'ites held merely 16 percent.[12]

The Shi'ite predicament in the contemporary state of Iraq can be traced back to the Ottoman era. Then Shi'ites were excluded

from power and persecuted by the authorities, in the overwhelmingly Sunni Ottoman Empire. It was further compounded by the
hostile, and violent, Shi'ite response to the ascendancy of King
Faisal I to the Iraqi throne, which reflected their fear of continued
Sunni domination in the newly established state of Iraq. Geographical disposition has also exerted an adverse impact on the
Shi'ite community. Unlike the Kurds who reside in a mountainous
terrain, far from the locus of state power, the central location
of the Shi'ite community makes them far more accessible to
the regime, and hence more controllable. Finally, the Shi'ites
lack a cohesive leadership and their social organization is saddled with deep divisions. The major schism has been between
the inhabitants of the cities and the rural concentrations, but
further significant divisions exist within the urban and rural
communities.[13]

The Shi'ites' deep-rooted feeling of discrimination gained
considerable momentum under the Ba'th regime. The lofty
Ba'thi slogan of "one Arab nation with an eternal mission" had
never prevented the Shi'ites from noticing that Iraq was being
ruled by an ever-tighter social group: "the Sunni triangle" and the
"Tikriti clique." This frustration with the rule of the few over the
many was exacerbated by the economic and social dislocations
attending the migration of large numbers of Shi'ites to the cities
during the 1970s, as a result of Saddam's urbanizing and modernizing development plans. Finding themselves substituting a
miserable suburban existence for their rural poverty, the new
underprivileged urban Shi'ites became a fertile soil for anti-
regime sentiments. The professed secularism of the Ba'th only
fueled the resentment by upsetting the Muslim foundations of
social order and antagonizing the religious Shi'ite authorities, the
ulama, whose traditional position was fundamentally threatened
by the Party's tight control over the state apparatus.

Organized Shi'ite opposition to the regime began surfacing as
early as in the late 1960s, when an underground religious party,
al-Da'wa al-Islamiyyah, the Islamic Call, was formed. Inspired by
the teachings of the prominent Iraqi Ayatollah Muhammad Baqir
al-Sadr, the *Da'wa* was not merely a reformist movement but
rather a revolutionary party, preaching the replacement of the
modern secular state by an Islamic socio-political order. This
vision could not have been more unwelcome to Saddam who
feared that the spread of religious fundamentalism might undermine the stability of the Ba'th regime. No such doctrines were,

therefore, to be allowed to infiltrate the masses. They had to be immediately uprooted. Accordingly, a special branch for handling Shi'ite opposition was established within the security services, and by the mid-1970s it was reported in the Western press that Shi'ite *ulama* were being secretly executed to deter organized opposition to the regime.[14]

These harsh measures, nevertheless, did not prevent the Shi'ite cauldron from boiling over again. In February 1977, during the *Ashura* ceremonies commemorating the martyrdom of the Hussein Ibn-Ali, widespread demonstrations, led by Shi'ite clergymen, erupted in the holy towns of Karbala and Najaf. For several days many thousands of Shi'ite pilgrims clashed with the security forces sent to restore order. When the violent confrontation subsided, Shi'ites had been arrested by the thousands, and an unspecified number of people had been killed or wounded.[15]

Saddam's response was prompt and relentless. At the end of the month, a special court was set up to try participants in the riots. Eight *ulama* were sentenced to death and 15 to life imprisonment. A few months later Saddam delivered a speech in which he vehemently rejected calls for compromising the Party's staunch secularism as a means of accommodating the growing Islamic sentiments. "What we must do," he argued, "is to oppose the institutionalization of religion in the state and society—and also to oppose the Revolution's intrusion into religion. Let us return to the roots of our religion, glorifying them—but not introduce it into politics."[16] The Ba'th was on the side of belief, he said, but it would never accept the use of religion as a cloak for subversive activities against the regime.

By way of underlining Saddam's determination to prevent "the institutionalization of religion in the state and in society," in March 1978 the regime took control over Shi'ite revenues.[17] Since until then Shi'ite endowments had been independent of government control, this move struck at the very heart of the Shi'ite establishment. It deprived the *ulama* of a central source of social and political power, effectively reducing them to the status of government officials. They no longer had the power to dispense financial resources at will. Now it was the regime which was to collect, to allocate and to regulate the methods of expenditure and the general upkeep of all Shi'ite shrines.

Saddam's choice of the stick in his dealings with the Shi'ite community backfired. The rise to power of a fundamentalist regime in Tehran played a key role in the resurgence of anti-government sentiments within the Iraqi Shi'ite community in 1979 and 1980. Yet it is equally true that much of the responsibility for inciting Shi'ite opposition could be laid at Saddam's own doorstep. Through his insensitivity to the adverse implications of his development plans for the socio-economic conditions of the Shi'ites, his staunch secularism and his repressive tactics toward the *ulama,* he had managed to buy the regime the unbounded hostility of the largest community in Iraq, well before the Iranian Revolution. No wonder, therefore, that Hussein's semi-official biographers go out of their way to play down his responsibility for the expulsion of the exiled Iranian spiritual leader, Ayatollah Ruhollah Khomeini, from Iraq in October 1978, a move which generated considerable Shi'ite resentment. Khomeini was not expelled from Iraq at the request of the Shah, argues one such biographer. On the contrary, he was welcome to stay as long as he observed the authorities' request to refrain from hostile activities against Iraq, but he decided to leave of his own free will:

> For six years Iraq supported the [Iranian] opposition groups; Khomeini was allowed to use Iraq as a center for his activities and was treated with the utmost respect.
>
> After the Algiers Agreement between Iraq and Iran in 1975, Iraq stopped the activities of the Iranian opposition groups on a reciprocal basis. But Khomeini continued his operations and stepped up his activities in 1978, causing the Shah to complain. The Iraqi authorities did not want relations to worsen with Iran, so they sent a member of the Revolution[ary] Command Council to ask Khomeini to respect the Iraqi stand. Khomeini refused to be flexible, and told the Iraqi official, "I will continue the struggle against the Shah's regime, and if the Iraqi authorities object, I will leave Iraq." A few days later Imam Khomeini left Iraq and headed for Kuwait, but the Kuwaiti authorities refused to allow him in. He contacted the Iraqi authorities from the border and asked to be allowed to return for a few days before finding another base. The Iraqi authorities immediately agreed. At the very moment that Imam Khomeini was at the border area, the Iranian embassy requested in the name of the Shah that Imam Khomeini not be allowed to remain in Iraq; the Iraqi authorities refused [to comply with this Iranian request]. Imam Khomeini then left Iraq for France.[18]

This description of the course of events leading to Khomeini's departure from Iraq could not be more far-fetched. As is well known, the aged Ayatollah did not leave Iraq of his own free will but was forced out by Saddam, at the request of the Iranian Shah. Hence, once Khomeini landed in Tehran to replace the deposed monarch, a massive wave of enthusiasm engulfed the Shi'ite community in Iraq and drove the *Da'wa* Party, which openly endorsed him as its spiritual leader, to step up its activities against the regime.

In February 1979 the regime responded to widespread demonstrations in support of Khomeini by dispatching a military force, including tanks, to Karbala and Najaf. In June 1979 riots erupted again in the two holy towns after Ayatollah al-Sadr, who had meanwhile emerged as the symbol of Iraqi Shi'ite opposition, had been denied the possibility of leading a procession to Iran to congratulate Ayatollah Khomeini. Martial law was reportedly imposed in southern cities and even in Baghdad itself. A harsh campaign was launched against *Da'wa* and its leaders. Membership in the party became punishable by death. Large numbers of suspected members of the organization were rounded up, including Sadr himself, who was placed under house arrest in Najaf and denied access to the outside world.[19]

This time, however, Saddam was willing to offer the Shi'ites his honey, besides his sting. Increasingly mindful both of the depth of Shi'ite alienation and of the potentially devastating consequences of such an alienation for the continued survival of the regime, he assiduously sought to cultivate their sense of belonging to the wider Iraqi nation. The memory of the traumatic events leading to the 1975 Algiers Agreement was still fresh in his mind. He knew that if Iran's manipulation of the Kurdish problem in the early 1970s had brought the Ba'th regime to its knees, the agitation of Iraq's largest community against its unelected leader could not but entail catastrophic consequences for his political survival.

To their astonishment, the Shi'ites heard their hitherto staunch secularist leader laud their patron Imam, Ali Ibn-Abi-Talib, and claim to be a true follower of his in the quest for "heavenly values." As an indication of his commitment to such "values," Saddam banned gambling at the beginning of 1979, and made generous allocations for religious purposes. Donning the traditional Shi'ite robe, the *abbaya,* he staged numerous televised visits to Shi'ite settlements, distributing money and television sets as gifts. To dispel any remaining doubts about the sincerity of his sudden transformation, he produced the ultimate "proof": a genealogical table connecting himself to the heart of Shi'ism. During a well-publicized visit to the holy city of Najaf in October 1979, it was pronounced that Saddam was a direct descendant of the Caliph Ali, hence of the Prophet Muhammad. "We have the right to say, and we will not fabricate history," he declared emotionally, "that we are the grandsons of Imam Hussein."[20]

The recruitment of Islam's holiest figures to Saddam's political ends reflected the extent both of his ruthless pragmatism and of his deep anxiety. He calculated that the nationalist and secularist Ba'thi message would be of little value in containing the mounting Iranian pressures on his regime. Khomeini wanted to overthrow him by fueling Shi'ite sentiments, and had therefore to be given his own medicine. If religion were to be the name of the game, then Saddam would have to master it. Throughout the coming decade, as he struggled to survive an eight-year war against Iran, he was to make extensive use of religious symbolism, placing Ba'thi ideology and rhetoric on the sidelines. Whatever its essence, ideology was worthy only to the extent that it served the ultimate goal of political survival.

Saddam's new tactics did not buy him the respite he so badly needed in 1979 and 1980. The Iranians, and the Iraqi Shi'ite underground organizations they supported, remained unmoved by his demonstrated piety, continuing their violent campaign against his regime. This, in turn, drove Saddam to accompany his efforts to appease the Shi'ites with the harsh repressive tactics which had brought him to the Presidential Palace. He clamped down on the Shi'ite underground organizations, countered the Iranian propaganda campaign by launching a series of verbal attacks against Ayatollah Khomeini, whom he called a "turbanned Shah," and supported Iranian separatist elements such as the Kurds and the Arabs in Khuzistan. He also accelerated the expansion of the Iraqi armed forces and attempted to rally the Arab states behind his regime by announcing the February 1980 National Charter which sought to solidify the Arab nation into a unified front against "external aggression."

Deeply shaken by Iran's ability to hit at the heart of his regime, especially the abortive attempt on Aziz's life, Saddam's perception of the Iranian threat rose sharply, manifesting itself in draconian measures against the Shi'ite opposition. Within two weeks of Aziz's narrow escape, Iraq's most prominent Shi'ite religious

authority, Ayatollah Muhammad Baqir al-Sadr, who had been
under house arrest for several months, was executed, together
with his sister. Following in the footsteps of their revered leader,
hundreds of Shi'ite political prisoners, most of them members of
the *Da'wa* Party, were placed before the firing squads. This killing
spree did not overlook the armed forces, where a few dozen
officers were executed, some of them on account of their failure
to stem the mounting tide of Iranian terrorist activities throughout Iraq, while others fell victim to the routine accusation of
plotting against the regime. Hussein effectively sealed the southern part of Iraq, denying foreign, particularly Iranian, worship-
pers any access to the Shi'ite holy shrines. The extent of his
anxiety was further illustrated by the expulsion of some 100,000
Iraqi Shi'ites from the country.

These countermeasures failed to impress the revolutionary
regime in Iran. Responding to Saddam Hussein's pledge to take
revenge for the attempt on the life of Aziz, Ayatollah Khomeini
called on the Iraqi Shi'ites on June 9, 1980, to overthrow
"Saddam's Government." Iran's Foreign Minister, Sadegh Ghotz-
badegh, revealed on the same day that his government had taken
the decision to topple the Ba'th regime in Iraq. The same theme
was reiterated two days later by the Iranian President, Abol Hasan
Bani Sadr, who also warned that Iran would go to war in case of
further deterioration in the situation on the border. And the
Iranian Minister of Defense did not hesitate to openly spell out
the actual implications of an Iraqi-Iranian war. "Should the
Iranian army enter Iraq," he said, "Iraqi Shi'ites would welcome
it with open arms."[21] By that time the Iranian-Iraqi confrontation
had already entered a new phase, with clashes along the common
frontier; in August these escalated into heavy fighting involving
tank and artillery duels and air strikes.

Iran's subversive activities in general, and the protracted and
escalating border fighting in particular, led Saddam Hussein to
the conclusion that he had no alternative but to contain the
Iranian threat by resorting to arms. Faced, for the second time
within a decade, with Iranian determination to reshape the
regional status quo to its own design and with the bitter memory
of armed conflict with Iran in the early 1970s on his mind,
Hussein seriously doubted whether his regime could sustain
another prolonged, exhausting confrontation with Iran. Added
to these concerns was the unique nature of the new theocratic

Iranian regime. The Shah, for all his military power and ambitious designs, was perceived by Hussein as rational, if unpleasant. Certainly his goals were opposed to Iraqi national interests, and their satisfaction came necessarily at Iraq's expense. However, the Shah did not seek to remove the Ba'th regime and his intervention in Iraq's domestic affairs was limited and purely instrumental, designed to assert Iran's superiority and prevent Iraq from competing militarily with it. Once the Shah's aspirations for Gulf hegemony were recognized, a deal (albeit disadvantageous to Iraq) could be struck and both parties could be expected to live up to it.

The revolutionary regime in Tehran, on the other hand, was a completely different type of rival—an irrational actor motivated by uncompromising ideology, and pursuing goals which were wholly unacceptable to Hussein and unaccepting of him. The clerics did not seek territorial aggrandizement, let alone the dismemberment of Iraq. They were after spiritual expansionism and, unlike the Shah, did not consider their intervention in Iraq instrumentally. Rather, they were adamant on overthrowing Hussein and the secular Ba'th regime. Given the growing evidence of the Iranian regime's real agenda, Hussein no longer felt able to live with the Iranian superiority he had tacitly recognized in 1975. Now, such superiority could eventually lead to his decline from power, if not his physical elimination. Consequently, he came to realize that the only way to contain the Iranian threat was to exploit Iran's temporary weakness following the revolution and to raise the stakes for both sides by resorting to overt, state-supported armed force. On September 7, 1980, Iraq accused Iran of shelling Iraqi border towns from territories which, according to the Algiers Agreement, belonged to Iraq, and demanded the immediate evacuation of Iranian forces from these areas. Soon afterwards Iraq moved to "liberate" these disputed areas and, on September 10, announced that the mission had been accomplished. A week later, Hussein formally abrogated the Algiers Agreement and the road from there to war was short.

Hussein's decision to go to war was not taken easily or enthusiastically. He did not embark on war in pursuit of a premeditated "grand design" but was pushed into it by his increasing anxiety about the threat to his own political survival. War was not his first choice but rather an act of last resort, taken only after trying all other means for deflecting Iran's pressure. It was a pre-emptive move, designed to exploit a temporary window

of opportunity, in order to forestall the Iranian threat to his
regime; a ruthless and calculated act of using the Iraqi people as
a shield to protect his political survival. If Saddam entertained
hopes or aspirations beyond the containment of the Iranian
danger—as he may have done—these were not the reasons for
launching the war but were incidental to it.

It was fear rather than greed that drove Hussein to invade
Iran: as late as the spring of 1980 he was publicly alluding to the
possibility of Iraq's disintegration into Sunni, Shi'ite and Kurdish
statelets.[22] In retrospect, these apprehensions turned out to be
grossly overrated as the majority of Iraqi Shi'ites were to spurn
Khomeini's militant brand of Islam. However, given the record of
Shi'ite unrest in the late 1970s, Iran's intense pressure on the
Ba'th regime and Hussein's obsessive preoccupation with ensuring his political survival, his concerns in the heated summer of
1980 were understandable.

The reluctant nature of Hussein's decision to invade Iran was
clearly reflected in his war strategy. Instead of dealing a mortal
blow to the Iranian army and trying to topple the revolutionary
regime in Tehran, he sought to confine the war by restricting his
army's goals, means and targets. His territorial aims did not go
beyond the Shatt al-Arab and a small portion of Khuzistan. As to
means, the invasion was carried out by less than half of the Iraqi
army—five of twelve divisions. Hussein's initial strategy avoided
targets of civilian and economic value in favor of attacks almost
exclusively on military targets. Only after the Iranians struck
non-military targets did the Iraqis respond in kind.

Saddam Hussein hoped that a quick, limited yet decisive
campaign would convince Iran's revolutionary regime to desist
from its attempts to overthrow him. By exercising self-restraint,
he sought to signal his defensive aims and an intent to avoid
all-out war with the hope that Tehran would respond in kind, and
perhaps even be willing to reach a settlement. In the words of
Tariq Aziz: "Our military strategy reflects our political objectives.
We want neither to destroy Iran nor to occupy it permanently
because that country is a neighbor with which we will remain
linked by geographical and historical bonds and common interests. Therefore we are determined to avoid any irrevocable
steps."[23]

This wishful thinking compounded Hussein's failure to grasp
the operational requirements of such a campaign. Rather than
allowing his forces to advance until their momentum was ex-

hausted, he voluntarily halted their advance within a week of the
outbreak of hostilities and then announced his willingness to
negotiate a settlement. This decision not to capitalize on Iraq's
early military successes by applying increased pressure had a
number of dire consequences which, in turn, led to the reversal of
the course of the war. It saved the Iranian army from a decisive
defeat and gave Tehran precious time to reorganize and regroup;
and it had a devastating impact on the morale of the Iraqi army
and hence on its combat performance. Above all, the limited Iraqi
invasion did nothing to endanger the revolutionary regime, nor
to drive Ayatollah Khomeini to moderation.

Most governments, of course, would react strongly to a
foreign armed intervention, but a revolutionary regime under
attack is all the more likely to respond with vehemence when it has
not yet gained full legitimacy and still has many internal enemies.
History has shown that attacking a destabilized civil society in the
throes of revolution tends to unify it, for the enemies within
suddenly seem much less threatening than those without. Like the
French almost two centuries earlier, the Iranians channeled
national (and religious) fervor into resisting the external threat.
Instead of seeking a quick accommodation, the authorities in
Tehran capitalized on the Iraqi attack to consolidate their claims,
diminish the power struggle within their own ranks and suppress
opposition to their regime. As a result, Hussein had to pay a far
higher price for a limited invasion than he had anticipated. As he
was to admit candidly a month after the outbreak of hostilities, at
the height of the Iraqi success: "Despite our victory, if you ask me
now if we should have gone to war, I would say: It would have
been better if we had not gone to war. But we had no other
choice."[24] He should have heeded the common wisdom about not
making a war on a revolution. However, since he perceived his
political survival to lie in the balance, Saddam did not look beyond
the immediate threat as he saw it. He was to pay a high price for
his shortsightedness.

7

Confronting the
Ayatollah

Ever since war was transformed in the late eighteenth century
from a contest between professional armies into a clash
between populations, its prosecution has become decisively linked
to the vicissitudes of national morale. No regime can sustain a
prolonged war unless a significant portion of the nation endorses
the effort and makes the necessary sacrifices.

This reality has never been lost on Saddam Hussein. He
reckoned that the Iraqi people could be rallied behind a cause of
grave national interest. Yet he had no illusions regarding the
people's willingness to make heavy sacrifices for the maintenance
of his personal rule. The war with Iran arose primarily from the
animosity between Hussein and Khomeini and, as such, the
support of the Iraqi people, especially the majority Shi'ite community, could not be taken for granted. The export of the Iranian
Revolution did not threaten Iraq as a nation state. Rather, it was
Hussein and the Ba'th leadership which were singled out as
"public enemies" by the aged Ayatollah. Khomeini had no territorial designs vis-à-vis Iraq. All he wanted was the substitution of
a pious leadership for the "infidel" regime in Baghdad.

Nor did Hussein view his repressive state machinery as
sufficient for mobilizing the nation in the first all-out war it had
initiated in Iraq's modern history. He knew all too well that
"terror can force people to take to the streets and to chant
enthusiastic slogans for the regime, but it cannot make them fight

150

a war far outside their own territory."[1] When war with Iran broke out, the Iraqis had to be convinced that they were fighting a just cause.

By way of persuading his subjects that his decision to make war was theirs, Hussein's image and voice became ubiquitous in all Iraqi public spaces and activities. The Iraqi people were inescapably exposed to the towering presence of the "Struggler President," from the moment they glanced at the morning paper, through their journey to work, to the family evening gathering in front of the television or the radio. They saw him posing with a rocket launcher on the front lines or paternally embracing young children; as a statesman meeting heads of state and a military leader discussing war plans; as an efficient bureaucrat in a trendy suit and an ordinary peasant, helping farmers in their harvest, scythe in hand. His portraits pervaded the country to such an extent that a popular joke put Iraq's population at 28 million: 14 million Iraqis and 14 million pictures of Saddam Hussein.[2] Schoolchildren sang hymns of praise and recited odes glorifying life under the "warm sun of the Commander President." Press articles and scholarly works began and ended with obsequious adulation of the "great hero, brave commander, astute politician . . . whose name will be written with glowing letters in the annals of history."[3] The members of the National Assembly, the rubber-stamp Iraqi parliament, signed in their own blood their oath of allegiance to Saddam Hussein.[4]

This personality cult was not a unique phenomenon in the political landscape of the Middle East. In the highly personalized politics of the region, where leaders often count more than state institutions, the notion of *l'Etat c'est moi* is no alien implant. Yet Hussein carried his campaign to an incredible peak of propaganda and forced adulation. He was at once the father of the nation and its glorious son, a fierce warrior and a thoughtful philosopher, a radical revolutionary and a practicing Muslim.

In this last respect Hussein proved himself a man for all seasons. Clothed in the habiliments of religious devotion, the secular and modernizing leader, hitherto one of the staunchest proponents of Ba'thi temporal ideology, set out to defend his own religious credentials. The Iranian diatribes against the Ba'th, he told his people, were baseless. Not only was the Party not opposed to religion but it "derived its spirit from heaven." Islam and Arab nationalism were indivisible, Hussein argued, and any attempt to separate the two was tantamount to the application of *Shu'ubi* ideas to contemporary conditions (the *Shuʻubia* was a movement in Islamic history originating in Iran and rejecting Arab cultural predominance). Who besides the Arabs, he pleaded emotionally, "carried and defended the banner of Islam until it reached the furthest corners of the earth, including the land on which Bani Sadr now stands?"[5] And who could embody in his personality this immortal bond between Islam and Arab nationalism better than Saddam, a direct descendant of the Prophet Muhammad?

Therefore, reasoned Hussein, it was inconceivable that a genuine Islamic movement would be hostile to Arab nationalism and to himself. The fact that the Iranian Revolution projected such an unbridled hostility cast serious doubt on its Islamic pretensions. It was not the spread of Islamic ideals, he reasoned, which really interested the mullahs. Rather, they were motivated by the desire to reverse the course of Islamic history, to undo the battle of Qadisiya (A.D. 635) where a numerically much inferior Arab army brought the Persian Empire to its knees and forced it to embrace Islam.[6] What the present *"Shuʻubists"* in Tehran failed to grasp, he cautioned, was that "when a clash is a patriotic and national duty, we shall wage it in all its forms." A second Qadisiya was in the making, with the Prophet's descendant, Saddam Hussein, replacing the great earlier Muslim commander, Saʻd Ibn-Abi-Waqqas, in teaching the Persians a historic lesson.[7]

The Prophet was not the only historical figure "recruited" in the attempt to project Hussein as the latest personification of Iraqi and Arab nationalism. The great pre-Islamic Mesopotamian rulers such as Hammurabi, Sargon and Nebuchadnezzar were equally instrumental. Nebuchadnezzar, the Babylonian king who in 587 B.C. occupied Jerusalem and destroyed the Jewish Temple, was particularly appealing to Hussein. Transformed by the Iraqi President into "a great Arab leader who fought Persians and Jews," Nebuchadnezzar represented everything that Hussein aspired to: glory, conquests, regional hegemony "from the Gulf to Egypt" and, above all, the embodiment of both distinct Iraqi patriotism and wider Arab nationalism. As Hussein himself put it:

> By God, I do indeed dream and wish for [assuming Nebuchad-
> nezzar's role]. It is an honor for any human being to dream of such
> a role. . . . I am reminded that any human being with broad
> horizons, faith and feeling can act wisely but practically, attain his

goals and become a great man who makes his country into a great
state. And what is most important for me about Nebuchadnezzar is
the link between the Arabs' ability and the liberation of Palestine.
Nebuchadnezzar was, after all, an Arab from Iraq, albeit ancient
Iraq. Nebuchadnezzar was the one who brought the bound Jewish
slaves from Palestine. That is why whenever I remember Nebuchadnezzar I like to remind the Arabs, Iraqis in particular, of
their historical responsibilities.[8]

Saddam Hussein may possess certain idiosyncrasies, but na-
ivete is not one of them. His impassioned rhetoric about a second
Qadisiya notwithstanding, he seriously doubted the impact of his
personality cult campaign on his Iraqi compatriots, and their
readiness to follow in the footsteps of their glorious ancestors in
"dying on horseback." Hence, once hostilities broke out between
Iraq and Iran, Hussein went out of his way to insulate the Iraqi
population at large from the effects of the war. Instead of
concentrating most of Iraq's resources on the military effort and,
like Iran, stressing the virtue of sacrifice, the Iraqi President
sought to prove to his people that he could wage war and
maintain a business-as-usual atmosphere at the same time. In
order to press ahead with ambitious development plans begun
prior to the war, public spending rose from $21 billion in 1980 to
$29.5 billion in 1982. The lion's share of this expanded budget
(up from only $13.9 billion in 1980) was spent on civilian imports
to prevent commodity shortages.[9]

The outcome of this guns-and-butter policy was that the
ferocious military offensive which raged on the battlefield was
hardly felt on the Iraqi home front. Instead, the country was
buzzing with economic activity, to the delight of numerous
foreign contractors, Western in particular, who leisurely carved
lucrative slices from the expanding pie of the Iraqi economy.
Construction projects of all kinds, begun prior to the war,
continued apace, and Baghdad was being transformed at a
feverish rate from a medieval into a modern city. Daily life in the
capital continued largely unaffected. Blackouts, imposed at the
beginning of the war, were quickly lifted once the seriously
disabled and dwindling Iranian air force was not able to extend
the war to the Iraqi hinterland. Most foodstuffs were readily
available, and the black color of mourning was not too visible in
the streets of Baghdad. The most salient signs of war were the
growing number of women in government offices and the swelling

numbers of Asian and Arab workers who poured into Baghdad to replace the Iraqis who were fulfilling their national duty at the front.[10]

To be sure, the effort to insulate the Iraqi population from the dislocations of the war could not be fully successful. After all, a nation of merely 14 million people can hardly remain impervious to many thousands of casualties (even the authorities were forced to admit some 1,200 casualties per month). However, the protective shield built by Hussein largely cushioned the Iraqi public from the hazards of war, and those directly involved in the fighting or personally affected by the war were handsomely rewarded by the authorities. The already high standard of living of the officer corps was further improved, and members of the armed forces were given priority for car and house purchases. Bereaved families, for their part, were granted a free car, a free plot of land and an interest-free loan to build a house.[11]

While eliminating potential public dissatisfaction with the war through his domestic policy, Hussein paid close attention to the only state organ which could effectively endanger his regime—the military. Forcing his colleagues in the ruling clique to follow him in substituting the ubiquitous battledress for their tailored suits, he transformed the Revolutionary Command Council into his military headquarters, thus maintaining tight control over war operations. This was clearly demonstrated by an apparent inflexibility and lack of initiative on the part of Iraq's field commanders. Battalion and brigade commanders were unwilling to make independent decisions in rapidly changing battlefield situations, instead referring back to division or corps headquarters, which in turn approached the highest command in Baghdad.

Hussein also extended the logic of his inconspicuous war to include the complete subordination of war operations to political considerations. Aware of the complex composition of Iraq's population and reluctant to risk significant losses within any of Iraq's sectarian groups, he instructed the military leadership to prepare and execute the invasion with the utmost caution, so as to minimize casualties. This instruction, which went against the view of Saddam's professional advisors, turned out to have devastating consequences. Not only did it fail to reduce casualties, it indeed increased them when Iraq, unable to exploit its initial successes, was forced to commit its troops in increasingly difficult operational conditions as Iran strengthened its defenses.[12]

The British military in World War I has often been described as "lions led by donkeys." The Iraqi armed forces were by no means lions. Yet their Commander-in-Chief appeared to be doing his best to prevent them from achieving a decisive victory over a disorganized and ill-equipped enemy. Like other totalitarian leaders in the twentieth century, Saddam Hussein was not willing to relinquish complete control, and heed the advice of military professionals, even in time of war. Not only did Hussein's general strategy—that of a limited war—make little sense from a military point of view, but his tight control of the war and his grave operational mistakes, particularly his failure to follow up Iraq's early military successes, ground the "second Qadisiya" to a disturbing halt.

Finding themselves entrenched for months in hastily prepared defensive positions and subjected to the hardships of the climate and the suicidal attacks of the Iranian militias, the Iraqi troops began to lose all sense of purpose. This loss of will, which was reflected in reports of discipline problems and a growing number of defections, as well as in the large numbers of Iraqi prisoners of war taken and weapons abandoned, was exploited to the fullest by the revolutionary regime in Tehran. In January 1981 Iran carried out its first major counteroffensive since the beginning of the war. The spring and autumn of 1981 witnessed a series of further successful Iranian counterattacks which dislodged the Iraqis from many of their strongholds in Khuzistan before the end of the year.[13]

Anxious to stem the mounting tide of Iranian successes, Baghdad quickly pleaded for peace. In February 1982 Taha Yasin Ramadan, Iraq's First Deputy Prime Minister and one of Hussein's closest associates, declared that Iraq was prepared to withdraw from Iran in stages before the conclusion of a peace agreement, once negotiations had begun "directly or through other parties" and showed satisfactory signs of progress.[14] A couple of months later the Commander-in-Chief in person further lowered Iraq's conditions for peace by stating his readiness to pull out of Iran, provided that Iraq was given sufficient assurances that such a move would lead to a negotiated settlement. The scornful Iranian response came in the form of a series of large-scale offensives which practically drove the Iraqi forces out of Iran. The last nail in the coffin of the Iraqi campaign was driven in late May 1982 by the recapture of Khorramshahr, one of the major cities occupied by Iraq since the beginning of the war. The panic-stricken Iraqi troops fled in large numbers,

leaving behind a substantial amount of military equipment and
some 12,000 of their own troops to become prisoners of war.

In one of his wisest strategic moves during the war, illustrative of
his readiness to lose face whenever his survival so required,
Hussein decided to bow to the inevitable, to withdraw from
Iranian territory still under Iraqi control and to deploy for a static
defense along the international border. He reckoned that his
demoralized and afflicted army was incapable of maintaining its
position in Iran, and that the only conceivable way of containing
the Iranian threat was through a formidable line of defense on
Iraqi territory along the border. Using the Israeli invasion of
Lebanon as a pretext, he offered Iran the chance of stopping
fighting and sending their troops to the Palestinians' aid, and on
June 20, 1982, he announced that his troops had started withdrawal from Iran and would complete it within ten days. This
move, however, failed to appease the clerics in Tehran and on
July 13, following a bitter debate within the Iranian leadership, a
large-scale offensive was launched in the direction of Basra, the
second most-important city in Iraq.

In mid-1982, then, a new and more dangerous stage in
Hussein's struggle for political survival began. Nothing remained
of the "second Qadisiya" apart from the smoking ashes of military
hardware, nearly 100,000 Iraqi corpses left on the battlefield and
flocks of prisoners in the Iranian detention camps. To make
things worse for Hussein, the guns-and-butter policy, perhaps the
main buttress of Iraqi national morale, had to be abandoned
because of the war's drain on the country's financial reserves and
the loss of oil revenues, due to the war with Iran and the world oil
glut; this predicament was compounded by Syria's closure of the
Iraqi pipeline to Banias on the Mediterranean (Damascus was
then Iran's closest Arab ally), which slashed Iraq's expected oil
revenues by $5 billion.[15] With Iraqi foreign reserves plunging
from $35 billion before the war to $3 billion at the end of 1983,
the government had to cut back on much non-essential spending
and to adopt austerity measures. Civilian imports dropped consequently from a peak of $21.5 billion in 1982 to $12.2 billion in
1983, and $10–$11 billion per annum between 1984 and 1987.[16]

Paradoxically, the reversal in Iraq's military fortunes facilitated Hussein's efforts to rally the nation behind him. Once Iraq
was no longer operating on foreign soil but rather defending its
own homeland, the armed forces regained their fighting spirit

and public morale became buoyant. Hussein was seemingly able to avoid the taint of defeat and to portray the war as a heroic defense of the nation, and by extension of the Arab world, against a bigoted and aggressive enemy who persistently sabotaged efforts for peace. In this he was assisted by the growing arrogance of the revolutionary regime in Tehran. Not only did the mullahs dismiss Iraq's successive peace initiatives out of hand, but they also escalated their declared war aims, beyond the demand for the overthrow of Saddam Hussein, to include $150 billion in reparations and the repatriation of the 100,000 Shi'ites expelled from Iraq before the outbreak of the war.[17]

Another factor which mitigated the potentially adverse consequences of the Iraqi debacle was the ability of the regime to assure a reasonable flow of consumer goods and to continue the generous provisions for the relatives of war victims, despite the imposition of austerity measures. This success, however, had less to do with Hussein's financial skills than with the mounting regional and international fear of the Islamic republic, a development which in turn improved Iraq's accessibility to international markets and brought in generous "loans" from the Gulf states.

Well before the war Hussein was assiduously harnessing Arab, particularly Gulf, support for his cause. The struggle against Khomeinism, he argued, was neither a personal vendetta nor solely an Iraqi venture. Rather, it was a defense of the eastern flank of the Arab world against a violent and aggressive enemy. Should Iraq fail to contain the Iranians at the gates of the Arab world, it would not be the only casualty of the Iranian Revolution; the entire Gulf would be devoured by the fundamentalist Persians.[18]

Hussein's claim to the Arab cause had already been illustrated by his National Charter of February 1980 which advocated, inter alia, a collective Arab rebuff of any aggression against an Arab state; those pretensions were even more vividly demonstrated by Iraq's initial demands for ending the war. When on September 28, 1980, less than a week after the outbreak of hostilities, Hussein announced for the first time his readiness to enter into peace negotiations with Iran, his conditions, which centered on Iran's non-interference in Iraqi domestic affairs, included the surrender to the United Arab Emirates of the three Arab islands at the mouth of the Gulf occupied by Iran in 1971.[19] Whether Hussein would have insisted on this demand had the Iranians agreed to cease fighting and to stop their pressure on the Iraqi

regime remains a matter of conjecture. It is clear, however, that
even at this stage in his career, Saddam was aware of the benefits
of linking his personal aims to broader Arab issues, a technique
which he was to carry to its extreme during the Kuwait crisis. His
portrayal of Iraq as the bastion of Arabism could not be taken
lightly by the Gulf regimes.

From his early days in power in Iran, Khomeini did not
conceal his contempt for the Gulf dynasties and his determination
to uproot them. "Islam proclaims monarchy and hereditary
succession wrong and invalid" he declared, setting in train a huge
wave of Shi'ite unrest throughout the Gulf.[20] In November 1979
and February 1980 widespread riots erupted in the Shi'ite towns
of the oil-rich Saudi province of Hasa, exacting dozens of casualties and leading to the closure of the Shi'ite areas. Similar
disturbances occurred in Bahrain during the summer of 1979 and
the spring of 1980, while Kuwait became the target of a sustained
terrorist and subversive campaign.

In these distressing circumstances the Gulf monarchies found
it increasingly difficult to decline the "protection" offered by their
strong "sister" to the north, Iraq, who, only half a decade earlier,
had openly demanded their heads. A brief and decisive military
encounter, they apparently reasoned, would be the least of all
evils. However risky, it might debilitate the two most formidable
powers in the Gulf and curb Iran's messianic zeal.

Hence, in the summer of 1980 Kuwait openly sided with
Baghdad, and during Saddam Hussein's first state visit to Saudi
Arabia in August 1980 he apparently received King Khalid's
blessing for the impending campaign against Iran. When war
broke out, these two states quickly threw their support behind
Iraq and their identification with the Iraqi cause grew as the
Iranian threat loomed larger. By the end of 1981 Saudi Arabia
had already extended some $10 billion worth of financial support
to Iraq while Kuwait had contributed an additional $5 billion.
During the war years this support reached some $50 billion, and
it was evident that these loans were given with the knowledge that
part of them at least might not be repaid in the future. In
addition, Saudi Arabia and Kuwait sold some oil on Iraq's behalf
and allowed the use of their ports for the shipment of goods to
and from Iraq, whose access to the Gulf had been severed at the
beginning of the war. Saudi Arabia even allowed the use of its
territory for the construction of an Iraqi oil pipeline to the Red
Sea, thereby enabling Baghdad to bypass Iran's naval superiority

in the Gulf and to export considerable amounts of oil.[21] Although Hussein was never satisfied with the level of Saudi and Kuwaiti support and tended to accuse these countries (let alone the rest of the Gulf states) of being "free riders" on "Iraq's heroic struggle on behalf of the Arab nation," these contributions were doubtless indispensable for his war effort. Without Saudi and Kuwaiti financial aid and logistical support, Hussein's ability to weather Iraq's growing economic plight would have been seriously impaired.

Just as military prowess may be counterproductive in that it projects too menacing an image, so a glaring vulnerability may often become an asset in rallying support for one's cause. This "power of the weak," conferred on Iraq following its humiliating expulsion from Iran, was masterfully exploited by Hussein for the consolidation of his regime. Threatening his neighbors and the world at large with the apocalyptic vision of a belligerent, fundamentalist Middle East, he managed to drive a group of the most unlikely bedfellows to do their utmost to ensure that Iraq did not lose the war. The Soviet Union, Iraq's staunchest yet problematic ally, which had responded to Iraq's invasion of Iran by declaring its neutrality and imposing an arms embargo on Baghdad, resumed arms shipments in mid-1981 once the pendulum had swung in Iran's favor. A year later, following the initiation of large-scale Iranian incursions into Iraq, the flow of Soviet arms turned into a flood, and Moscow also extended an offer (albeit modest) of economic support to Baghdad. In return, Hussein declared a general amnesty for the communists and released many of them from jail.[22]

The United States, whose diplomatic relations with Iraq had been severed following the 1967 Six Day War, did not shy away from supporting the Iraqi war effort either. In February 1982 Baghdad was removed from the U.S. government's list of states "supporting international terrorism," thus paving the way for a significant boost in U.S.-Iraqi trade relations. Three months later, as the mullahs in Tehran were deliberating the invasion of Iraq, Secretary of State Alexander Haig strongly warned Iran against expanding the war. The French went a step further in supporting Iraq. While speaking softly to the Iranians, they unequivocally tied their fortunes to the Iraqi cause from the beginning of the war, taking great pains to accommodate Iraq's growing needs for commercial credits and military hardware: during the first two years of the war France provided Iraq with $5.6 billion worth of

weapons. This generosity was not difficult to understand. With
the Iraqi debt to France growing from 15 billion francs in 1981 to
$5 billion in 1986, the survival of Saddam Hussein was not only a
matter of containing fundamentalist Islam but had also become a
prime economic interest.[23]

In his dealings with his neighbors and the great powers
Hussein displayed the resilient pragmatism which had reaped
him abundant rewards during the 1970s. The removal of Iraq
from the West's list of states supporting terrorism, for example,
was responded to by Saddam's expulsion of the notorious international terrorist, Abu Nidal, from Baghdad. The Iraqi media,
for their part, significantly reduced their blatant attacks on the
United States as the leader of "world imperialism," thereby
facilitating the re-establishment of U.S.-Iraqi diplomatic relations.
Indeed, despite his long-standing assertion that bilateral relations
with the United States would be restored only when the interests
of the "Arab nation" had been satisfied, Hussein was not deterred
from such a move when it suited his needs. No country is an
island, he told his subjects, and Iraq's technological and economic
progress would be seriously impaired without external supply and
support. Besides, he argued, this move was essential for bringing
the war to an end. And in any event, nobody had the right to tell
Iraq how to conduct its affairs; Iraq would befriend whomever it
found suitable in accordance with its national (rather than pan-
Arab) interests.[24] Saddam's political survival was at stake and
anything necessary to guarantee his well-being was permissible.
Neither principle nor policy was an obstacle when the issue was
survival.

The lavish American returns were not long in coming. In
December 1984, merely a month after the re-establishment of
diplomatic relations, the newly opened U.S. Embassy in Baghdad
began supplying the Iraqi armed forces with much-needed military intelligence. At the same time, Washington nearly doubled its
credits for food products and agricultural equipment from $345
million in 1984 to $675 million in 1985; in late 1987 Iraq was
promised $1 billion credit, the largest loan of its kind to any single
country worldwide.

The way Hussein exploited the American support to promote
his own personal position is most revealing. Whenever U.S.
intelligence reports enabled the Iraqi armed forces to anticipate
and ward off an Iranian offensive, the success was immediately
attributed to Hussein's military ingenuity. Whenever Iraq failed

to make appropriate use of the invaluable information, the failure
was blamed on the United States which was accused of deliberately
misleading Baghdad. Such accusations were occasionally leveled
even when the Iraqis scored a military success, so as to heighten
the military acumen of the Commander-in-Chief.

This tendency to milk the cow and kick it at the same time,
which had become one of Hussein's main hallmarks, was vividly
illustrated by his reaction to Iran's capture of the Fao Peninsula in
February 1986, undoubtedly one of the most severe Iraqi setbacks
in the war. Faced with penetrating criticism from some of his
military commanders over his tight control of the war operations
which precluded flexibility and innovation at the front, Hussein
did not hesitate to point an accusing finger in the direction of
Washington. The United States, he argued via his closest associates, had intentionally given Iraq false information regarding the
Iranian offensive in order to prolong the war indefinitely.[25]
Astutely gauging America's frustration with Iran's unyielding
mullahs, Saddam knew that the United States would suffer his
indignities in order to guarantee their regional interests.

Hussein's occasional outbursts against the United States could
hardly disguise the fact that by mid-1982 he had abandoned for
pragmatic reasons much of his self-styled championship of the
Arab cause. If in March 1979 Hussein, then still the official number two man, triumphantly hosted the Baghdad Summit which
expelled Egypt from the Arab League on account of its peace
treaty with Israel, three years later he urged his Arab allies to
readmit the outcast into their ranks regardless of its peace treaty.
This fundamental change of heart was hardly surprising, given
the fact that during the war Egypt developed into one of the most
solid rocks to which Hussein could anchor his hopes for survival.

The supply of arms between the two countries had been
established toward the end of 1980, when Hussein swallowed his
pride and approached the excommunicated Egyptian President,
Anwar Sadat, with a plea for military support. Sadat, while
publicly condemning the Iraqi invasion of Iran, acquiesced to
Hussein's request, justifying his decision as a token of gratitude
for the Iraqi support to Egypt in 1974, when the latter was
subjected to a Soviet arms embargo. Substantial amounts of
Egyptian weaponry and spare parts arrived in Iraq in 1981, and
within a year Egypt had supplied Iraq with $1 billion worth of war
materiel. By 1983 the aggregate value of Egyptian military aid

had amounted to $2.7 billion and a further $2 billion arms deal was signed in 1985. Some 30,000 Egyptian "volunteers" were reportedly deployed in the Iraqi armed forces, while more than 1 million Egyptian workers serviced the over-extended Iraqi economy. In March 1984 Egypt promised Iraq all the necessary material aid it required, and a year later, when the Iraqis faced one of the largest Iranian offensives of the war, the Egyptian President, Husni Mubarak, arrived in Baghdad, together with King Hussein of Jordan, to express his profound solidarity.[26]

Saddam reciprocated. In 1984, and again in 1985, he reiterated his call for Egypt's readmission into the Arab League. "Arab solidarity," he argued heatedly, "would never be the same without Egypt. It is simply too large and important to be left outside the Arab camp. Besides, Mubarak was not Sadat. He was an honorable man, whose contribution to the Arab cause exceeded by far that of many Arabs who spent their time speaking about Arabism."[27] Hussein's efforts on Egypt's behalf were crowned with success in November 1987 when the Arab League summit in Amman allowed the member states to re-establish diplomatic relations with Egypt. Iraq quickly seized the opportunity, followed by the rest of the Arab World, with the exception of the two hard-line Arab states Syria and Libya, as well as Lebanon. By paving the way for the re-incorporation of Egypt into the mainstream of Arab politics without its renunciation of the peace with Israel, Hussein not only rewarded the latter's generous support and cemented the strategic alliance between the two countries, but he also managed to ostracize his erstwhile enemy, Hafiz Asad, in the Arab World.

If the thaw in Iraqi-Egyptian relations implied an acquiescence to the hitherto blasphemous idea of peace with Israel, Hussein proved even willing "to sup with the devil" in order to promote his ceaseless quest for survival. To be sure, he would capitalize on any opportunity to implicate Israel in the conflict. In his account of the war with Iran, it was "the Zionist entity" which ignited the war, both by agitating the mullahs to take on Iraq and by feeding Baghdad with false information (through the Shah's former generals who fled Iran after the revolution) about the actual strength of the Iranian armed forces; and it was Israel which gave Iran the weapons necessary for sustaining the war. What could provide better evidence of the "Zionist-Persian" collusion, he asked, than the Israeli destruction of Iraq's nuclear reactor in

June 1981 and the revelations of 1986 regarding Israel's involvement in the supply of American weapons to Iran (the so-called "Iran-Contra affair")?[28] By linking Israel to the Gulf conflict Hussein managed to reap two important propaganda gains: to present his war as a pan-Arab crusade on behalf of the Palestinian cause despite the fact that Iraqi troops faced Tehran rather than Jerusalem; and to ridicule Khomeini's spiritual authority by portraying him as a "Zionist stooge." The ability to generate these fictions and disseminate them with deep conviction and righteousness made Saddam his own most potent propaganda instrument.

Yet, at the same time when he targeted his pointed arrows at Israel, Hussein was seeking to placate the Jewish state. In 1982 he shed the rejectionist mantle and participated in the Fez Arab Summit which tacitly accepted a two-state solution to the Arab-Israeli conflict—Israel and a Palestinian state on the West Bank and the Gaza Strip. He even went so far as to voice public support for peace negotiations between the Arabs and Israel, emphasizing that "no Arab leader looks forward to the destruction of Israel" and that any solution to the conflict would require "the existence of a secure state for the Israelis."[29] And as if to underline the legitimacy of Israel's concern over its national security, the then Iraqi Ambassador to the United States, Nizar Hamdoon, distributed an Iranian map of the envisaged Middle East which straightforwardly stated that the Iran-Iraq War was the first step on the long road to "the liberation of Jerusalem and the banishment of Israel from the face of the earth."[30]

Accidentally or not, the distribution of the Iranian map coincided with a covert Iraqi effort to secure Israel's consent to the laying of an oil pipeline through Jordanian territory to the port of Aqaba. Since Aqaba lies in Jordan but right on the Israeli border, Israel could easily have obstructed the export of Iraqi oil through that port, as well as the flow of arms to Iraq. An Israeli acquiescence to the project therefore became a prerequisite for its implementation. In February 1985, at the initiative of the American engineering conglomerate Bechtel, which sought the contract for the Iraqi pipeline, a Swiss businessman of Israeli origins, Mr. Rappaport, approached the then Israeli Premier, Shimon Peres, with the request that Israel not sabotage the project. What happened in the corridors of power in Jerusalem remains shrouded in mystery. An official American investigation of the affair several years later suggested that Israel was offered $700 million over ten years in return for its acquiescence to the Iraqi pipeline. It was even implied that this substantial sum was promised to Mr. Peres's Labor Party rather than to the Israeli government. While these insinuations were vehemently denied by Peres, he admitted having discussed the matter with the relevant cabinet ministers, including Defense Minister Rabin and Foreign Minister Shamir. Whatever the truth, two weeks after his meeting with Rappaport, Peres signed a written understanding that Israel would not interfere with the Iraqi project. This, nevertheless, failed to satisfy Hussein who would have nothing less than watertight guarantees of full financial compensation in case of an Israeli attack on the pipeline. Since his American associates were unable to deliver, the project was eventually shelved.[31] Saddam would only sacrifice his credibility on Israel if he got exactly what he wanted. If not, he would simply try another avenue of opportunity.

The aborted attempt of 1985 did not dissuade Hussein from approaching Israel yet again through the American channel. In March 1986, a month after the devastating fall of the Fao Peninsula, when Iran seemed to be on the verge of breaching Iraq's line of defense, Saddam was reported to show keen interest in the Israeli-made Drone, a sophisticated, unmanned reconnaissance mini-aircraft. American efforts to convince Israel that its best interest lay with the arming of Iraq, which it perceived as the major obstacle to the spread of Islamic fundamentalism as well as a bitter foe of Israel's enemy Syria, were of no avail. Entrenched in their view of Iraq as a relentless foe and in the belief that Iran still represented the "big prize" in the Gulf, decision makers in Jerusalem would agree neither to delivering Israel's state-of-the-art reconnaissance plane to Iraq, nor to selling it Soviet weaponry captured in previous Arab-Israeli wars.[32] Nevertheless, signals of Iraqi interest in ties with Israel continued as late as the autumn of 1987, withering away gradually given the lukewarm Israeli response and the significant improvement in Baghdad's military position due to Soviet and Western military aid.[33]

Whether a more positive Israeli attitude would have led to a breakthrough in Iraqi-Israeli relations is difficult to tell. Arabs often accuse Western observers of the Middle East of downplaying the depth of Arab, and by extension Iraqi, compassion for the Palestinian cause. Yet this compassion was hardly evident in Hussein's behavior during the Iran-Iraq War. Quite the reverse in fact. Hussein's flexibility on the Arab-Israeli conflict, let alone his dealings with Israel in 1982 when Israeli forces were battering

Palestinian strongholds in Lebanon, reflected an unscrupulous readiness to subordinate even the most sacred Arab taboos to momentary considerations of political expediency.

Even worse, the attempt on the life of the Israeli Ambassador in London, Shlomo Argov, which was carried out by the Baghdad-based Abu Nidal terrorist group and which sparked the 1982 Lebanon War, the PLO's gravest military defeat since the 1970 Black September, was conceived by Saddam Hussein.[34] It is inconceivable that Abu Nidal (who was later expelled from Baghdad) could have carried out such an operation without his host's approval. It was also common knowledge at the time that any Palestinian attack on Israeli targets was bound to lead to a general conflagration. Israel had publicly announced it determination to remove the Palestinian military threat to its civilian settlements in the Galilee, and was impatiently looking for an excuse to make good on its promise.

What could Hussein gain by providing the bellicose Israeli Defense Minister, Ariel Sharon, with a long-sought pretext to unleash Israeli troops on the Palestinian and Syrian forces in Lebanon? The diversion of Iran's attention from the war against Iraq, to the "treacherous attack by Zionism and imperialism" on brotherly Muslim states, who incidentally also turned out to be Tehran's main Arab allies. But even if Tehran failed to live up to his expectations, an Israeli-Syrian-Palestinian confrontation in 1982 would still debilitate Iran's two most prominent Arab allies, thereby ensuring Iraq's western border against a perennial rival.

Saddam's pragmatic maneuvering was sufficient for rallying the international community behind the Iraqi war effort. However, in his struggle to survive the window of extreme personal vulnerability to which he was exposed following Iraq's "voluntary withdrawal" from Iran in June 1982, Hussein had to exploit to the full his resourceful ruthlessness. In an attempt to inexorably implicate the Iraqi leadership in his policy, he took the unprecedented step of convening an extraordinary joint meeting of the RCC, the Regional and National Commands of the Ba'th, and the Military Command in his absence, which pleaded with Iran for a cease-fire.[35] The predictably dismissive Iranian response provided a fresh reminder, if such were needed, of the fate awaiting the entire Iraqi leadership in the event of an Iranian victory. Yet Hussein did not trust his associates, even under these extreme circumstances. During the Ninth Regional Congress of the Ba'th

Party, convened in late June 1982 after a lapse of eight years to reconfirm Hussein's absolute control over the Party and state, he reshuffled the country's major power centers. Eight of the 16 members of the RCC were removed, and seven of them also lost their seats at the Party's Regional Command. The cabinet was similarly purged, with eight ministers being replaced. The most symbolic change was the dismissal of General Sa'dun Ghaydan, the last of the officers who brought the Ba'th to power in 1968, both from the RCC and the cabinet.[36]

Interestingly enough, these reshuffles were not accompanied by the customary manifestations of violence. None of the victims was jailed or executed, and many of them were compensated by handsome positions outside the government. The only exception was the ill-fated Minister of Health, Riyadh Ibrahim Hussein, who was executed in the summer of 1982. The government claimed that the Minister was executed for profiteering from distributing tainted medicine. But the popular view in Baghdad was that the Minister paid the ultimate price for saying the unsayable. During a cabinet meeting he reportedly suggested that Saddam Hussein step down temporarily in favor of Ahmad Hasan al-Bakr, in order to pave the way to a negotiated cease-fire. The Iraqi President, the story goes, showed no sign of irritation at this heretical idea. "Let us go to the other room and discuss the matter further," he suggested. The minister agreed and the two left the room. A moment later, a shot was heard, and Hussein returned alone to the cabinet as though nothing had happened. The question of his resignation did not come up again.[37]

Whether or not Hussein personally executed the Health Minister, the incident certainly reinforced one of the major components of his personality cult—his alacrity with the gun. In the highly macho Iraqi society, lack of military training or experience is a serious liability for would-be leaders. To overcome this persistent gap in his career and to build up his manly credentials, Hussein has skillfully nurtured the popular myth of his perfect mastery of the pistol and his unwavering readiness to put it to use. Hussein's coterie never tire of reiterating how he received his first pistol at the age of ten, when he decided to leave his mother's village and return to Khairallah's home in Tikrit, and how he managed as a young revolutionary to hold off for a whole day dozens of security men who sought to arrest him until his gun ran out of ammunition. Nor do they shy away from pointing out how he used his gun to kill several traitors such as the communist ministers in 1979 and the Minister of Health in 1982. One of the more graphic descriptions of Hussein's legendary mastery of the gun relates to a meeting of the National Assembly in the eventful summer of 1982. According to the story, as Hussein addressed the Assembly he noticed a man in the audience passing a note to another man. Without thinking twice the President drew his pistol and killed both of them. His assumption that the note informed the second man what time to kill the President was quickly proved correct.[38]

For those who would not be deterred by this demonstration of resolve in the Assembly, Hussein reserved the firing squads. In the summer of 1982 some 300 high-ranking officers were executed, while many others were purged. In an interview with the West German magazine *Stern,* Hussein admitted to having executed two Divisional Commanders and one Brigade Commander for what he described as "failing their duties." Poor combat performance was also the official explanation for the purge of the Commanders of all four corps of the Iraqi army a year later.[39] Someone had to pay for the military failures against the Iranian forces.

Hussein also clamped down on the last remnants of Shi'ite opposition. In the spring of 1983 he arrested some 90 members of the prominent al-Hakim family, relatives of Hojjat al-Islam Muhammad Baqr al-Hakim, head of the Supreme Council of the Islamic Revolution of Iraq (SCIRI), an exiled military group trained and operated by Iran. Six of the detainees were executed, and the exiled leader received a personal message from Hussein threatening him with further executions should he continue his subversive activities; the threat was carried out two years later with the killing of another ten members of the Hakim family.[40]

By that time, however, the Shi'ite challenge to the regime had for all intents and purposes disappeared. In effect, Shi'ite behavior during the war demonstrated that Hussein's suspicions of the community's disloyalty had been grossly exaggerated. Not only did the Shi'ites fail to welcome their self-styled liberators, but they fought shoulder to shoulder with their Arab compatriots to rebuff the Persian threat. Hence, with the exception of isolated terrorist activities by the dwindling *Da'wa* and the Iranian-sponsored SCIRI which were easily contained, the Shi'ite community sealed its social contract with the Iraqi state with the blood of its sons. They just would not fight alongside the Iranians against their Arab brothers. Had Hussein been aware of this Shi'ite state of

mind in 1979 or 1980, the war might have been averted altogether. As things stood, he was able to accompany the sporadic
repressive convulsions against the Shiʻite community with regular
demonstrations of generosity. An important symbolic act of
goodwill was the guarantee, both in the 1980 and 1984 elections
to the National Assembly, that some 40 percent of those elected
would be Shiʻites and that the Speaker of the 250-member legislature would also be a Shiʻite.[41] On the material level, Hussein
took much care to improve the standard of living of the Shiʻites
and to renovate their holy shrines. Particular attention was paid to
the tomb of Ali Ibn-Abi-Talib, the Shiʻa's patron Imam, which was
paved with special marble tiles imported from Italy.

Hussein also found the Kurdish threat during the early war years
less ominous than previously anticipated. The tribal and linguistic
fragmentation of the Kurdish community and the long-standing
enmity between its two main resistance groups, Masʻud Barzani's
KDP and Jalal Talabani's PUK, precluded a joint Kurdish strategy
and enabled the regime to pit them against each other. It was only
after Iran had launched its first major offensive into Kurdistan in
the summer of 1983 that the Kurdish opposition became a real
irritant to the central regime. Yet even then Hussein managed to
keep the two Kurdish organizations apart. While the KDP was
brutally repressed, with some 8,000 members of the Barzani clan
imprisoned, the PUK was carefully courted through substantial
financial inducements and ambiguous political pledges. In late
1983 the talks between the government and the PUK culminated
in a truce agreement. In the agreement, whose contents have
never been made officially public, the government reportedly
agreed to hold "free and democratic elections" for legislative and
executive councils of an autonomous region in Kurdistan, as well
as to allocate 30 percent of the state budget to rehabilitate war
damage. The PUK reciprocated by undertaking to form a 40,000-
strong popular army "to protect Kurdistan against foreign
enemies."[42]

Before long, however, Talabani discovered that he had been
double-crossed by Hussein who had no intentions whatsoever of
rehabilitating Kurdistan or promoting Kurdish autonomy at the
expense of the central government. Frustrated and angry, he
curtailed the dialogue with the authorities, buried his differences
with Barzani and joined the KDP campaign against the regime.
Thus, by early 1985, Hussein was confronted with a full-scale

insurrection in Kurdistan. In a last-ditch effort to deflect the Kurdish (and to a lesser extent Shi'ite) insurgency, the Iraqi President offered a general amnesty "for all Iraqis who conducted activities hostile to their country." When this offer was spurned by the disillusioned Kurds, a ferocious campaign was launched against them. With the passage of time and the deterioration in Iraq's military position, this campaign assumed genocidal proportions, when the Iraqi forces retaliated for what they viewed as treacherous Kurdish behavior. Not only were the 8,000 "prisoners" captured in 1983 executed, along with hundreds of other members of the Kurdish opposition, but the government embarked once more on a systematic effort to uproot the rebellious population from its native environment. By the end of the Iran-Iraq War in the summer of 1988, more than half of the villages and numerous towns in Kurdistan had been razed and their populations deported. Some half a million Kurds were placed either in easily controllable settlements in the vicinity of the main towns in Kurdistan, or in concentration camps in the south-western Iraqi desert.

Commanded by Hussein's paternal cousin, Ali Hasan al-Majid, this punitive campaign witnessed the extensive use of chemical weapons, including mustard gas, cyanide, and Tabun nerve agent against the unprotected civilian population. The first attacks of this kind were reported in May 1987, when some 20 Kurdish villages were gassed in an attempt to deter the civilian population in Kurdistan from collaborating with the advancing Iranian forces. A month later several Kurdish villages in Iran were given the same "medicine," with some 100 people dead and 2,000 injured. The most appalling attack took place in March 1988, when the specter of a major Iranian breakthrough in Kurdistan drove Hussein to employ gas on an unprecedented scale against the Kurdish town of Halabja. As the thick cloud of gas spread by the Iraqi planes evaporated into the clear sky, television crews were rushed into the town by the Iranians and the world discovered the full extent of this horrendous massacre. Five thousand people—men, women, children and babies—were killed that day. Nearly 10,000 suffered injuries.[43]

The Kurds, of course, were not the sole victims of Iraq's chemical arsenal. Iranian troops had been subjected to gas attacks as early as 1982. Surprisingly enough, Hussein displayed far greater circumspection in his use of chemical warfare on the battlefield than he did against his own civilian population. Chemical weapons were used only at critical moments when there was no other way to check Iranian offensives.

The same circumspection was applied to air raids on Iranian population centers which were limited in scope, intensity and duration, and were usually preceded by a prolonged warning campaign intended to leave room for a change in Iranian policy or an evacuation of citizens. When affairs seemed likely to get out of control, as during the ferocious strikes against Iranian and Iraqi cities, the so-called First War of the Cities in February 1984, Hussein quickly reached an agreement with Iran not to strike indiscriminately at each other's civilian populations, and honored that agreement relatively well. Moreover, he did not push the superiority of the Iraqi air force to its logical end and would often back down once his strategy had begun to yield positive results. The most vivid illustration of this apparently illogical behavior is, perhaps, offered by the Second War of the Cities (March and April 1985), when the Iraqi campaign was abruptly halted despite its success in triggering widespread demonstrations in Tehran against the Iranian regime.[44] Saddam's strategy confused observers, seeming to defy military expectations and practice.

And yet, his restraint did not stem from normative or moral considerations, but was rather grounded in very practical concerns. Hussein was willing to use chemical weapons whenever he deemed it necessary and he had no moral qualms whatsoever about doing so. As General Maher Abd al-Rashid, one of Iraq's most prominent commanders during the war and the then father-in-law of Hussein's younger son Qusai, put it: "If you gave me a pesticide to throw at these swarms of insects to make them breathe and become exterminated, I would use it."[45] Saddam, however, was unwilling to antagonize his Arab supporters (Saudi Arabia and Kuwait, in particular) which feared the possibility of Iran's broadening the conflict in retaliation for an Iraqi chemical attack. The Soviet Union, too, was reported to have pressured Iraq to avoid any irrevocable escalation of the war. Hussein's restraint was indicative as well of his reluctance to hazard his air force, for serious losses (especially of its trained pilots) could destroy Iraq's most effective reserve of military force. It would seem that the fierceness of Iran's reaction to attacks on its population centers served to modify Hussein's calculations. Though the scope and intensity of Iranian retaliation could not match that of Iraq (after 1982 Iran possessed only a handful of operational fighting aircraft), what little Iranian air force retaliation there was nevertheless appears to have exposed the fragility of Iraq's public morale and frustrated Hussein's attempts to insulate the home front from the war. In general, Hussein's circumspection reflected his fundamental wish to keep the war limited so as to secure his rule and foreign suppliers and to avoid irreversible damage to future Iraqi-Iranian relations.

This set of considerations was fundamentally upset in 1986. Faced with catastrophic developments on the battlefield—the fall of Fao in February and the town of Mehran on the central front four months later—and the collapse of oil prices with its devastating impact on the debilitated Iraqi economy, Hussein made yet another desperate plea for peace. Gone were his earlier pretensions to Gulf, let alone Arab, leadership. Apart from the vague reference to future Iraqi-Iranian collaboration over the stability of the Gulf (a far cry from his previous demand for Iran's return of the Gulf islands to Arab hands), Hussein's conditions for peace centered on the security of his regime, namely, a mutual guarantee to respect each other's choice of government.[46] When Tehran remained as adamant as ever on his removal from power, Hussein apparently concluded that his only hope of persuading the Iranian authorities to desist from their efforts to overthrow him was to appeal to them indirectly by making life still more unpleasant for their constituents. Accordingly, an unprecedently ferocious aerial campaign was launched against Iranian strategic targets, primarily its main oil export terminal at Kharg Island, and major population centers—including Tehran, Isfahan and Kermanshah—were subjected to heavy raids. On August 12, 1986, Iraqi aircraft mounted the first successful raid on the Iranian oil terminal of Sirri Island (150 miles north of the Strait of Hormuz), thereby signaling to Tehran that no strategic targets were beyond Iraq's operational reach.

Iraq also intensified its attacks on civilian shipping, particularly tankers, making their way to and from Iran. The so-called Tanker War was launched by Hussein in early 1984 with the idea of shifting the war from the stalemate of the battlefield to a new and potentially more rewarding arena. Both sides had, of course, carried out attacks against each other's merchant shipping from the early stages of the war; between September 1980 and February 1984, 23 Iraqi and 5 Iranian attacks were recorded. In 1984 alone, however, there were 37 Iraqi and 7 Iranian attacks.[47]

The Tanker War differed from the previous campaign against

shipping not only in its scope but also in its strategic rationale. Unlike earlier Iraqi attacks on non-military shipping, which were directed solely against Iran and aimed at convincing it of the futility of continuing the war, the Tanker War sought to draw external actors—the Western powers in particular—into the war, in the hope that they would support Iraq or help to bring about a peaceful settlement. The idea seems to have been that intensifying the attacks would provoke Iran into extreme actions, such as attempts to close the Strait of Hormuz, which would leave Western oil consumers with no other alternative but to intervene.

Iran's response to these moves to escalate the war did not live up to Hussein's expectations. Fully aware of the rationale behind the new Iraqi strategy, Iran not only avoided any attempts to block the Strait of Hormuz but went out of its way to keep its responses at the lowest possible level; it refrained from public acknowledgement of its attacks on civilian shipping, and reiterated its disinterest in the closure of the Strait since "the Islamic Republic of Iran would be the first to suffer as a result of such a move."[48] Iranian naval attacks were essentially limited to ships trading with Saudi Arabia and Kuwait, in the hope that these two countries, Iraq's staunchest economic supporters, would exert economic pressure on Baghdad to end its attacks.

To Hussein's dismay, Iran's caution succeeded in keeping the Western powers relatively aloof. Although the eruption of the Tanker War increased U.S. anxiety, and reportedly led to a review of Gulf contingency plans, it was not followed by any concrete action. It was only in late 1986, after the intensification of the Iraqi campaign against Iranian economic targets and commercial shipping, that Iranian caution began to falter. Responding to the Iraqi escalation by intensifying its own attacks on Iraqi-bound shipping, Tehran intimidated Kuwait to the point that it approached both superpowers with the request to protect a number of its tankers against naval attacks: in March 1987 the United States informed the Kuwaiti government of its willingness to escort that country's 11 tankers through the Gulf, provided they would fly the U.S. flag, and a month later Kuwait chartered 3 tankers from the USSR which were put under the Soviet flag. By the end of 1987 Iran was confronted with a formidable multi-national armada of nearly 50 warships.[49]

Shielded by the West from Tehran's wrath, Hussein could intensify his attacks on Iranian-bound shipping and Iran's oil infrastructure with virtual impunity. He did exactly that in the hope that the Iranians would sooner or later provide the West with a pretext to unleash its power on them. Although this assessment proved misconceived, as Tehran did its best to signal its interest in de-escalation (with the exception of a minor encounter between American and Iranian vessels, a direct U.S.-Iranian confrontation was averted until April 1988, when the American navy sank several Iranian naval craft), the Iraqi pressure further damaged the Iranian economy, while the multinational presence in the Gulf exacerbated the deepening feeling of isolation and hopelessness within the Iranian leadership.[50]

Fortunately for Hussein, the "peace camp" within the Iranian leadership reflected a broader and long-standing segment within the Iranian public. The sense of purpose among Iranians declined after mid-1982 when they were no longer defending their own territory but were engaged on Iraqi soil. Economic dislocations occasioned by fighting gave rise to great frustration as shortages of basic commodities grew worse, and a black market and corruption flourished. A mounting human toll caused a deep war weariness.

Declining morale in Iran showed in manifestations of discontent, including a drop in the number of army volunteers after late 1984 and anti-war and anti-government demonstrations, most notably in mid-1985. Morale plunged sharply in 1987 as the regime responded inadequately to intensified Iraqi missile attacks on population centers. The decline in volunteers for the front assumed alarming proportions after the costly failure to capture Basra in the winter of 1987. Growing discontent among the poor who constituted the mainstay of the regime's support was particularly disconcerting for the clerics.

Popular dissatisfaction echoed within the councils of the Iranian revolutionary regime as early as mid-1982, when a loose coalition of military and political figures began to question the logic of taking the war into Iraq on the grounds of its human, material and political costs. As national spirits fell, such skeptical voices became increasingly influential. Nevertheless, it took nearly five years of growing dissatisfaction before the authorities could fully reconcile themselves to the futility of the conflict.

This acceptance of the inevitable, however, did not come without a final blow from Baghdad. Seeing the light at the end of the tunnel for the first time since the early months of the war, in February 1988 Hussein ordered the most ferocious campaign ever. During the next two months over 150 missiles and numerous air raids battered Iran's major population centers. The risks of this escalation for Iraq were negligible. Iran was in no position to launch a ground offensive due to the lack of volunteers for the front, nor was it capable of extending the war to Iraq's hinterland, given its glaring strategic inferiority. All Tehran could do was to intensify attacks against Iraqi-bound shipping; but such a move involved the risk of a direct confrontation with the United States which Iran was anxious to avoid.

Indeed, this attack on the cities turned out to be the straw that broke Iranian morale. With government employees joining citizens in fleeing Tehran *en masse*, the regime was paralyzed and national morale was shattered to the core. The road from there to the total collapse of the military's fighting spirit was short. In April 1988, after nearly six years in a defensive posture in the ground war, Iraq moved to the offensive, and in 48 hours of fierce fighting recaptured the Fao Peninsula, whose loss in 1986 had signified Baghdad's lowest ebb during the war. A major psychological victory for Hussein, the recapture of Fao signaled the final shift in the fortunes of the war. It was soon followed by a string of military successes: in May Iraq drove the Iranians out of their positions in Salamcheh (east of Basra), and a month later dislodged them from the Majnoon islands, held by Iran since 1985. In early July Iraq drove the remaining Iranian forces out of Kurdistan and later that month gained a small strip of Iranian territory in the central part of the Iran-Iraq border.

Confronted with these setbacks, the mullahs in Tehran were desperately urging their spiritual mentor to sanctify the cessation of hostilities. Iraq is not the only enemy facing Iran, they reasoned in an attempt to convince the aged Ayatollah to accept the unthinkable. Rather, a worldwide coalition of imperialist forces, headed by the Great Satan (the United States), vied for Iranian blood. Therefore, and in view of the social and economic conditions in Iran, any prolongation of the war could but play into the aggressors' hands and would endanger the great achievements of the Islamic Revolution. What could provide a better proof of imperialist ruthlessness, they retorted, than the shooting down of an Iranian civilian plane by the U.S. navy and the killing of its 290 innocent passengers?

This reasoning seems to have convinced Khomeini that the overthrow of his mortal enemy would not take place in his lifetime. On July 18, 1988, after a year of evasion and hesitation, Iran accepted Security Council Resolution 598 on a cease-fire in the Iran-Iraq War. A month later the guns along the common border fell silent. The deadliest threat to Saddam Hussein's political survival until then had been temporarily removed.

After eight years of a war he had initiated, Saddam could claim a major success. Despite his often bewildering and sometimes self-defeating strategies, he had managed to achieve some notable political successes. He had projected himself as the reasonable and progressive Arab leader confronting the tide of irrational and fanatical hordes from Iran, whose openly stated policy was to export their Islamic Revolution. This had earned him the financial and military support of his conservative Gulf neighbors as well as that of almost the entire international community. He had shown himself to be a wily foe whose total commitment to his own survival enabled him to pursue unconventional warfare as he deemed necessary and engage in domestic repression despite its threat to morale. He had made clear that no sacrifice was too great to keep him in power, neither that of his armies nor of his civilians. He would only end the conflict when his political survival was assured, at least for the immediate future.

8

The Rule of Fear

Like other absolute leaders, such as Stalin and Hitler, whose power base resided in political systems whose ideological acts permeated every facet of their respective societies, Saddam Hussein has predicated his personal rule on the Ba'th Party. His logic, like that of his predecessors, has been strikingly simple: since the Party possesses the organizational infrastructure and ideological basis for controlling people's actions and minds, it would control the masses and the state machinery while he would control the Party.

To this end, the Ba'th has been transformed from a nucleus Party numbering a couple of thousand full members with little popular basis, to a mass organization boasting some 25,000 full members and 1.5 million supporters. This impressive growth in the Party's power, however, has been matched by a steady decline in its hold on the real reins of power. During his years in power—both as de facto leader under President Bakr and in the top spot—Saddam has fully subordinated the Ba'th to his will, sterilized its governing institutions and reduced the national decision-making apparatus to one man, surrounded by a docile flock of close associates. He has done this by preempting any dissent through systematic purges, and by subordinating all domestic and foreign policies to one and only goal: his political survival.

Saddam always considered that the road to national servility had to begin with the education of the young, who have not yet been "corrupted by backward ideas."[1] "The boy and the youth have no social awareness or political affinities," he stated after assuming the Presidency, "therefore the Party and the State

176

should be their family, their father and mother."[2] Hence, from their first days at kindergarten Iraqi children are introduced to Baʻthi terminology and, of course, learn to adulate their glorious leader. As they grow up they join the Party's various youth organizations where they are thoroughly brainwashed with the xenophobic anti-"imperialist" mentality of their President. They are not only taught not to trust anybody, not even their parents, but to serve as the Party's extension into the family, keeping a vigilant eye on their parents' behavior, always ready to report them to the authorities, should they "misbehave." In this respect, the nightmare vision of a totalitarian state in George Orwell's *1984* has become reality in present-day Iraq. As Saddam observed: "You must encircle the adults through their sons in addition to other means and instruments. Teach students and pupils to contradict their parents if they hear them discussing state secrets. . . . You must place in every corner a son of the revolution, with a trustworthy eye and a firm mind who receives his instruction from the responsible center of the revolution."[3]

Having laid the ideological foundations for unquestioning submission to the Party in early youth, the next step for Iraqi citizens is their incorporation into the Party's organizational infrastructure. Since the Baʻth, according to Hussein's populist reasoning, represents the general will, it should absorb the largest possible number of Iraqis into its ranks. As he picturesquely put it: "With God's will we shall leave nobody outside the ship, for this time this ship is big enough to encompass the whole of Iraq."[4]

By way of filling the "big ship," Party membership has become essential for a public career, with non-Baʻthists being removed from their positions to make room for dedicated Party members and supporters. All state organs—the army, the bureaucracy and even the trade unions and the mass organizations—have come under the Party's complete domination. In January 1980 a special bureau for mass organizations was set up under the auspices of the RCC. One of the more visible constituent organizations of the bureau has been the National Union of Iraqi Students, which specializes in harassing dissident Iraqi students abroad. To reduce the number of such potential dissidents in the first place, scholarships for foreign study have been confined to Party members and "offenders" risk a penalty of up to 15 years' imprisonment with hard labor. Moreover, thousands of non-Baʻthist students have been denied admission to vocational and higher education institutions in Iraq or have been expelled from them.[5] Academic

standards have indeed become a farce as senior Party officials
have pressured lecturers to award academic degrees to their
relatives and fellow Party members. Saddam himself obtained his
law diploma this way.[6]

Party service, though, may be demanding. While low-level
membership is open to all, entailing few privileges and multiple
obligations, full membership is limited to an exclusive club of the
"chosen few" who have reached a high level of "maturity." Not
everyone can reach this stage which, in any case, requires five to
ten years of dedicated work and absolute commitment. Those
who fail this sacred duty of dedication to the Party face the
ominous specter of Article 200 of the Iraqi Penal Code which
entails the death penalty for such "crimes" as leaving the Ba'th
and joining another political party, concealing previous political
affiliations upon joining the Ba'th or maintaining contacts with
other political organizations. In order to ensure that such "devi-
ations" are reduced to the barest minimum, Party members are
subjected to permanent supervision by their vigilant comrades
who would gladly report any "suspicious" activity on the part of
neighbors, workmates, friends and even family members.

The methods employed to ensure absolute loyalty within the
ranks of the Ba'th pale in comparison with the Party's treatment
of political dissidents, whether imaginary or real. With one in
seven Iraqis a Party member of one rank or another, the common
definition of Iraq as a state of informers can hardly be considered
an exaggeration. No ordinary Iraqi is immune to the regime's
arbitrariness or to the vindictiveness of disenchanted neighbors,
friends or even family members. Eavesdropping, spies and informers are a constant threat. A joke or derogatory comment
about the President, the RCC, the Ba'th Party or the National
Assembly can cost people their lives according to a state decree
of November 1986 which prescribes the death penalty for the
deliberate and public insult of these institutions.[7] They may find
themselves detained and tortured without having the slightest
clue about the reason for their plight. The luckier detainees may
shortly return to their families with no explanation given for their
absence; the less fortunate may face long prison terms or even
execution. These sentences, as reports by Amnesty International
indicate, are likely to be issued by state officials rather than
judges.[8]

The notorious security services have been the main arm
through which Saddam has kept his house in order. With re-

sponsibility for the Party's security apparatus entrusted to him as early as the mid-1960s, Saddam has transformed this establishment into the major agent for promoting his political program. By diminishing the influence of the military within the Party, and by purging potential contenders for leadership, he has let only the Party's security branch survive as a political force. In order to prevent his creation from rising against him, Hussein has resorted to a strategy of divide and rule, making sure that all branches of his security services operate independently and report to him separately. This has given him full control over the formidable apparatus as well as allowed him to use each of the security services to spy on the other. As a final security valve Hussein has placed his fellow Tikritis, whose kinship ties continue to have significance for him, in key positions within the security apparatus.[9]

From the regime's point of view, however, even the tortured and executed should be grateful for their fate. *"Qasr al-Nihayyah* is a beautiful palace," Saddam told a Western correspondent when asked about the use of torture in this notorious prison, "it is the palace where the members of the royal family were killed in 1958. Throughout our underground days we hoped to see this royal palace. It is a great honor to be detained there."[10] This sarcastic response to an inquiry into Iraqi punishment was carried a step further by the Director General of the Ministry of Culture and Information. Answering a Danish journalist's query about executions in Iraq, he said: "You let a spy spend the rest of his life in prison. We prefer to free him and give him eternal peace immediately. Is this not more humane?"[11]

Nor does Saddam see anything morally wrong in executing those of his subjects who dare joke at his expense. "Does not the law in your country punish whoever tries to insult the President?" he asked ABC television network correspondent Diane Sawyer when pressed on this issue. "No, Mr. President," she said, "half of the country would be in prison." "And no measures are taken against anybody who insults the President?" he continued, not believing his ears. "No, they are even given their own TV show." "Well," he said, visibly stunned by what he had just heard, "in Iraq the President is regarded by the people as a symbol representing something."[12]

Beyond the chilling insight it gives into Saddam's psyche and value system, this interview provides a vivid illustration of his limited understanding of Western attitudes and values, an im-

pression which may be further corroborated by the following
story. An Arab journalist who went to interview Saddam found
himself giving his interviewee a lengthy exposition on the working
of the American political system. Having patiently listened to his
guest explain the concept of checks and balances, and the
separation of executive, legislative and judicial functions, Saddam
finally asked: "Who, then, am I supposed to deal with?"[13]

With the Ba'th Party reduced to a rubber stamp, Saddam has
ruled the country through a small clique of longtime Party
associates and family members, as well as more distant relatives
from the Tikriti clan. Saddam's deep affection for his mother's
family, the Talfahs, dating back to his fond memories of the years
he spent at Khairallah's home, was manifested in his marriage to
his uncle's daughter, Sajidah, and his lifetime association with
Khairallah's son, Adnan. Nor have Hussein's family on his father's
side, the Majids, or his stepfather's side, the Ibrahims, been
deprived of their share in power. The most recent climber to the
top has been General Hussein Kamil Hasan al-Majid, the President's cousin and a son-in-law, who serves as Minister of Industry
and Military Production. An ambitious and shrewd operator, the
young and energetic minister is regarded by many as a rising star
if not a potential successor to Hussein. The best indication of
Kamil's growing importance is his responsibility for developing
Iraq's non-conventional arms industry, including the nuclear
project, the feather in Saddam's cap. Kamil also commands the
country's long-range missile units where his brother, Saddam
Kamil, serves as a Colonel. Another cousin of Saddam Hussein,
Ali Hasan al-Majid, who conducted the atrocious campaign
against the Kurds in 1987–1988, served for a few months as
Governor of Kuwait following the Iraqi invasion.[14]

Saddam's half-brothers on his stepfather's side have been
equally indispensable for his regime. Barzan al-Tikriti, Hussein's
younger brother and the closest to him among the Ibrahims, was
promoted to the key position of Head of the notorious Party
Intelligence (*Mukhabarat*) as early as 1974, a position which he
held until the fall of 1983, when he was dismissed and placed
under house arrest. Wathban Ibrahim, demoted with Barzan in
1983, served as the governor of Hussein's native province of Salah
al-Din (with Tikrit at its center), while Sibawi Ibrahim was the
Deputy Chief of Police, before he was removed together with his
brothers.

What exactly happened between Hussein and his half-brothers in 1983 is not entirely clear. One explanation is that they were implicated in a coup against their senior brother. According to this version, Barzan was approached by military officers who offered him the Presidency and his brothers were tempted to join him. Another explanation is that the three, Barzan in particular, were sacked for failing to detect a plot against Hussein. Barzan, at least, should have known better: in 1982 he published a book entitled *Attempts to Assassinate Saddam Hussein*, in which he described seven alleged plots against Saddam Hussein (some of which took place before Saddam's ascent to the Presidency), and accused foreign countries, including Iran, Syria, the United States and Israel, of masterminding these "plots."[15] Yet, despite these conjectures of rebelliousness, some observers believe that the Ibrahims' fall from grace had nothing to do with a coup attempt but was rather related to a bitter family feud. The death of Saddam's mother in August 1983 was also said to have facilitated the removal of the Ibrahims from power, as she had been their main "protector."

That this latter version is more plausible than the other two can be gauged not only from Saddam's public admission that Barzan was no conspirator, but from the fact that the three were not punished and, moreover, were brought in from the cold to key posts three years later: Sibawi assumed Barzan's previous influential position as Head of the *Mukhabarat*, Wathban was made head of State Internal Security (*Amn*), while Barzan was appointed Ambassador to the United Nations in Geneva. Had the three been involved in a conspiracy against Saddam, such a "comeback" would have been inconceivable.[16]

Hussein has also used his children as pawns in the tangled web of dynastic loyalties around him. His eldest son, Udai, is married to the daughter of Izzat Ibrahim, Deputy Chairman of the RCC. His younger son, Qusai, had been married to the daughter of General Maher Abd al-Rashid before this marriage was reportedly dissolved following Abd al-Rashid's fall into disfavor when his victories in the Iran-Iraq War transformed him into a threat to Saddam's absolute power. The President's eldest daughter, Raghd, is married to Hussein Kamil Hasan, while his younger daughter, Rina, is married to Saddam Kamil, Hussein Kamil's brother. Raghd's betrothal to Hussein Kamil Hasan in 1983 is believed to have triggered the bitter confrontation between Saddam and his half-brothers, who feared that the forthcoming marriage would strengthen the al-Majid clan at their expense.[17]

The Ibrahims had good reason to dread the future. Life under their half-sibling has been extremely rewarding. By the time of his death in 1989, Adnan Khairallah reportedly owned more than 500 cars. His father and the family's "Godfather," Khairallah Talfah, has accumulated a fabulous fortune in real estate deals, having forced landowners to sell him their property at ridiculous prices.[18] Hussein Kamil Hasan is rumored to have made millions in commissions on arms deals, while Saddam's eldest son, Udai, has used his privileged position to reap abundant financial benefits. According to the London weekly, the *Observer*, in 1985 he imported a shipment of cows from India without the necessary health documentation, and although the entire shipment had to be slaughtered due to disease, he insisted on receiving his fee. In addition, Udai reportedly owns a vast network of businesses, including the National Meat Company, an ice cream factory and a retail chain producing food products. In 1988, Udai made more than $20 million in one transaction by forcing the central bank to sell him foreign currency at the official rate and exchanging it on the black market. His fleet of cars is only surpassed by that of his late uncle, Adnan.[19]

While Saddam has not really fought corruption among his entourage and has apparently even encouraged it, as yet another form of leverage over them, he would occasionally launch "anti-corruption" campaigns to allay public restiveness and to signal to his associates where the locus of real power resides. Thus, the execution of the Minister of Health in 1982 was officially attributed to profiteering, as was the dismissal of his successor, Sadeq al-Wash, six years later. Similarly, in June 1986 a former Mayor of Baghdad, Abd al-Wahab Mufti, was hanged for alleged corruption. Although it is not at all clear how corrupt he really was, particularly since his execution coincided with the "exposure" of yet another "Syrian plot," it was a clear signal of Saddam's determination to keep his administration "clean."

Another means of concealing the depth of Tikriti entrenchment in power from public eyes was the abolition, in the late 1970s, of family names denoting the place of origin.[20] Saddam himself had dropped his place of origin from his surname as early as 1973, adopting instead his late father's name—Hussein. Ever since he has gone to extraordinary lengths to hide his narrow provincial origins and to present himself as the embodiment of Iraqi unity:

Western journalists say that Saddam Hussein is a Tikriti. I say to them with pity: Saddam Hussein was born in a village in the southern part of Tikrit province; Tikrit province is part of the *muhafaza* [district] of Salah al-Din, and he is an Iraqi. Saddam Hussein was born in the *muhafaza* of Salah al-Din but he is not (only) a son of the *muhafaza* of Salah al-Din because he is a son of the province of Arbil, of Sulaimania, he is a son of Anbar, of the Tigris and Euphrates, a son of Barada, and of Jordan, and of the Nile, of Damascus and Amman, Cairo and Casablanca, and a son of every Iraqi city and a son of the Iraqi people, of the Iraqi soil and of the Iraqi air and of the Arab homeland and of the Arab nation.[21]

The rules of the game for Hussein's coterie are simple and straightforward: they give their ruler unconditional loyalty and obedience in return for political prominence and economic advantage. But the footing at the top of the pyramid is treacherous. Should a member of the inner circle find his loyalty called into question, or should he become too popular, his political career will quickly go into decline, whatever his former standing, and whether he is a member of Hussein's family or not.

Take the case of Adnan Khairallah Talfah, who died mysteriously in a helicopter crash in May 1989. The official explanation was that the helicopter had flown into a sandstorm. Few believe it. Too many senior military officials had met their end in similar accidents following the Iran-Iraq War. Even the most trusting Iraqis found it difficult to comprehend why they seemed to be losing more helicopters in peacetime than at the height of the war.[22]

Even in a regime that thrives on purges Adnan Khairallah's case was remarkable, given his unusually close relationship with Saddam. The two spent most of their childhood in the same home and were brought up as virtual brothers rather than cousins. It was a seven-year-old Adnan who, in 1947, convinced his illiterate cousin, then ten years old, to defy his family, leave his village and seek education in Tikrit.[23]

Friendship was rewarded. Though a lackluster officer with no record of military excellence or national standing, in 1977 Staff Colonel Adnan Khairallah became Minister of Defense and one of the few military representatives on the Revolutionary Command Council and the Regional Command. Any doubts about who had pulled the strings behind this promotion were dispelled two years later when Hussein, now President, appointed Adnan

Deputy Prime Minister and Deputy Commander-in-Chief of the
Armed Forces. Adnan Khairallah repaid his benefactor by insur-
ing the absolute loyalty of the armed forces through systematic
purges, and by serving as Saddam's right hand during the eight
years of war against Iran.

Yet none of this mattered once Talfah reportedly sided with
his sister in a family feud over Hussein's romantic involvement
with Samira Shahbandar, ex-wife of the Chairman of Iraqi
Airways and member of a respected Baghdadi family. Unlike
previous presidential romances, which had carefully been kept
secret, Hussein's affair with Shahbandar became public knowledge, rocking his marriage and damaging the President's carefully
nurtured image as a faithful husband and devoted family man.

To make matters worse, Hussein's eldest son, Udai, decided to
avenge his mother's lost honor by publicly clubbing to death the
presidential food taster, who happened to perform services in
addition to his gastronomical responsibilities. It was he who had
introduced Ms. Shahbandar to Hussein and had served as a
go-between for the two lovers. Furious, Hussein put his son
behind bars and pledged to try him on murder charges, but after
a highly emotional campaign by his wife and Adnan Khairallah he
relented and sent Udai into luxurious exile in Switzerland. This
move was presented to the public as a gesture to the family of the
deceased which had, allegedly, written the President pleading
with him to stop the investigation against his son, since "what
happened was God's will."[24]

Hussein's wrath was not difficult to understand. For some
years he had been grooming Udai for high office, if not as a
potential successor. Having graduated from engineering college
in 1984, with a grade of 99.5 percent, a not-too-surprising result
for the leader's son, Udai became the President of Saddam
University and Head of Iraq's Olympic Committee. Yet his
flamboyant and undisciplined behavior caused Saddam public
embarrassment on a number of occasions. Udai was reported to
have killed at least two other people before murdering the
presidential food taster. His first victim was an army colonel who
opposed Udai's attempts to seduce his teenage daughter, while
the second was an army officer who dared resist Udai's pass at his
wife in a Baghdad discotheque. Interestingly enough, in the
twisted logic of the Presidential Palace, Udai's previous murders
were apparently taken to his credit as his mother questioned

Saddam's decision to punish their son for the particular murder of the food taster, while he had turned a blind eye to Udai's previous killings. "Why arrest him?" she reportedly asked her husband. "After all, it is not the first time he has killed. Nor is he the only one in his family who has killed."[25]

Although relations within the family eventually thawed (Udai was allowed to return to Baghdad in the spring of 1990 and to resume his previous posts), Hussein never forgave Adnan Khairallah for his involvement in the affair, which embarrassed him before the public. A few months after the scandal, he ferociously attacked the Minister of Defense, accusing him of failing to respond effectively to a coup attempt in early 1989. The handwriting was on the wall.

In truth, with or without the "Shahbandar affair," Adnan was already a marked man. Whatever his immediate mistakes, he had committed the unforgivable "sin" of sharing glory for the "victory over the Persian enemy" with Saddam Hussein. For this sin, there could be no absolution, as any number of prominent generals were also to find out. Maher Abd al-Rashid and Hisham Sabah Fakhri, national heroes after liberating the Fao Peninsula from Iranian occupation in April 1988, were relieved of their commands later that year and are believed to be under house arrest or even executed. Nobody, no matter how close he was to Saddam, was ever to be allowed to reach a position that might even theoretically endanger the President, either in popularity or in power.

Adnan Khairallah's unhappy fate notwithstanding, surprisingly few of Hussein's inner circle have fallen into disrepute during the 1980s, suggesting that even in a system permeated by distrust and betrayal, a feeling of solidarity, whether tribal or terror-induced, is not completely unknown.[26]

This solidarity does not rest, however, on the nobler emotions of faith and fidelity. Not only has Hussein managed to purge, during his gradual rise to absolute power, all potential rivals and to surround himself with subservient yes-men, but he has also tied his inner circle to his policies and, consequently, to his own fate. Those were the people who formed the foundations of the regime, who had made Saddam's rise to absolutism possible, reaped abundant rewards in his service and risked losing all in the event of his demise. Many of them have played a highly visible role in the purges (Na'im Haddad, it may be recalled, headed the

special tribunal that ordered the notorious executions of 1979);
most of them, it has been rumored, have picked up a rifle and
joined Hussein on firing squads.

The links binding Iraq's ruling clique to Hussein were further
tempered during the Iran-Iraq War. Mindful that they, too, and
not only their master, had been singled out as enemies by the
clerics in Tehran, and well aware of the merciless retribution
meted out by Hussein for indecisiveness in those fateful days, the
inner circle rallied more closely than ever around the only person
who, in their view, could save the day.

No one knew better than Tariq Aziz the dire consequences an
Iranian victory would mean for him and his associates, following
his narrow escape from an assassination attempt in April 1980.
The gray-haired, soft-spoken politician who since 1983 has held
the post of Foreign Minister in addition to that of Deputy Prime
Minister, is widely regarded as the moderate face of the regime.
This image, however, owes more to Aziz's articulation and fluency
in English (he holds a B.A. in English language and literature
from Baghdad University) than to the substance of his message. A
Christian in a Muslim administration, he is largely a creature of
Saddam, attending carefully to his master's voice and amplifying
his wishes and views. A well-known joke in diplomatic circles in
Baghdad tells that during a late-night meeting of the RCC,
Saddam turned to Aziz and asked him what hour it was. "Whatever hour you like, Mr. President," came the answer.

During the early 1970s, as Chief Editor of the Party's organ,
al-Thawra, Aziz put the newspaper at Saddam's disposal, playing a
crude role in building up the latter's public image and sanctioning
the ruthless actions of his security services. When in 1969 the
West expressed its indignation at the ghastly scenes attending the
hanging of Jews in Baghdad, Aziz retorted vehemently: "One
should not think that the hundreds of thousands of people who
enjoyed going out to look at the hanged bodies, are barbaric or
primitive. This would be an injustice and also a false impression.
That event was a monument of confidence staged by the revolution in the most important square in Baghdad to prove to the
people that what had been impossible in the past was now a fact
that could speak for itself."[27] A decade later, when the communists were purged in large numbers, Aziz proved equally ruthless.
"There is no need for a Communist Party in our country," he said.
"If the communists want to become martyrs, we will oblige
them."[28]

Aziz's predecessor in the Foreign Ministry, Sa'dun Hammadi, is a somewhat more agreeable person. One of the founding fathers of the Iraqi Ba'th, the elderly Shi'ite is the only person in Saddam's coterie who has been exposed to Western education (in 1957 he obtained a Ph.D. in agricultural economics from the University of Wisconsin). Yet, he has showed no indication throughout his career that this experience increased his openness to democratic ideals. Since the early 1970s he has devotedly backed Hussein, helping him carry out his policies from the influential post of Foreign Minister, to which he was appointed in 1974. In 1983 he resigned from the Foreign Ministry for health reasons but remained Deputy Prime Minister, a member of the RCC and the President's trusted advisor on economic affairs. In these capacities, he was the person assigned the delicate task of pressuring the Kuwaitis, during the year preceding the invasion, to forgive their wartime loans to Iraq and to agree to subsidize his country's economic reconstruction.

While Aziz and Hammadi speak softly for the regime, Taha Yasin Ramadan carries the big stick. A graduate of the Baghdad Military Academy in 1958, he was dismissed from the army because of his Ba'th leanings and became a bank clerk. His close association with Saddam dates back to the mid-1960s, when he assisted him in establishing the Party militia, which he came to command several years later.[29] Like his benefactor, Ramadan is well-practiced in anti-Western, nationalistic rhetoric and, unusual among those surrounding Hussein, is endowed with personal charisma. This quality has enabled him to build up a certain power base, as evidenced by his position as First Deputy Prime Minister. Yet it also drove Hussein to take much care to keep him on a short leash. Saddam's treatment of Ramadan is vividly illustrated by the following story. "Just before the end of the Iran-Iraq War, the President decided that all fat Iraqis should diet. Cabinet ministers had their actual weights and target weights published in the press, with exhortations to measure up—and fast. The corpulent Mr. Ramadan had to lose more than 60 pounds—and he did."[30]

Another harsh voice in Saddam's close entourage is that of the Minister of Information and Culture, Latif Nusseif Jasim. A fifty-year-old Shi'ite from the small town of Rashidiya in the Baghdad province, Jasim joined the Ba'th Party in 1957 at the age of 16, and had a spell of prison life in the mid-1960s under the Arefs' regime. In 1974 he became Director General of the state

radio and television, a position which he used in order to build up
the public image of his patron—Saddam Hussein. He was generously rewarded for his services. Upon Saddam's ascent to the
Presidency, he was promoted to the important post of Minister of
Information, which he has held ever since. He played a key role
during the Kuwait crisis, amplifying his master's messages to the
world. His domestic face is even harsher than his international
image. Iraqi political exiles have often been taken aback by his
rude language and the poor Baghdadi dialect he uses. "What a
low ebb Iraq plunged to if such a person can be Minister of
Information and Culture," sighed one of them.[31]

Hussein's personal experience has also led him to deal cautiously with his official number two, Izzat Ibrahim al-Duri. Bearing
in mind his own success in using the Deputy Chairmanship of the
Revolutionary Command Council as a springboard to absolute
power, Hussein has kept his deputy an essentially ceremonial figure, denying him any real hold on the levers of power. Unlike
Hussein, whose portrait appears on every corner, Izzat Ibrahim
remains a largely anonymous figure; rarely do his subjects see him
on television, hear him on the radio or read his speech in the press.
This must not have been too difficult a task, for Ibrahim's main
asset has been his dogged devotion to his superior. A rather in-
troverted person who, prior to the Ba'thist takeover, made his
living by selling ice blocks, the red-haired, 50-year-old Deputy has
never had any ambitions beyond his present post. His failing health
has also made him an unlikely challenger to Hussein's power.
Ibrahim's value for Hussein is his religious piety, which has made
him the Ba'th's main negotiator with Iraq's Shi'ite clergy.

Their political prominence and material affluence notwithstanding, Hussein's closest dependents have always found themselves
between Scylla and Charybdis. They have staked their political
future, indeed their lives, on the success of Hussein's policies,
while exercising virtually no influence on his major decisions.
Were he to be deposed, they would most likely go down with him;
should they over-achieve in his service, he would reap the fruits of
their labors, while they would be left to count their blessings at not
being purged for their successes. At most, Hussein's inner circle
has served as an echo chamber, amplifying his wishful thinking
and backing those political options it believes he is inclined to
adopt.

Police states do not make a habit of divulging information about their decision-making process. Evidence of what actually happens in the dark corridors of power must be gathered from second- and third-hand sources. Often it is flimsy. However, as far as can be ascertained, no one in Iraq's political leadership contested Hussein's decision to take on the aged Ayatollah Khomeini in September 1980. Rather, the inner circle rallied sheep-like around their leader during the tense year preceding the war. When Hussein hoped to contain the Iranian threat without going to war, his associates backed him wholeheartedly; once he had made up his mind to resort to arms, they quickly forgot their previous moderation and insisted on the advantages of invading Iran.

As with other megalomaniacal leaders such as Nicolae Ceausescu and the latest Shah of Iran, Muhammud Reza Pahlavi, who were only told what they wanted to hear, Hussein's judgment of the real world has been fundamentally distorted by the Byzantine atmosphere of flattery and self-abasement surrounding him. In a cabinet meeting in November 1989, according to a broadcast by the state-controlled radio, he boasted that were he to sell pebbles in the streets of Baghdad, "a thousand Iraqis and foreigners may be there to offer one million dinars for one single pebble, and tell him: 'Saddam Hussein, you are carrying a gem, not a pebble, without knowing.' "[32]

In non-democratic systems, force is the main agent of political change. Hussein knows this only too well, and he has spared no effort to transform the military into an "ideological force," loyal only to him. The general guiding principles for such an "ideological army" were already laid down in 1974 by the Eighth Congress of the Ba'th:

> From the earliest days, the Party had urgently to tackle two basic tasks. The first was to consolidate its leadership in the armed forces; to purge them of suspect elements, conspirators and adventurers; to cultivate pan-Arab and socialist principles among the soldiers; to establish the ideological and military criteria which would enable the armed forces to do their duty as well as possible and would immunize them against the deviations which the Qassem and Aref regimes and their military aristocrats had committed in the army's name; and thus to integrate the armed forces with the people's movement, directed by the Party.[33]

Accordingly, scores of party commissars have been deployed within the armed forces down to the battalion level. Organized political activity has been banned; "unreliable" elements have been forced to retire, or else purged and often executed; senior officers have been constantly reshuffled to prevent the creation of power bases. The social composition of the Republican Guard, an elite corps within the army which made the Ba'th takeover possible and has ensured its survival ever since, has been fundamentally transformed to draw heavily on conscripts from Tikrit and the surrounding region.

Like his archenemy, the revolutionary regime in Tehran, Hussein has sought to counterbalance the military through a significant expansion of the Party's militia, the Popular Army. Established in the late 1950s as a para-military organization, the militia (then called the National Guard) played a key role in the overthrow of Qassem in 1963 and in buttressing the first Ba'th regime. It was reorganized in the late 1960s by Saddam Hussein as part of the security apparatus he established. Though transformed into a more orderly military force since the mid-1970s, the Popular Army has never been subordinated to the armed forces. Rather, it has served as the Party's main vehicle for rallying the masses behind the regime and suppressing actual and potential opposition. The Popular Army has its own recruitment and training infrastructure, and militia members are thoroughly indoctrinated during their two-month annual training period. To encourage volunteering for the militia, employers are reimbursed by the authorities for the absences of employees, and students are exempted from their studies.[34]

Within less than a year after Saddam's seizure of absolute power in 1979, the Popular Army was more than doubled—from 100,000 to 250,000 men. During the Iran-Iraq War it was to become an ominous force some one-million strong, using heavy weaponry and participating in some of the war operations.[35] This has by no means put the Popular Army on a par with the professional military, which continues to enjoy far superior equipment and training. Yet, by denying the latter monopoly over the state's means of violence, it has widened the regime's security margins against potential coups.

Thus, through sustained effort, Hussein has created a docile and highly politicized military leadership, vetted and promoted on the principle of personal loyalty and kinship rather than on professional excellence. Consequently, when the Iran-Iraq War

broke out in September 1980, the military was no more courageous than the politicians, challenging neither Hussein's war
strategy, which made little military sense, nor his conduct of the
war operations.

The first rumblings of discontent from the military with the
over-centralized control of the war came in the summer of 1982,
when Iraq was already defending its own territory against Iran's
human wave attacks. Although this feeble criticism did not reflect
any organized opposition within the ranks of the military, Hussein took no chances. Some 300 high-ranking officers were
executed, along with a small number of Party officials; others
were purged. It was reported that Hussein himself executed an
officer who ordered a tactical retreat. According to the story, the
hapless officer was thrown in front of his Commander-in-Chief,
who calmly drew his pistol and shot the man in the head.[36] Word
of this decisive act, which occurred at about the same time that
Hussein was said to have murdered his Minister of Health, sent a
clear signal to the military. To dissent was to commit suicide.

This time, however, Saddam went out of his way to accompany
the use of the stick with a generous resort to the carrot. Mindful
that exclusive reliance on terror could demoralize the military and
undermine the successful prosecution of the war, he sought to
gain the hearts of the officer corps through a series of inducements. To reward professional competence, he personally conferred numerous medals and decorations on the military. Those
who distinguished themselves in combat and won three medals
became members of the honorific "club" of "Saddam Hussein's
friends." This prestigious affiliation entailed many material benefits on top of the substantial plot of land given to any recipient of
a decoration.

By way of demonstrating his solidarity with the armed forces
and underscoring his close involvement in military affairs, Saddam began to pay regular and widely publicized visits to the front
lines. The military leaders, for their part, were given greater
exposure in the Iraqi media, and the high command was incorporated into a process of an apparently collegial decision making
with the political leadership.[37]

This marriage of convenience between Saddam and his generals lasted until 1986 when it was marred by an impressive series
of Iranian victories. The public nature of the Iraqi setbacks—
particularly the fall of the Fao Peninsula in February 1986 where
Iraq lost 10,000 soldiers in one week, and the failure to compen-

sate for this loss by the occupation of the Iranian town of Mehran four months later—led to bitter recriminations between Saddam and his leading generals. For the first time in his career, Saddam was confronted by what nearly amounted to an open mutiny. With the Iranian army at the gates of Basra, the military leadership rose up in an attempt to force Hussein to win the war despite himself. They did not demand political power. Nor did they try to overthrow the leader who had divided, intimidated, and battered them for nearly two decades. All they wanted was the professional freedom to run the war according to their best judgment, with minimal interference from the political authorities.

Perhaps the most vivid illustration of this "rebellious" state of mind is offered by the oft-repeated story of Hussein's clash in the winter of 1986 with his kinsman and son's father-in-law, General Maher Abd al-Rashid. According to the story, Rashid was ordered to report back to Baghdad following his failure to dislodge the Iranian forces from the Fao Peninsula, and his candid admission in an interview with the Kuwaiti press of high casualties on the Iraqi side. Well aware what the order meant, Rashid's officers transmitted a warning to Hussein, implying that they would refuse to prosecute the war should anything happen to their Commander. On arriving at the Presidential Palace, Rashid was decorated by a beaming Hussein, who deferred vengeance until later.[38]

The officers' exceptional determination to stand up to Saddam saved Iraq from disaster. Threatened by military defeat, Hussein grudgingly gave in to his Generals (though not without instantly purging their ranks). His concession led to a series of Iraqi successes that culminated in Tehran's agreement to a cease-fire after eight years of fighting.

Yet, in retrospect it can be seen that the Generals apparently missed an ideal opportunity to settle accounts with Hussein at one of the lowest points in his career. Had they tried to topple him, their success would by no means have been a foregone conclusion; but their chances of achieving this objective were better than on any other occasion during the previous two decades. Having failed to seize the moment, Hussein moved swiftly to reap the fruits of victory and wipe out any traces of his "indecisiveness." The Iraqi victories were presented as yet another product of his great leadership whereas those who had actually made this achievement possible, first and foremost, Generals Abd al-Rashid and Fakhri, faded into obscurity, if not into physical demise.

The end of the Iran-Iraq War in the summer of 1988 ushered in a new stage of Hussein's relations with the military. The belief, common in the military, that avoiding any taint of political activity provided some insurance against the whims of the Saddam regime was shattered by the purges of the heroes of the war against Iran. However, Hussein's concessions to the military during the war proved that even he was not invincible.

Hussein's ceaseless quest for survival was not yet over. The repressive system he had so laboriously constructed over a long period of time might still crack under certain conditions. His main instrument of national repression, the Ba'th Party and its security services, remained fully subservient to his wishes. His control over his subjects had been equally tightened during the eight-year war, due to a mixture of terror, a massive indoctrination into Saddam's personality cult, economic inducements and—above all—fear of the Iranian enemy. Yet, Saddam's grip over the officer corps, the main potential threat to his personal rule, had been somewhat loosened. During the Iran-Iraq War the Iraqi armed forces had expanded to an unprecedented size. A new generation of professional and combat-hardened commanders was evolving. Their loyalty to Saddam's person was still guaranteed through the political control mechanisms in the military, personal opportunism, and occasional purges; however, it could not be taken for granted in the long run unless new and more sophisticated means for controlling them were developed.

One such means of control could be the engagement of the military ranks in a venture abroad that would satisfy their yearning for national gratitude (for saving Iraq from the Iranian threat), while keeping them at a safe distance from the locus of power in Baghdad. And what constituted a more suitable target for such a venture than Kuwait, Iraq's tiny neighbor to the south, whose independence had been repeatedly contested by Baghdad, and whose fabulous riches could finance the ambitious economic programs on which Hussein's political survival hinged. Given these organizational and economic considerations, another violent stage in Saddam Hussein's incessant struggle for personal control and political survival seemed only a matter of time.

9

The Road to Kuwait

For Ayatollah Ruhollah Khomeini, the end of the Iran-Iraq War was tantamount to drinking from the poisoned chalice. For Saddam Hussein, it was the elixir of life. After all, had he not managed to emerge unscathed from eight years of savage struggle for survival against a fanatic enemy who had openly demanded his head? In the summer of 1988 Iran was debilitated; Iraq's military power was greater than ever, having steadily expanded during the war. In Tehran an agonizing reckoning was already under way; in Baghdad millions were dancing in the streets.

Yet not even such euphoric circumstances would lure a professional survivor like Hussein into a false sense of security. He had no illusions whatsoever, realizing that the celebrations would give way to a hangover; that a bill for the dislocations of the war would be presented in one form or another. He knew that even in the most repressive police state there are limits to what people are willing to endure or the sacrifices they are prepared to make. The removal of the Iranian threat, the main factor cementing Iraqi society during the war years, generated an urgent need for new means of rallying public support and enthusiasm behind Saddam. In terms of his political survival, the war may have ended, but the domestic battle for hearts of the Iraqis may have only just begun.[1]

Paradoxically, Hussein's strategy in this latest struggle for political survival seemed to betray his own self-interest. Had he

194

presented his subjects with a somber analysis of the situation, explained the consequences of the war's termination and called for a national effort to reconstruct the damage wrought by the "brutal Persians," popular sentiment might have been effectively harnessed to the government's policy. Instead, fearful as ever about projecting the slightest sign of weakness, he chose to present the end of the war as a momentous triumph of both Iraq and the Arab nation. This, in turn, created a wave of popular expectations for a tangible improvement in fortunes which Hussein would find impossible to deliver.

The most extravagant demonstration of the alleged Iraqi victory was the imposing *arc de triomphe* which appeared in central Baghdad in the immediate wake of the war. It consists of two pairs of giant crossed swords, held by huge bronze fists embedded in concrete. Not surprisingly, the sense of power and grandiosity embodied by the monument has been inextricably linked to Hussein: the fists holding the sabers were actually modeled on those of the Iraqi President.[2] Indeed, if Hussein's personality cult during the war was preposterous even by Middle Eastern standards, it was to be surpassed after the cessation of hostilities as the manipulation of Iraq's Mesopotamian legacy was carried to unprecedented heights in the service of his rule.

In 1989 Hussein held official burial ceremonies for the remains of the Babylonian kings and built new tombs on their graves. At the same time a hectic reconstruction of Babylon was under way. Whole sections of ancient ruins were razed to give way to yellow bricked walls; tens of thousands of bricks bore a special inscription reminding future generations that "the Babylon of Nebuchadnezzar was rebuilt in the era of the leader President Saddam Hussein." A $1.5 million prize was promised to the architect who would re-create the Hanging Gardens of Babylon, one of the Seven Wonders of the Ancient World.[3]

In a sinister shift in direction which took both Iraqis and foreign observers of Iraq by surprise, Saddam enrolled the Hashemite monarchy which ruled Iraq until 1958 in his effort to inscribe his name among former illustrious and aristocratic leaders. The ill-fated dynasty, whose last monarch's body was dragged through the streets of Baghdad by a rampaging mob, suddenly gained legitimization and respectability. No longer were the Hashemites branded as British lackeys and servants of world imperialism; instead, Faisal I, the "founding father" of modern Iraq, was lauded as a "giant Arab nationalist," and the monarchy described by Iraqi

officials as "a symbol of Iraqi unity and continuity." The royal
cemetery containing the remains of the Hashemite kings was ren-
ovated at a cost of $3.2 million, and a bronze statue of Faisal I was
returned to its pedestal in central Baghdad.[4]

The apparently inexplicable rehabilitation of the monarchy
generated a flurry of speculations that Hussein was paving the
way for the restoration of monarchical rule with himself as king
and was grooming his eldest son, Udai, as his heir apparent.
These rumors were fueled both by the building of a new palace,
envisaged by Hussein as the "new wonder of the world that would
overshadow the Pyramids," and by his claim of blood relatedness
to the Prophet which also made him a relative of the Hashemites.

It is not at all clear whether Hussein has ever entertained such
royal aspirations. Had he toyed with the idea of creating a new
dynasty he apparently gave it up, at least temporarily, in the fall
of 1988 when Udai, the heir apparent, was exiled to Switzerland
after killing his father's food taster. In any event, by restoring the
Hashemites and their former glory in Iraqi political consciousness
and implying his continuation of their line, Hussein clearly put
himself above the Ba'th Party and shed his earlier images of a
sober, committed socialist and an ascetic, modest ruler. These
were replaced by an assumed air of grandeur and pomp. Hussein
was not simply another great leader. He was the living embodiment of Iraqi history, from Babylonian to Hashemite rule. The
assumption of this weighty historical and noble legacy seemed to
assert to his people and the world that his rule was predestined
and inviolable, part of a multi-millennial chain.

Just as Hussein has cultivated Iraq's Mesopotamian identity at the
expense of the sacred Ba'thist ideal of Arab nationalism, so he has
subordinated the Party's other article of belief, "socialism," to
short-term considerations of political expediency. The liberalization of the Iraqi economy, begun in the mid-1970s, gained
considerable momentum during the war. In 1983 the regime gave
its blessing to the privatization of agriculture, and four years later
Hussein officially announced that the private sector would be
encouraged to play an active role in the economy alongside the
state sector. Subsidies were lifted across the board, with the
exception of some basic items.

Although the main beneficiaries of this policy were the
entrepreneurs who made huge sums of money, the relatively
uninterrupted supply of foodstuffs to Baghdad during the war

was indispensable for Hussein's effort to insulate his population against the effects of the conflict. It was only natural, therefore, that he would assign the private sector an important role in the postwar economic reconstruction of Iraq, hoping that its more dynamic nature would help revive the debilitated economy. Consequently, many state-owned corporations were sold off to the private sector at very attractive prices, and there was much talk about the eventual privatization of all state enterprises except oil and military supplies. Price controls on all goods were lifted. Iraqis with (illegal) accounts abroad were encouraged to open import business accounts, no questions asked. An attempt was made to attract capital from Gulf states and foreign, mainly Western, companies, and $2 billion worth of import licenses were issued to private enterprises. Far-reaching economic ideas such as the formation of an Iraqi stock exchange and the privatization of the banking sector were circulated.[5]

To many external observers these measures seemed more serious than similar actions in the past since they were accompanied by unprecedented indications of an openness to change on Hussein's part, designed to prove to the Iraqi public that the end of the war had ushered in a truly new era. In an address to the Iraqi Bar Association on November 27, 1988, three months after the cessation of hostilities, he announced a general pardon to political prisoners and pledged to establish a democratic multi-party system in Iraq. A month later he started floating the idea of a new constitution that would arrange for direct elections to the Presidency, allow the formation of opposition parties and a free press, and provide for the dismantling of the Revolutionary Command Council. To underscore the seriousness of his intentions, in January 1989 Hussein convened a joint meeting of the RCC and the RC which endorsed his proposals for political reforms and set up a special committee to draft a working paper on a new constitution.[6]

In April 1989 the Iraqis went to the polls for the third time since 1980 to elect a new National Assembly. As in the past, flocks of western journalists were flown into the country so they could observe the flourishing "democratic process" firsthand. At the same time, the Arab press was being recruited to Saddam's propaganda campaign through a very direct and extravagant technique: leading editors in Egypt, for example, reportedly received "spanking new red, white, blue and light brown Mercedes Benz 230 cars. . . . Lesser figures received Toyotas."[7] Much was made about the fact that non-Ba'thists were free to stand for election and that half of the elected representatives were defined as "independent." What the authorities did not emphasize, though, was that people defined as "dangerous to the state" were not allowed to submit their candidacy.[8]

Other signs of political relaxation followed suit. At the University of Baghdad a "Freedom Wall" was established where students were supposed to air their grievances. The state-controlled media began to carry a considerable number of public complaints about difficulties in daily life, such as high prices and petty incidents of corruption. This, in turn, enabled the Minister of Information and Culture, Latif Nusseif al-Jasim, to declare proudly that "there is no censorship in Iraq. No person is asked about what he has written. The only limitations relate to issues of national security."[9]

The ostensible "democratization" of the Iraqi polity was not solely motivated by domestic political considerations. Nor was it mainly aimed at laying the political infrastructure for the liberalization of the economy. It was equally targeted at the West in an attempt to improve the image of Iraq's human rights record, particularly in view of public indignation about the atrocities against the Kurds which were taking place at the time.

As in 1975, the Kurds were the main victim of the new Iraqi-Iranian understanding. With the Iranian threat to his personal rule removed, Hussein turned against the Kurds with great ferocity. It appeared that he had made up his mind to impose his "final solution" on the Kurdish independence movement and to eliminate any remnants of Kurdish national aspirations. Within a couple of months after the end of the war, some 65 Kurdish villages came under chemical attack. No fewer than 5,000 people perished in the "winds of death," while 100,000 fled in the direction of the Turkish and Iranian frontiers. The lucky ones among these refugees managed to cross the border and were given temporary shelter by the local authorities. The less fortunate ones were captured by the Iraqis and divided into male and female groups: the women were sent to detention camps in Kurdistan whereas the men "disappeared," that is, were most probably executed. Within a year the number of Kurdish refugees in Turkey and Iran grew to 250,000, while a similar number were forcefully "relocated," either to the large Kurdish community in concentration camps in the western desert or to special hamlets built by the regime in western Kurdistan.[10]

The plight of the Kurds aroused an international wave of public sympathy and confronted Hussein with severe criticism. The U.S. Congress voiced vocal support for sanctions against Baghdad, while the European Parliament condemned Iraq and called for a community ban on all weapons deliveries to that country. Madame Danielle Mitterrand, the French President's wife, issued an emotional plea for support following a visit to Kurdish refugees in Turkey in May 1989.[11]

Hussein was surprised and irritated by the intensity of the international response. Dismissing this criticism as a "Zionist plot" to discredit Iraq after its "glorious victory" over Iran, he launched a propaganda campaign aimed at portraying the relocation of the Kurds as a humanitarian act.[12] "Throughout modern history, many states have removed parts of their population from a certain area for civil or military reasons," ran the Iraqi argument. "Why, then, does the world focus on Iraq?" Moreover, he argued, the relocation of the Kurds was a humanitarian issue: "Iraq is clearing the border strip of the entire population, including Kurds and others living there to protect them from the threat of additional Iranian bombardments."[13]

Whether or not the contrived Iraqi rationale had any impact on its intended audience, Hussein was greatly relieved to realize that the moral condemnation of public opinion was not matched by the political actions of the respective governments. In the United States the drive in the Congress toward sanctions was effectively obstructed by the Administration. In France, at the time when Madame Mitterrand was emotionally pleading on behalf of the Kurds, scores of businessmen were bidding at the international military hardware fair in Baghdad for lucrative arms contracts. Similarly, while the then British Foreign Minister, Sir Geoffrey Howe, criticized Iraq's treatment of the Kurds, Trade Minister Tony Newton doubled British export credits to Iraq from 175 million in 1988 to 340 million in 1989. A feeble request by the United States, made in collaboration with Britain, West Germany and Japan, that the UN Secretary-General send a special team on a fact-finding mission to Kurdistan, was easily side-stepped by Iraq. Another Western attempt to condemn Iraq at the UN Human Rights Commission for the use of chemical weapons against the Kurds met a similar fate. Finally, in their eagerness to defuse the escalation with Iraq, the Western powers contented themselves with Hussein's pledge not to use chemical weapons in the future, forgoing the convening of the Security

Council to discuss the issue.[14] It was clear that lucrative financial gains had superceded moral imperatives.

Another major consideration working in Hussein's favor vis-à-vis the West was the continuation of his seemingly cooperative policies toward his neighbors. Not only did he not revert to his pre-war "rejectionist" rhetoric but he sustained and expanded collaboration with the moderate Arabs in an attempt to orchestrate them into a unified bloc that would resist Iranian hegemony, promote the Palestinian cause, and pressure Syria. This objective was crowned with success in February 1989 with the formation of the Arab Cooperation Council (ACC), comprising Egypt, North Yemen, Jordan and Iraq. Although the raison d'être for the newly established bloc was economic, it was evident from the outset that it would address political affairs as well and would serve as a vehicle for the reassertion of Hussein's regional influence, albeit within a moderating framework. A month later, during an official visit to Baghdad by King Fahd of Saudi Arabia, a bilateral non-aggression pact was concluded.

Hussein also played an important role, together with President Mubarak of Egypt, in sponsoring the PLO's historic recognition of Israel's right to exist in November and December 1988: had it not been for their readiness to shield the PLO from Syrian wrath, the Palestinians' political maneuverability would have been severely constrained. As in the past, however, Hussein's attitude toward the PLO was not so much dictated by compassion for the Palestinian cause as it was by the desire to improve his bargaining position vis-à-vis the hated Syrian President, Hafiz Asad.[15]

During the 1982 Lebanon War, in which Israel fought Palestinian and Syrian forces, relations between the Syrians and the Palestinians hit their lowest point. In the summer of 1983 Yasser Arafat was disgracefully expelled from Damascus in a clear display of Syrian indignation toward his leadership. Asad produced an armed revolt against Arafat's authority by pro-Syrian elements within al-Fatah, the PLO's main constituent organization. By November 1983 the rebels had managed to push Arafat's supporters from the Lebanese valley into Tripoli; a month later a humiliating evacuation of PLO forces from Lebanon took place— the second that year, though this time from Tripoli, rather than from Beirut, and under Syrian, rather than Israeli, pressure.

The rift between Syria and the PLO was a blessing in disguise for the Iraqi President, who did not fail to exploit this breach of Arab unity in order to extend his support of the Palestinian cause.

Thus, within less than a decade after engineering Abu Nidal's attempt on the life of the Israeli Ambassador in London which led to the outbreak of the Lebanon War and to the PLO's greatest military setback alongside the 1970 Black September, Saddam Hussein had effectively become the main "protector" of the Palestinian organization.

The burning desire to punish Asad for his "treacherous" support for Iran during the Iran-Iraq War manifested itself in other channels apart from the Palestinian one. Although Hussein publicly pledged in the wake of the war with Iran not to interfere in the domestic affairs of other Arab countries, his chieftain, Taha Yasin Ramadan, made it clear that this undertaking did not apply to Syria. "Has not the time come," he posed a rhetorical question, "to get rid of Hafiz Asad and his gangs in the interest of the Arab nation?"[16] Indeed, the fall of 1988 witnessed the beginning of an intensive Iraqi intervention in the Lebanese civil war in the form of financial and military support to General Michel Aoun, the self-styled Maronite President who declared "a war of liberation" to drive the Syrians out of Lebanon.[17]

Iraq's growing intervention in Lebanon led to the evolution of tacit collaboration with Israel. For, just as Syrian-Israeli hostility improved Hussein's standing vis-à-vis Asad, so did Iraqi-Syrian acrimony widen Israel's security margins. This collaboration was mainly expressed in Israel's abstention from intercepting Iraqi arms shipments to the Christians despite the ability of the Israeli navy to do so. There were also reports that the Israeli port of Haifa was used by Iraq as a transit station for shipping tanks and heavy equipment to General Aoun. In November 1988 Hussein stated his readiness to collaborate even with Israel for the "liberation of Lebanon from Syrian occupation," though this far-reaching statement (which was immediately retracted) passed virtually unnoticed.[18]

Neither Hussein's domestic efforts nor his international maneuvers could disguise the fact that Iraq had emerged from the war a crippled nation. The Iraqi economy was wrecked. Economic estimates put the cost of reconstruction at $230 billion.[19] Even if one adopted the most optimistic (and highly unrealistic) assumption that every dollar of oil revenues would be directed to the reconstruction effort, it would require nearly two decades to repair the total damage. As things stood a year after the termination of hostilities, Iraq's oil revenues of $13 billion did not even suffice to cover ongoing expenditures: with civilian imports approximating $12 billion (of which $3 billion was for foodstuffs), military imports exceeding $5 billion, debt repayments totaling $5 billion, and transfers by foreign workers topping $1 billion, the regime needed an extra $10 billion per annum to balance its current deficit, before it could embark on the Sisyphean task of reconstruction.

Iraq's $80 billion foreign debt was extremely disturbing for Hussein, since repayment arrears and the consequent reluctance of foreign companies and governments to extend further credits implied that economic reconstruction, on which Hussein's political survival hinged, would have to be shelved.[20] By way of addressing this problem, Hussein resorted to a variety of tactics: he dealt with his creditors separately, pitting one against the other and ensuring that they would not consolidate their interests. He also promised that those who showed the greatest generosity in extending credits would be favored in the award of contracts. In order to reduce expenditures and to secure jobs for the first demobilized soldiers returning to the labor market, Hussein began to squeeze out of Iraq two million migrant workers, mainly Egyptians, and slashed the remittances they were allowed to send home. These measures were to no avail; the burden remained unabated.

Domestic economic problems seemed equally ominous. Not only did the intensive privatization measures taken by Hussein since the late war years prove to be no panacea, they in fact created a severe backlash. The high expectations aroused among various groups of the society were only matched by soaring inflation, forcing Saddam to reintroduce price controls and to give the public its seasonal quota of scapegoats: in the spring of 1989 the Finance Minister, Hikmat Mukhalif, and the Acting Agriculture Minister, Abdallah Bader Damuk, were removed from their positions on grounds of incompetence.

These measures, nevertheless, only scratched the surface of the Iraqi economic malaise. The truth of the matter was that privatization had never stood any chance under Saddam Hussein. With the real reins of economic power—the oil industry which accounts for some 95 percent of Iraq's income—remaining in the hands of the state, there was no viable basis for the creation of a significant private sector. Moreover, given the repressive nature of the regime and its periodic convulsions, entrepreneurs were likely to remain wary of the system and would, therefore, try to

reduce their risks by investing the barest minimum in future
expansion and reaping as much profit as they could in the short
run. Like the Chinese, Hussein seemed to believe that economic
liberalization could work without real political reconstruction. In
both cases, the disillusionment of the leader proved agonizing for
the subjects. In China it assumed the form of the Tiananmen
Square massacre. In Iraq it constituted an important watershed
on Hussein's road to Kuwait.

Nor could Hussein provide his people with glowing foreign
successes: quite the reverse. Apart from the formation of the ACC
which boosted his prestige in the Arab World, Hussein's regional
policy soured. The clash he initiated with Syria in Lebanon
brought no results, as the maverick General Michel Aoun made
no headway toward his declared goal of "liberating Lebanon from
the Syrian occupation." Moreover, at the Arab summit in Casablanca in May 1989 Hussein suffered a public humiliation when
his proposal for the replacement of the Syrian military presence
in Lebanon by a genuine Arab League force was rejected in the
face of tough opposition by President Hafiz Asad.

More significantly, Hussein failed to make even the slightest
progress on the most important foreign policy issue: a peace
agreement with Iran. If Iraq did in fact win the war, as its people
were urged to believe, then the fruits of victory had to be formally
sealed, the hatchets officially buried. The 65,000 Iraqi prisoners
of war could then return to their families, alongside hundreds of
thousands of demobilized troops. Life would return to normal.
Reconstruction would be under way.

None of these things happened. The UN-orchestrated peace
talks in Geneva quickly ran into a blind alley as Iran would not
negotiate directly with Iraq; successive Iraqi initiatives using the
carrot and the stick led nowhere. In the lack of progress Hussein
was forced to look to his guns. His formidable army remained by
and large mobilized, costing the destitute Iraqi treasury a fortune.
The social consequences were no less worrisome. An entire
generation was being wasted: hundreds of thousands of young
conscripts who had been 18 when the war started were 26 by its
end and still under arms. They had no private life; they could not
study, they could not work and could not get married. Now that
war had been "won" they began questioning the necessity of their
continued mobilization. Hussein's attempt to defuse this seething
social problem by ordering partial demobilization in 1989 backfired, as it proved beyond the capacity of the shaky Iraqi economy

to absorb the huge numbers of young men pouring into the labor market.

By 1990, then, Hussein had probably begun to suspect that, as far as his personal position was concerned, the termination of the war might not have been the light at the end of the tunnel but rather, the tunnel at the end of the light. The nature of the threat to his regime had, of course, fundamentally changed. The mullahs in Tehran no longer demanded his downfall, at least not for the foreseeable future. Instead, he faced the potential risk of arousing the Iraqi people against him, should he fail to deliver the promised fruits of the "historic victory." An immediate economic breakthrough had thus become, literally, a matter of life and death.

On paper, the cure for Iraq's economic plight was strikingly simple: a decisive reduction in expenditures and a significant increase in revenues. In practice, however, the attainment of these goals was a far more difficult task which required heavy reliance on coercive diplomacy. Hussein did not flinch before such a challenge, especially since his political survival was at stake. During the war he had already pressured the Gulf states, Saudi Arabia and Kuwait, to forgive their loans to Iraq. The war had not been Iraq's private business, he told them, but, rather, a defense of the eastern flank of the Arab World against fundamentalist Islam. While the Gulf states were not asked to pay with rivers of blood for the protection of their own security, since Iraq did that on their behalf, they could not expect to take a "free ride" on Iraq's heroic struggle.

These pressures were significantly intensified in the postwar era. At a summit meeting of the Arab Cooperation Council in Amman in February 1990, celebrating the organization's first anniversary, Saddam asked King Hussein of Jordan and President Mubarak of Egypt to inform the Gulf states that Iraq was not only adamant on a complete moratorium on its wartime loans, but urgently needed an immediate infusion of additional funds, say, some $30 billion. "Let the Gulf regimes know," he added, "that if they did not give this money to me, I would know how to get it"; and this covert threat was accompanied by Iraqi military maneuvers in the neutral zone on the Kuwaiti border.[21] The message was immediately passed to Saudi Arabia by the Jordanian monarch.

Two months later President Mubarak had another firsthand

opportunity to learn the intensity of Hussein's yearning for cash. In a visit to Baghdad in early April, he was lectured yet again on the deplorable evasion by the Gulf states of their pan-Arab responsibilities. This time, however, Hussein took care to give public expression to his grievance. While denying any desire on his part to benefit from "Arab economic or financial capability" despite the "special economic circumstances which Iraq was undergoing," he argued that the Iran-Iraq War could have been shortened or even averted, had Iraq been more generously supported by the Gulf states. And by way of illustrating the nature of such possible support he said:

> For Iraq to maintain its national security, it requires for instance, 50 infantry and armored divisions in the ground forces alone. But if Iraq were part of overall pan-Arab security, it perhaps would need only 20 divisions, and the cost of the 30 other divisions could be used for economic development and for upgrading the standard of living of the Iraqi people. From this perspective, it does not hurt Iraq to earmark the cost of 5 of these 30 divisions for strengthening the national security of other fraternal Arab countries.[22]

Bullying the Gulf states into forgiving their loans and raising further contributions to the Iraqi treasury was only one aspect of Saddam's strategy. The other, and equally delicate component of this policy involved the manipulation of the world oil market to accommodate Iraq's financial needs. It is an elementary law of economics that excessive supply tends to depress prices while surplus demand has the opposite effect. Following the war, Iraq (as well as Iran) demanded that other members of the Organization of Petroleum Exporting Countries (OPEC) reduce their quotas in order to enable the former combatants to increase their own production without pushing prices down.

This demand was completely ignored. Even worse, instead of reducing their oil quota to make more room for increased Iraqi production, some OPEC members, most notably Kuwait and the United Arab Emirates (UAE), continued to exceed their quotas by far, putting a downward pressure on world oil prices. Since Hussein was intent on pushing oil prices up without relinquishing his plans for enhanced production, an immediate change in Kuwaiti and UAE policy became a matter of great urgency.

In a working visit to Kuwait in February 1990, the Iraqi Oil Minister, Isam Abd al-Rahim al-Chalabi, apparently pressured his hosts to abide by the new oil quota set by OPEC earlier that year. Then he proceeded to Riyadh to deliver a personal message from Saddam Hussein to King Fahd and to ask the Saudis to convince the rest of the Gulf states not to exceed their oil quotas. Three months later, during a meeting of OPEC ministers in Geneva, Chalabi reiterated the need to adhere to the organization's established production quota of 22 million barrels a day (MBD) and urged his counterparts to raise oil prices to $18 a barrel. The Iraqi First Deputy Prime Minister, Taha Yasin Ramadan, was far more outspoken in his criticism of quota violations, deploring such an act as "detrimental to Iraqi interests."[23]

If the Gulf states still had any illusions regarding the intensity of the Iraqi anxiety over the stability of the oil market, they were completely dispelled during the discussions at the Arab summit meeting in Baghdad in May 1990. In an extraordinary closed session with the visiting heads of state, Hussein put forth his grievances against the Gulf oil states in the harshest possible manner. "For every single dollar drop in the price of a barrel of oil," he told his guests, "our loss amounts to $1 billion a year. Is the Arab nation in a position to endure a loss of tens of billions, . . . especially as the oil markets, or let us say, the clients are, at least, prepared to pay up to $25 a barrel for the next two years, as we have learned or heard from the Westerners who are the main clients in the oil market?"

The answer to this question, in Hussein's opinion, was an unequivocal no. In his eyes, the continued violation of oil quotas by some Arab states amounted to a *declaration of war on Iraq*. "War," he said, "is fought with soldiers and much harm is done by explosions, killing, and coup attempts—but it is also done by economic means. Therefore, we would ask our brothers who do not mean to wage war on Iraq: this is in fact a kind of war against Iraq." "Were it possible," he concluded, "we would have endured. But I believe that all our brothers are fully aware of our situation . . . we have reached a point where we can no longer withstand pressure."[24]

Surprisingly enough, Kuwait and the UAE were unmoved by Hussein's uncharacteristically candid admission of weakness and his consequent blatant threat. While replacing his Oil Minister in a clear attempt to appease Saddam, the Emir of Kuwait would neither reduce oil production nor forgive his wartime loans to Iraq nor extend Baghdad additional grants. A Gulf tour in June 1990 by Dr. Sa'dun Hammadi, Hussein's chief economic advisor, as well as several tough warnings by Iraq's Oil Minister failed to bend Kuwait (and the UAE) into submission. Even a direct attack by Saddam on this policy as a "conspiracy against the region's economy which serves Israel directly" had no discernible impact.[25] It was only on July 10, during a coordination meeting of the Gulf oil ministers in Jedda, that the two states succumbed to combined Saudi, Iranian and Iraqi pressure and agreed to abide by their oil quotas.[26]

This concession, nevertheless, was too little too late. By that time Hussein was expecting far more from Kuwait. He probably had not yet made up his mind to invade the tiny principality, but he was certainly determined to extract substantial grants on top of a complete moratorium on war loans. Nothing less than that would satisfy him, particularly in light of the widespread international pressure which he faced at the time following the execution of Farzad Bazoft, an Iranian-born journalist working for the London weekly, the *Observer*. Bazoft was arrested in September 1989 while probing into a mysterious explosion in a secret military complex near Baghdad. In March 1990 he was put on trial on charges of espionage and executed shortly afterwards.

Why did Hussein execute Bazoft and thus set in motion a dangerous process of international escalation? The grim answer must be that Bazoft was yet another link in the long chain of victims of Hussein's paranoiac obsession with his personal and political survival. Since the cease-fire with Iran in July 1988 Hussein had escaped several attempts on his life. The first took place in November 1988 and reportedly involved a plan to shoot down Hussein's plane on his way home from a state visit in Egypt. Another attempt, which apparently took place in northern Iraq in late 1988 or early 1989, was ruthlessly suppressed with dozens, if not hundreds, of officers executed. The attempt was particularly worrisome for Saddam since it involved officers from the Republican Guard, his elite bodyguard force. A third coup attempt was aborted in September 1989, at a time when the Iraqi leader was hailed as a new Nebuchadnezzar at a national cultural festival in Babylon. Finally, in January 1990 Hussein narrowly escaped an assassination attempt by army officers while he was riding in his car through Baghdad.[27]

These incidents were sufficient on their own to ring the strongest alarms in the mind of the ever-vigilant leader. But coming against the backdrop of the collapse of the communist regimes in Eastern Europe, their impact was magnified several-fold. For the West, the historic events in Europe were a rare moment of spiritual uplift. For Saddam Hussein, like most Arab leaders, they were a development fraught with grave dangers. In his view, the decline of Soviet power and the disintegration of the Eastern bloc had deprived the Arab World of its traditional allies and had left the arena open for a U.S.-Israeli "dictate." It is an open secret that the fall of the Romanian dictator, Nicolae Ceausescu, who, like Hussein, had predicated his rule on a combination of fear and personality cult, was particularly trau-matic for the Iraqi leader. Whether or not he actually ordered the heads of his security services to study the videotapes of Ceauses-cu's overthrow, as has been widely claimed in the West, this event undoubtedly made him extremely wary.

Under these distressing circumstances, Hussein apparently reasoned that the execution of the British journalist Farzad Bazoft, despite pleas for clemency from the West, would send a resounding message to potential plotters that the Iraqi leader was as adamant as ever on exacting the ultimate price from "traitors." It was certainly not the first occasion he had resorted to such draconian measures. The exposure of fabricated plots and the punishment of their "perpetrators" had been one of Saddam's favorite methods of eliminating political dissent and deterring "treacherous conspiracies" against the regime. These ranged from the hanging of the "Zionist spies" in 1969, to the execution of his RCC colleagues in 1979, to the execution of the ill-fated Minister of Health in 1982. The execution of Bazoft, however, was different from these earlier executions in one crucial respect. The other victims were Iraqis, so that Hussein could keep the purges an internal Iraqi affair, whereas Bazoft's British affiliation unleashed an international response.

Whether Hussein might have avoided Bazoft's execution had he foreseen the intensity of Western indignation is difficult to say. It is clear, however, that Saddam's overriding preoccupation with his own survival and his meager understanding of the West resulted, not for the first or last time, in a gross underestimation of the Western response. How could he have imagined that the "lawful" execution of one foreign "spy" would arouse a far harsher international outcry than the fate of the entire Kurdish community?

The execution of Bazoft put Hussein under unprecedented

international "siege." Unlike the wave of criticism over the Kurdish issue two years earlier, the worldwide wave of public shock and indignation confronting Hussein was accompanied by a determined effort on the part of several Western governments to subvert his program of non-conventional weapons. Hussein's act against the British journalist had finally persuaded the West of the barbaric and arbitrary nature of his rule. On March 22, 1990, a Canadian ballistics expert, Dr. Gerald Bull, was assassinated in Brussels. Since Bull was involved in developing a "supergun" for Iraq that would supposedly be capable of launching non-conventional warheads for thousands of miles, the assumption was made by many that he was murdered by a Western security service, or possibly Israel's Mossad. Soon afterwards, the U.K. Customs confiscated eight Iraqi-bound large steel tubes, manufactured by a Sheffield company and believed to be destined to form the barrel of Dr. Bull's 40-ton "supergun." During the next few weeks other parts of the "supergun" were intercepted in Greece and Turkey.[28] Another blow to Iraq's non-conventional program was dealt on March 28, when a joint U.S.-U.K. Customs operation culminated in the seizure at Heathrow Airport of 40 electrical capacitors, sophisticated devices designed to be used as nuclear triggers.[29]

These actions were interpreted by Hussein as a smear campaign aimed at paving the way for military aggression against Iraq, a suspicion which was aggravated by his conviction that Israel would never allow any Arab state to blunt its technological edge.[30] More immediately, however, he feared that the massive influx of Soviet Jews into Israel would boost the self-confidence of the Jewish state and would lure it into military adventures beyond its frontiers.[31] Reports in the Western media at the time about secret meetings between Israeli and Syrian representatives in Europe were viewed by the Iraqi President as further indications of "a dangerous conspiracy" against Iraq.[32] In January 1990 he warned Israel that any attack on Iraq's scientific or military installations "would be confronted by us with a precise reaction, using the means available to us according to the legitimate right to self-defense."[33] A month later, during a visit to Baghdad, Ambassador Richard Murphy, former U.S. Assistant Secretary of State for Near Eastern and South Asian Affairs, was told by his hosts that they had reliable information of an imminent Israeli strike against Iraq's non-conventional arms industry, modeled on the 1981 attack on Iraq's Osiraq reactor.[34] A similar message was delivered to the British chargé d'affaires in Baghdad in late March, during his meeting with Iraq's Under Secretary of Foreign Affairs, Nizar Hamdoon.[35]

By early April the anxious Hussein had concluded that the only way to forestall the impending attack was to amplify his threat against Israel. In a speech on April 2 before the General Command of the Iraqi Armed Forces, he denied that Iraq sought to develop nuclear weapons as it was already in possession of what he argued to be equally destructive chemical weapons. However, he cautioned, the Western powers "will be deluded if they imagine that they can give Israel a cover in order to come and strike at some industrial metalworks. By God, we will make fire eat half of Israel if it tries to do anything against Iraq." "Yet," he added by way of underlining the purely defensive nature of his threat, "everyone must know his limits. Thanks be to God, we know our limits and we will not attack anyone."[36]

As in the case of the "Bazoft affair," the American (and Israeli) response to Hussein's threat ran counter to his initial expectations. Not only did it fail to take the heat off Iraq, but President Bush hurried to deplore the statement in strong words. Israel, ignoring the conciliatory part of the threat, was said to have hinted that an Iraqi chemical attack might be met by a nuclear response.[37] Yet Saddam's bellicosity proved useful from his point of view: it threw him into a position of regional prominence, as the Arab World unanimously hailed his "heroic stand against the Zionist machinations." In the following months, then, the Iraqi President would try to strike a delicate balance between the desire to translate his newly gained inter-Arab eminence into financial support for Iraq's economic needs and the wish to avert a regional conflagration.

The outcome was a rather incoherent policy combining blatant threats with attempts at appeasement. Hussein increasingly leaned on the vibrant pan-Arab rhetoric which he had essentially abandoned more than a decade earlier, expanding his "burn-Israel" pledge to cover potential Israeli aggression against any Arab state rather than against Iraq alone. However, he also took great pains to reassure decision makers in Jerusalem and Washington that his bellicose statements should not be construed "in the context of threats or demonstrations of power." "Iraq does not want war," he said, "it fought for eight years and it knows what war means." "Nor should it be assumed," he argued, that if the Arabs have a certain weapon, they will use it while others will not. We talked about using chemical weapons, should Israel threaten us or threaten any Arab nation militarily, including using nuclear weapons that it owns. . . . when anyone threatens us with aggression, or tries to raise slogans of aggression, against Iraq or any part of the Arab homeland, then it would be natural for the Arabs to say to him: "if you try to attack us, we will retaliate against your aggression with the weapons we have."[38]

This dialectical combination of impotence and omnipotence, of a deep economic plight and fears of an Israeli attack, on the one hand, and an undisguised air of self-importance, on the other, sealed the fate of Kuwait. In the permanently threatened mind of the Iraqi leader, where personal interests are nationalized and national affairs personalized, the Kuwaiti indifference to Iraq's desperate needs at a time when it faced an "imperialist-Zionist plot" amounted to "stabbing Iraq in the back with a poisoned dagger."[39] Conversely, full of his newly gained prominence, Hussein felt that he had gone out of his way to plead the Iraqi case and that further begging would only cause him (and, by extension, Iraq) public humiliation which he was unwilling to endure.

On July 16, the pressures on Kuwait were decisively stepped up. In a letter to the Secretary-General of the Arab League, the Iraqi Foreign Minister, Tariq Aziz, reiterated the accusation that Kuwait and the UAE had "implemented an intentional scheme to glut the oil market with a quantity of oil that exceeded their quotas as fixed by OPEC." According to Aziz, this policy had a devastating impact on the Middle East: "the drop in oil prices between 1981 and 1990 led to a loss of $500 billion by the Arab states, of which Iraq sustained $89 billion." To add insult to injury, Kuwait had directly robbed the Iraqi treasury by "setting up oil installations in the southern section of the Iraqi Rumaila oil field and extracting oil from it." In the Iraqi assessment, the value of the oil "stolen by the Kuwaiti Government from the Rumaila oil field in this manner that conflicts with fraternal relations" amounted to $2.4 billion.

While conceding that the Gulf states provided "various kinds of assistance" to Iraq during the Iran-Iraq War, Aziz argued that this support covered merely a small fraction of Iraq's tremendous costs. Moreover, "a simple calculation will show that the UAE and Kuwaiti loans to Iraq were not entirely from their treasuries but from the increases in their oil revenues as a result of the drop in

Iraqi oil exports over the war years." In order to rectify this behavior and to help Iraq recover from the dire economic plight that it now faced due to its defense of "the [Arab] nation's soil, dignity, honor and wealth," Aziz presented several demands: the raising of oil prices to over $25 a barrel; the cessation of Kuwaiti "theft" of oil from the Iraqi Rumaila oil field and the return of the $2.4 billion "stolen" from Iraq; a complete moratorium on Iraq's wartime loans; and the formation of "an Arab plan similar to the Marshall Plan to compensate Iraq for some of the losses during the war."[40]

A day later Saddam escalated the situation further. In an address to the nation on the twenty-second anniversary of the Ba'th "Revolution," he accused Kuwait and the UAE yet again of conspiring with "world imperialism and Zionism" to "cut off the livelihood of the Arab nation," threatening that Iraq would not be able to put up with such behavior for much longer, since "one would be better off dead than having one's livelihood cut off." The two states had therefore to come "back to their senses," he said, preferably through peaceful means. However, he cautioned, "if words fail to afford us protection, then we will have no choice but to resort to effective action to put things right and ensure the restitution of our rights."[41]

The substance of the Iraqi demands was not new. They had been presented to the Kuwaiti and Arab governments on several previous occasions. Yet by stating in public what had hitherto been said behind closed doors, Hussein had effectively crossed the Rubicon. He had committed himself to certain objectives in such a way that any compromise on his part would have been seen as a humiliating capitulation. In his view, there was no room left for bargaining or procrastination. Kuwait had to accept his demands in full or face the grave consequences.

Unfortunately, the Kuwaitis failed to grasp the seriousness of their situation. However startled they may have been by the harsh Iraqi rhetoric, they remained amazingly complacent, interpreting Saddam's demands as a bargaining chip rather than an ultimatum. The prevailing view within the Kuwaiti leadership was that surrender to such extortionist methods would only lead to unlimited demands in the future. They suspected that some concessions might be necessary, but were determined to reduce them to the barest minimum. They felt that military action could not be ruled out but believed that it was extremely unlikely, and that in the worst case it would be confined to a small disputed area such as

the Rumaila oil field and the Bubiyan and Warba islands, which in
the past Iraq had consistently sought to lease.[42] Thus, less than 24
hours after Saddam's speech, Kuwait had dispatched to the
Secretary-General of the Arab League a strongly-worded memorandum refuting the Iraqi accusations, and expressing strong
indignation at Iraq's behavior. This was not the way to treat a
sister country who had always been at the forefront of the Arab
national struggle, argued the message, the Iraqi "expressions are
out of line with the spirit of the existing fraternal relations
between Kuwait and Iraq, and conflict with the most fundamental
bases on which we all wish to govern our Arab relations. The sons
of Kuwait, in good as well as in bad times, are people of principle
and integrity. By no means will they yield to threat and
extortion."[43]

This defiant response was the last nail in the Kuwaiti coffin.
Not only was it taken by Hussein as a vindication of his long-
standing perception of Kuwait as a parasitic state thriving on
Iraq's heavy sacrifices, it was also viewed as a personal affront
made by a minor neighbor. In Hussein's opinion, the Kuwaitis did
not treat him (i.e., Iraq) with due respect, or take his word
seriously. They were playing their devious game of procrastination, believing that they could yet again evade their responsibilities
to Iraq. But not for much longer. As friendly persuasion would
not make Kuwait recognize its fraternal obligations, Iraq had no
choice but to take by force what belonged to it.

Apart from Hussein's sense of urgency and loss of patience
with the Kuwaitis, the temptations of the military option must
have seemed irresistible to the hard-pressed President. By adding
Kuwait's fabulous wealth to the depleted Iraqi treasury, Hussein
hoped to slash Iraq's foreign debt and launch the ambitious
reconstruction programs he had promised his people in the wake
of the war with Iran. Given Iraq's historic claim to Kuwait, its
occupation could enhance Hussein's national prestige by portraying him as the liberator of usurped Iraqi lands. Furthermore, the
capture of Kuwait could improve Iraq's access to the Gulf and
give it a decisive say in the world oil market. In short, in one
stroke Hussein's position would be permanently secured.

Once set on the military option, Saddam moved resolutely
forward. On July 21, against the backdrop of an exceptionally
virulent propaganda campaign against Kuwait, some 30,000 Iraqi
troops began moving in the direction of the joint border. Although this move was generally interpreted as saber rattling,

Egypt's President, Husni Mubarak, rushed to Baghdad where he was reassured by Hussein that he would not move against Kuwait before the exhaustion of diplomatic avenues. Yet, by now, the Iraqi President probably had little intention of negotiating. His public readiness to continue a dialogue with Kuwait was merely a smoke screen aimed at gaining international legitimization for the impending military action. The most important audience for this apparent delay was the United States.

Given his conviction that Moscow's irreversible decline from its superpower status had left the United States as the only power capable of jeopardizing his plans, either via direct intervention or through pitting its Israeli (or Arab) "lackeys" against Iraq, Hussein was anxious to harness tacit American support, or at least neutrality, for his Kuwaiti venture. He had reasonable grounds to anticipate such an attitude. Despite the harsh criticism of Iraq following the "Bazoft affair," the Bush administration did not fail to signal its keen interest in cultivating bilateral relations. When a group of five U.S. senators, headed by Robert Dole, visited Baghdad in mid-April, ostensibly to denounce Hussein's quest for chemical and nuclear weapons, they privately reassured the Iraqi leader that his problems were not with the American people but rather with its "haughty and pampered" press.[44] Later that month the U.S. Assistant Secretary of State for Near Eastern Affairs, John Kelly, sought to block a congressional initiative to impose sanctions on Iraq by telling the House's Foreign Affairs Committee that such a move would be counterproductive to U.S. national interest and that the administration would not "see economic and trade sanctions imposed at this point." Two months later he told the same committee that although Iraq had not relented in its quest for non-conventional weapons and continued to violate human rights, it nevertheless took "some modest steps in the right direction."[45]

The American double-talk continued throughout July. While responding to the concentration of Iraqi forces along the Kuwaiti border by deploying six combat vessels in the Gulf and deploring Iraq's coercive tactics, the Department of State took care to emphasize that the United States was not bound by a defense treaty to any of the Gulf states. The conciliatory policy toward Hussein was also sustained: a couple of days before the invasion the administration was still opposed to a Senate decision to impose sanctions against Iraq. Given these mixed signals, Hussein decided to secure his "American flank."

On July 25, he summoned the U.S. Ambassador to Baghdad, Ms. April Glaspie, to what was to become one of the most crucial, and controversial, milestones on Iraq's road to Kuwait. According to the Iraqi transcript of the meeting (the State Department has not released its own version, but neither has it challenged the authenticity of the Iraqi transcript) Hussein gave Ms. Glaspie a lengthy exposition of Iraq's economic plight and his grievances against the Gulf states. He accused the United States of supporting "Kuwait's economic war against Iraq" at a time when it should be grateful to Baghdad for having contained fundamentalist Iran. He then went on to threaten the United States with terrorist retaliation should it sustain its hostile policy against Iraq. "If you use pressure, we will deploy pressure and force," he said, "we cannot come all the way to you in the United States but individual Arabs may reach you."

Ignoring Hussein's bellicose rhetoric, Glaspie went out of her way to assure him of Washington's goodwill. His fears of an American conspiracy were completely unwarranted, she said: "President Bush is an intelligent man and he is not going to declare an economic war against Iraq." On the contrary, not only had the administration blocked successive attempts by the Congress to impose economic sanctions on Iraq but it fully understood Hussein's desperate need for funds and his desire for higher oil prices to strengthen Iraq's economy; indeed, many Americans from oil-producing states within the United States would like to see prices rising even further. When Hussein stated his determination to ensure that Kuwait did not cheat on its oil quota, Glaspie empathetically conceded that "my own estimate after 25 years of serving in the area is that your aims should receive strong support from your brother Arabs." This was an issue for the Arabs to solve among themselves, she continued, and the United States had "no opinion on inter-Arab disputes such as your border dispute with Kuwait . . . and Secretary of State Baker had directed our official spokesman to reiterate this stand."

When Glaspie dared at long last to ask Hussein "in the spirit of friendship, not of confrontation" what his intentions were regarding Kuwait, he reassured her of his preference for a peaceful solution to the dispute: "We are not going to do anything until we meet with [the Kuwaitis]. When we meet and when we see that there is hope, then nothing will happen." However, he stressed, since Kuwait's "economic war" was depriving "Iraqi children of the milk they drink," Iraq could not be expected to sit idle for much longer: "If we are unable to find a solution, then it will be natural that Iraq will not accept death, even though wisdom is above everything else."[46]

Whether or not Ambassador Glaspie voiced a remonstration of sorts against the use of force as a means of resolving the conflict, as a source familiar with her cable to the State Department has suggested, is immaterial.[47] Her servility in front of the Iraqi leader and the conciliatory language she used were construed by Saddam as an American "green light" for a move against Kuwait. After all, did he not tell the Ambassador that Iraq "will not accept death," and did not Glaspie express her empathy with Iraq's economic plight, as well as her government's neutrality toward the Iraqi-Kuwaiti conflict? And if there remained any doubts in his mind after the meeting concerning U.S. neutrality, they were probably dispelled three days later by a personal message from President Bush which, apart from describing the "use of force or the threat of using force" as "unacceptable," expressed his keen interest in improving relations with Baghdad.[48]

Apparently confident of American neutrality, Hussein proceeded to the last stage of his plan. On July 31, he gave Mubarak and Bush the promised political dialogue by sending the Deputy Chairman of the RCC, Izzat Ibrahim al-Duri, for negotiations with Kuwaiti representatives in the Saudi town of Jedda. Although the outcome of the meeting was probably irrelevant for Hussein, having already decided to invade Kuwait, the Kuwaitis certainly played into his hands by remaining as defiant as ever regarding Iraq's financial demands.[49] On August 1, the negotiations collapsed amidst a bitter exchange of accusations. Twenty-four hours later Kuwait was no longer a sovereign state. It had become the latest casualty of Saddam Hussein's ceaseless quest for survival.

10

Against the World

Thursday, August 2, 1990, was no ordinary day for the Iraqis. Those who rose early and bothered to turn on the radio, heard the announcer overtaken with excitement. "O great Iraqi people, pearl of the Arabs' crown and symbol of their might and pride," he rejoiced,

> God helped the liberals from among the honest ranks to undermine the traitorous regime in Kuwait, who is involved in Zionist and foreign schemes. The liberals from the sons of dear Kuwait appealed to the Iraqi leadership to provide support and backing to prevent any possibility [of takeover] by those who desire foreign interference in Kuwait's affairs and the end of its revolution. They have urged us to help restore security to spare the sons of Kuwait any harm. The Revolutionary Command Council has decided to respond to the request made by Kuwait's free provisional government and to cooperate with it on that basis, leaving citizens of Kuwait to decide their own affairs by themselves.

"We will withdraw when the situation becomes stable and when Kuwait's provisional government asks us to do so," he reassured his listeners, *this may not exceed a few days or a few weeks.*"[emphasis added][1]

This projection was, on the face of it, based on solid ground. The occupation of Kuwait was nothing like the agonizing invasion of Iran a decade earlier. It was a virtual walkover. In a lightning operation, 100,000 Iraqi troops and 300 tanks effectively crushed

217

the 16,000-strong Kuwaiti army, and gained control over the principality. The panic-stricken royal family just managed to escape the country in time.

Saddam was euphoric. He had carried out his pledge to teach the al-Sabah dynasty an unforgettable lesson. Kuwait was in the palm of his hand. A "provisional revolutionary government" had been declared. What was required at this point was to transform Kuwait into an extension of Iraq's will, though not necessarily through formal annexation and maintenance of a permanent military presence. Iraqi's strategic needs could be satisfied by the annexation of the Bubiyan and Warba islands, together with some territories along the joint boundary including the southern Ru- maila oil fields. Kuwait's financial subservience to Saddam's wishes would be guaranteed by an Iraqi-installed puppet regime. His domestic and regional position would be immeasurably enhanced and consolidated.

Saddam's euphoria, however, proved short-lived. The unpro- voked occupation of an unsuspecting neighbor aroused an un- precedented wave of international indignation. Within hours of the invasion, President George Bush imposed an economic em- bargo against Iraq and ordered the aircraft carrier *Independence* to move from the Indian Ocean to the Persian Gulf. All Kuwaiti and Iraqi assets and property in American banks and companies worldwide were frozen, and the movement of people and goods to and from Iraq was fully suspended. In an exceptional show of unity, the United States and the Soviet Union issued a joint condemnation of the invasion. An equally compelling consensus was demonstrated at the UN Security Council, where 14 of the 15 members, Yemen excluded, joined forces to pass Resolution 660 condemning the Iraqi occupation of Kuwait and calling for an immediate and unconditional Iraqi withdrawal.[2]

Events unfolded at an amazing pace. Against the backdrop of reports in the Western media about Iraqi troop movements toward the Saudi border, the European community and Japan followed the United States in imposing economic sanctions against Iraq, while the Soviet Union and China suspended all arms shipments. On August 6, the economic noose around Iraq was further tightened when the Security Council passed yet another measure, Resolution 661, ordering worldwide economic sanctions and an arms embargo on Iraq.[3] The following day Turkey shut off the Iraqi oil pipeline running through its territory.

Saddam was trapped. For him the invasion of Kuwait was not a matter of personal whim or greed. It was a measure stemming from dire necessity, a desperate bid to gain the vital financial resources on which his political future hinged. It was essential for his survival and thus, to him, a justifiable act. Moreover, he had taken all the necessary precautions to reduce the attendant risks of this step to the barest minimum: he had warned the Kuwaitis time and again not to continue their "economic conspiracy against Iraq." He had even sought, and in his view received, a "green light" from the United States for an action against Kuwait.

Now, all of a sudden, his scheme turned sour. Instead of the simple, straightforward operation he believed he had mounted, he found himself facing a nightmare scenario. It was no longer a conflict between Iraq and Kuwait but, rather, a feud between Iraq and almost the entire international community. Instead of securing survival for the foreseeable future, Saddam realized that he had just entered, perhaps, the most precarious stage in his career. From that moment onward, all his energies would be geared toward a single goal: emerging intact from the latest quagmire into which he had maneuvered himself.

Even a cursory examination of Saddam's political record would reveal that his instinctive inclination, whenever faced with overwhelming opposition, was to appease rather than to confront, to try to defuse tensions, rather than to escalate. His initial response to the buildup of international pressures following the invasion of Kuwait was no exception. While threatening to turn the Gulf into "a graveyard for those who think of committing aggression," he took great care to emphasize the temporary nature of the Iraqi intervention, reiterating his pledge to withdraw the Iraqi forces "as soon as the situation settles down and the evil grip is loosened on Arab Kuwait."[4]

Moreover, within less than 36 hours of the invasion, the Iraqi public learned, through a special announcement of the RCC, that their valiant armed forces had completed "their honest national and pan-Arab duties" of defending Kuwait, and were to begin withdrawing from the principality on August 5, "unless something emerges that threatens the security of Kuwait and Iraq." The deep anxiety underlying this hasty statement was vividly illustrated by its vehement denial that the decision to withdraw came in response to "the empty hubris voiced here and there by tendentious parties to whom we attach no weight at all"; it was equally visible from the Iraqi warning that any attack against Kuwait or Iraq would be "confronted by decisiveness that would sever its arm from its shoulder." On August 5, Iraq announced that the withdrawal had begun.[5]

A special emphasis in Saddam's conciliating campaign was placed on denying any possibility of an impending Iraqi act of aggression against Saudi Arabia. "Some news agencies have reported fabricated news about what they called the approach of Iraqi forces toward the Saudi border," read an official statement. "Iraq categorically denies these fabricated reports. Causing confusion between the Kingdom of Saudi Arabia, which is a fraternal country with which we have normal cordial relations, and Kuwait's case is tendentious."[6] This message was quickly conveyed to the heads of Arab states, Egypt and Saudi Arabia in particular, by high-ranking officials. More importantly, it was directly relayed to President Bush in an oral message from Saddam Hussein, transmitted at a meeting with the U.S. chargé d'affaires in Baghdad, Joseph Wilson, on August 6.

During the meeting, Hussein was far more affable than in his bellicose encounter with Ms. Glaspie a fortnight earlier. "Iraq is firmly willing to respect the United States' legitimate international interests in the Middle East," he told Mr. Wilson, "and is interested in establishing normal relations with the United States on the basis of mutual respect." Dismissing the reports on Iraqi military deployments along the Saudi border as fabrications, aimed at providing "pretexts to interfere in the region's affairs and to justify an aggression against Iraq," he reassured his interlocutor that Iraq harbored no evil intentions whatsoever against Saudi Arabia, with which it was tied in a bilateral treaty of non-aggression.[7]

Neither Saddam's reassurances nor the alleged beginning of the Iraqi withdrawal from Kuwait impressed the U.S. administration. On the contrary, in an extraordinary televised address to the American nation in the early morning hours of August 8, President Bush announced his decision to acquiesce in a Saudi request and to deploy U.S. troops to the desert kingdom in order to shield it from an imminent Iraqi attack. Labeling Hussein as an "aggressive dictator threatening his neighbors," Bush defined the four guiding principles behind his policy as the immediate, unconditional and complete Iraqi withdrawal from Kuwait; the restoration of the legitimate Kuwait government; the ensurance of Gulf security and stability; and the protection of the lives of American citizens abroad.[8]

The American decision to take irrevocable action and to commit itself to the restoration of the pre-invasion situation caused Saddam to shift his strategy. An immediate withdrawal from Kuwait was no longer a viable option. Withdrawal after the installment of a "liberal regime" in Kuwait that would ensure Iraq's economic and strategic interests there was one thing, but an unconditional pullout due to American pressure would be an admission of weakness and failure which he felt unable to afford. Any loss of face at this precarious moment, particularly when caused by an "infidel" Western power, was viewed as devastating to his position. To make things worse for Hussein, the Kuwaitis did not rise in large numbers to greet their self-styled liberators. Notwithstanding the immediate collapse of the Kuwaiti military, armed resistance continued throughout the principality. From a practical point of view, this resistance was merely a nuisance for the formidable Iraqi contingent. Yet its political consequences were far-reaching, for no other reason than that it sent an unmistakable signal to Hussein that his puppet regime stood no chance of survival, unless propped up by Iraqi bayonets. Under these circumstances of ongoing popular defiance in Kuwait and mounting international economic and military pressures, the Iraqi President felt that he had no alternative but to escalate by digging in and solidifying his position: on August 8 the Revolutionary Command Council announced the merger of Iraq and Kuwait.

If Saddam's mind had been set on the annexation of Kuwait from the outset, there was nothing in the references of the Iraqi state-controlled mass media at the time of the invasion to indicate it. Quite the reverse. The overthrow of the ruling dynasty in Kuwait was presented as an indigenous uprising, and the Iraqi intervention—as a temporary measure, of days or weeks at the most, aimed at shoring up the new "liberal regime" against external aggression. Indeed, the "satellization" of Kuwait, as opposed to its official incorporation into Iraq, made eminent sense for Saddam in that it would have given him everything he wanted from Kuwait without incurring the attendant risks from foreign intervention of an outright annexation.[9] Above all, an official annexation could always wait for a later, more suitable occasion, well after the initial storm had subsided.

As things developed, Saddam's script had to be re-written.

From as early as August 7, a change of heart in the Iraqi media could be detected. No longer was the intervention described as a short-lived step. Instead, it was argued that "Kuwait is part of Iraqi territory that was severed at some point in the past. The Iraqis and the Kuwaitis were one family united by a common destiny."[10] A day later, it was reported that the provisional government in Kuwait had "appealed to [their] kinfolk of Iraq—the valiant men of Qadisiya, the honorable, generous, chivalrous guards of the eastern gateway of the Arab homeland, led by the knight of the Arabs and the leader of their march, the hero leader President Field Marshal Saddam Hussein—to approve the return of the sons to their family, the return of Kuwait to great Iraq, the motherland." Naturally, the RCC agreed on August 8 "to return the part and branch, Kuwait, to the whole root, Iraq." Three weeks later, on August 28, Kuwait officially became the nineteenth province of Iraq.[11]

Whatever Saddam's original plans, he knew that with the annexation of Kuwait he had significantly raised the stakes for all parties, making it virtually impossible for him to back down unconditionally. What he apparently hoped to achieve by this brinkmanship was to convince the international coalition of the irreversibility of the situation, so as to weaken its resolve to confront the Iraqi aggression.

Since war could not help him in any way but would instead entail devastating consequences for his personal survival, Saddam went out of his way to discredit this option by underlining the horrendous nature of a military confrontation. "Death is better than humiliation and subordination to the foreigner," he warned. "The Iraqi people are capable of fighting to the victorious end which God wants [and] the blood of our martyrs will burn you."[12] This threat was amplified by Saddam's various chieftains, most notably the Minister of Information, Latif Nusseif Jasim. "If fire breaks out with an immense force now," he threatened, "the flames will reach the sky and sparks will fly in all directions. Heaps of corpses will be seen in the desert." In his view, there was no way the West could win such a war: "For us, death is an honor. We would be martyrs. As for them, they have no cause." "I would like to seize this opportunity," he concluded on a macabre note, "to warn foreign and U.S. pilots that they might be eaten up by the people when their aircraft are downed."[13] And to show the seriousness of these threats, chemical bombs were openly loaded and unloaded on Iraqi planes, a large-scale mobilization of reservists was declared and a sustained effort was launched to transform Kuwait into an impermeable military fortress.

These military preparations were accompanied by nationwide measures aimed both at strengthening the Iraqis' fighting spirit for their second Herculean military campaign within a decade, and at demonstrating the intensity of Iraq's resolve to resist the international pressures. "The Iraqis are ready to eat the soil and not to bow their heads to the aggressive invaders," Hussein declared emphatically.[14] Yet he did everything within his power to prevent his subjects from having to resort to such desperate means. In a personal call to Iraqi women "to reorganize the family's economic life," Saddam pleaded that they spend only on the necessary victuals and see that "the quantities of food placed in cooking pots and on the table only meet the needs of our new life."[15] Two months later, when his decision to ration gasoline and motor oil supplies aroused widespread discontent, he backtracked within days, sacking his Oil Minister on the grounds of providing him with false information. As in the Iran-Iraq War, Hussein was attempting to protect his home front from the privations of war (and now sanctions, too), in order to protect his political power base from domestic threats.

To ensure an orderly supply of basic foodstuffs, Saddam resorted to his tried technique of the "stick and the carrot." On August 11 he decreed that the hoarding of foodstuffs for commercial reasons would be considered "a crime and an act of subversion that affected national and pan-Arab security" and would, therefore, be punishable by death. A month later the RCC ordered the expropriation without remuneration of private agricultural lands which were not cultivated "in accordance with the scheduled agricultural density." At the same time, the authorities began to issue the population ration cards for the purchase of basic foodstuffs.[16]

Alongside these harsh measures, the Iraqi farmers were offered a series of incentives designed to induce them to increase their production. These included exemption of peasants from military reserve service and the duties of the Popular Army, permission to cultivate certain state-owned lands, reduction in the price of seeds and fertilizers, and higher financial returns for wheat, rice and barley bought from farmers. Campaigns were launched to encourage conservation and higher production, and competitions were held to develop indigenous substitutes for food

products. In accordance with Saddam's conviction that the future
lay with the young, the Iraqi children were exposed to a personal
indoctrination by their supreme leader on the merits of frugality:
"My beloved children of Iraq. I am aware that you love sweets. . . .
However, the shortage or unavailability of sweets is less harmful
compared to what Bush wants. Bush wants to enslave you after
enslaving your fathers and mothers. Shame on him and shame on
those who stand behind him with bowed heads and shameless
faces."[17]

As in the Iran-Iraq War, the effort to rally the masses behind
the regime was essentially predicated on Saddam's personality.
The crisis around Kuwait was thus portrayed as the direct
extension of "Saddam's Qadisiya," with the Americans replacing
the Persians as the villains. And just as the Persians had learned
the hard way the strength of the "Iraqis' belief in their rights and
their adherence to their dignity," so the "new invaders" would be
taught a historic lesson:

> Be damned O impudent imperialist [i.e., President Bush]. We raise
> Saddam Hussein as our sword, banner, and leader, because he
> said: No. He said it through acts, construction, capability and
> determination. We renew our pledge of allegiance because he is
> one of us and speaks with our tongue, mind, aspirations, and will.
> And because of this, all Arabs, Muslims, and all poor and honest
> people in the world shout his name.[18]

Whether or not "all honest people in the world shout[ed] his
name," Saddam displayed extreme sensitivity to his image
throughout the crisis, retaliating harshly against any insinuation
regarding his integrity. When President Bush argued that the
Iraqi leader had deceived the United States twice—by invading
Kuwait and by promising to withdraw within a few days—he was
immediately labeled by the Iraqi press as a liar, seeking "to be in
harmony with the band of little agents that he had gathered." The
then British Prime Minister, Margaret Thatcher, was even more
strongly rebuked for her personal attacks on Saddam, being
called "an old hag" with a "canine, harsh voice," who behaved in
a "selfish and inhuman way." When voices in the West threatened
that Saddam and the Iraqi leadership might be put on trial for
war crimes, should something happen to the hostages they had
taken, the Iraqi Bar Association began organizing a popular
tribunal to try the U.S. President, George Bush, for his "terrible

crimes against humanity," including his (alleged) invasion of Grenada, and his "occupation of Najd and Hijaz (that is, Saudi Arabia)."[19]

President Mubarak of Egypt was subjected to much harsher treatment. Having accused Saddam of lying to him by promising not to invade Kuwait, he received a scornful personal letter from the Iraqi leader, in which Saddam lauded his own credentials and ridiculed those of the Egyptian President. How did Mubarak, who came of an undistinguished Egyptian family "that had nothing to do with the princes and kings who ruled before the July 1952 Revolution," dare to smear Saddam—"a descendant of the Mu-hammadan Quraishi [the tribe of the Prophet Muhammad] family, whose family's lineage goes back to our master and forefather, Hussein, who is the son of Ali Ibn Abi-Talib"?[20]

Even Saddam's son, Udai, was recruited to the campaign to boost his father's image. In an article in the Ministry of Defense's organ, *al-Qadisiya*, entitled "The Other Face of Saddam Hussein," he sought to discredit the insinuations that the invasion of Kuwait had been motivated by Saddam's desire to add the Kuwaiti riches to his depleted treasury. Saddam had always "hated money and got annoyed when people used to talk about it," he argued. "On two occasions, Saddam donated his presidential salary, and even sold his sheep, to help build tombs for his late mother and the late founder of the Ba'th Party, Michel Aflaq. Iraqis would be surprised to know how generous he is to widows, orphans, families of martyrs, and the needy." According to Udai's account, Saddam feared nothing except God and the people; there was nothing that could make him happier and more reassured than supporting his people and feeling "that they were solidly behind him." "When we returned from our minor pilgrimage [to Mecca]," he revealed, "we told Saddam Hussein about the palaces and the possessions of the Saudi kings and princes as related to us by the Saudis themselves. So, we joked about that and told him: 'People should not call you the knight of the Arabs but the poor man Saddam Hussein.' He retorted: 'When I see Iraq and my people prosperous, I feel rich.' "[21]

Udai was correct in one thing. The economic well-being of the Iraqi people, particularly after eight years of dislocations, had given his father many sleepless nights, if only because popular discontent threatened his regime. It was Saddam's desperate need for funds which had driven him to invade Kuwait, and now, because of Kuwait, he was forced to ask his subjects yet again to suffer economic privations. Fortunately for the Iraqi leader, the emergence of a new enemy, the imperialist West, at the gates gave him a crucial respite. Prior to the invasion of Kuwait, he had to deliver the promised economic reconstruction without delay. Once Iraq had been thrown again into a state of emergency, he could resort to his favorite technique of putting the blame for the consequences of his aggression on the victim, and asking his subjects to trade the hazardous present for a rosy picture of the future. As he argued in his address to Iraq's women, "the large wealth and the future which will be secured after the victory is achieved, are contingent on the success of [your present sacrifices]."[22]

Economic reconstruction was not the only adverse consequence of the Iran-Iraq War which Saddam could temporarily delay, due to the international siege. So too were his unmet political demands on Tehran. The lack of any progress toward an enduring settlement with Iran, it may be recalled, had been a major impediment to Iraq's return to normal after the war, and consequently, a paramount concern for Saddam. Yet, until August 2 there was virtually nothing he could do about this. He could not, and did not, admit to his people that he had embroiled them in eight years of horrendous war only to save his regime. Nor was he willing to concede that the war had not actually been won. Hence, his hands were tied; he could make no concessions to Iran lest the complete futility of his "second Qadisiya" be exposed.

All of these pressures were abruptly removed following the occupation of Kuwait. In order to effectively resist the formidable power of the United States and its lackeys, Saddam argued, Iraq had to free itself of any possible distraction, even at a certain cost. On August 14, Saddam conveyed a message to the Iranian President, Ali Akbar Hashemi-Rafsanjani, suggesting that the two countries accept the terms of the 1975 Algiers Agreement, agree to exchange prisoners of war and withdraw their forces from respective occupied territories. The surprised Rafsanjani immediately seized the opportunity, and on August 18, the exchange of prisoners of war began.

Bearing in mind the humiliating circumstances under which the 1975 Algiers Agreement had been concluded, and the fact that the abrogation of this treaty topped the list of the Iraqi demands from Iran following the 1980 invasion, Hussein's peace proposals were startling. In a letter to Rafsanjani only three days

before the invasion of Kuwait, he had still been adamant that
sovereignty over the Shatt al-Arab should "belong to Iraq as its
lawful historical right."[23] Now, not only were these demands
dropped altogether, but the Iraqi people were told for the first
time that "the eight-year war was not over the 1975 agreement,
which the Iranians implicitly cancelled and denounced."[24]

Once again Iran proved to be an important key to Saddam's
political survival. In 1975 he had boxed himself into a corner and
was consequently compelled to make the most far-reaching concession in his career until then in order to buy a vital respite to
deal with the crippling Kurdish problem. In 1980, when Tehran's
goodwill could not be bought, he opted for war to deflect the
relentless hostility of the revolutionary regime. In 1990 he was
obliged to appease his large neighbor to the east in order to untie
his hands for the looming confrontation in the south.

While assiduously mending fences with Iran, Saddam showed a
staunch, principled face to Iraq's other neighbors, seeking to
"Zionize" the Gulf crisis from the outset. By linking his Kuwaiti
venture to the Palestinian problem, he hoped to portray himself
as the champion of the pan-Arab cause, thereby eradicating any
conceivable opposition to his move in the Arab World. If the
"restoration of Kuwait to the motherland" was the first step
toward "the liberation of Jerusalem," how could any Arab leader
be opposed to it? The aggressor would be transformed into a
liberator and a hero. The gratitude of the Arab World, in the
form of generous financial contributions to the empty Iraqi
treasury, would be secured.

The annexation of Kuwait was thus described as "a dear
pan-Arab goal, through which we would comprehensively, eter-
nally and radically rectify what colonialism had imposed on our
country."[25] Similarly, once the first American units arrived in
Saudi Arabia, Saddam quickly insinuated Israeli participation in
the conflict. He argued that Israeli pilots and troops had been
deployed in the kingdom, and that the United States and Israel
had "divided aggressive duties among themselves." Within this
framework, he argued, "Israel had painted its planes and put on
them the signs of American planes. Some of its pilots, who will
carry out the aggressive missions, have been provided with
American names and identification cards to escape Iraq's direct
military reaction against Israel." "However," he cautioned, "Iraq
is vigilant and cannot be misled by the U.S. markings on Zionist

fighter planes. . . . It will respond in kind to any hostile action by Israel."[26] Similar allegations of Israel's military contribution to the international coalition, and threats to attack Israel should hostilities break out, were to become a regular theme in Saddam's statements throughout the crisis.[27]

On August 12, in the first official presentation of his "peace initiative," Saddam revealed his optimum scenario for resolving the crisis. He linked the Kuwaiti issue to the Palestinian problem by suggesting a comprehensive solution for "all issues of occupation, or the issues that have been depicted as occupation, in the entire region." In his view, such a solution should include "the immediate and unconditional withdrawal of Israel from the occupied Arab territories in Palestine, Syria, and Lebanon, Syria's withdrawal from Lebanon, and a withdrawal between Iraq and Iran." Only after all these problems had been settled, *in chronological order*, "an arrangement for the situation in Kuwait" could be reached, "taking into consideration the historical rights of Iraq to its land and the choice of the Kuwaiti people."[28] Iraq's material interests had become merely one part of a great moral crusade undertaken by Saddam on behalf of the whole Arab World.

Had this proposal been accepted, let alone implemented, it would have represented a shining achievement for Saddam. With one stroke he would have projected himself as the architect of a new Middle Eastern order and the champion of the Palestinian cause, resolved the frustrating deadlock on the Iranian front, reversed 15 years of Syrian efforts in Lebanon, and become the undisputed Arab leader, with the Arab World, the wealthy oil states in particular, more subservient than ever to his financial wishes. Above all, in making this proposal he risked precious little. Whatever the outcome of his initiative, he would emerge the winner since his sweeping demands articulated the cherished hopes of the majority of people in the Arab World. By leaving the resolution of the Kuwait crisis at the bottom of the list, Saddam gave himself ample time to change the demographic balance in the tiny principality (as he had done in Kurdistan in the early 1970s) so that when the "Kuwaiti people would be given a chance to determine their own future," the outcome would be a foregone conclusion. According to a report published on December 19, 1990, by the human-rights organization, Amnesty International, some 300,000 Kuwaitis, nearly a third of Kuwait's citizens, had fled the country since the invasion. Those who stayed behind were subjected to a systematic campaign of terrorism, aimed at extin-

guishing Kuwait as an independent nation: "Residents have had
to change street names, identity documents and car number
plates. The time difference between Kuwait and Baghdad had
been abolished. For reasons unknown, the Iraqi army bans
Kuwaitis from growing or wearing beards. Some offenders are
punished by having their beards plucked out with pliers."[29]

Not surprisingly, Saddam's "peace proposal" was dismissed by
the West, Israel, Syria and Egypt, with the rest of the Arab states
lukewarm at best.[30] It was only two days earlier that an emergency
meeting of the Arab League, convened in Cairo, had decided to
dispatch Arab troops to the international coalition facing
Saddam.[31] Yet the seeds of a pan-Arab solution had been sown,
and during the following months Saddam would persistently
strive, both directly and through his chief Arab advocates, Yasser
Arafat and King Hussein of Jordan, to establish a linkage between
his personal predicament and the Palestinian problem. To this
end he would exploit all explosive incidents. When in early
October Israeli security forces killed some 20 Palestinians during
clashes on Temple Mount in Jerusalem, Saddam immediately
connected the tragic incident to the American presence in Saudi
Arabia: "After the Zionists thought that the American occupation
of the sanctities in Najd and Hijaz and the desecration of Mecca
and the tomb of the Prophet, may God's peace and blessing be
upon him, provide them with a golden opportunity to entrench
their occupation of Jerusalem . . . they attempted to destroy the
al-Aqsa mosque after they failed to burn it and to destroy it
through excavations."[32]

Before too long Saddam's strategy began to yield results.
Dreading a linkage with the Arab-Israeli conflict established at
Saddam's instigation, but reluctant to allow him to monopolize the
Palestinian cause, the Arab members of the coalition did not fail
to indicate to their Western partners that a positive response to a
settlement of the Palestinian problem was desirable, though not in
the context of a compromise with Iraq. Their anxiety was not
difficult to understand. Donning the spiritual mantle of his late
archenemy, Ayatollah Ruhollah Khomeini, Saddam was zealously
agitating the Arab masses to launch a holy war (*jihad*) against the
corrupt Saudis who had defiled Islam's holiest shrines by allowing
the presence of Western troops on their territory:

> Arabs, Muslims, believers in God, wherever you are. This is the day
> for you to stand up and defend Mecca, which is the captive of the

spears of the Americans and Zionists. . . . The rulers there not only
disregarded their people and the Arab nation; not only challenged
their people and the Arab nation; but challenged God when they
placed Mecca and the tomb of the prophet Muhammad under
foreign protection.[33]

Subsequently, allusions to a comprehensive peace conference
began to emerge from other sources. The first positive reference
to the possibility of an international conference came from the
Soviets, the spiritual parents of the idea some two decades earlier,
in the wake of the 1973 Yom Kippur War. On September 4, the
Soviet Foreign Minister, Edward Shevardnadze, explicitly linked
the Gulf crisis to the Arab-Israeli conflict, arguing that Israel's
agreement to participate in an international conference could
exert a "positive influence" on the events in the Gulf.[34]

France went a step further. In his speech at the United
Nations General Assembly on September 24, President François
Mitterrand linked the occupation of Kuwait with the Arab-Israeli
conflict. While demanding that Iraq comply with the UN resolutions by withdrawing unconditionally from Kuwait, Mitterrand
appeared to have recognized the legitimacy of some of Iraq's
territorial claims on Kuwait, and, no less importantly, to suggest
that the resolution of the Kuwaiti crisis would be followed by a
comprehensive peace conference on the Middle East.[35]

Even though the Americans were visibly embarrassed by
Mitterrand's proposals, a week later Bush himself used the same
forum to link the Gulf crisis with the Arab-Israeli conflict. Like his
French counterpart, he reiterated the call for an unconditional
Iraqi withdrawal from Kuwait, and criticized in strong words the
destruction wrought by Iraq in Kuwait. Then, in a turn that took
many observers by surprise, he argued that an Iraqi withdrawal
would pave the way "for Iraq and Kuwait to settle their differences
permanently; for the Gulf states to build new arrangements for
stability; and for all the states and peoples of the region to settle
the conflict that divides the Arabs from Israel."[36] A similar
position was taken a couple of days later by the British Foreign
Minister, Douglas Hurd, who argued that the five permanent
members of the Security Council should start preparing a Middle
Eastern peace conference once Iraq had withdrawn from
Kuwait.[37]

These declarations were still a far cry from Hussein's expectations. They neither called for a simultaneous resolution of all

regional conflicts, nor agreed to leave the Kuwaiti issue at the
bottom of the agenda. Instead, they predicated any progress on
the Arab-Israeli conflict on Iraq's unconditional withdrawal from
Kuwait. Moreover, the American and British response did not fail
to show the mailed fist under the velvet glove: they remained as
adamant as ever on dislodging Iraq by force should the latter
refuse to abide by the UN resolutions. Yet these public allusions to
the Arab-Israeli conflict were viewed by Saddam as an important
breach in the fortified wall of Western hostility, which he was
determined to expand in order to erode the international commitment to the military option. His strategy of shifting the onus of
responsibility for the stalemate from his own aggression to the
long-standing Palestinian issue had its effect.

From the beginning of the crisis Saddam sought to contain the
international coalition confronting him by relying on his favorite
strategy of divide and rule, which had served him so faithfully
during his long political career. Once faced with the specter of
military action, he sought to limit the hostile coalition to the
Western states, and then—to sow divisions among the Western
members of the coalition. To keep Third World countries out of
the coalition he offered them financial inducements, most notably
his mid-September offer to supply "any needy country" with Iraqi
oil free of charge (although how he proposed to export the oil
under the UN sanctions remains a mystery). Similar financial
incentives were reportedly offered to the Soviet Union and
China.[38] As far as the Western states (and Japan) were concerned,
Saddam took great pains to convince them that they were in effect
"victims of the covetousness of America" and would be the first to
suffer from the outbreak of war. In his view, the real motive
behind the United States' response to the annexation of Kuwait
was its desire "to control the oil of the Middle East to the extent of
being able to dictate to France, England, Italy, or Japan, the
amount of oil, its type, and price, and a list of the amounts to
reach European markets." "Is it in Europe's interest to see this
happen?" he asked. Moreover, "if war breaks out, the oil fields in
Iraq would not be the only ones to be set on fire, but also those in
other areas." "Should this happen, a good deal of the amount
allotted to the West would be cut off, because when oil is ablaze it
cannot flow to France, England or Japan." "At any rate," he
argued, "America will be in a better position to acquire its quota
than Europe or Japan." But oil was not the only commodity which

the United States wanted the Europeans to sacrifice: it also wanted their blood. How else, he asked, ignoring the real situation on the ground, could one explain the fact that the Americans were deployed far from the front line, leaving the rest of the forces, the French in particular, to absorb the most telling blows?[39]

Indeed, fear of the exorbitant cost of an armed confrontation was the main stick that Saddam waved in front of Western eyes, threatening them not only with the direct consequences of such a war, but also with terrorist activities. Already in his famous conversation with Ambassador Glaspie prior to the invasion of Kuwait, Saddam had expressed his readiness to hit American targets throughout the world should the United States confront Iraq militarily. Now he seemed to expand the threat to America's allies. In an interview with the French News Agency on August 31, Tariq Aziz implied the possibility of terrorist attacks against the West, arguing that Iraq would consider itself "free of any moral constraint" if attacked. In a press conference in Baghdad two weeks later, Abu Abbas, head of the Palestine Liberation Front, a constituent organization of the PLO which was responsible for the hijacking of the *Achille Lauro* cruise liner and the murder of an American passenger, Leon Klinghoffer, vowed to attack targets in Europe and the Middle East if war broke out. "If America attacks Iraq, we will fight with our Iraqi brothers in our own way," he said, admitting that he had to confine his operations to Europe due to technical shortcomings. "We would love to reach the American shore, but it is difficult."[40]

An even more pointed signal to the West regarding the detrimental consequences of war was transmitted on August 9, in the form of an Iraqi statement that the thousands of foreigners in Iraq and Kuwait would not be allowed to leave the country. This, in turn, kindled widespread fears that Saddam was about to use Western nationals as hostages to prevent a military attack against Iraq. An indication that this terrifying scenario was in the offing was provided within days. In a radio interview, the Iraqi Ambassador to Paris, Abd al-Razzaq al-Hashimi, implied that the fate of the foreign nationals in Iraq and Kuwait would depend on the behavior of their respective governments, and expressed the hope that the militancy of the Western powers would be curbed by their concern for the safety of their nationals.[41]

On August 19, Saddam in person revealed his plans concerning the foreign nationals. In an "open letter" to the families of foreigners in Iraq, broadcast by Radio Baghdad, he expressed his "pain" at having to confine their loved ones to Iraq. However, he argued that this move, particularly in the case of those "whose governments have a hostile position and are taking part in the preparations for aggression and the economic embargo against Iraq," was designed to open "a deep dialogue" for a peaceful resolution of the crisis and the averting of war. Should the West pull out of the Gulf and undertake not to attack Iraq, these people would be immediately released. For the time being, "their presence with the Iraqi families working in the vital targets may prevent military aggression." And to underscore his determination to host "the foreign guests," as he preferred to call them, Saddam decreed that "every citizen, regardless of nationality, harboring foreigners—who are forbidden to leave the country— would be sentenced to death."[42]

Saddam's decision to use the foreign hostages as a bargaining chip afforded yet another vivid illustration of his stark worldview. One's own survival justified all and any means. There was no room for legalistic or moral niceties. Mindful of Western sensitivity to human life, he was determined to exploit this Achilles' heel to the full. The lamentable response of the Carter administration to the unlawful detention of American diplomats by the revolutionary regime in Tehran in 1979 and 1980, and the undisguised concern of the West for the safety of its hostages in Lebanon, reinforced Saddam in his belief that in the hostages he had found his trump card. Through their very presence in Iraq he hoped to generate public pressure on the Western governments to forgo a military action altogether. By using the hostages as "a human shield" he sought to deter military strikes against Iraq's strategic locations, particularly its non-conventional arms industry, and to limit a potential ground war to Kuwaiti territory. By conditioning the hostages' release on the behavior of their respective governments, he hoped to drive a wedge between the governments and their constituents, and among the various members of the anti-Iraq coalition. To this end, he would occasionally release hostages, usually after a well-publicized visit to Baghdad by a public figure, as a means of indicating to Western audiences that his quarrel was not with them but rather with their aggressive leaders. This theme was already evident in his "open letter" of August 19, in which he addressed the hostages' families as "beloved children of God, dear and beloved children in Europe and the United States," while simultaneously invoking curses on their respective governments for "starving the Iraqi people to death."[43] The world watched and listened to his every utterance, which is just what he wanted.

However, Saddam's propaganda ploy backfired, as Western public opinion was appalled by his cynical manipulation of the hostages. Particularly loathsome was a television spectacle showing Saddam paying a "goodwill visit" to a group of British hostages. Having explained to his hapless "guests" why their stay in Iraq served the cause of peace, Saddam took seeming personal interest in the well-being of a seven-year-old boy, Stuart Lockwood. "Did Stuart have his milk today?" he asked in Arabic, patting the boy's head. The boy's terrified expression sent chills down the spines of hundreds of millions of spectators throughout the world.

Yet Saddam proved a fast learner. Recognizing the damage done to his cause by the "Stuart Lockwood affair," he quickly changed tack and on August 28, ordered the release of all women and children, keeping the men at strategic locations throughout Iraq.[44] In the coming months he would show greater skill in manipulating the hostages for his political ends, drawing to Baghdad a long procession of foreign dignitaries to plead for the release of the hostages. The first such pilgrim was the Austrian President, Kurt Waldheim, who arrived in Baghdad as early as August 25. The only Western head of state to visit Iraq during the crisis, Waldheim joined Saddam at a well-attended press conference, which enabled the Iraqi President to present the case for his "hostages policy." Waldheim was generously rewarded, being allowed to leave with all the 140 Austrians held in Iraq and Kuwait.[45] The former Democratic presidential contender in the United States, the Reverend Jesse Jackson, arrived at the heels of Waldheim, only to leave Baghdad with a handful of American citizens suffering from health problems, and a large group of women and children, whose release had been decided by Saddam independently of Jackson's visit. In the following months Waldheim and Jackson were to be followed by a procession of foreign visitors, from the veteran boxer Muhammad Ali to the former Premiers Willy Brandt, Edward Heath, and Nakasone Yasuhiro. Most of these visitors returned with a batch of hostages, whose size reflected each one's relative importance for the Iraqi propaganda campaign.

In addition to the worldwide news coverage gained from the constant stream of dignitaries to Baghdad, Saddam sought to exploit the hostage question to extract concrete returns. In early September, for example, Iraq offered to release all the Japanese hostages if Tokyo agreed to partly lift its economic sanctions. At the same time, Saddam allowed a number of French nationals to leave the country, expressing the hope that France "would refrain from linking its interests to the aggressive U.S. policies in the world."[46] Indeed, with the passage of time Saddam gradually turned the release of hostages into his main instrument for courting, or "punishing," certain governments for their behavior.

The main target of this policy was France, on which Saddam pinned his hopes for the collapse of the coalition confronting him. When in mid-September Iraqi troops forced their way into the residence of the French Ambassador in Kuwait, seizing several people, Saddam quickly apologized and released the sick and the elderly among the French hostages. A similar gesture was made following President Mitterrand's UN speech, when nine French hostages were allowed to leave Iraq. But the most adroit Iraqi manipulation of the French hostages took place in late November when Hussein suddenly announced that he would ask Iraq's National Assembly to approve the release of all 327 French "guests" held in Iraq and Kuwait. According to Hussein, his decision was a gesture of goodwill to the French people, who "have rejected Bush's aggressive methods . . . and have proven that they are a people who understand the meaning of the required correct stand toward events." Tariq Aziz was more elaborate. In a speech at the National Assembly following its approval of Saddam's recommendation to free the hostages, he hailed the long record of Franco-Iraqi friendship and expressed his hope that the positive changes in French policy would affect the other European states, since "France plays a key role in Europe and the French stand always reflects on the European stands in one way or another."[47]

Not surprisingly, the unexpected Iraqi move generated a whirlwind of speculations about a bilateral deal. Initially, the Iraqis denied these rumors;[48] however, on November 10, they changed their version and argued that the release of the hostages had been agreed upon in a secret meeting in Tunis between Tariq Aziz and Claude Cheysson, the former Foreign Minister under Mitterrand. In the Iraqi account this meeting had been mediated by the PLO and had taken place with the full approval of the French Foreign Minister, Roland Dumas.[49]

The Iraqi revelations were not accidental. Rather, they were a deliberate spoiling tactic, timed to coincide with the arrival in Paris of the U.S. Secretary of State, James Baker, to coordinate

the coalition's Gulf strategy. Reflecting Saddam's irritation with
what he perceived as French ingratitude for his generous gesture,
the revelations sought to drive a wedge between the two allies.
Saddam's strategy managed to embarrass the French—Dumas
hastened to deny the Iraqi allegations, but Cheysson remained
mute, neither denying nor confirming them. Yet, embarrassing as
they were, the Iraqi revelations failed to stop the swing of the
pendulum in an ominous direction from Saddam's point of view:
a special UN resolution authorizing the use of force to dislodge
Iraq from Kuwait.

Realizing that war might be closer than he had anticipated,
Saddam played all the cards in his hand to prevent the passage of
the impending UN resolution. On November 8, as Secretary
Baker was about to gain Soviet support for the forthcoming
Security Council resolution, Saddam allowed Willy Brandt to
leave Baghdad with nearly 200 hostages. Ten days later he
offered to release all hostages, in batches, over a three-month
period starting from Christmas. His logic was transparent—the
postponement of war until March 25. "If after that date [President
Bush] still has the devil in his head," he said, "and if he decides to
attack us, we shall then count on God to meet any eventuality."[50]
The dismissive American response did not dissuade Saddam. A
day later he announced his decision to release all the German
"guests," and on November 29, a few hours before the convocation of the Security Council, he promised Moscow to carry out his
pledge, which he had broken before, and allow 1,000 Soviet
workers to leave Iraq.[51] Simultaneously he made a last-ditch
attempt to forestall the impending resolution by putting on a
brave face and promising to fight rather than to suffer humiliation
from the United States.[52] He failed. On the same day, UN
Security Council Resolution 678 was passed, calling upon Baghdad to leave Kuwait by mid-January and authorizing the use of
military force should it fail to abide by this deadline.
    The immediate Iraqi response to the new resolution was
defiant: "Great Iraq, under the leadership of Saddam Hussein
and his excellent management of the conflict, will remain proud
and firm, challenging the gathering of evil-doers and tyrants."[53]
Yet Saddam was disconcerted. Wherever he looked, the choices
seemed bleak. Unconditional withdrawal would most probably
damage his position beyond repair. The economic plight which
pushed him to occupy Kuwait had not only remained but had

been significantly aggravated by the sanctions. Iraq's political system had not become kinder, and the nation's patience with its leader would soon be running thin. Plots were certain to lurk around each corner.

The alternative boded equally ill. Once the full impact of the economic sanctions had sunk in, public discontent was bound to force Saddam into a hasty withdrawal. An all-out war which would destroy Iraq's military machinery and strategic infrastructure was a recipe for his political destruction. Saddam's only hope, therefore, lay in the collapse of the international coalition before sanctions had been given sufficient time to bite, or full-scale hostilities had broken out. But how realistic were these scenarios after the passing of Resolution 678? How likely was the coalition to collapse? Who could guarantee that the Americans would play into his hands and limit the war to Kuwait?

At this moment of great anxiety a rope was offered from an unexpected direction. On November 30, a day after scoring the most significant point in his struggle against Saddam, George Bush made a dramatic move: he announced his readiness to go an "extra mile for peace" and offered direct talks between the United States and Iraq on a peaceful resolution to the Gulf crisis. He was willing to send Secretary Baker to Baghdad and to receive Foreign Minister Aziz in Washington, to meet himself and representatives of the international coalition. Yet he emphasized that his offer should not be construed as the initiation of negotiations, but rather as a last attempt to drive home to the Iraqi leader the seriousness of his situation, so as to bring about Iraq's unconditional withdrawal from Kuwait.[54]

Notwithstanding these qualifications, Saddam was ecstatic. "Bush's initiative is a submission to Iraq's demand, on which it has insisted and is still insisting," rejoiced the Iraqi mass media, "namely, the need to open a serious dialogue on the region's issues. This is because the Gulf crisis, as they call it, is in fact a reflection of a chronic crisis, the Palestine crisis."[55]

This elation was not difficult to understand. From the beginning of the crisis Saddam had opted for direct negotiations with the United States. Less than a week before the passing of Resolution 678 he had voiced such interest, only to be rebuffed by a White House spokesman: "Our position is unchanged. We see no reason for any special envoy."[56] Now, when his position was at its lowest, the Americans were suddenly willing to negotiate. Perhaps he had been right, after all, in telling Ambassador

Glaspie, during their conversation in July, that the United States
did not have "the stomach" for a costly war. Perhaps the Americans would be willing to reach a compromise that would leave him
with that part of Kuwait which he had originally sought. Perhaps
it was possible, after all, to emerge from the crisis with a real gain
that would thrust him into regional prominence and ensure his
political survival for the foreseeable future.

Saddam's sudden surge of optimism was further fueled by a
series of encouraging developments. In early December Defense
Minister Jean Pierre Chevènement, perhaps the staunchest sympathizer of Iraq in the French cabinet, indicated the possibility of
redrawing Kuwait's borders if Hussein withdrew from the principality, and called for an international conference on the Middle
East after the Iraqi pullout. His call was echoed by Foreign
Minister Dumas, who also implied that he might follow Secretary
Baker's footsteps and visit Baghdad.[57] Most importantly, in an
about-face in American long-standing opposition to an international conference on the Middle East, on December 5 the U.S.
Ambassador to the United Nations, Thomas Pickering, implied
his government's readiness to consider such an idea.[58]

Even though Pickering's statement remained an exception to
the otherwise unabated, outspoken determination of the U.S.
administration not to link the Gulf crisis with the Arab-Israeli
dispute, Saddam felt that, whatever his original intentions, President Bush had unleashed forces that might prove beyond his
ability to control. The drive toward war appeared to have slowed
down. The "peace camp" capitalized on the unexpected gesture to
push the demand for a political resolution of the crisis with
greater vigor. A public controversy over whether the President
had the constitutional powers to move the nation toward war,
without clear authorization from the Congress, was under way.
Senior Democrats like Edward Kennedy and Sam Nunn were
questioning the prudence of military action and demanding that
sanctions be given more time.

What was needed at this critical juncture, Saddam seemed to
believe, was a dramatic move that would tip the scales in favor of
the "peace camp." And what could be more dramatic than the
release of all foreign hostages in Iraq and Kuwait? Such a move
was bound to be seen as a major show of goodwill and was likely,
therefore, to set in train a political momentum that would be
difficult to contain. If handled skillfully enough, this move might
enable him to retain some of his newly acquired possessions and

might even lead to the convocation of an international conference, thereby diverting world attention from Kuwait to the Palestine problem. Conversely, the hostages had outlived their usefulness. Given the clear UN mandate for the use of force against Iraq after January 15, they could hardly shield him from American wrath as they had done before.

Saddam believed that a unique opportunity to ride out the storm was at hand, and that he had an irreversible chance, albeit by no means without risk, to rebound, to emerge from his confrontation with the world with a real achievement. Not only might he survive with dignity, but he might attain new international power. Given this balance of risks and opportunities, Saddam decided to strike while the iron was still hot. On December 6 he played his trump card: he announced the release of all foreign hostages.

Saddam's ploy failed. Before long it became evident to him that despite the deep relief worldwide over the hostages' release, the U.S. administration would not budge from the demand for Iraq's unconditional withdrawal from Kuwait. In President Bush's view, his offer of direct talks on a peaceful resolution to the conflict had given Saddam a last chance to save his skin without losing face, and it was up to him to decide whether or not to seize the opportunity. To Hussein, however, the situation seemed fundamentally different. He had not occupied Kuwait for reasons of power-seeking or political aggrandizement, though certainly his prestige across the Arab World and among his own subjects would have grown enormously with a successful takeover of Kuwait. Rather, the invasion had been a desperate attempt to shore up his regime in the face of dire economic straits. Hence, an unconditional withdrawal, or even withdrawal with a cosmetic face-saving formula, were totally unacceptable from the outset, since they did not address the fundamental predicament underlying the invasion. Only a substantial *quid pro quo*—such as being given a chunk of Kuwait—that would boost his regional standing and cow the Arab Gulf states into subservience with his future wishes, could lead to a peaceful withdrawal from Kuwait. Since Bush showed no inclination to move in this direction despite the release of the hostages, Hussein calculated that his only hope of avoiding war was to try to circumvent the January 15 deadline by postponing his meeting with Secretary of State Baker to the last possible moment.

When he first raised the idea of bilateral talks, President Bush suggested meeting the Iraqi Foreign Minister, Tariq Aziz, in Washington after December 10, and sending James Baker to Baghdad between December 20 and January 3. Saddam agreed to dispatch Aziz to Washington on December 17, but refused to meet Baker before January 12. Irritated by this transparent procrastination ploy, the U.S. administration countered by offering four alternative dates, between December 20 and January 3, for Baker's meeting with Saddam. Yet Baghdad would have none of these. "Iraq will not allow anyone to set the date for his meeting with its President," insisted the mass media. "It is up to Iraq to set appropriate dates for visits to its capital and talks with its President."[59] As the administration remained unimpressed by this argument, Saddam made a significant step toward the brink, threatening to call the talks off. "We will not go to the United States to receive orders," he said. "If the U.S. President George Bush insists on repeating the UN resolutions, then there will be no reason for us to go."[60]

Saddam meant what he said. As the UN deadline for Iraq to withdraw from Kuwait neared, it became increasingly evident that the Iraqi leader was gradually reconciling himself to the inevitability of war. On December 12, 1990, the Iraqi Minister of Defense, General Abd al-Jabbar Khalil Shanshal, was replaced by Lieutenant General Sa'di Tumah Abbas, a seasoned veteran of the Iran-Iraq War.[61] An elderly professional soldier of a rather taciturn personality, Shanshal had assumed his position in mid-1989, following Adnan Khairallah Talfah's mysterious death. It had been clear from the beginning that his appointment was temporary, designed to eliminate mutterings of discontent in the military regarding the cause of Khairallah's death. His removal at that particular stage in the crisis, however, reflected Saddam's growing conviction of the imminence of war.

Also indicative of this conviction was the intensification of the regime's efforts to improve Iraq's military and civilian preparedness. Saddam held several well-publicized meetings with the military and the political leadership. Peasants, who at the beginning of the crisis had been exempted from military service as a means to combat the economic sanctions, were ordered to report immediately to their units. The public was given elaborate instructions regarding self-protection against chemical and nuclear attacks, and was told to black out homes and to store a medicine cabinet in every apartment. Individuals and institutions were ordered to clear their shelters for immediate use, and to store oil products for an emergency. Civil defense drills were held, including a large-scale exercise of an evacuation of Baghdad, involving hundreds of thousands of people.[62]

The expectations of war were also heard in the references of the Iraqi mass media to the crisis. Alongside the already-standard doomsday scenarios of a "second Vietnam," and threats to draw Israel into the conflict, a somber, perhaps even apologetic tone crept into the official commentaries. The Iraqi people were asked to brace themselves for yet another imposed war which was not of their leadership's choice. "Iraq has given peace every chance it deserves, and has repeatedly proved that it is seeking peace," argued the Iraqi press, "but given the U.S.-Western insistence on war and aggression, Iraq will not hesitate to engage in confrontation and fighting to destroy the invading forces."[63] And Saddam put his acceptance of the inevitability of war in a somewhat fatalistic fashion: "If it is God Almighty's will that we fight this battle to cleanse the Arab homeland of all this rottenness, so be it."[64]

The die had been cast. Saddam's mind had been made up. War, it is true, would not have been his first choice. However, caught between the hammer and the anvil, between the certain demise attending an unconditional withdrawal and the hazardous opportunities and possible rewards offered by an armed confrontation, the choice seemed self-evident. Were he to succeed in holding on against the coalition for some time, war would not only offer Saddam the best chance for political survival but would enable him to emerge victorious. Just as Nasser had managed to turn Egypt's military defeat in the 1956 Suez Crisis, against a British-French-Israeli coalition, into a resounding political victory, so Saddam hoped that the loss of Kuwait in a war with the allies would make him a hero, to be lauded by the Arab masses as a new Nasser, a leader who defied world imperialism and survived.

Given this state of mind, a last-minute reversal in the Iraqi position was inconceivable. Saddam's readiness to send Tariq Aziz to Geneva to meet Secretary of State Baker on January 9 was merely a propaganda ploy, not unlike his agreement to hold the Jedda talks with the Kuwaitis prior to the invasion. He knew that George Bush had proposed the Geneva meeting only due to congressional pressures, and that he would offer Iraq nothing except an unconditional withdrawal. Yet, he felt that the Geneva avenue had to be exploited in order to convince his subjects that

the war they were about to face, merely two years after the end of
its fearful predecessor, was an inevitable consequence of America's intransigence.

Not surprisingly, the Geneva meeting turned out to be a
fiasco. After six hours of talks, which aroused widespread speculation about a possible diplomatic breakthrough, but were in
effect a dialogue of the deaf, a somber Baker emerged from the
conference hall to announce the failure of his mission. "I heard
nothing which showed any Iraqi flexibility whatsoever," he told a
press conference, expressing his dismay at Aziz's refusal to deliver
a personal letter from George Bush to Saddam Hussein, despite
reading it "very slowly and very carefully." "The conclusion is
clear," he said, "Saddam Hussein continues to reject a diplomatic
solution."[65]

That Baker's prognosis was correct was evidenced by Iraq's
blatant rebuff of last-minute mediation attempts by anxious third
parties. A request by Jacques Poos, Luxembourg's Foreign Minister and the European Community's rotating President, to go to
Baghdad on behalf of the Community was dismissed out of hand,
as was his suggestion to meet Foreign Minister Aziz in Algeria.
The United Nations' Secretary-General, Javier Pérez de Cuéllar,
was not much luckier: he was allowed to travel to Baghdad, only
to realize at first hand that Hussein's mind was set on war. Nor did
the French President, François Mitterrand, escape a humiliating
snub from the Iraqi leader. As his last-ditch attempt to engineer
a UN resolution linking the Kuwaiti issue with the Palestinian
problem was under way, much to the irritation of France's
partners in the coalition, Saddam rebuffed his initiative. He had
convinced himself that only unyielding resistance and a bold
righteous stance would win him the hearts of the Arab World and
perhaps even the war.

It is arguable, of course, that the French initiative came too
late to be taken seriously by Saddam. However, the truth of the
matter is that the idea of an international conference had never
stood any real chance of driving Iraq out of Kuwait. Saddam had
never implied any readiness to trade the occupation of Kuwait for
the convocation of an international conference on the Middle
East. In fact, he had not even referred to such a conference. What
he meant by raising the notion of a linkage was that the Palestinian
problem (as well as the Syrian presence in Lebanon) would have
to be *resolved*, and not merely addressed, before the Kuwaiti issue
could be tackled. Given the complexity of the Arab-Israeli conflict

and the lengthy time required for its resolution, the concrete consequence of Saddam's "linkage" was that he would be given an indefinite respite to keep Kuwait, while at the same time gaining enormous prestige in the Arab World and "Iraqizing" Kuwait. And as if to dispel any remaining hopes that Iraq would be willing to leave Kuwait in return for an Israeli withdrawal from the territories, the Revolutionary Command Council issued a special communiqué stating the nature of Iraq's perception of a linkage:

> When we stand for linkage as stated in the August 12 initiative, the belief that Kuwait is part of Iraq is unshakable, and that it is the nineteenth province is a fact treated by our people and their Armed Forces as a great gain. . . . It has become a symbol of honor and virtue in this major battle—the mother of battles. We have wanted to establish a link between any gain for the [Arab] nation and any [Iraqi] national gain.[66]

Against this backdrop, there was nothing that could be done to stop the countdown to war. On January 12, the U.S. Congress authorized President Bush to use military force to evict Iraq from Kuwait. The Iraqi National Assembly countered by endorsing Saddam Hussein's grim determination to fight. They called the Iraqi people to "proceed toward holy *jihad*," and gave their absolute leader "full constitutional authority to deal with all that is necessitated by the decisive confrontation to preserve the right and dignity of Iraq and the Arab nation."[67] Western diplomats fled Baghdad *en masse* as the UN deadline approached. Thousands of peace activists marched in European and American cities. At midnight on January 15 the threshold between peace and war had been crossed, though the region remained conspicuously tranquil. The following night war came to Iraq.

11

The "Mother of All Battles"

War came on Thursday, January 17, 1991, at approximately 2 A.M., Baghdad time, some 26 hours after expiration of the UN deadline. Two hours into the new day, sirens in Iraq went off, as waves of U.S.-led allied planes systematically pounded military, strategic and political targets through the country. Radar and communications bases, early warning stations and air defense batteries were hit in the first wave, to pave the way for extensive precision bombings. These included airfields, command and control centers, troop concentrations in Kuwait, oil refineries and surface-to-surface ballistic missiles, those targeted at Israel in particular. Baghdad took the brunt of the allied assault. Buildings vibrated as huge explosions rocked the capital, and the skies were lit up by anti-aircraft fire. When people emerged from their shelters in the morning, they realized that their President's Palace had been largely demolished, together with the headquarters of the ruling Ba'th Party and the Ministry of Defense.

Iraqi resistance to the initial air offensive was light. Even though it had been evident to Saddam that war was inevitable, and that it was bound to come sooner than later, the timing and intensity of the allied attack took him by surprise. He apparently shared the prevailing view at the time that hostilities were not likely to erupt for a few more days, as the coalition was expected to soften Saddam's stance by forcing the Iraqis to spend several more sleepless nights in anticipation of the impending attack.[1]

244

Subsequently, the Iraqi air force did not try to challenge the allied aircraft, and those planes that managed to take off did so in an attempt to escape to airfields in northern Iraq. Anti-aircraft fire was dense but inaccurate, as the guidance systems of Iraq's more lethal air defense weapons, the surface-to-air missiles, had been effectively jammed or destroyed by the coalition. Not a single allied aircraft was lost during the first night of fighting.

Saddam's recovery from the initial shock, though, was prompt and impressive. At 4:18 A.M., two hours after the outbreak of hostilities, the state radio broadcast a defiant presidential statement which informed the Iraqis that "the mother of all battles" had begun, and urged them to live up to their glorious reputation: "O great Iraqi people, sons of our great people, valiant men of our courageous armed forces. . . . Satan's follower Bush committed his treacherous crime, he and the criminal Zionism. The great duel, the mother of all battles, between victorious right and the evil that will certainly be defeated has begun, God willing."[2]

broadcast

A few hours later Iraqis could watch televised footage of their President visiting a Baghdad street. Donning his ubiquitous battledress, Saddam was greeted by a handful of cheering people, hardly more than the number of his bodyguards. A hysterical old woman kissed his hand with great reverence, while soldiers accompanying him waved their rifles enthusiastically. Saddam looked relaxed and calm, visibly enjoying the carefully staged demonstration of affection.[3]

Having underscored his defiance, in the following weeks Saddam would go out of his way to convince his subjects of their ultimate victory. Within hours of the beginning of the allied offensive, "the air defense heroes and the valiant hawks in the planes of confrontation" allegedly downed 14 aircraft. By the evening this figure had risen to 44, and at the close of the first day of fighting 60 allied aircraft had allegedly been brought down (the figure given by the allies was 8 aircraft). A day after the outbreak of hostilities, Iraq had already claimed victory. "The battle was settled in our favor," Minister of Information and Culture Latif Nusseif Jasim told journalists. "We are confident of victory and heading toward victory. What counts is the human factor and high morale. What is lost is nothing."[4]

These reports of glowing successes were accompanied by fiery rhetoric, abounding in religious terminology that sought to portray the conflict as a holy war between pious Islam and the evil forces of infidelity. Harping on a sensitive nerve, the Iraqis vehemently attacked King Fahd for defiling the Holy Land by allowing Israel to position 60 of its aircraft on Saudi territory. They also accused the allies of intentionally attacking the holy Shi'ite shrines in Karbala and Najaf, vowing to avenge this "lowly behavior" in the most decisive fashion: "Najd and Hijaz will be liberated [i.e., the Saudi dynasty toppled], the invaders will be defeated; usurped Palestine will be liberated from the filth of the Zionists; the midget entity—Israel, the protégé of U.S. imperialism—will disappear forever."[5]

As in the earlier stages of the crisis, Saddam used his eldest son, Udai, to promote his cause. When the foreign media insinuated that Saddam's wife and children had fled the country to Mauritania, the Iraqi radio countered by producing an adulatory letter by Udai to his father, in which he bid him farewell before (allegedly) departing for the front:

> Greetings to you, source of bravery, heroism and love, greetings to you, symbol of Iraq and its loyal leader. I am writing to you as I leave for southern Iraq, where the lions and the brave men of Iraq are stationed to counter the tyrants. I would have liked to have seen you or met you before I left. However, I hope that I will return and see you in perfect health. . . . Since my childhood I have seen you as the lofty mountain and the ever-glittering banner. I will be there, where I will endeavor to obtain God's blessing, repay the homeland's debt, and will seek competition and cooperation among brave men. Like father like son. This is a family that does not hesitate to make any sacrifices for the land, even their children and souls. My sincerest regards to you, my father. I pray that God will preserve you for us as a family and for our people in general.[6]

Udai had good reason to pray for heavenly supervision. His father's high rhetoric about the "mother of all battles" apart, Saddam's need to prove to his subjects that his family "does not hesitate to make any sacrifices for the land, even their children and souls," indicated his doubts regarding their readiness to face the new predicament into which he had maneuvered them. On the face of it, Iraq's capacity for a protracted conflict seemed unlimited, having sustained an extremely bloody, eight-year war against Iran and emerged intact. And yet, nobody knew better than Saddam that this apparent resilience was largely misleading. He recalled that the persistence of the Iran-Iraq War was not of his own choice: it had been imposed on him by a fanatic foe which openly demanded his downfall. When he invaded Iran in September 1980 he envisaged a brief campaign of days or weeks at the most. Merely five days after the outbreak of hostilities he had already sued for peace, a plea which he was to reiterate for eight years before Khomeini would give up his declared goal of overthrowing him.

Nor did Saddam have any illusions about the staying power of the Iraqi nation. He knew too well that his ability to survive the Iran-Iraq War had largely stemmed from his success in shielding the Iraqi public from the effects of the conflict. Due to Iran's inability to extend the war to the Iraqi home front, and to financial help from the Gulf states, Saddam managed to keep the war confined to the battlefield and to preserve, by and large, an atmosphere of "business as usual" for the Iraqi population. Whenever Iran had managed to reach the Iraqi home front, during the so-called Wars of the Cities, Saddam quickly backed down.

Above all, Saddam knew that even Iraq's defensive capability, its main military strength, was far less impressive than met the eye. The Iraqi operations during the Iran-Iraq War had been conducted under ideal circumstances. Iraq's firepower had been far superior to that of Iran, and it had enjoyed mastery of the air. Yet its formidable defenses had been repeatedly breached by the ill-equipped Iranian teenagers, whose advance had been contained with great difficulty and, at times, through the use of chemical weapons. If Iran had not been severed from its main arms suppliers and if Saddam had not enjoyed the massive military support of almost the entire international community, he would undoubtedly have lost the war.

All of this meant that the position of the Iraqi leader was far more precarious than he would have liked the world, and his subjects, to believe. Given his awareness that the conflict would not be confined to the front lines, he knew that the longer it dragged on, the dimmer his chances became of surviving the postwar situation. The economic plight which had pushed him to occupy Kuwait was significantly aggravated after the invasion, and a protracted war was bound to deal a devastating blow to his hopes for the economic reconstruction of Iraq, on which his political survival would continue to hinge. A sustained conflict was also likely to erode national, and in consequence military, morale and to force him into a humiliating withdrawal from Kuwait, not on his own terms.

Hence, from the onset of hostilities Saddam's war strategy was

geared toward a single goal: drawing the coalition into a premature ground offensive in Kuwait that would bring the war to a
quick end, even at the cost of many Iraqi lives. Such an encounter
offered him his best chance of inflicting heavy casualties on the
allies, thereby driving the disillusioned Western public opinion to
demand an early cease-fire. As he put it: "Not a few drops of
blood, but rivers of blood would be shed. And then Bush will have
been deceiving America, American public opinion, the American
people, the American constitutional institutions."[7]

But even if this optimistic scenario failed to materialize, the
specter of a quick but honorable withdrawal from Kuwait in the
course of a bloody encounter, as opposed to having to evacuate
the principality under allied pressure and without such a battle,
did not augur too badly. It could enable him to live up to the
meaning of his name, "the one who confronts," and to emerge
from the conflict as a new Nasser who had defied "world imperialism" and survived.

The Israeli card was the first to be played by Saddam in his
attempt to lure the allies into a premature ground assault. By
striking at Israel's main population centers he not only hoped to
be cheered by the Arab masses, and to put the Arab members of
the coalition in a difficult position, but he also laid the ground for
an Israeli retaliation. Such a response, in turn, could be expected
to force the allies—who feared the Arab-Israeli conflagration
might fracture the war coalition—to try to preempt this eventuality by moving earlier than planned to a ground offensive in
Kuwait.

An indication that Israel was indeed an integral component of
Saddam's war strategy had already been given during the first day
of the war, when the Iraqi Ambassador to Belgium, Ziad Haidar,
revealed that the decision to attack Israel had been taken and that
such an attack was imminent.[8] Before long Haidar's promise was
made good: in the early-morning hours of January 18, three Iraqi
ballistic missiles landed in Tel Aviv and two in the northern port
city of Haifa.

Though causing few fatalities the attacks punctured the
bubble of euphoria in the coalition following the initial air
offensive, and aroused apprehensions of an Israeli response. The
Israelis themselves were disconcerted. For the first time since the
establishment of their state, its main population centers had come
under indiscriminate military attack by a regular Arab army. No

less frustrating for the Israelis was the painful awareness that they had been "hijacked" into a war that was not theirs, without being able to do anything about it. Retaliation, one of the main foundations of Israel's strategic thinking over the past four decades, seemed to offer no solution to the newly posed challenge. The underlying logic of retaliation had been to deter attacks against Israel by impressing upon would-be aggressors that their losses were bound to exceed any potential gains. Yet, this rationale was completely irrelevant to this situation, for no reason other than that Saddam's aggression was designed to trigger a response, not to avoid one.

If retaliation could only play into Saddam's hands, inaction entailed its own risks. Not only did it go against the grain for Israelis to turn the other cheek, but it could erode Israel's future deterrent posture. Given the acrimonious legacy between Arabs and Jews and the fundamental misperceptions on both sides, there was no guarantee that the Arabs would take Israel's restraint for what it was, a sign of maturity and strength. Indeed, to judge by the jubilant response of the Arab masses to the Iraqi attack, this move was interpreted as a demonstration of Arab strength and Israeli weakness.

Torn by these contradictory considerations, the Israeli government tilted in the direction which Saddam, and many Israelis, least expected—restraint. It is true that this decision was heavily affected by pressures and reassurances on the part of the U.S. administration and some other members of the coalition. In a telephone conversation with Premier Shamir, George Bush pleaded for restraint and promised "the darndest search and destroy operation ever in the region [for remaining Iraqi mobile missile launchers]."[9] It is also true that some decision makers in Jerusalem were inclined to retaliate. The Israeli Chief of Staff, Lieutenant General Dan Shomron, stated that "an attack on our civilians cannot pass without a response," and his superior, Defense Minister Moshe Arens said that an Israeli retaliation was a foregone conclusion: "We have said publicly and to the Americans that if we were attacked we would react; we were attacked, we will react, certainly. We have to defend ourselves."[10] Yet, the decision to hold back reflected the keen awareness that, without relinquishing the right to retaliation at the appropriate moment, the short- and long-term advantages of restraint exceeded by far the immediate satisfaction of revenge.

Israel's restraint shuffled Saddam's cards. While gloating that

"Nebuchadnezzar will feel proud in his grave" and that "Saladin al-Ayyubi is shouting God is great," he realized that his ploy to draw Israel into the conflict at its initial stage had failed. Not only did the Arab members of the coalition fail to applaud his action, but the Syrians, who were likely to face the greatest embarrassment in the case of an Israeli-Iraqi clash, ridiculed the Iraqi action. "You are free to fight the whole world alone," the Syrian Minister of Defense, Mustafa Tlas, said scornfully to Saddam, "but you are not free to claim wisdom and reason. You are especially not free to call on other people to join you in this folly."[11] And the Syrian Foreign Minister, Faruk al-Shara, reassured foreign ambassadors in Damascus that Syria would not be dragged into war with Israel in order to satisfy Saddam Hussein, even in the case of Israeli retaliation.[12]

Frustrated with his failure to trigger an automatic Israeli response, but mindful of his ability to strike at Israel with virtual impunity due to its policy of restraint, Saddam continued his missile campaign against the Jewish state. Within the first two weeks of the war, Israel was subjected to nine missile attacks, exacting a toll of nearly 200 wounded and 4 dead. These attacks, nevertheless, were of no avail. Not only did they fail to provoke Israel into action, but they led to the intensification of U.S.-Israeli relations, with the tacit approval of the Arab members of the coalition. Several batteries of Patriot anti-missile missiles, together with their U.S. crews, were deployed in Israel, improving its protection against intruding missiles and reducing the urge for retaliation. A special bilateral agreement on the "status of forces" was signed, giving American military personnel in Israel and Israeli personnel in the United States a "privileged status." Israel also presented the administration with a request for an additional $13 billion in foreign aid, including $3 billion to cover loss of revenues due to the Gulf War, and $10 billion for the absorption of Soviet Jewish immigrants. Germany, for its part, offered Israel $165 million in "humanitarian aid" and $700 million in military aid, in an attempt to allay the latter's irritation at the substantial involvement of German companies both in Iraq's chemical weapons program, and in the extension of the Scud missiles' range. By February, Israel had already taken the first delivery of German military supplies, including antidotes to counteract the effects of chemical and biological weapons, and Patriot missiles.[13]

As the attack on Israel did not trigger the anticipated allied response, Saddam drew another strategic arrow from his quiver: oil. On January 22 Iraq set fire to several oil installations in Kuwait, causing huge fires and dense smoke. While this action made some military sense by creating a smoke screen that could complicate allied operations, its main aim was to underline to the coalition the devastating consequences of a protracted war for the world oil market and the region's ecology. This signal was amplified shortly afterwards, when Iraq began pumping oil into the Persian Gulf from the Ahmadi loading complex, south of Kuwait City. Flowing at the pace of some 200,000 barrels a day, the oil slick soon became the worst-ever oil-related ecological disaster, covering an area of at least 240 square miles. This slick made its way slowly in the direction of Saudi Arabia, polluting long stretches of the Saudi coastline and threatening the desalination plants that provide most of the kingdom's eastern provinces' drinking water. This was not the first time that Saddam had proved willing to inflict horrendous ecological damage in order to bring about a quick ending to a war: in 1983 the Iraqi army blew up the Norwuz oil platform, west of Iran's main oil export terminal at Kharg Island, causing the Iranian wells to leak for some eight months.[14]

The ecology was not the only victim of Saddam's anxiousness to entice the allies into an early attack in Kuwait. So were the Western prisoners of war. Already on the first day of hostilities the Iraqi media called upon "the brave men of the armed forces to apply the law on prisoners [of war] and not to kill them. We will benefit greatly from the pilots being kept alive as military intelligence may get information from them."[15] To encourage people to hunt for allied pilots, the authorities announced that such an act "would please God and would be a national honor." For those Iraqis who still required a more earthly inducement, the government promised a handsome reward of 10,000 dinars ($32,000) for any captured pilot; non-Iraqis were promised a smaller reward of "merely" $20,000.[16]

Before long it transpired what the Iraqi authorities meant by "applying the law on prisoners of war." On January 20, seven allied pilots—three Americans, two British, one Italian and one Kuwaiti—were shown on Iraqi television. Questioned about the nature of their military missions, they gave answers that had been clearly scripted for them, criticizing the war against "peaceful Iraq." It was evident from their subdued voices and general

appearance that they had been subjected to considerable psychological and physical pressure. "Our losses were very great," said
one of them, "and this was one of the main reasons for the fear of
American pilots flying against the Iraqi defense. We were talking
together and we felt that Iraq had some of the best anti-aircraft
systems and the losses caused by these systems to our aircraft have
been very great and were leading to American pilots objecting to
being in this conflict." Another pilot expressed his opposition to
the unjust war in strong terms: "Myself and the other pilots talked
about what interest the United States had for going to war, and we
could find none. This was before the war. And now, we wonder
whether American blood can be so cheap in the eyes of our
government officials."[17]

Once again, Saddam's ploys failed to produce the desired
result. To be sure, his ruthless behavior brought him the increasing contempt of Western public opinion, but this indignation was
not translated into actual pressure on the political leadership to
proceed to the ground offensive. Even worse from Saddam's
point of view, the callous treatment of the captured pilots and his
threat to deploy them as "human shields" at Iraq's strategic sites
touched a sensitive nerve in the American public and generated
calls to expand the war aims beyond the liberation of Kuwait to
include the removal of the Iraqi leader from power. President
Bush pledged to hold Saddam accountable for the consequences
of his deeds, and argued that the "human shield" strategy would
not affect allied strategy. A similar warning came from the British
Prime Minister, John Major, who said that the Iraqi forces would
be held responsible for their "inhuman and illegal" behavior,
implying that Saddam and others responsible could be tried for
war crimes after the war.[18]

To judge by the decreased manipulation of war prisoners by
Iraq, these warnings seemed to have been well taken by Saddam.
His desire to bring about the early termination of the war,
though, remained unabated. On the face of it, he was as defiant as
ever. "Our ground forces have not entered the battle so far, and
only a small part of our air force has been used so far," he told his
subjects on January 20, in the second personal statement since the
beginning of the war. "When the battle becomes a comprehensive
one with all types of weapons, the deaths on the allied side will be
increased with God's help. When the deaths and dead mount on
them, the infidels will leave and the flag of Allahu Akbar will fly
over the mother of all battles."[19]

This public confidence was reiterated a week later in Saddam's first interview with a Western journalist since the war began. In his meeting with Peter Arnett, a Cable News Network (CNN) correspondent, Saddam looked rested and relaxed. He was more casual than usual and showed no sign of anxiety. In his view, Iraq had managed to maintain its "balance" by using only conventional weapons, and would undoubtedly "win the admiration of the world with its fighting prowess." When asked whether he had any doubts about obtaining a military victory he unhesitatingly answered: "Not even one in a million."[20]

Yet this remarkable exercise in self-control could hardly disguise the deepening anxiety of the Iraqi President. In the interview he argued that Iraq had the capability to fix nuclear, chemical and biological warheads to its missiles and vowed to escalate the conflict if he had to. "I pray to God I will not be forced to use these weapons," he said, "but I will not hesitate to do so should the need arise." This threat rang familiar and ominous bells from the Iran-Iraq War. During that war Saddam often warned the Iranians before resorting to chemical attacks, and his use of this weapon against them (as opposed to his reckless gassing of the defenseless Kurds) had always taken place at critical moments, when there had been no other way to check Iranian offensives. Since non-conventional weapons had always been a means of last resort for Saddam when confronted by a formidable foe, the raising of the chemical threat in the CNN interview unintentionally exposed his growing awareness that the moment of truth was nearing.

An equally revealing illustration of Saddam's exasperation was afforded by his harsh attack on those "hypocritical" Western politicians, who had promised him that by releasing the foreign hostages he would be able to avert war. Apart from implying his dissatisfaction with the course of the war (had it progressed smoothly, he would presumably have been less troubled by the release of the hostages), Saddam's unprecedented public admission of a mistake was completely out of line with the image of the infallible leader he had so carefully nurtured during his twelve-year Presidency. He had never publicly expressed self-doubt before, and his inadvertent slip of the tongue revealed how disconcerted he really was. Indeed, in an Iraqi television report showing Saddam conferring with his commanders in a military van, the Iraqi leader looked exhausted and distressed. He sat quietly, nervously clasping his hands and listening anxiously to his generals' explanations. There was nothing in this scene reminiscent of the confident Saddam of the CNN interview.

Saddam's distress was not difficult to understand. The aerial *blitz* of the first night of the war continued apace. In what turned out to be the largest and most extensive air campaign since the Second World War, allied aircraft rained devastation on Iraq, proceeding methodically from north to south, and from Iraq to Kuwait. The feather in Saddam's cap, the cherished nuclear program, had been essentially reversed as the allies wiped out Iraq's four primary nuclear research reactors. His chemical and biological weapons facilities had been badly damaged as well. The economic and strategic infrastructure of Iraq was being systematically destroyed: roads, bridges, power stations and oil installations. His armed forces were subjected to heavy bombardments, with their command and control systems and logistical lines severely disrupted. The Iraqi air force was virtually paralyzed. Although a small fraction of its 700 fighting aircraft had been actually destroyed, it not only failed to challenge the allies, but within the first two weeks of the war some 100 combat and transport planes, including many top-quality aircraft such as Soviet MiG-29s and SU-24s, and French Mirage-F1s, fled to Iran in search of sanctuary.

The exact reasons for this mass air exodus to a country with which Iraq had just fought a bloody, eight-year war, were not entirely clear. It was believed that this move was a ploy by Saddam "to retain his best aircraft for when the conflict is over so he will have some military assets to keep him in power." (In similar fashion, Saddam had sent some of his aircraft to Jordan for safekeeping during the Iran-Iraq War.) An alternative explanation suggested that the escape of the Iraqi planes was linked to a coup attempt by senior air force officers against Saddam, after he had executed his Air Force and Air Defense Commanders for failing to resist the allied attack. A related version maintained that by sending his planes to Iran, Saddam removed a group of potentially rebellious officers who could, at a certain point, challenge his decision to prosecute the war. Finally, Iranian sources argued that the air exodus was, in effect, mass defection of Iraqi pilots who flew to Iran without Saddam's authorization. This last version was questioned by Western sources which attributed it to Tehran's anxiety to avoid any taint of Iraqi-Iranian collusion. Israeli officials, for their part, tended to doubt the rumors about an attempted coup, suspecting Saddam of leaking

false reports in this regard in order to lull the allies into the belief
that his high command structure had been seriously disrupted.[21]
That this skepticism was warranted to some extent could be
inferred from the expansion of the exodus beyond the air force:
before long Iraqi naval vessels as well tried to escape to the
Iranian haven.

Whatever the explanation, the positioning of aircraft in a
neutral country denied Iraq a crucial component of military
power and indicated the depth of Saddam's strategic plight, and
his consequent need for a quick ending to the war. Since neither
the Israeli nor the oil cards had succeeded in pushing the allies
into a premature offensive in Kuwait, they had to be augmented
by other means. And what would constitute a better means for
this purpose than initiating a limited ground encounter in Kuwait.
It is true that such a move entailed grave risks, as allied air
supremacy meant that the Iraqi forces would be exposed to heavy
air attacks. Yet the advantages of an Iraqi attack seemed to
outweigh its potential risks. It could enable Saddam to seize the
initiative from the allies, at least temporarily, and to give the
morale of his battered troops in Kuwait a much-needed boost. In
addition, the attack could be used to underscore his credentials as
the "daring knight of Arabism" who was not deterred from taking
on the "assembled forces of world imperialism." Most importantly,
if sustained over a sufficient period of time, it could create a
momentum that would suck the reluctant coalition into a ground
offensive.

On Tuesday night, January 29, an Iraqi force, apparently
comprising two infantry and one tank battalions, crossed the
Kuwaiti border in the south-eastern front and headed in the
direction of Khafji, a deserted Saudi town, some 12 miles from
the frontier. Taking the small Saudi garrison by surprise, the
Iraqis occupied the town and resisted allied attempts to dislodge
them for nearly two days. In the ensuing fighting the Americans
suffered their first casualties in ground fighting when 11 marines
were killed (7 of them from friendly fire). The Iraqi losses in men
and equipment were far higher, amounting to dozens of dead and
hundreds of prisoners.

Both parties quickly claimed victory for the first significant
ground encounter of the war. The Iraqis described their action as
"a lighting strike into the kingdom of evil." They argued that it
had been planned by Saddam, together with the Revolutionary
Command Council and the military leadership, and that the

President had visited his troops in Basra a couple of days prior to the battle to personally issue the command for the attack. The coalition, for its part, downplayed the significance of the battle, and the commander of the allied forces, General Norman Schwarzkopf, said that it was "about as significant as a mosquito on an elephant."[22] The fact of the matter is that both claims were partly justified. Despite allied denials, the Iraqis had apparently achieved a measure of tactical surprise, and their ability to hold on for some time was clearly an important propaganda gain for Hussein. Yet, the Iraqis were decisively defeated and failed to achieve any concrete military objective.

Indeed, before long it transpired that, from the Iraqi point of view, the Khafji incursion was part of a wider planned offensive. "Bush tried to avoid a meeting of men face to face, one on one, and substituted for such confrontation technology that fires from afar," stated the Iraqi radio. "However, the men of faith, chivalry, and honor in the Iraq of glory and heroism would not allow Bush and Fahd not to understand the truth about their meager value, which is the quality of every infidel, traitor, and ungrateful person. . . . Thus, the first signs of dawn on January 30, began to illuminate the battlefield on the ground, giving hope to all Arabs, honest men in the world and believers."[23]

This threat was accompanied by large troop movements in the direction of the Saudi border. On January 31, allied sources reported that four Iraqi mechanized divisions with some 240 tanks and 60,000 soldiers were massing near the south-western Kuwaiti border town of Wafra. Together with a ten-mile-long Iraqi column making its way through Kuwait, these units were subjected to ferocious air assaults, which exacted a heavy toll and aborted the intended Iraqi attack.

Saddam's decision to take his troops into the open despite their glaring vulnerability to allied air power was, correctly, interpreted by the West as an indication of his growing desperation to force the coalition into the decisive ground encounter. President Bush quickly announced that he would not fall for this latest ploy, and that the land offensive would be launched "if and when the time was right."[24] Saddam's instinctive response to this cool-headed statement was to threaten the allies with the escalation of the conflict to a more extreme level. "We will use whatever power and weapons are at our disposal," cautioned al-Qadisiya on February 2, "from kitchen knives to weapons of mass destruction."

Even though this threat was taken seriously by the allies, the Iraqi leader remained faithful to his past pattern of exhausting all available options before resorting to the extreme means of chemical warfare. During the Iran-Iraq War he had effectively exploited the ominous specter of Iranian fundamentalism in order to rally domestic and international support behind his personal struggle for survival. Now, trapped again in a war of his own making, he sought to divert public opinion from his brutal occupation of Kuwait and portray Iraq as a hapless victim of Western aggression by exaggerating the extent of material damage and civilian casualties caused by the allied air campaign.

His rhetorical and media strategy was simultaneously targeted at three different audiences. The Iraqi people, who could no longer be convinced that their "valiant eagles" were dealing telling blows at the allied air forces, were encouraged to translate their anger at Western "atrocities" into unquestioning support for the war effort. The Arab masses, who took great pride in Iraq's defiant stance, were expected to give public expression to their exasperation with their own leaders and to pressure the Arab members of the coalition to desist from their "despicable behavior." Finally, the televised scenes of (allegedly) indiscriminate bombings were designed to strengthen the "peace camp" in the West and to provoke a public debate there about the legitimacy of the strategic air campaign.

By way of implementing this propaganda, Western journalists, expelled from Iraq at the beginning of the war, were allowed back into the country and taken to selected sites from which they transmitted pictures of collateral damage caused by allied air raids. Though these scenes were fully controlled by the Iraqis (who denied the Western media any information regarding damage to military targets), and although it was evident to spectators outside Iraq that the actual scope of civilian suffering was far smaller than that claimed by the Iraqis, Saddam's latest ploy proved highly effective. In Morocco some 300,000 people took to the streets, forcing King Hasan into an apologetic explanation of his participation in the anti-Saddam war coalition. King Hussein of Jordan, for his part, responded to Iraq's publicized plight by expressing his support for Saddam and blaming the allies for "committing war crimes under the disguise of UN resolutions." Even President Bush could not remain indifferent to the mounting ferment in the Arab World. In a special phone conversation with Hafiz Asad, he reassured the

Syrian President that the coalition was doing its best to avoid civilian casualties. More significantly, some uneasiness about the progress of the air campaign induced him, on February 7, to send his two senior military advisors—Secretary of Defense Cheney and Chairman of the Joint Chiefs of Staff Powell—to Saudi Arabia, to discuss with the Field Commanders the timing of the ground offensive.

To Saddam's exasperation, this high-ranking visit failed to produce the anticipated change of strategy. Upon returning to Washington, Cheney and Powell reportedly informed President Bush that, in the opinion of the Field Commanders, the air campaign had significantly eroded the might and the morale of the Iraqi armed forces but not sufficiently to begin a ground war; thus they recommended sustaining aerial bombardments for some time longer, perhaps up to a month, in order to maximize their effect. This development could not be more disconcerting for Saddam. His troops in Kuwait were being systematically decimated, with growing numbers of Iraqis surrendering themselves to the coalition forces. According to official allied data, some 1,300 Iraqi tanks out of a total of 4,280 in the Kuwaiti theater of operations had been destroyed or severely damaged. More than 1,110 of Iraq's 3,100 artillery pieces had been taken out, together with 800 of its 2,870 armored personnel carriers. Iraq's military casualties in the Kuwait war theater were estimated to have exceeded 50,000.[25] Civilian life in Iraq was becoming equally unbearable. There was no electricity or running water in Baghdad and Iraq's other major cities, with the residents of Baghdad faced with the threat of cholera and typhoid epidemics. By early February the government was forced to announce an indefinite halt to the sale of fuel, thereby leading to the complete collapse of vehicular civilian transportation. At this low ebb, when the desired ground encounter seemed to be edging away again and the specter of an unconditional withdrawal loomed larger than ever, Saddam scored a crucial propaganda coup: on February 13 American bombers destroyed an air raid shelter in the Baghdad neighborhood of Amiriya, killing some 300 civilians.

The Iraqis did not fail to seize this golden opportunity to discredit the allied air campaign which, they contended, was aimed at destroying Iraq rather than liberating Kuwait. Foreign journalists were rushed to the scene, and disturbing pictures of bodies retrieved from the wrecked shelter were shown throughout the world. The U.S. administration responded by laying the blame for the tragic incident at Saddam's doorstep. According to the White House spokesman, Marlin Fitzwater, the bunker was a well-known command and control center, and the civilians should not have been there in the first place. The Director of Operations for the Joint Chiefs of Staff, General Thomas Kelly, went a step further, arguing that one could not rule out "a cold-blooded decision on the part of Saddam Hussein to put civilians without our knowledge into a facility and have them bombed. He had to know we knew this was a military facility."[26]

Whether inadvertently or by design, the tragic incident played into Saddam's hands. The allies quickly announced that they might revise their air strategy by shifting its focus to the Iraqi troops in Kuwait, and by giving prior notice of forthcoming strategic bombings deep inside Iraq. No less importantly from Saddam's point of view, there were suggestions in Washington that progress toward a land offensive should be speeded up.[27] Simultaneously, a new diplomatic avenue was opened as Moscow responded to the unexpected escalation by sending a special envoy to Baghdad, Yevgeny Primakov, to explore the possibility of a cease-fire.

At this point Saddam decided that the moment was ripe for a radical move to bring matters to a conclusion, either through provoking a ground war or, even better, a diplomatic solution. Capitalizing on Primakov's visit and a special session of the UN Security Council to discuss the Gulf War, on February 15 the Revolutionary Command Council announced "Iraq's readiness to deal with Security Council Resolution 660 of 1990, with the aim of reaching an honorable and acceptable solution, including withdrawal."

The Iraqi statement took the world by surprise. This was the first time since August 5, 1990, that the Iraqi President had referred to the possibility of leaving Kuwait, Iraq's nineteenth province for the past six months. Rays of light seemed to emerge at the end of the tunnel. People in Baghdad were jubilant. "It is high time we withdraw from Kuwait," a young Baghdadi told foreign television correspondents with uncharacteristic frankness, "this war is unbearable. Baghdad is no longer a city. It has become a desert."

Before long, however, this initial euphoria gave way to a

painful disillusionment, as it transpired that Saddam's readiness to withdraw from Kuwait was accompanied by a string of conditions which nullified the letter and spirit of Resolution 660. Not only was an Iraqi withdrawal conditional on an Israeli withdrawal "from Palestine and the Arab territories it is occupying in the Golan and southern Lebanon," and the cancellations of all UN resolutions against Iraq, but it was also predicated on international guarantees for "Iraq's historical rights on land and at sea," which implied general recognition of Iraq's claim to Kuwait and, possibly, of its continued occupation of the principality in whole or in part. In addition, Saddam compiled a list of demands, including the cancellation of Iraq's $80 billion foreign debt and the economic reconstruction of Iraq by the allied countries and at their expense.

Not surprisingly, these demands were dismissed as a "cruel hoax" by George Bush, who called upon "the Iraqi military and the Iraqi people to take matters into their own hands, to force Saddam Hussein the dictator to step aside."[28] Iraq responded by renewing its threat of employing chemical weapons. "If the high-altitude bombings against Iraq are not stopped," warned the Iraqi Ambassador to the UN, Abd al-Amir al-Anbari, "we would have no choice but to resort to weapons of mass destruction." This statement, just as the Iraqi "peace initiative," was interpreted by the Pentagon as a further indication of Saddam's growing desperation. The air campaign was intensified, preparations for the land war were consequently speeded up, and, although the administration denied a French assertion that a date for the decisive offensive had already been set, President Bush promised the Kuwaitis that their nightmare was going to end "very, very soon."

The American assessment of Saddam's despair was soon confirmed. On February 18, 1991, Tariq Aziz visited Moscow where he was presented with a Soviet plan for a cease-fire. Three days later, with international attention focused on Iraq, Aziz carried Saddam's response to the Soviet capital. The world then learned that the Iraqi leader had accepted the Soviet proposal agreeing to a full and unconditional withdrawal from Kuwait in accordance with UN Resolution 660.

Even though the Soviet proposal fell short of the allies' war aims in that it stipulated the cancellation of all other resolutions against Iraq and the cessation of sanctions before completion of an Iraqi withdrawal, it doubtless constituted a critical Iraqi concession. In agreeing to the Soviet proposal, Saddam, in effect, accepted the loss of Kuwait and abandoned his posture as champion of the Palestinian cause. The attempt to link his personal survival to broader Arab aspirations, begun with his "peace initiative" of August 12, 1990, had come to an abrupt end. True to his nature, at this dire moment, he chose to concentrate on those conditions posing the greatest threat to his own political survival: war crimes trials, reparations to Kuwait, and the end of economic sanctions. That Saddam already had the post-war situation on his mind was further illustrated by his belligerent speech, delivered a few hours before his acceptance of the Soviet proposal. Once more portraying the conflict as a battle between the noble forces of Islam and the evil forces of the infidels, Saddam pledged to continue the struggle "irrespective of the nature of the political efforts which we are exerting and whose formulation and directions Tariq Aziz carried to Moscow."[29] By presenting his concessions to Moscow as the natural culmination of his six months' defiance of the Western world, Saddam sought to prepare his subjects by casting the inevitable withdrawal from Kuwait as an act of national greatness.

Saddam's concessions were too little too late. Having already set the date for the ejection of Iraqi forces from Kuwait (though keeping this fact secret at the time), and sensing the extent of Saddam's anxiety, President Bush would not tolerate any delaying tactics that could benefit the Iraqi leader. "The coalition will give Saddam Hussein until noon Saturday [8 P.M. Iraqi time, February 23] to do what he must do—begin his immediate and unconditional withdrawal from Kuwait," he said. "We must hear publicly and authoritatively his acceptance of these terms."[30]

Despite his desperation, Saddam could not allow himself to submit to an American ultimatum before his people. Such capitulation, in his view, was tantamount to signing his own death warrant. Remaining adamant, he sought to revive the Soviet peace initiative which offered his only hope of portraying an Iraqi withdrawal as a morally responsible act, a generous acquiescence to the request of a friendly great power. Tariq Aziz offered the Soviets further concessions. These peace feelers were accompanied by indications that the Iraqis were bracing themselves for the land war and possibly the evacuation of Kuwait: an accelerated scorched-earth policy, as the Iraqi forces in Kuwait set fire to nearly half of Kuwait's 950 oil fields, and mass executions of Kuwaitis.

That Saddam had reconciled himself to the inevitability of the ground campaign was soon underscored by his public rejection of the ultimatum. A ground encounter had been his strategic goal from the beginning of the war, and, though losing much of its appeal due to the devastation wrought on the Iraqi forces by the allied air campaign, this option was still viewed by Saddam as more conducive to his survival than an unconditional surrender.

President Bush's response to the Iraqi rebuff of his ultimatum came within hours. At 4 A.M. (Iraqi time) on Sunday, February 24, he announced that the Commander-in-Chief of the coalition forces in Saudi Arabia, General Norman Schwarzkopf, had been instructed "to use all forces available, including ground forces, to eject the Iraqi army from Kuwait." Twelve hours later, in his first official briefing since the beginning of the land offensive, General Schwarzkopf informed scores of foreign journalists that the offensive was "progressing with dramatic success" and that the allied forces had already "reached all of their first day objectives," while incurring "remarkably light casualties."

Despite the signs of an overwhelming allied success, Saddam once more exhorted his soldiers to put death before humiliation. Invoking Islam and quoting from the Koran, Saddam remained bellicose and unyielding. He continued to proclaim Iraq's glorious victory in "the mother of all battles."

As events unfolded at an amazing pace, Schwarzkopf's description of the campaign was soon dated. Within less than forty-eight hours of fighting, the backbone of the Iraqi army had been broken. The apparently formidable line of defense in Kuwait, the so-called "Saddam line," collapsed as allied forces pushed through the Iraqi lines and stormed into Kuwait. Iraqi troops were surrendering en masse: by the end of the first day of fighting some 14,000 prisoners of war had been taken, and by the end of the second day this number had exceeded 20,000 and was growing by the hour. At the same time allied forces were moving rapidly inside Iraq, in a determined thrust to reach the Baghdad-Basra highway and thus encircle Saddam's elite units, the Republican Guards, deployed on Iraqi territory just north of the Kuwaiti border. More than 370 Iraqi tanks had been destroyed, and American intelligence sources reported that at least seven Iraqi divisions—up to 100,000 men—reported to their supreme headquarters that they could no longer fight.

From his bunker in Baghdad, Saddam watched with increasing dread the developments on the front. Not only had his hopes of giving the coalition a "bloody nose" been dashed, but "the mother of all battles" turned out to be a military catastrophe of the rarest stamp. Unless halted immediately, the allied offensive would culminate not only in a humiliating Iraqi withdrawal from Kuwait, but in the collapse of Saddam's own rule, as well.

The Iraqi leader moved swiftly to contain this formidable threat. As on many past occasions, when his personal and political survival lay in the balance, long-standing public commitments and pronouncements were reversible. Around midnight of February 25, some forty hours after the beginning of the land war, the Iraqi people were told by their state radio that "orders have been issued to our armed forces to withdraw in an organized manner to positions they held prior to August 1, 1990. This is regarded as practical compliance with Resolution 660. Our armed forces, which have proven its ability to fight and stand fast, will confront any attempt to harm it while it is carrying out their order."

Saddam's attempt to salvage his position was quickly spurned by the United States. Although there were reports of Iraqi units turning north in what appeared to be the beginning of a withdrawal, and although Mikhail Gorbachev personally made a phone call to President Bush, informing him that Saddam no longer demanded the abolition of all UN resolutions as a condition of withdrawal, the Administration refused to take the Iraqi bait. "We do not consider there is anything to respond to," said the White House spokesman, Marlin Fitzwater, "the war goes on."[31] The White House demanded that President Saddam Hussein "personally and publicly" commit to a speedy withdrawal and that Iraq comply fully with the twelve UN Security Council resolutions.[32]

This demand could not be more disconcerting for Saddam. Public humiliation was his worst possible scenario, no less alarming than the decimation of his army. In a society where words most often substitute for deeds, and where loss of face is the gravest dishonor,[33] the public admission of a mistake as devastating as the Kuwaiti invasion could not but pose a mortal threat to Saddam's survival. The larger-than-life image of the infallible "President Struggler," on which he had predicated his rule for more than a decade, would be supplanted by that of the bungling leader whose poor judgment had brought nothing but suffering and humiliation to his people. The carefully constructed barrier of public fear and adulation which in the past had shielded him from criticism and accountability would then be irrevocably destroyed.

Caught between the hammer and the anvil, between the suicidal consequences of continuing the battle and the hazards of admitting defeat, Saddam tried to have it both ways, complying with the American demand for a personal commitment to withdrawal, but, at the same time, keeping his proud image intact. In a personal address to the Iraqi nation, broadcast by Baghdad radio in the early morning hours of February 26, he announced that "our great armed forces will continue their withdrawal from Kuwait and complete it on this day."

An orderly withdrawal of a large army within a brief period of time, conducted in the course of full hostilities, is virtually impossible. Saddam's order, in effect, granted permission to his troops to run for their lives. Yet, to avoid the taint of defeat he rhetorically portrayed this hasty withdrawal as an Iraqi victory, achieved in the face of all adversity: "Applaud your victories, my dear citizens. You have faced 30 countries and the evil they have brought here. You have faced the whole world, great Iraqis. You have won. You are victorious. How sweet victory is." He did not renounce Iraq's claim to Kuwait but, rather, reminded his subjects that "the gates of Constantinople were not opened before the Muslims in their first struggling attempt." Whatever the future held for Iraq, he claimed, "the Iraqis will remember and will not forget that on August 8, 1990, Kuwait became part of Iraq legally, constitutionally and actually. They remember and will not forget that it continued in this state for a period of time between August 8, 1990, and until last night, when withdrawal began."[34]

President Bush responded angrily to this delusional posture. Nothing short of Saddam's acknowledgment of his defeat, underscored by his unconditional acceptance of all relevant Security Council resolutions, would be satisfactory. In a televised statement from the White House rose garden, Bush argued that Saddam was interested not in peace but in regrouping to fight another day, so as "to save the remnants of power and control in the Middle East by every means possible. And here, too, Saddam Hussein will fail. . . . The coalition will continue to prosecute the war with undiminished intensity. We will not attack unarmed soldiers in retreat. We have no choice but to consider retreating combat units as a threat and respond accordingly. Anything else would risk additional U.S. and coalition casualties."[35]

Bush's demands were followed by intensified military action.

As the Iraqi troops in Kuwait followed the order of their Commander-in-Chief and fled the advancing forces in large numbers, the allies reported the decimation of 21 of Iraq's 40 divisions in the Kuwaiti theater, and the tightening encirclement of the Republican Guards in Iraq. In the evening hours of February 26, on the thirtieth anniversary of Kuwait's independence, the Kuwaiti flag was flown again in Kuwait City.

Desperate to salvage whatever he could from his devastated war machine (within hours after Bush's speech, eight more Iraqi divisions had been rendered ineffective and the number of Iraqi war prisoners had exceeded 50,000), Saddam further softened his position. In a personal message to the President of the Security Council and the United Nations Secretary General, Foreign Minister Aziz announced Iraq's readiness to rescind its official annexation of Kuwait, to release all prisoners of war, and to pay war reparations in return for an immediate cease-fire and an end to the sanctions.[36] The proposal was immediately rejected by the Security Council, which remained adamant on Baghdad's compliance with all twelve UN resolutions. This compliance came shortly afterwards when the Iraqi Ambassador to the United Nations, Abd al-amir al-Anbari, informed the Security Council that Baghdad was willing to abide by the remaining Security Council resolutions. The last Iraqi soldier had left Kuwait at dawn, he said, and there was no further justification for sustaining the international sanctions against Iraq.[37]

With 150,000 casualties the Iraqi armed forces, a few days earlier the fourth largest military establishment in the world, lay in their death throes. Kuwait was free, and the Republican Guards were routed. There was no need to continue the war operations, which came increasingly to be seen as a one-sided battering of a defenseless foe. At 5 A.M. on February 28 (Iraqi time), six weeks after the launching of operation Desert Storm, and one hundred hours after the beginning of the ground war, President Bush announced that the allied forces would suspend offensive combat operations within three hours. "Kuwait is liberated," he said, "Iraq's army is defeated. Our military objectives are met. It was a victory for all the coalition nations, for the United Nations, for all mankind, and for the rule of law." In his view, it was now up to the Iraqis to determine whether the cessation of hostilities would be followed by a permanent cease-fire. They were to refrain from firing on any coalition forces or launching Scud missiles against any other country, to release all prisoners of

war and Kuwaiti detainees, and to send within forty-eight hours a
military delegation to discuss the details of a cease-fire.[38]

The American announcement was received with great relief
by Saddam, who lost no time in telling his subjects that the
cessation of hostilities was the result of the "glorious Iraqi
victory":

> You have won, Iraqis. Iraq is the one that is victorious. Iraq has
> succeeded in demolishing the aura of the United States, the empire
> of evil, terror, and aggression. Iraq has punched a hole in the myth
> of American superiority and rubbed the nose of the United States
> in the dust. The Guards have broken the backbone of their
> aggressors and thrown them beyond their border. We are confi-
> dent that President Bush would have never accepted a cease-fire
> had he not been informed by his military leaders of the need to
> preserve the forces fleeing the fist of the heroic men of the
> Republican Guards.[39]

This vibrant rhetoric notwithstanding, Saddam knew that he had
committed the gravest miscalculation of his political career. In
four days of fighting, the coalition forces managed to achieve
what the Iranians had failed to do during eight years of bloody
conflict—to reduce the Iraqi army to rubble and to occupy a
significant chunk of Iraq's territory, triggering widespread and
ferocious clashes in Shi'ite towns of southern Iraq and posing the
most deadly threat to his personal rule. From the outset of the
Kuwaiti crisis in the summer of 1990, there was an absolute
certainty in Saddam's mind of what could not be sacrificed: the
political survival of the ruler. Kuwait, the Palestinian cause, Iraqi
lives—all of these were important only so long as they served the
self-perpetuation of Saddam. When they did not, they became
dispensable. In his world of a war of "all against all," the
termination of one battle is merely the beginning of the next. As
the Iraqi people and the rest of the world looked hopefully to the
period of peace which would follow the war, Saddam braced
himself for what was to come. As far as he was concerned, the
Gulf War might have ended, but the most dangerous stage in his
never-ending struggle for personal and political survival had just
begun.

Epilogue

Whatever the long-term consequences of the Gulf War, Saddam Hussein will go down in history as one of those modern tyrants who brought their countries to the peak of their military might, only to embroil them later in catastrophic foreign adventures. Saddam's trail of destruction is long and painful—hundreds of thousands of deaths, as well as untold economic wreckage and ecological disaster. Upon his ascendancy in 1979 Iraq was a regional economic superpower, boasting some $35 billion in foreign exchange reserves. Twelve years later, after two devastating wars of its leader's making, it was reduced to dire poverty, with $80 billion in foreign debt and a shattered economic and strategic infrastructure.

The most prevalent image of Saddam Hussein, which gained more currency following the occupation of Kuwait in the summer of 1990 and the outbreak of the Gulf War six months later, is of an irrational, impetuous, yet cunning, megalomaniac, driven by an unbridled ambition to impose his domination over the entire Middle East. The most widely used historical analogy is that of the German dictator, Adolf Hitler.

Such a view, however, is largely misconceived. Saddam is no Hitler. To be sure, the two leaders share some striking similarities. Both Hitler and Hussein espoused a Darwinian worldview in which only the fittest survive, and where the end justifies all means. Both lacked the ability for personal empathy and possessed neither moral inhibitions nor respect for human life. As heads of ideological parties professing a mixture of nationalism and socialism, they transformed their countries into terrifying totalitarian systems, and embarked on large-scale acts of aggression against external neighbors. And yet, there are fundamental differences between the two. Hitler was willing to pursue his vision of the Third Reich to the destruction of his nation and his own death. Saddam might drive his people to misery and sacrifice but he always sought to avoid irreparable damage to himself and Iraq. In the Iran-Iraq War he opted for a cease-fire after 5 days of fighting; in the Gulf War, 48 hours of the ground operation forced him to search for a way out. Hitler was driven by a socio-political vision, however perverse, which he doggedly sought to achieve. Saddam, conversely, carries no ideological baggage whatsoever. Quite the reverse. From his point of view, ideology is purely a means for the promotion of the one and only goal which has guided him from the beginning of his political career: to reach the country's top position and to stay there for as long as he can. Political survival in one of the region's most hazardous political systems is the name of the game, and he would use whatever ideological acrobatics were required to achieve this objective. For Saddam, nothing is sacred; every principle is violable.

This can be most clearly seen in Saddam's actions concerning the Palestinian question, one of the core precepts of "Arab nationalism" and, allegedly, the issue dearest to Saddam's heart. "If the Americans ask us to first discuss the Gulf issue, and then the Palestinian question," Saddam responded to President Bush's offer for talks late in November 1990, "we will reply that if oil is the most important thing for you, Jerusalem is the most important thing for us."[1] As far as the Gulf crisis was concerned, the statement of intentions could not have been more sincere, for no other reason than that linkage of the Kuwaiti issue with the Arab-Israeli feud was highly instrumental for Saddam's political survival. It offered him both a possible avenue for regional prominence, and a dignified cover for the indefinite retention of Kuwait. By insisting on addressing the Palestinian problem prior to any discussion of the occupation of Kuwait, without ever committing himself to the evacuation of that country after the resolution of the Arab-Israeli conflict, he sought to give himself the necessary breathing space to reshape the human landscape of the tiny principality so that when the question were to be eventually discussed, the world would be faced with a *fait accompli*.

Yet, whenever the Palestinian question did not serve his personal ends, Saddam's attitude toward it ranged from indifferent aloofness to impatient hostility. When the Palestinian resistance movement experienced one of its greatest tragedies, during the Black September of 1970, Saddam was one of the foremost opponents of any Iraqi intervention on the Palestinians' behalf. Nor was he more responsive to the Palestinians' plight at another dark moment in their history—the 1982 Lebanon War. To the contrary. He provided Israel with the pretext to unleash a general assault on the PLO by authorizing the Abu Nidal group, then based in Baghdad, to carry out an assassination attempt on the Israeli Ambassador in London. And, when the Soviet Union proposed a cease-fire in February 1991, which omitted any mention of the Palestinian cause, Saddam, needing to end the Gulf War, accepted its terms.

Similarly, notwithstanding Saddam's vociferous recriminations against the Egyptian President, Anwar Sadat, for his separate peace treaty with Israel, when Saddam's lauded "second Qadisiya" against Iran ground to a halt and the Soviet Union proved reluctant to supply him with the necessary military hardware, he was not deterred from approaching Sadat with a request for military supplies. During the following years, as Egypt developed into an important military provider, Saddam would toil tirelessly to pave the way for that country's reincorporation into the mainstream of Arab politics, regardless of its peace treaty with Israel.

This friendship with Egypt was sustained beyond the Iran-Iraq War, as the two countries became founding members of a new regional organization, the ACC. Yet, when Saddam had decided to invade Kuwait, he did not hesitate to deceive his ally, President Mubarak, by giving his word of honor not to take this action until fully exploring diplomatic channels.

Even more, whenever his personal survival so required, Saddam had no qualms about seeking contacts with the "Zionist entity," either in the form of gaining Israeli acquiescence in the laying of an Iraqi oil pipeline to the Jordanian port town of Aqaba, or of attempting to acquire sophisticated Israeli military equipment. Saddam's interest in the Israeli channel did not disappear even after his personal survival had been (temporarily at least) secured: in the wake of the Iran-Iraq War, when the "punishment" of Damascus figured prominently on his agenda, he (tacitly) collaborated with Israel against Syrian interests in Lebanon. His contacts with Israel were illustrated most vividly by a series of meetings held by Major-General Abrabam Tamir, a senior Israeli official between 1984 and 1988, with Tariq Aziz,

Sa'dun Hammadi and Nizar Hamdoon. However, when his insecurity was exacerbated in the early months of 1990 due to a series of adverse domestic and international developments, he once more assaulted Israel in fiery rhetoric, and later with Scud missiles, in order to displace opprobrium from himself to the Jewish state. As with Egypt, Saddam's attitude toward Israel was purely instrumental.

Nor did Saddam show a more principled stand with regard to what is, perhaps, the Ba'th's most sacred article of faith—unity of the "Arab nation." It is true, of course, that he skillfully played on the theme of Arab nationalism in accordance with his shifting needs. In February 1980, for example, fearful of the revolutionary regime in Tehran, he enunciated the pan-Arab Eight-Point National Charter in an attempt to rally the Arab World behind his regime. During the following eight years of the Iran-Iraq War he would extract generous financial support from the Arab Gulf states by portraying his personal struggle for survival as the defense of "the eastern flank of the Arab World." Throughout the Kuwaiti crisis he made excessive use of the standard anticolonialist argument, accusing the West of preventing the emergence of a unified Arab state in the wake of the collapse of the Ottoman Empire, by carving the region into many small states, so as to keep it divided and weak.

And yet, when in the late 1970s the first real opportunity to rectify this "historic wrong," by taking a significant stride toward the unification of "the Iraqi and Syrian regions of the Arab nation" presented itself, Saddam unscrupulously obstructed this chance. It simply did not coincide with his own plans at the time. Moreover, by way of disguising his virtual inaction on the pan-Arab front after the mid-1970s, due to his overwhelming preoccupation with the consolidation of his domestic position, he gradually swayed the Ba'thi concept of commitment to the wider Arab nationalism (qawmiyya) in the direction of a distinct Iraqi identity (wataniyya). By concentrating on its own development, he argued, Iraq was in effect promoting the Arab cause, since "the glory of the Arabs stems from the glory of Iraq."

Nor did he pay any respect to the idea of Arab solidarity. In his pan-Arab Charter of 1980, he himself had formulated the principle that "disputes between Arab states should be settled through peaceful means." Ten years later, in his desire for Kuwaiti riches, Saddam violated his own highly lauded principle by his armed invasion of the neighboring principality.

The other fundamental precepts to which Saddam has declared himself committed have been no more strictly observed. His socialism has been nothing but a patchy populism, combining a tightly controlled state economy with a measure of free enterprise, geared toward one goal: the strength and security of his own political position. While ostensibly seeking to narrow the social and economic gaps within Iraqi society, Saddam has effectively created a new *nouveau riche* class, which owes its sole allegiance to him. The "liberation" of the Iraqi woman, an issue in which Saddam has taken great pride, has been similarly viewed instrumentally. Whenever he deemed that promoting women's rights could tarnish his regime, he would quickly backtrack, as illustrated most vividly by the 1990 law allowing male members of a family to kill their "misbehaving" female relatives with impunity. Finally, the Ba'thi commitment to a secular, modernizing society continues to be sacrificed on the altar of Saddam's survival. When the mullahs in Tehran began to demand his head in 1979, Saddam quickly disabused himself of his long-standing, staunch secularism, donning the mantle of religious piety. Nowhere has this transformation been more visible than during the Kuwaiti crisis and the ensuing war, where Saddam has resorted to zealous religious rhetoric that would have brought him the respect and admiration of the late Ayatollah Khomeini.

The subordination of policies to the ultimate goal of survival was also evident in Saddam's approach to the less ideological issues in Iraq's domestic and external affairs. His deep anxiety to consolidate the Party's position against mounting domestic pressures and growing Iranian hostility, for example, led him to make far-reaching concessions to the Kurdish minority in the March Manifesto of 1970. Five years later, having boxed himself into a corner, he made one of the most significant, and humiliating, foreign policy concessions of his career by concluding the Algiers Agreement of March 1975, which involved significant territorial losses, and constituted a de facto recognition of Iran's hegemony in the Gulf.

Yet these two agreements, like many other lesser understandings reached during Saddam's political career, were not worth the paper on which they had been signed, once the raison d'être for their conclusion disappeared. For Saddam there has been nothing permanent in political situations; everything is transitory and subjected to the ultimate goal of self-interest. In pursuing this objective he has relied on his unique mixture of capabilities:

obsessive caution, endless patience, tenacious perseverance, impressive manipulative skills and utter ruthlessness; and he has been adamant about preventing any factor—whether the Iraqi military, domestic factionalism, or external enemies—from dislodging him from power, regardless of the cost involved.

The employment of physical force for the promotion of domestic and foreign political ends has been the main hallmark of Saddam's career. This has ranged from his first significant Party assignment, participation in the abortive attempt on Qassem's life, to the notorious purges of 1979; from his formation of and control over Iraq's formidable security apparatus, through the mass gassing of the Iraqi Kurds, to the invasions of Iran and Kuwait, and his brutal suppression of the Shi'ite opposition to his rule in the wake of the Gulf War. This excessive use of force, however, has never been implemented in a hasty or uncontrolled manner. For all his ruthlessness, during his steady drive to the Presidential Palace Saddam proved himself cunning and calculating. He was willing to share power with President Bakr, standing in the shadows under the official epithet of "Mr. Deputy," for more than a decade before feeling confident enough to push his superior to the sidelines. He proved ready to allow the temporary ascendancy of political rivals if it served the long-term purpose of removing more lethal foes. His caution and deliberate machinations showed him to be less an *enfant terrible* than a ruthless tyrant who would use any means at his disposal to survive.

Even the two most dangerous decisions of his career—the invasions of Iran and Kuwait—were not taken in the heat of the moment. In both cases war was not Saddam's first choice but rather an act of last resort, taken only after trying other means for shoring up his position in the face of great adversity. In both instances the actual decision to use military force was taken only a short while before the outbreak of hostilities, following a prolonged process during which Saddam's anxiety escalated daily. The Iranian campaign—an extremely risky move—was aimed at containing a fanatical and uncompromising enemy who openly called for Hussein's blood. The occupation of Kuwait—a rather minor operation in the view of the Iraqi leader—was designed to provide the financial resources on which Saddam Hussein's political survival hinged.

While these decisions were undoubtedly fraught with grave miscalculations, it is clear that Hussein has probably been the most powerful Iraqi ruler during the past half century. Concentrating in his hands unprecedented political power, he has dictatorially ruled one of the less governable political systems in the Middle East, transforming it from an "ordinary" Third World authoritarian regime into a more modern totalitarian state, wielding awesome control over its subjects. No less significantly, he has turned Iraq into a military giant, towering over its neighbors. Most importantly, from his point of view, Saddam has managed to hold the reins of power for more than two decades: first as de facto leader under President Bakr and then as absolute ruler. No other leader in Iraq's modern history can make such a claim.

Yet, for all his brutal methods and malleable ideology, Saddam has largely become the captive of his own success. Like many tyrants before him, he has gradually maneuvered himself into domestic, regional and global positions which require raising the stakes incessantly in order to survive. Each acquisition of power engenders more fear of losing it. In the violent manner of Iraqi politics, either one subdues the system or is devoured by it. Saddam has managed for the present to subject the system to his will, at an exorbitant cost of domestic repression and external aggression. But he has failed to eradicate all potential dangers. By way of deflecting the Iranian threat, he created an economic monster that was about to destroy him; by way of fighting this economic monster, he managed to implicate himself in a far more complex and costly action in Kuwait, one that pitted him against the world and condemned him to ever greater threats to his survival.

The truth of the matter is that in the politics of the Middle East, where conflicting loyalties, disputed boundaries, religious, ethnic and tribal conflicts, as well as insecure rulers abound, Saddam's vision of a wild jungle where only the strongest and most adaptable survive has kept him in power for over two decades. Yet, even this stark approach can last only as long as the leader's ceaseless surveillance and tyrannical control of the country's governing mechanisms. Unless democracy emerges in Iraq, there will be no solution to the fundamental predicament confronting the person at the top of the political pyramid. Whether Sunni or Shi'ite, Ba'thist or Islamic fundamentalist, military or civilian, he will continue to confront dissent and disaster at every turn, and will be constantly preoccupied with his personal survival.

One can only hope that the readiness of the international community to go to such great lengths to subvert naked aggression by a regional superpower against a hapless neighbor will convince whoever reigns in Baghdad, as well as other local tyrants, that their perennial struggle for political survival must be subject to certain limits and norms of behavior. Only then, when physical force has outlived its usefulness as the primary instrument for settling political issues is there some hope that Saddam Hussein and his like will be discredited, and that life in the Middle East will emerge into the twenty-first century less "nasty" and "brutish" and more promising of peace.

Notes

Introduction: The Man and His World

1. Saddam Hussein's interview with the *Independent Television Network* (*ITN*), October 11, 1990; his address to the Iraqi nation as brought by *Baghdad Domestic Service*, July 17, 1990.
2. *Radio Moscow*, August 10, 1990.
3. Thomas Hobbes, *Leviathan* (1651), part I, chapter 13.
4. Personal interview.
5. Cited in H. Batatu, *The Old Social Classes and the Revolutionary Movements of Iraq* (Princeton: Princeton University Press, 1978), p. 25.
6. S. al-Khalil, *Republic of Fear: The Politics of Modern Iraq* (London: Hutchinson Radius, 1989), p. 169.
7. P. Marr, *The Modern History of Iraq* (Boulder, Colo.: Westview and London: Longman, 1985), p. 157.
8. Batatu, *The Old Social Classes*, p. 990.

Chapter 1: The Making of a Ba'thist

1. P. Hitti, *The Arabs: A Short History* (Chicago: Gateway, 1970), p. 248.
2. S. Lloyd, *Twin Rivers: A Brief History of Iraq from the Earliest Times to the Present Day* (Oxford: Oxford University Press, 1943), p. 126.
3. Like many other details in his life, Saddam's date of birth is somewhat shadowy. A certificate of the civil status of Saddam Hussein and his family, reproduced in one of his semi-official biographies, states 1939 as the year of his birth. The reasons for this contradiction with the official date are not entirely clear. One possibility is that it stems from a bureaucratic mistake by the registry clerk who prepared the certificate. It is also conceivable that Saddam himself does not know the exact date of his birth, not a completely uncommon phenomenon in rural Iraq. Alternatively, Saddam may have chosen to add two years to his age, either because his wife, Sajidah Talfah, was two years his senior, or because he thought that being older might buy him more respectability among his Party members during his meteoric climb

to the top. For the official version, see A. Iskandar, *Saddam Hussein: Munadilan, wa Mufakiran, wa Insanan* (Paris: Hachette, 1981), p. 17; for the personal status certificate, see F. Matar, *Saddam Hussein: The Man, the Cause and the Future* (London: Third World Centre, 1981), p. 71.

4. Edith Penrose and E. F. Penrose, *Iraq: International Relations and National Development* (London: Ernest Benn, 1978, and Boulder, Colo.: Westview, 1978), pp. 85, 88.

5. For the text of the 1930 Treaty, see J. C. Hurewitz, ed., *Diplomacy in the Near and Middle East: A Documentary Record* (Princeton, NJ: D. VanNostrand, 1966), vol. 2, pp. 178–181.

6. Matar, *Saddam Hussein,* p. 228.

7. Saddam Hussein, *al-Dimuqratiyya Masdar Quwwa li al-Fard wa al-Mujtama* (Baghdad: al-Thawra, 1977), p. 20.

8. C. M. Alexander, *Baghdad in Bygone Days: From the Journals and Correspondence of Claudius Rich, Traveller, Artist, Linguist, Antiquary, and British Resident at Baghdad, 1808–1821* (London: John Murray, 1928), p. 239.

9. Batatu, *The Old Social Classes,* p. 1088.

10. Goverment of Iraq, Ministry of Economics, *Statistical Abstract for the Eleven Financial Years 1927/28–1937/38* (Baghdad: The Government Press, 1939), p. 8.

11. G. L. Harris et al., *Iraq, Its People, Its Society, Its Culture* (New Haven, Conn.: Harf Press, 1958), p. 246; S. H. Longrigg and F. Stoakes, *Iraq* (London: Ernest Benn, 1958), p. 165.

12. Saddam's interview with ABC correspondent, Diane Sawyer, on June 24, 1990, as brought by the *Iraq News Agency* (*INA*), June 30, 1990.

13. J. Bulloch and H. Morris, *Saddam's War* (London: Faber & Faber, 1991), pp. 31–32.

14. Iskandar, *Saddam Hussein,* p. 19.

15. Ibid., p. 18.

16. *Guardian* (London), August 14, 1990.

17. Ibid.

18. M. Khadduri, *Socialist Iraq: A Study in Iraqi Politics since 1968* (Washington, D.C.: The Middle East Institute, 1978), p. 72.

19. For a good account of the formation of the Baghdad Pact, see J. C. Campbell, *Defense of the Middle East* (New York: Harper, 1960), Chapters 4–6.

20. On Ba'thi evolution and ideology, see J. Devlin, *The Ba'th Party: A History from Its Origins to 1966* (Stanford, Calif.: Hoover Institution Press, 1976); M. H. Kerr, *The Arab Cold War* (Oxford: Oxford University Press, 1971); P. Seale, *The Struggle for Syria* (Oxford: Oxford University Press, 1965).

21. M. Khadduri, *Independent Iraq, 1932–1958* (Oxford: Oxford University Press, 1960), pp. 358–364.

22. Ibid., pp. 299–302.

23. Personal interview.

24. *Al-Thawra* (Baghdad), February 2, 1987.

25. Bulloch and Morris, *Saddam's War,* p. 32.

26. Cited in al-Khalil, *Republic of Fear,* p. 17, n. 21.

27. According to Islamic opposition sources, Saddam also killed a relative of

his at the instigation of Hasan Ibrahim. There is, however, lack of evidence to substantiate this widely circulated story. See *Who Is Saddam Tikriti?* (Lawrence, Kan.: The Islamic Union of the Iraqi Students, n.d.), p. 5.

28. M. Khadduri, *Republican Iraq: A Study in Iraqi Politics since the Revolution of 1958* (Oxford: Oxford University Press, 1969), p. 87.

29. For an objective description of the assassination attempt, see Ibid., pp. 126–132. For a laudatory account, see Iskandar, *Saddam Hussein,* Chapter 5.

30. Matar, *Saddam Hussein,* p. 34.

31. Iskandar, *Saddam Hussein,* p. 45.

32. Penrose and Penrose, *Iraq,* pp. 362–363; *Koteret Rashit* (Tel Aviv), September 7, 1988, p. 34.

33. Matar, *Saddam Hussein,* p. 211.

34. E. Mortimer, "The Thief of Baghdad," *The New York Times Review of Books,* September 27, 1990, p. 8.

35. See, for example, *al-Qadisiya* (Baghdad), August 14, 1990.

36. P. Mansfield, *Nasser's Egypt* (Harmondsworth, England: Penguin, 1965), p. 123; K. Wheelock, *Nasser's New Egypt: A Critical Analysis* (London: Stevens & Sons, 1960), pp. 114–115.

37. *Observer* (London), September 28, 1980; A. Baram, "The Ruling Political Elite in Ba'thi Iraq, 1968–1986: The Changing Features of a Collective Profile," *International Journal of Middle East Studies,* Vol. 21 (1989), p. 483.

38. Matar, *Saddam Hussein,* p. 220; Iskandar, *Saddam Hussein,* pp. 77–78.

39. Bulloch and Morris, *Saddam's War,* p. 37.

40. Matar, *Saddam Hussein,* p. 237; Khadduri, *Socialist Iraq,* p. 74.

41. Kerr, *The Arab Cold War,* p. 20.

42. Al-Khalil, *Republic of Fear,* p. 29.

43. Marr, *The Modern History of Iraq,* p. 189; Penrose and Penrose, *Iraq,* p. 312.

44. Iskandar, *Saddam Hussein,* pp. 80–81.

45. I. Deutscher, *Stalin,* (Hardmondsworth, England: Penguin, 1966), p. 67.

46. Iskandar, *Saddam Hussein,* pp. 92–93.

47. Ibid., p. 101.

48. Cited in P. J. Vatikiotis, *Nasser and his Generation* (New York: St. Martin's Press, 1978), p. 15. For an excellent account of the decline of Arab nationalism, see F. Ajami, *The Arab Predicament* (Cambridge: Cambridge University Press, 1983).

49. *Middle East Record* (*MER*) (Jerusalem), Nos. 5–6, (1969–70), p. 516.

50. Ibid., No. 4 (1968), pp. 515–517.

51. Penrose and Penrose, *Iraq,* p. 376, n. 2.

52. Iskandar, *Saddam Hussein,* p. 110.

53. Ibid.

Chapter 2: Second among Equals

1. *Baghdad Domestic Service,* July 17, 1968.

2. In an account of the "July 17 Revolution," sympathetic to the Ba'thi takeover, Saddam Hussein's role is conspicuously missing. See Khadduri, *Socialist Iraq,* pp. 21–24.

3. Iskandar, *Saddam Hussein,* pp. 116–120; Matar, *Saddam Hussein,* pp. 46–47.

4. *Baghdad Domestic Service,* July 30, 1968.
5. A. Kelidar, *Iraq: The Search for Stability,* Conflict Studies, No. 59 (London: The Institute for the Study of Conflict, 1975), pp. 8–10.
6. Iskandar, *Saddam Hussein,* p. 111.
7. Matar, *Saddam Hussein,* p. 48.
8. See, for example, A. Baram, "Saddam Hussein: A Political Profile," *The Jerusalem Quarterly,* No. 17 (Fall 1980), pp. 117–118.
9. Iskandar, *Saddam Hussein,* pp. 108–109.
10. Batatu, *The Old Social Classes,* p. 1075.
11. *Economist* (London), June 24–30, 1978, p.78.
12. See Batatu, *The Old Social Classes,* pp. 1088–1090; Kelidar, *Iraq,* p. 6.
13. *Baghdad Domestic Service,* March 20, 1971.
14. Bulloch and Morris, *Saddam's War,* p. 31.
15. *Yediot Acharonot Weekly Magazine* (Tel Aviv), August 17, 1990, p. 13.
16. M. Farouk-Sluglett and P. Sluglett, *Iraq since 1958: From Revolution to Dictatorship* (London and New York: KPI, 1987), pp. 120–123; Marr, *The Modern History of Iraq,* pp. 213–214.
17. *Anwar* (Beirut), September 17, 1968.
18. Khadduri, *Republican Iraq,* p. 188.
19. *INA,* December 14, 1968; *Baghdad Observer,* December 13, 1968.
20. Al-Khalil, *Republic of Fear,* p. 292.
21. *Baghdad Domestic Service,* February 3, 1969.
22. Bulloch and Morris, *Saddam's War,* p. 71.
23. Khadduri, *Socialist Iraq,* p. 51; L. K. Kimball, *The Changing Pattern of Political Power in Iraq, 1958–1971* (New York: Robert Speller, 1972), p. 148.
24. See J. B. Schechtman, "The Repatriation of Iraq's Jewry," *Jewish Social Studies,* Vol. 15 (1953), pp. 151–172; Kimball, *The Changing Pattern of Political Power in Iraq,* p. 147.
25. Al-Khalil, *Republic of Fear,* pp. 49–50.
26. *Sunday Times* (London), February 28, 1969.
27. *Baghdad Domestic Service,* February 19, 1969; *Middle East News Agency* (*MENA*), February 26, 1969.
28. *Al-Jumhuriyya* (Baghdad), January 22, 1970.
29. B. al-Tikriti, *Muhawalat Irtiyyal al-Rayis Saddam Hussein* (Baghdad: Matbaat al-Dar al-Arabiya, 1982), pp. 45–79; *Baghdad Domestic Service,* January 21, 22, 1970.
30. *Baghdad Domestic Service,* January 21, 1970; March 2, 1970.
31. Farouk-Sluglett and Sluglett, *Iraq since 1958,* p. 118.
32. J. Bulloch, *The Making of War: The Middle East from 1967 to 1973* (London: Longman, 1974), p. 131.
33. Matar, *Saddam Hussein,* p. 227.
34. Batatu, *The Old Social Classes,* p. 1100.
35. Marr, *The Modern History of Iraq,* p. 190.
36. Khadduri, *Socialist Iraq,* p. 60.
37. *Guardian* (London), July 4, 1973.
38. *Baghdad Domestic Service,* March 29, 1970.
39. Iskandar, *Saddam Hussein,* p. 81.
40. A Baram, "The Ruling Political Elite in Ba'thi Iraq, 1968–1986," p. 452.

41. Al-Khalil, *Republic of Fear*, pp. 6–7; Khadduri, *Socialist Iraq*, pp. 63–67.
42. Kelidar, *Iraq*, p. 9.
43. *Al-Nahar* (Beirut), July 7, 1973.
44. For a description of the course of events during the "Kazzar affair," see, for example, *Times* (London), July 9, 1973; *New York Times*, July 13, 1973; *Le Figaro* (Paris), July 20, 1973; *Financial Times* (London), July 25, 1973.
45. *Al-Thawra* (Baghdad), July 9, 1973; *Baghdad Domestic Service*, July 7, 8, 1973.
46. *Al-Hayat* (Beirut), July 10, 1973; *MENA*, July 6, 1973.
47. *Baghdad Domestic Service*, August 30, 1971
48. Ibid., October 17, 1971.

Chapter 3: The Ruthless Pragmatist

1. S. Hussein, *Saddam Hussein on Current Events in Iraq*, trans. by K. Kishtainy (London: Longman, 1977), p. 64.
2. See, for example, *al-Thawra* (Baghdad), June 4, 1970.
3. *Near East Report* (Washington, D.C.), February 4, 1969, p. 10.
4. *Al-Thawra* (Baghdad), September 18, 1970; *Baghdad Domestic Service*, September 16, 20, 1970.
5. Farouk-Sluglett and Sluglett, *Iraq since 1958*, pp. 133–134.
6. *Baghdad Domestic Service*, September 26, 1970.
7. *Akhbar al-Yawm* (Cairo), October 24, 1970.
8. Bulloch, *The Making of War*, p. 135.
9. *Al-Hawadith* (Beirut), October 2, 1970.
10. Saddam's interview with *al-Siyasa* (Kuwait), January 17, 1981.
11. Matar, *Saddam Hussein*, pp. 244, 253.
12. E. O'Ballance, *No Victor, No Vanquished: The Yom Kippur War*, (San Rafael, Calif. and London: Presidio, 1978), p. 195, as cited in E. Kienle, *Ba'th v Ba'th* (London: I. B. Tauris, 1990), p. 72.
13. *Al-Thawra* (Baghdad), October 30, 1973.
14. *Baghdad Domestic Service*, October 29, 1973.
15. *Al-Jumhuriyya* (Baghdad), May 13, 1970; *al-Thawra* (Baghdad), September 28, 1970.
16. Ba'th Party, *The 1968 Revolution in Iraq. Experience and Prospects*. The Political Report of the Eighth Congress of the Arab Ba'th Socialist Party in Iraq, January 1974 (London: Ithaca Press, 1979), p. 133.
17. For the text of the agreement, see Hurewitz, *Diplomacy in the Near and Middle East*, Vol. 1, pp. 218–219.
18. For the text of the agreement, see ibid., pp. 269–270.
19. G. Lenczowski, *The Middle East in World Affairs*, 4th edition (Ithaca and London: Cornell University Press, 1980), pp. 661–662; Khadduri, *Socialist Iraq*, pp. 163–159; Marr, *The Modern History of Iraq*, pp. 78, 122, 180–181.
20. Khadduri, *Socialist Iraq*, p. 155.
21. Ibid., p. 157.
22. Marr, *The Modern History of Iraq*, p. 291.
23. The Shah emphasized his views on many occasions, as reported by the *Guardian* (London), October 9, 1971; *Agence France-Presse* (*AFP*), June 24, 1974; *Deutsche Presse Agentur* (*DPA*), June 10, 1976.

24. For a discussion of the Iranian-Iraqi relationship, see E. Karsh, "Geopolitical Determinism: The Origins of the Iran-Iraq War," *Middle East Journal*, Vol. 44, No. 2 (Spring 1990), pp. 256–268.
25. Saddam's interview with *al-Ahram* (Cairo), February 21, 1975.
26. E. Karsh, *The Iran-Iraq War: A Military Analysis*, Adelphi Papers, No. 220 (London: The International Institute for Strategic Studies, 1987), p. 8.
27. For background on the Kurdish problem, see C. Kutschera, *Le Mouvement national kurde* (Paris: Flammarion, 1979); E. Ghareeb, *The Kurdish Question in Iraq* (Syracuse, N.Y.: Syracuse University Press, 1981).
28. *Financial Times* (London), March 15, 1969.
29. *Kurdish Affairs Bulletin*, No. 6 (1969), p. 1.
30. For the text of the March Manifesto, see Khadduri, *Socialist Iraq*, Appendix C, pp. 231–240.
31. *Al-Thawra* (Baghdad), March 12, 1970.
32. *Al-Jumhuriyya* (Baghdad), March 16, 1971.
33. *Le Monde* (Paris), May 25, 1971.
34. O. Bengio, *Mered ha-Kurdim be-Iraq* (Tel Aviv: Hakibutz Hameuchad, 1989), pp. 67–69.
35. Ibid., p. 75.
36. For the text of the agreement, see *New Middle East*, June 1972, p. 42.
37. Marr, *The Modern History of Iraq*, pp. 223–224; Farouk-Sluglett and Sluglett, *Iraq since 1958*, p. 145.
38. *Middle East Economic Survey (MEES)*, December 24, 1967.
39. Matar, *Saddam Hussein*, p. 233. See also, S. Hussein, *On Oil Nationalisation in Iraq* (Baghdad: al-Thawra House, 1973).
40. G. Golan, *Soviet Policies in the Middle East from World War II to Gorbachev* (Cambridge: Cambridge University Press, 1990), p. 167.
41. Saddam's interview with *al-Nahar* (Beirut), April 13, 1972.
42. Karsh, *The Iran-Iraq War: A Military Analysis*, pp. 6–7.
43. Farouk-Sluglett and Sluglett, *Iraq since 1958*, pp. 158–160, 164–170.
44. *Washington Post*, June 22, 1973.
45. S. Hussein, *Saddam Hussein on Current Events in Iraq*, p. 38.
46. S. Hussein, *Khandaq Wahid am Khandaqan* (Baghdad: Dar al-Thawra, 1977), p. 31.
47. S. Jawad, "Recent Developments in the Kurdish Issue," in T. Niblock (ed.), *Iraq: The Contemporary State* (London: Croom Helm and Exeter: Centre for Arab Gulf Studies, 1982), p. 53.
48. J. M. Abdulghani, *Iraq and Iran: The Years of Crisis* (Baltimore: Johns Hopkins University Press and London: Croom Helm, 1984), p. 142.
49. Saddam's interview with *al-Ahram* (Cairo), February 21, 1975.
50. See S. Hussein, *Discours du Président Saddam Hussein à l'Assemblée Nationale*, réunie en séance extraordinaire le 17 septembre 1980, pp. 16–18; *INA*, March 27, 1979.
51. Abdulghani, *Iraq and Iran*, pp. 156–157.
52. Penrose and Penrose, *Iraq*, p. 137.
53. Kutschera, *Le Mouvement national kurde*, pp. 322–323.
54. For the text of the Algiers Agreement, see *INA*, March 6, 1975; *New York Times*, March 8, 1975.

55. For such an argument, see, for example, Marr, *The Modern History of Iraq*, p. 233.
56. See, for example, *al-Ba'th* (Damascus), April 9, 1975; *Damascus Domestic Service*, April 18, 1975.
57. *Financial Times* (London), March 24, 1975.
58. Ramadan's interview with *al-Tadamun* (London), October 29, 1990, pp. 25–27.

Chapter 4: The Strong Man of Baghdad

1. Matar, *Saddam Hussein*, pp. 231–232.
2. Ibid.
3. Ibid., p. 231.
4. Ibid.
5. *Baghdad Domestic Service*, February 25, 1977.
6. *Middle East* (London), July 1977, p. 49.
7. Farouk-Sluglett and Sluglett, *Iraq since 1958*, p. 206.
8. Karsh, *The Iran-Iraq War: A Military Analysis*, pp. 10–11.
9. Mortimer, "The Thief of Baghdad," p. 12.
10. L. Trotsky, *Stalin* (London: Hollis & Carter, 1947), p. 421.
11. G. Gilbar, *Kalkalat ha-Mizrah ha-Tichon* (Tel Aviv: Ministry of Defense Publishing House, 1990), pp. 181–182.
12. Marr, *The Modern History of Iraq*, pp. 242, 336.
13. R. Springborg, "Infitah, Agrarian Transformation, and Elite Consolidation in Contemporary Iraq," *Middle East Journal*, Vol. 40, No. 1 (Winter 1986), pp. 33–52; Marr, *The Modern History of Iraq*, pp. 240–243, 250–251.
14. A. Sousa, "The Eradication of Illiteracy in Iraq," in Niblock (ed.), *Iraq*, pp. 102–105.
15. *Official Gazette* (Baghdad), February 20, 1978.
16. I. al-Khafaji, "The Parasitic Base of the Ba'thist Regime," in CARDRI, *Saddam's Iraq* (London: Zed Books, 1989), pp. 80–82; S. Jain, *Size Distribution of Income* (Washington, D.C.: World Bank, 1975).
17. Springborg, "Infitah."
18. *INA*, April 14, 1977.
19. Ibid., January 27, 1990.
20. *Al-Thawra*, as cited in CARDRI, *Saddam's Iraq*, p. 104.
21. Ba'th Party, *The 1968 Revolution in Iraq*, pp. 115–116.
22. Al-Khalil, *Republic of Fear*, p. 91.
23. Ibid., pp. 88–93.
24. Hussein, *al-Dimuqratiyya*, pp. 14–15.
25. Saddam Hussein, *Social and Foreign Affairs in Iraq*, trans. by K. Kishtainy (London: Croom Helm, 1979), p. 31.
26. *Guardian* (London), April 19, 1990.
27. Hussein, *Saddam Hussein on Current Events in Iraq*, p. 71.
28. See *Times* (London), June 7, 1972; Penrose and Penrose, *Iraq*, pp. 434–435.
29. Penrose and Penrose, *Iraq*, p. 377, n. 21.
30. *Middle East Contemporary Survey* (*MECS*) (London and New York, 1978–1981), all editions from 1976–77 through 1979–80.

31. *Der Spiegel* (Hamburg), August 6, 1990, p. 118.
32. A. Dawisha, "Iraq: The West's Opportunity," *Foreign Policy*, 1980, pp. 136–137.
33. Karsh, *The Iran-Iraq War: A Military Analysis*, p. 44.
34. *Observer Foreign News Service* (London).
35. Personal interview.
36. *MECS, 1978–79*, p. 568.
37. Kutschera, *Le Mouvement national kurde*, p. 324.
38. Farouk-Sluglett and Sluglett, *Iraq since 1958*, pp. 182–186.
39. *Financial Times* (London), May 27, 1978; *Daily Telegraph* (London), June 7, 1978.
40. *Middle East* (London), May 1978.
41. *Washington Post*, April 28, 1975.
42. A. Baram, "Qawmiyya and Wataniyya in Ba'thi Iraq: The Search for a New Balance," *Middle Eastern Studies*, Vol. 19, No. 2 (April 1983), pp. 188–200.
43. *Al-Jumhuriyya* (Baghdad), October 29, 1974.
44. *MECS, 1978–79*, p. 573.
45. *Al-Thawra* (Baghdad), September 5, 1975.
46. Kienle, *Ba'th v Ba'th*, p. 95.
47. *INA*, February 1, 1978.
48. *Baghdad Domestic Service*, October 1, 1978.
49. For the text of the Charter of Joint National Action, see Kienle, *Ba'th v Ba'th*, pp. 176–178.
50. M. Wight, *Power Politics* (Harmondsworth, England: Penguin, 1979), p. 157.
51. Kienle, *Ba'th v Ba'th*, p. 142.
52. P. Seale, *Asad: The Struggle for the Middle East* (London: I. B. Tauris, 1988), p. 355.
53. See, for example, Baram "Qawmiyya and Wataniyya"; Matar, *Saddam Hussein*, pp. 65–70.
54. *MECS, 1978–79*, p. 575.
55. Matar, *Saddam Hussein*, p. 51.
56. *MECS, 1978–79*, p. 560.

Chapter 5: President at Last

1. Matar, *Saddam Hussein*, p. 49.
2. *INA*, July 16, 1979.
3. Ibid.
4. *Baghdad Domestic Service*, July 17, 1979.
5. Matar, *Saddam Hussein*, p. 54.
6. *Baghdad Voice of the Masses*, July 15, 1979.
7. *INA*, July 28, 1979.
8. This account draws heavily on al-Ahram (Cairo), August 5, 1979, and al-Tikriti, *Muhawalat Irtiyyal al-Rayis Saddam Hussein*, pp. 139–160.
9. Saddam's public address, *INA*, August 8, 1979.
10. *MECS, 1978–79*, p. 564.
11. *Baghdad Domestic Service*, August 8, 1979.
12. *INA*, August 8, 1979.

13. *Guardian* (London), April 11, 1980.
14. *Observer* (London), August 5, 1979.
15. *MECS, 1979–80*, p. 505.
16. O. Bengio, "Saddam Hussein's Quest for Power and Survival," *Asian and African Studies*, Vol. 15 (1981), pp. 328–329.
17. *INA*, December 23, 1970.
18. Ibid., June 30, 1980.
19. *Al-Thawra* (Baghdad), May 3, 1980.
20. *New York Times*, June 21, 1980.
21. Matar, *Saddam Hussein*, p. 219; *al-Qadisiya* (Baghdad), August 14, 1990.
22. G. Roux, *Ancient Iraq* (Harmondsworth, England: Penguin, 1980), p. 274. The discussion in this section draws heavily on this excellent book.
23. For a detailed discussion of Saddam's efforts to create "a new Mesopotamian man," see: A. Baram, "Culture in the Service of *Wataniyya:* The Treatment of Mesopotamian-Inspired Art in Ba'thi Iraq," *Asian and African Studies*, Vol. 17 (1983), pp. 265–313; and his "Mesopotamian Identity in Ba'thi Iraq," *Middle Eastern Studies*, Vol. 19 (1983), pp. 426–455.
24. Hussein, *Saddam Hussein on Current Events in Iraq*, p. 51.
25. *Times* (London), July 17, 1980.
26. *Observer* (London), April 28, 1980.
27. Personal interview.
28. Karsh, *The Iran-Iraq War: A Military Analysis*, p. 12.
29. Saddam Hussein, *Muqtatafat min Ahadith Saddam Hussein* (Beirut: Dar al-Tali'ah, 1979), pp. 172–173.
30. Matar, *Saddam Hussein*, p. 217.
31. The discussion of Iraq's nuclear program draws mainly on the following sources: F. Barnaby, *The Invisible Bomb* (London: I. B. Tauris, 1989); L. Spector, *Going Nuclear* (Cambridge, Mass.: Ballinger, 1987); L. Spector, *Nuclear Ambitions* (Boulder, Colo.: Westview, 1990); J. Snyder, "The Road to Osiraq: Baghdad's Quest for the Bomb," *Middle East Journal*, Vol. 37, No. 4 (1983), pp. 565–593.
32. *Times* (London), July 22, 1980.
33. Snyder, "The Road to Osiraq," p. 569.
34. *MECS, 1979–80*, p. 509.
35. *Baghdad Domestic Service*, July 22, 1980.
36. Ibid., July 17, 1981.
37. *Independent* (London), September 12, 1990.
38. *Sunday Times* (London), September 2, 1990.
39. Matar, *Saddam Hussein*, p. 104.
40. *MECS, 1978–79*, p. 577.
41. *International Herald Tribune*, July 10, 1978.
42. See, for example, *Baghdad Domestic Service*, January 6, 1980; *INA*, January 31, 1980.
43. Hussein, *Social and Foreign Affairs in Iraq*, p. 101.
44. Hussein, *Saddam Hussein on Current Events in Iraq*, p. 63.
45. *MECS, 1979–80*, p. 527; A. Baram, "Iraq: Between East and West," in E. Karsh (ed.), *The Iran-Iraq War: Impact and Implications* (London: Macmillan and New York: St. Martin's Press, 1989), p. 80.

46. *MECS, 1977–78*, p. 528, *1979–80*, p. 526; *Times* (London), July 22, 1980; *Observer* (London), May 20, 1979.
47. *MECS, 1979–1980*, pp. 224–225.

Chapter 6: Deciding on War

1. Iraq's Ministry of Foreign Affairs, *Iraqi-Iranian Conflict: Documentary Dossier* (Baghdad: January 1981), pp. 208–214.
2. See, for example, S. Bakhash, *The Reign of the Ayatollahs* (New York: Basic Books, 1984), p. 125; R. K. Ramazani, *Revolutionary Iran: Challenge and Response in the Middle East* (Baltimore, Md.: Johns Hopkins University Press, 1988), p. 57; A. Cordesman, *The Gulf and the Search for Strategic Stability* (Boulder, Colo.: Westview, 1984), pp. 645–646.
3. *INA*, December 31, 1979.
4. E. Kanovsky, "Economic Implications for the Region and World Oil Market," in Karsh (ed.), *The Iran-Iraq War: Impact and Implications*, pp. 231–232.
5. *INA*, February 14, 1979.
6. Ibid., February 13, 1979.
7. See, for example, interview with President Bakr in British Broadcasting Corporation (BBC), *Summary of World Broadcast*, May 22, 1979, ME/6122/A 1–2.
8. Ramazani, *Revolutionary Iran*, pp. 58–59.
9. *Tehran Domestic Service*, July 24, 1982.
10. *BBC Summary*, June 8, 1979, ME/6144/A5 and June 9, 1979, ME/6145/A7.
11. C. Brockelman, *History of the Islamic People* (New York: Capricorn Books, 1960), pp. 45–76.
12. P. Marr, "Iraq's Leadership Dilemma: A Study of Leadership Trends, 1948–1968," *Middle East Journal*, Vol. 24 (1970), pp. 288–289.
13. O. Bengio, "Shi'is and Politics in Ba'thi Iraq," *Middle Eastern Studies*, Vol. 21, No. 1 (1985), pp. 1–14; C. Tripp, "The Consequences of the Iran-Iraq War for Iraqi Politics," in Karsh (ed.), *The Iran-Iraq War: Impact and Implications*, pp. 65–69; E. Kedourie, "The Iraqi Shi'is and Their Fate," in M. Kramer (ed.), *Shi'ism, Resistance, and Revolution* (Boulder, Colo.: Westview, 1987), pp. 135–157.
14. *Times* (London), January 8, 1975. For a general discussion of Shi'ite opposition to the regime, see H. Batatu, "Iraq's Underground Shi'a Movements: Characteristics, Causes and Prospects," *Middle East Journal*, Vol. 35 (1981), pp. 578–594.
15. *MECS, 1976–77*, pp. 405, 408.
16. Saddam Hussein, *Nadhra fi al-Din wa al-Turath* (Baghdad: Dar al-Hurriyah, 1978), pp. 12–13.
17. *Al-Thawra* (Baghdad), March 7, 1978.
18. Matar, *Saddam Hussein*, pp. 141–142.
19. *MECS, 1978–79*, p. 571.
20. *INA*, August 8, 1979.
21. *Guardian* (London), April 3, 1980; *Financial Times* (London), April 12, 1980; *International Herald Tribune*, April 10, 1980; *Daily Telegraph* (London), April 9, 1980.

22. See, for example, *al-Thawra* (Baghdad), February 9, June 21, 1980.
23. *Foreign Broadcast Information Service (FBIS-MEA)*, September 11, 1981, p. E2.
24. Cited in S. Chubin and C. Tripp, *Iran and Iraq at War* (London: I. B. Tauris, 1988).

Chapter 7: Confronting the Ayatollah

1. Saddam's interview with *al-Siyasa* (Kuwait), January 17, 1981.
2. B. Rubin, *Modern Dictators* (New York: New American Library, 1987), p. 229.
3. Hilal Abd al-Rida al-Dagili and Sa'd Abd al-Wahab al-Samarra'i, *Saddam Hussein: Batal al-Nasr wa al-Salam* (Baghdad: Dar al-Shu'un al-Thakafiyya al-Amma, 1989), p. 83.
4. Chubin and Tripp, *Iran and Iraq at War*, p. 96.
5. *Baghdad Domestic Service*, April 15, 1980.
6. Saddam's interview with *al-Mustaqbal* (Paris), October 13, 1979; *al-Thawra* (Baghdad), December 14, 1979.
7. *Baghdad Domestic Service*, April 15, 1980.
8. Matar, *Saddam Hussein*, pp. 235, 266.
9. Kanovsky "Economic Implications," p. 236.
10. R. King, *The Iran-Iraq War: The Political Implications*, Adelphi Papers, No. 219 (London: The International Institute for Strategic Studies, 1987), pp. 17–18; *Financial Times* (London), July 14, 23, 1981; December 17, 1981.
11. *Financial Times* (London), March 26, 1982.
12. Karsh, *The Iran-Iraq War: A Military Analysis*, p. 43.
13. For an analysis of the military conduct of the Iran-Iraq War, see Karsh, ibid.; A. Cordesman and A. Wagner, *The Lessons of Modern War, Vol. II, The Iran-Iraq War* (Boulder Colo.: Westview, 1990); E. O'Ballance, *The Gulf War* (London: Brassey's, 1988).
14. *International Herald Tribune*, March 16, 1982.
15. D. Hiro, "Chronicle of the Gulf War," *MERIP Reports*, Vol. 14, No. 6/7 (July–September 1984), p. 8.
16. Kanovsky, "Economic Implications," pp. 242–246.
17. *International Herald Tribune*, June, 21, 22, 1982.
18. See, for example, *BBC Summary*, July 31, 1979, A10/11.
19. Saddam Hussein, "Address to the Nation," *Baghdad Domestic Service*, September 28, 1980.
20. Ayatollah Ruhollah Khomeini, "Islamic Government," in his *Islam and Revolution*, trans. by H. Algar (Berkeley: Mizan, 1981), pp. 31, 48.
21. Chubin and Tripp, *Iran and Iraq at War*, pp. 140–142.
22. E. Karsh, *Soviet Arms Transfers to the Middle East during the 1970s* (Tel Aviv: Tel Aviv University, 1983), JCSS Paper No. 22, p. 18.
23. J. Garçon, "La France et le conflit Iran-Iraq," *Politique Etrangère*, February 1988, pp. 357–366.
24. *BBC Summary*, January 5, 1983, A6.
25. A. Baram, "Iraq: Between East and West."
26. F. Axelgard, *A New Iraq?* (New York: Praeger for the CSIS, 1988), pp. 77–78; *Financial Times* (London), April 1, 2, 1981.
27. Saddam's interview with *al-Siyasa* (Kuwait), May 24, 1982; Chubin and Tripp, *Iran and Iraq at War*, p. 147.

28. *Saddam Hussein's Press Conference*, November 10, 1980; Chubin and Tripp, *Iran and Iraq at War*, p. 144.
29. *International Herald Tribune*, November 27, December 5, 1984.
30. Ibid., May 20, 1985.
31. See, for example, *Washington Post*, January 31, 1988; *International Herald Tribune*, January 30–31, February 1, 1988; *Financial Times* (London), February 24, 1988.
32. *Daily Telegraph* (London), March 24, 1986.
33. *Hadashot* (Tel Aviv), November 13, 15, 1987; *Davar* (Tel Aviv), November 12, 1987.
34. J. Bulloch and H. Morris, *The Gulf War* (London: Methuen, 1989), pp. 81–88.
35. *BBC Summary*, June 11, 1982, A19–20; June 14, 1982, A23–24.
36. Bengio, "Saddam Hussein's Quest for Power and Survival," pp. 326–328.
37. This story has received wide coverage in the Western press. See, for example, *Wall Street Journal* (New York), August 27, 1990.
38. *Christian Science Monitor* (International Edition), August 18–24, 1986.
39. Cited in al-Khalil, *Republic of Fear*, p. 34.
40. *Guardian* (London), June 28, 1983.
41. Bengio, "Shi'is and Politics in Ba'thi Iraq," pp. 1–14.
42. *Guardian* (London), January 19, February 13, 1984.
43. For the Iraqi campaign against the Kurds in the summer of 1988, see, for example, *Daily Telegraph* (London), March 4, 1988; *Financial Times* (London), February 26, 1988; *Times* (London), March 22, 1988.
44. E. Karsh, "Military Lessons of the Iran-Iraq War," *Orbis*, Spring 1989, pp. 209–220.
45. *Newsweek*, March 19, 1984.
46. O'Ballance, *The Gulf War*, pp. 185–186.
47. On the Tanker War, see Karsh, *The Iran-Iraq War: A Military Analysis*, pp. 28–30; Cordesman and Wagner, *The Lessons of Modern War*, pp. 530–591.
48. *Tehran Domestic Service*, May 17, 1984.
49. On the reflagging operation, see T. McNaugher, "US Policy and the Gulf War: A Question of Means," in C. C. Joyner (ed.), *The Persian Gulf War* (New York: Greenwood Press, 1990), pp. 111–127.
50. For the breakdown of Iranian morale, see S. Chubin, "Iran and the War: From Stalemate to Ceasefire," in H. W. Maull and O. Pick (eds.), *The Gulf War: Regional and International Dimensions* (London: Pinter, 1989), pp. 5–17.

Chapter 8: The Rule of Fear

1. See, for example, Saddam Hussein, *For Youth Nothing Is Impossible* (Baghdad: Dar al-Ma'mun, 1984).
2. S. Hussein, *al-Thawra wa al-Nadhra al-Jadidah* (Baghdad: Dar al-Hurriyah, 1981), p. 149.
3. Hussein, *al-Dimuqratiyya*, p. 19.
4. *Al-Thawra* (Baghdad), February 12, 1979.
5. *MECS, 1979–80*, p. 505.
6. *Observer* (London), September 28, 1980.
7. *Guardian* (London), June 8, 1960.

8. See, for example, Amnesty International, *Iraq: Evidence of Torture* (London: Amnesty International Publications, 1981).
9. The best available account of the Iraqi security apparatus is offered in Samir al-Khalil's *Republic of Fear.*
10. Saddam's interview with *al-Nahar* (Beirut), April 13–14, 1972.
11. *MECS, 1979–80,* p. 510.
12. Saddam's interview on June 24, 1990.
13. Bulloch and Morris, *Saddam's War,* p. 29.
14. In mid-November 1990 he was removed from his post and replaced by Aziz Saleh al-Nouma. *Al-Jumhuriyya* (Baghdad), as cited by the *Independent* (London), November 15, 1990.
15. Al-Tikriti, *Muhawalat Irtiyyal al-Rayis Saddam Hussein.*
16. On Saddam's feud with his half-brothers, see, for example, the *Guardian* (London), November 7, 1983; *Times* (London), October 27, 1983; *Christian Science Monitor* (International Edition), August 3, 1984.
17. *Mideast Markets* (London), January 8, 1990.
18. *Guardian* (London), June 9, 1990.
19. *Observer* (London), June 3, 1990.
20. Chubin and Tripp, *Iran and Iraq at War,* p. 94.
21. M. Farouk-Sluglett and P. Sluglett, "Iraqi Ba'thism: Nationalism, Socialism, and National Socialism," in CARDRI, *Saddam's Iraq* (1986 edition), p. 105.
22. For the official version of Adnan Khairallah's death, see *INA,* May 6, 1989.
23. Iskandar, *Saddam Hussein,* pp. 22–23.
24. On the "Shahbandar affair," see *Sunday Times* (London), March 26, 1989; *Financial Times* (London), May 8, 1989; *Mideast Markets,* May 15, 1989; *Ma'ariv* (Tel Aviv), May 7, 1989; *Jerusalem Post* (Jerusalem), March 29, 1989.
25. *Observer* (London), June 3, 1990; *Sunday Times* (London), March 26, 1989.
26. C. Tripp, "The Consequences of the Iran-Iraq War for Iraqi Politics," in Karsh (ed.), *The Iran-Iraq War: Impact and Implications,* pp. 60–64.
27. Cited in al-Khalil, *Republic of Fear,* p. 55.
28. *MECS, 1978–79,* p. 568.
29. Baram, "The Ruling Political Elite in Ba'thi Iraq," p. 485.
30. *Wall Street Journal* (New York), August 27, 1990.
31. Personal interview.
32. *INA,* December 12, 1989.
33. Ba'th Party, *The 1968 Revolution in Iraq,* p. 103.
34. Al-Khalil, *Republic of Fear,* p. 31.
35. Baram, "Saddam Hussein: A Political Profile," pp. 122–125.
36. Al-Khalil, *Republic of Fear,* p. 28.
37. *MECS, 1983–84,* pp. 470–473; Chubin and Tripp, *Iran and Iraq at War,* p. 117.
38. Chubin and Tripp, *Iran and Iraq at War,* pp. 116–119.

Chapter 9: The Road to Kuwait

1. Tripp, "The Consequences of the Iran-Iraq War," p. 76.
2. *Independent* (London), August 30, 1989.
3. *Daily Telegraph* (London), November 18, 1989; *Independent* (London), August 14, 1989; *Times* (London), November 21, 1989.

4. *Guardian* (London), August 17, 1989; *Independent* (London), March 16, 1989.

5. On the privatization measures, see M. Farouk-Sluglett, "Iraq after the War: The Role of the Private Sector," *Middle East International* (London), March 17, 1989, pp. 17–18; *Christian Science Monitor* (International Edition), December 12–18, 1988; *Financial Times* (London), December 5, 1988; *Middle East Economic Digest* (*MEED*), November 25, 1988, June 23, September 4, 1989.

6. *Guardian* (London), April 1, 1989.

7. *Wall Street Journal* (New York), February 15, 1991.

8. *Guardian* (London), April 3, 1989.

9. Ibid., April 1, 1989; *Times* (London), November 29, 1988; *Independent* (London), August 30, 1989; *Christian Science Monitor* (International Edition), December 12–18, 1988, February 1, 1990.

10. For the Iraqi campaign against the Kurds, see the *Independent* (London), November 9, 1988; February 3, March 16, 1990; *International Herald Tribune*, September 14, 16, 1988.

11. *Financial Times* (London), March 16, May 22, 1989; *Times* (London), March 16, 1989.

12. *Guardian* (London), September 23, 1988; *Daily Telegraph* (London), September 13, 1988.

13. *Christian Science Monitor* (International Edition), August 31–September 6, 1989.

14. *Financial Times* (London), March 16, 1989.

15. Ibid. (London), April 12, 1989; *Times* (London), August 28, 1988; *Guardian* (London), October 12, 1988.

16. *Guardian* (London), October 12, 1988.

17. *Christian Science Monitor* (International Edition), December 12–18, 1988.

18. E. Karsh, "Regional Strategic Implications of the Iran-Iraq War," in S. Gazit (ed.), *The Middle East Military Balance, 1988–1989* (Boulder, Colo.: Westview, 1989), pp. 100–114.

19. *Independent* (London), July 20, 1988.

20. About half of the debt was owed to Arab Gulf states, Saudi Arabia and Kuwait in particular. Guaranteed trade debt to Western countries amounted to between $16 billion and $20 billion. Most of the rest were military debts, much of them owed to the Soviet Union. See, for example, the *Economist* (London), September 30, 1989, August 4, 1990; *Middle East*, December 1989; *Independent* (London), March 16, 1990.

21. *Observer* (London), October 21, 1990.

22. *INA*, April 8, 1990.

23. *INA*, February 17, 20, May 1, 1990; *Baghdad Domestic Service*, February 20, 1990; *al-Sharq al-Awsat* (London), May 18, 1990.

24. *Baghdad Domestic Service*, July 18, 1990.

25. *INA*, June 19, 26, 1990; Saddam's interview with the *Wall Street Journal* (New York), June 16, 1990.

26. J. Miller and L. Mylroie, *Saddam Hussein and the Crisis in the Gulf* (New York: Times Books, 1990), p. 15.

27. On the various coup attempts, see, for example, the *Economist* (London),

February 11, 1989; *Times* (London), September 11, 1989; *International Herald Tribune*, February 3, 1989.

28. On the "supergun affair," see *Times* (London), April 14, 1990; *Independent* (London), April 16, 1990; *Financial Times* (London), April 17, 1990; *International Herald Tribune*, April 4, 6, 22, May 26, 1990.

29. See, for example, *Financial Times* (London), March 30, 1990.

30. See, for example, Taha Yasin Ramadan's interview with *al-Ahali* (Cairo), May 16, 1990.

31. See, for example, *al-Jumhuriyya* (Baghdad), February 20, 1990; *al-Qadisiya* (Baghdad), March 6, 1990.

32. *Al-Thawra* (Baghdad), March 2, 1990.

33. *Baghdad Domestic Service,* January 5, 1990.

34. Interview with Richard Murphy, November 1, 1990.

35. *INA,* March 29, 1990.

36. *Baghdad Domestic Service,* April 2, 1990.

37. *Economist* (London), September 20, 1990.

38. *INA,* April 7, 8, 1990; *al-Thawra* (Baghdad), April 10, 1990; *Baghdad Domestic Service,* April 19, 1990.

39. *Baghdad Domestic Service,* July 17, 1990.

40. Ibid., July 18, 1990.

41. Ibid., July 17, 1990.

42. Personal interview.

43. *Al-Qabas* (Kuwait), July 20, 1990; *al-Ray al-Amm* (Kuwait), July 26, 1990.

44. *Economist* (London), September 29, 1990.

45. United States Department of State, *Current Policy, No. 1273,* April 26, 1990; *International Herald Tribune*, August 9, 1990.

46. *International Herald Tribune*, September 17, 1990; *Economist* (London), September 29, 1990; *Observer* (London), October 21, 1990.

47. Personal interview.

48. *International Herald Tribune*, October 22, 1990.

49. See a statement by a Kuwaiti official to *Radio Monte Carlo in Arabic* (Paris), August 1, 1990.

Chapter 10: Against the World

1. *Baghdad Voice of the Masses,* August 2, 1990 (emphasis added).

2. *Economist* (London), August 4, 1990.

3. For the text of Resolution 661, see *Times* (London), August 7, 1990.

4. *INA,* August 3, 1990.

5. Ibid.

6. Ibid.

7. *Baghdad Domestic Service,* August 6, 1990. According to the *Washington Post* of August 7, during his meeting with the American chargé d'affaires Saddam threatened to attack Saudi Arabia if it prevented the flow of Iraqi oil through its territory. This allegation was vehemently denied by the Iraqis. See, for example, *INA,* August 7, 1990.

8. For the text of President Bush's speech, see *Financial Times* (London), August 9, 1990.

9. A similar view has been suggested by Sir Anthony Parsons, a former British Ambassador to Iran and the United Nations. *Times* (London), December 8, 1990.

10. See, for example, *INA*, August 6, 1990.

11. *Baghdad Domestic Service*, August 8, 1990; *INA*, August 28, 1990.

12. *INA*, August 7, 1990; *Financial Times* (London), August 9, 1990.

13. Interview with *Der Spiegel* (Hamburg), October 8, 1990; *INA*, August 20, 1990.

14. *INA*, August 28, 1990.

15. *Baghdad Domestic Service*, August 12, 1990.

16. Ibid., October 19, 22, 28, 1990.

17. Ibid., October 12, 1990.

18. *INA*, September 17, 1990.

19. *Baghdad Domestic Service*, August 16, 1990; *Baghdad Voice of the Masses*, September 1, 1990; *INA*, September 4, 24, 1990.

20. *Baghdad Domestic Service*, August 23, 1990.

21. *FBIS-NES*, August 28, 1990, p. 31.

22. *Baghdad Domestic Service*, August 12, 1990.

23. For the Iraqi-Iranian correspondence over a political settlement, see *Kayhan International* (Tehran), September 29, October 13, 1990; *Baghdad Domestic Service*, August 15, 1990.

24. Taha Yasin Ramadan's interview with *al-Tadamun* (London), October 29, 1990, pp. 20–24.

25. *Baghdad Domestic Service*, August 8, 1990.

26. *INA*, August 9, 1990; *Baghdad Domestic Service*, July 8, 11, 1990.

27. See, for example, *INA*, September 18, 1990; *Baghdad Domestic Service*, September 23, 1990; *Times* (London), September 24, 1990.

28. *Baghdad Domestic Service*, August 12, 1990; *Financial Times* (London), August 13, 1990.

29. *Economist* (London), December 22, 1990, p. 80.

30. See, for example, *Damascus Domestic Service*, August 14, 1990; *Middle East News Agency* (*MENA*) (Cairo), August 13, 1990. Iraq's main Arab allies, the PLO and Jordan, adopted, naturally, a far more positive attitude toward the proposal.

31. Of the 20 League members attending the Cairo Summit, 12 voted in favor of the decision while 3 (Libya, the PLO, and Iraq) voted against. See the *Independent* (London), August 11, 1990; *International Herald Tribune*, August 11–12, 1990.

32. *Baghdad Domestic Service*, October 9, 1990.

33. Ibid., August 10, 11, 1990.

34. *INA*, August 20, 1990; *Radio Moscow in English*, September 5, 1990; *Financial Times* (London), September 5, 1990.

35. *Guardian* (London), September 25, 1990.

36. *Times* (London), October 2, 1990.

37. *Financial Times* (London), October 5, 1990.

38. For Iraq's overtures toward the Soviet Union and China, see, for example, *INA*, September 6, 1990; *Baghdad Domestic Service*, September 5, 8, 1990; *Times* (London), November 12, 23, 1990; *al-Madinah* (Jedda), October 21, 1990.

39. *INA*, August 8, 28, 1990.
40. *AFP* (Paris), August 31, 1990; *Times* (London), September 23, 1990; *INA*, September 28, 1990.
41. *Radio Monte Carlo in Arabic* (Paris), August 14, 1990.
42. *Baghdad Domestic Service*, August 19, 1990; *INA*, August 21, 1990.
43. Ibid.
44. *INA*, August 28, 1990.
45. For the joint press conference, see *Baghdad Domestic Service*, August 25, 1990.
46. *INA*, August 23, September 2, 1990.
47. *Baghdad Domestic Service*, October 22, 1990; *INA*, October 23, 1990.
48. *Radio Monte Carlo in Arabic* (Paris), October 24, 1990; *Baghdad International Service in English*, October 25, 1990.
49. *Times* (London), November 8, 10, 1990.
50. Saddam's interview with *Antenne 2 Télévision* (Paris), December 2, 1990.
51. *Times* (London), November 19, 28, 30, 1990.
52. Ibid., November 30, 1990.
53. *Al-Thawra*, December 2, 1990.
54. *Times* (London), December 1, 1990.
55. *Baghdad Domestic Service*, December 4, 1990.
56. *International Herald Tribune*, November 11, 1990.
57. *Times* (London), December 4, 5, 1990.
58. *Economist* (London), December 8, 1990, pp. 16, 85.
59. *INA*, December 11, 1990.
60. *Radio Monte Carlo in Arabic* (Paris), December 18, 1990.
61. *Baghdad Domestic Service*, December 12, 1990.
62. Ibid., December 7, 24, 1990; *al-Thawra* (Baghdad), December 11, 12, 1990; *INA*, December 14, 20, 21, 1990; *AFP*, December 21, 1990.
63. *Al-Qadisiya* (Baghdad), December 20, 1990.
64. *INA*, December 13, 1990.
65. *Independent* (London), January 10, 1991.
66. *Baghdad Domestic Service*, December 17, 1990.
67. *INA*, January 14, 1991.

Chapter 11: The "Mother of All Battles"

1. Personal interview.
2. *Baghdad Domestic Service*, January 17, 1991.
3. It is difficult to determine when the film was actually shot. No signs of physical damage could be detected, and the camera focused on the cheering group rather than the street in which they were standing. Yet, the meager size of the festive gathering and the extremely controlled way in which it was shown might indicate that it was indeed shot after the beginning of the war.
4. *Times* (London), January 19, 1991.
5. *Baghdad Domestic Service*, January 18, 1991.
6. Ibid., January 17, 1991.
7. *INA*, January 18, 1991.
8. *Times* (London), January 18, 1991.
9. Ibid., January 19, 1991.

10. Ibid.
11. *Al-Thawra* (Damascus), January 21, 1991.
12. *Times* (London), January 21, 1991.
13. Ibid., February 2, 1991.
14. Ibid., January 28, 1991.
15. *Baghdad Domestic Service,* January 17, 1991.
16. Ibid., January 19, 1991.
17. Ibid., January 23, 1991.
18. *Independent* (London), January 22, 1991.
19. *Baghdad Domestic Service,* January 20, 1991.
20. Saddam's interview with Peter Arnett, January 28, 1991.
21. *Times* (London), January 24, 30, 1991; *Sunday Times* (London), February 3, 1991.
22. *Times* (London), February 1, 1991.
23. *Baghdad Domestic Service,* January 31, 1991.
24. *Times* (London), February 2, 1991.
25. *Sunday Times* (London), February 16, 1991.
26. *Times* (London), February 14, 1991.
27. Ibid., February 15, 1991.
28. Ibid., February 16, 1991.
29. *New York Times,* February 22, 1991.
30. *Times* (London), February 23, 1991.
31. *Times* (London), *Independent* (London), both February 26, 1991.
32. *New York Times,* February 26, 1991.
33. R. Patai, *The Arab Mind* (New York: Charles Scribner's Sons, 1976), pp. 104–105.
34. *Baghdad Domestic Service,* February 26, 1991.
35. *Times* (London), February 27, 1991.
36. *Baghdad Domestic Service,* February 27, 1991.
37. *Times* (London), February 28, 1991.
38. *Ibid.*
39. *Baghdad Domestic Service,* February 28, 1991.

Epilogue

1. *INA,* December 15, 1990.

Select Bibliography

Abdulghani, Jasim M. *Iraq and Iran: The Years of Crisis*. Baltimore: Johns Hopkins University Press and London: Croom Helm, 1984.

Amnesty International. *Amnesty International Report*. London: Amnesty International Publications, various editions.

————. *Iraq: Evidence of Torture*. London: Amnesty International Publications, 1981.

Axelgard, Frederick W. (ed.). *Iraq in Transition: A Political, Economic and Strategic Perspective*. Boulder, Colo.: Westview, and London: Mansell Publishing, 1986.

————. *A New Iraq?* New York: Praeger for the Center for Strategic and International Studies, 1988.

Baram, Amazia. "Culture in the Service of *Wataniyya:* The Treatment of Mesopotamian-Inspired Art in Ba'thi Iraq." *Asian and African Studies*, Vol. 17 (1983), pp. 265–313.

————. "Mesopotamian Identity in Ba'thi Iraq." *Middle Eastern Studies*, Vol. 19. (1983), pp. 426–455.

————. "Qawmiyya and Wataniyya in Ba'thi Iraq: The Search for a New Balance." *Middle Eastern Studies*, Vol. 19, No. 2 (April 1983), pp. 188–200.

————. "The Ruling Political Elite in Ba'thi Iraq, 1968–1986: The Changing Features of a Collective Profile." *International Journal of Middle East Studies*, Vol. 21 (1989), pp. 447–493.

————. "Saddam Hussein: A Political Profile." *The Jerusalem Quarterly*, No. 17 (Fall 1980), pp. 115–144.

Barnaby, Frank. *The Invisible Bomb. The Nuclear Arms Race in the Middle East*. London: I. B. Tauris, 1989.

Batatu, Hanna. "Iraq's Underground Shi'a Movements: Characteristics, Causes and Prospects." *Middle East Journal*, Vol. 35 (1981), pp. 578–594.

————. *The Old Social Classes and the Revolutionary Movements of Iraq: A Study of Iraq's Old Landed and Commercial Classes and of Its Communists, Ba'thists and Free Officers*. Princeton: Princeton University Press, 1978.

Ba'th Party. *The 1968 Revolution in Iraq. Experience and Prospects*. The Political Report of the Eighth Congress of the Arab Ba'th Socialist Party in Iraq, January 1974. London: Ithaca Press, 1979.

Bengio, Ofra. "Saddam Hussein's Quest for Power and Survival." *Asian and African Studies*, Vol. 15 (1981), pp. 323–341.

———. "Shi'is and Politics in Ba'thi Iraq." *Middle Eastern Studies*, Vol. 21, No. 1 (1985), pp. 1–14.

Bulloch, John. *The Making of War: The Middle East from 1967 to 1973*. London: Longman, 1974.

CARDRI (Committee against Repression and for Democratic Rights in Iraq). *Saddam's Iraq: Revolution or Reaction?* new ed. London: Zed Books, 1989.

Chaliand, Gérard (ed.). *Les Kurdes et le Kurdistan*. Paris: François Maspero, 1978.

Chubin, Shahram, and Tripp, Charles. *Iran and Iraq at War*. London: I. B. Tauris, 1988.

Dann, Uriel. *Iraq under Qassem: A Political History. 1958–1963*, New York: Praeger, 1969.

Davies, Charles (ed.). *After the War: Iran and Iraq and the Arab Gulf*. Chichester: Carden Publications, 1990.

Devlin, John. *The Ba'th Party: A History from Its Origins to 1966*. Stanford, Calif.: Hoover Institution Press, 1976.

Farouk-Sluglett, Marion, and Sluglett, Peter. *Iraq since 1958: From Revolution to Dictatorship*. London and New York: KPI, 1987.

Ghareeb, Edmond. *The Kurdish Question in Iraq*. Syracuse, N.Y.: Syracuse University Press, 1981.

Guerreau, Alain, and Guerreau-Jalabert, Anita. *L'Irak, le développement*. Paris: Le Sycomore, 1978.

Hussein, Saddam. *The Arab Strategy in Meeting Challenges*. President Saddam Hussein's speech on opening the Tenth Arab Summit, Tunisia, November 20, 1979, trans. Namir A. Mudhaffer. Baghdad: Dar al-Ma'mun, 1981.

———. *The Close Link between Political and Economic Liberation: Saddam Hussein on the Inauguration of the Strategic Oil Pipeline*. Documentary Series 47 (1976). Baghdad: Ministry of Information, 1976.

———. *Al-Dimuqratiyya Masdar Quwwa li al-Fard wa al-Mujtama*. Baghdad: al-Thawra, 1977.

———. *Discours du Président Saddam Hussein à l'Assemblée Nationale*, réunie en séance extraordinaire le 17 septembre 1980.

———. *For Youth Nothing Is Impossible*. President Saddam Hussein addresses delegates to the Second Baghdad Seminar for Arab Youth Solidarity on October 3, 1983, trans. Samir Abd al-Rahim al-Chalabi. Baghdad: Dar al-Ma'mun, 1984.

———. *Islam's Verdict on Iran's Aggression*. President Saddam Hussein's address and proceedings of the Second Popular Islamic Conference held in Baghdad, April 22–25, 1985, trans. Samir Abd al-Rahim al-Chalabi. Baghdad: Dar al-Ma'mun, 1985.

———. *Khandaq Wahid am Khandaqan*. Baghdad: Dar al-Thawra, 1977.

———. *Muqtatafat min Ahadith Saddam Hussein*. Beirut: Dar al-Tali'ah, 1979.

———. *Nadhra fi al-Din wa al-Turath*. Baghdad: Dar al-Hurriyah, 1978.

———. *On Oil Nationalisation in Iraq*. Baghdad: al-Thawra, 1973.

———. *President Saddam Hussein Addresses the National Assembly on Iran's Aggression*. Baghdad: Dar al-Ma'mun, 1982.

———. *Saddam Hussein on the Conflict with Iran*. A press conference held on

November 10, 1980. London: Press Office of the Embassy of the Republic of
Iraq, 1980.
————. *Saddam Hussein on Current Events in Iraq*, trans. Khalid Kishtainy.
London: Longman, 1977.
————. *Social and Foreign Affairs in Iraq*, trans. Khalid Kishtainy. London: Croom
Helm, 1979.
————. *Tariquna Khass fi Bina' al-Ishtirakiyah*. Baghdad: Dar al-Hurriyah, 1977.
————. *Thus We Should Fight Persians*. Baghdad: Dar al-Ma'mun, 1983.
————. *Two Letters to Iranian Peoples*. Baghdad: Dar al-Ma'mun, 1983.
Iskandar, Amir. *Saddam Hussein: Munadilan, wa Mufakiran, wa Insanan*. Paris:
Hachette, 1981.
Karsh, Efraim. "Geopolitical Determinism: The Origins of the Iran-Iraq War."
Middle East Journal, Vol. 44, No. 2 (Spring 1990), pp. 256–268.
————. *The Iran-Iraq War: A Military Analysis*. Adelphi Papers, No. 220. London:
International Institute for Strategic Studies, 1987.
————. "Military Lessons of the Iran-Iraq War." *Orbis*, Vol. 33, Spring 1989,
pp. 209–220.
————. "Military Power and Foreign Policy Goals: The Iran-Iraq War Revisited."
International Affairs, Vol. 64, No. 2 (Winter 1987–88).
————. (ed.). *The Iran-Iraq War: Impact and Implications*. London: Macmillan and
New York: St. Martin's Press, 1989.
Karsh, Efraim, and Rautsi, Inari. "Why Saddam Hussein Invaded Kuwait"
Survival, January–February 1991, pp. 18–30.
Kelidar, Abbas. *Iraq: The Search for Stability*. Conflict Studies, No. 59. London:
The Institute for the Study of Conflict, 1975.
Khadduri, Majid. *Independent Iraq: A Study in Iraqi Politics from 1932 to 1958*, 2nd
ed., Oxford: Oxford University Press, 1960.
————. *Republican Iraq: A Study in Iraqi Politics since the Revolution of 1958*. Oxford:
Oxford University Press, 1969.
————. *Socialist Iraq: A Study in Iraqi Politics Since 1968*. Washington, D.C.: The
Middle East Institute, 1978.
al-Khalil, Samir. *Republic of Fear: The Politics of Modern Iraq*. London: Hutchinson
Radius, 1989.
Kienle, Eberhard. *Ba'th v Ba'th*. London: I. B. Tauris, 1990.
Kimball, Lorenzo Kent. *The Changing Pattern of Political Power in Iraq, 1958 to
1971*. New York: Robert Speller, 1972.
King, Ralph. *The Iran-Iraq War: The Political Implications*. Adelphi Papers, No.
219, London: International Institute for Strategic Studies, 1987.
Kramer, Martin (ed.). *Shi'ism, Resistance, and Revolution*. Boulder, Colo.: West-
view, and London: Mansell Publishing, 1987.
Kutschera, Chris. *Le Mouvement national kurde*. Paris: Flammarion, 1979.
Longrigg, Stephen. *Iraq, 1900 to 1950: A Political, Social and Economic History*.
Oxford: Oxford University Press, 1953.
Marr, Phebe. "Iraq: Its Revolutionary Experience under the Ba'th" in Peter J.
Chelkowski and Robert J. Pranger (eds.). *Ideology and Power in the Middle East*.
Durham and London: Duke University Press, 1988, pp. 185–209.
————. *The Modern History of Iraq*. Boulder, Colo.: Westview and London:
Longman, 1985.

Matar, Fuad. *Saddam Hussein: The Man, the Cause and the Future*. London: Third World Centre, 1981. (Reprinted in 1990 under the title *Saddam Hussein: A Biographical and Ideological Account of His Leadership Style and Crisis Management*.)

The Middle East Contemporary Survey. (An edited annual series, Tel Aviv and New York.)

The National Action Charter, Documentary Series 16. Baghdad: Ministry of Information, 1971.

Niblock, Tim (ed.). *Iraq: The Contemporary State*. London: Croom Helm and Exeter: Centre for Arab Gulf Studies, 1982.

O'Ballance, Edgar. *The Gulf War*. London: Brassey's, 1988.

———. *The Kurdish Revolt, 1961–1970*. London: Faber & Faber, 1973.

Penrose, Edith, and Penrose, E. F. *Iraq: International Relations and National Development*. London: Ernest Benn, and Boulder, Colo.: Westview, 1978.

Penrose, E. F. "L'Irak en 1963, une année de coups d'état." *Orient*, Vol. 28 (1963).

Roux, Georges. *Ancient Iraq*. Harmondsworth, England: Penguin, 1980.

Sader, Makram. *Le Développement industriel de l'Irak*. Beirut: CERMOC (Centre d'Etudes et de Recherches sur le Moyen-Orient Contemporain), 1983.

Saint-Prot, Charles. *Saddam Hussein: un "Gaullisme" Arabe?* Paris: Albin Michel, 1987.

Sassoon, Joseph. *Economic Policy in Iraq 1932–1950*. London: Frank Cass, 1987.

Snyder, Jed C. "The Road to Osiraq: Baghdad's Quest for the Bomb." *Middle East Journal*, Vol. 37, No. 4 (1983), pp. 565–593.

Spector, Leonard. *Going Nuclear*. Cambridge, Mass.: Ballinger, 1987.

———. *Nuclear Ambitions*, Boulder, Colo.: Westview, 1990.

Springborg, R. "Infitah, Agrarian Transformation, and Elite Consolidation in Contemporary Iraq." *Middle East Journal*, Vol. 40, No. 1 (Winter 1986), pp. 33–52.

Tahir-Kheli, Shirin, and Ayubi, S. (eds.). *The Iran-Iraq War: New Weapons, Old Conflicts*. New York: Praeger, 1983.

Tarbush, Mohammad A. *The Role of the Military in Politics: A Case Study of Iraq to 1941*. London: Kegan Paul, 1982.

al-Tikriti, Barzan. *Muhawalat Irtiyyal al-Rayis Saddam Hussein*. Baghdad, 1982.

Vernier, Bernard. *L'Irak d'aujourd'hui*. Paris: Armand Colin, 1963.

Winstone, H. V. F., and Freeth, Zahra. *Kuwait: Prospect and Reality*. London: Allen & Unwin, 1972.

Index

297

Acknowledgments

Our thanks are due to many individuals in Europe, the Middle East and the United States who generously shared their time and knowledge with us. In addition to those who wish to remain anonymous, we are particularly indebted to Fred Halliday, Charles Tripp, Peter Sluglett, Richard Murphy, Lawrence Freedman, Ofra Bengio, Philip Sabin and Joseph Mekelberg.

A good editor is of immeasurable help. We were fortunate to have one in the person of Joyce Seltzer.

Needless to say, the responsibility for what follows is ours and ours alone.

309